# MINORITIES
## RACE AND ETHNICITY IN AMERICA

ISSN 1532-1185

# MINORITIES
## RACE AND ETHNICITY IN AMERICA

Melissa J. Doak

**INFORMATION PLUS® REFERENCE SERIES**
Formerly Published by Information Plus, Wylie, Texas

GALE
CENGAGE Learning·

Detroit • New York • San Francisco • New Haven, Conn • Waterville, Maine • London

**Minorities: Race and Ethnicity in America**

Melissa J. Doak

Kepos Media, Inc.: Paula Kepos and Janice Jorgensen, Series Editors

Project Editors: Kimberley McGrath, Kathleen J. Edgar, Elizabeth Manar

Rights Acquisition and Management: Margaret Chamberlain-Gaston, Kimberly Potvin

Composition: Evi Abou-El-Seoud, Mary Beth Trimper

Manufacturing: Cynde Lentz

For product information and technology assistance, contact us at
**Gale Customer Support, 1-800-877-4253.**
For permission to use material from this text or product,
submit all requests online at **www.cengage.com/permissions.**
Further permissions questions can be e-mailed to
**permissionrequest@cengage.com**

Cover photograph: © digitalskillet/Shutterstock.com.

While every effort has been made to ensure the reliability of the information presented in this publication, Gale, a part of Cengage Learning, does not guarantee the accuracy of the data contained herein. Gale accepts no payment for listing; and inclusion in the publication of any organization, agency, institution, publication, service, or individual does not imply endorsement of the editors or publisher. Errors brought to the attention of the publisher and verified to the satisfaction of the publisher will be corrected in future editions.

Gale
27500 Drake Rd.
Farmington Hills, MI 48331-3535

ISBN-13: 978-0-7876-5103-9 (set)
ISBN-13: 978-1-4144-8146-3

ISBN-10: 0-7876-5103-6 (set)
ISBN-10: 1-4144-8146-2

ISSN 1532-1185

This title is also available as an e-book.
ISBN-13: 978-1-4144-9726-6 (set)
ISBN-10: 1-4144-9726-1 (set)
Contact your Gale sales representative for ordering information.

Printed in the United States of America
1 2 3 4 5    16 15 14 13 12

FD290

# TABLE OF CONTENTS

# PREFACE

*Minorities: Race and Ethnicity in America* is part of the *Information Plus Reference Series*. The purpose of each volume of the series is to present the latest facts on a topic of pressing concern in modern American life. These topics include the most controversial and studied social issues of the 21st century: abortion, capital punishment, care for the elderly, crime, the environment, health care, immigration, social welfare, women, world poverty, youth, and many more. Even though this series is written especially for high school and undergraduate students, it is an excellent resource for anyone in need of factual information on current affairs.

By presenting the facts, it is the intention of Gale, Cengage Learning to provide its readers with everything they need to reach an informed opinion on current issues. To that end, there is a particular emphasis in this series on the presentation of scientific studies, surveys, and statistics. These data are generally presented in the form of tables, charts, and other graphics placed within the text of each book. Every graphic is directly referred to and carefully explained in the text. The source of each graphic is presented within the graphic itself. The data used in these graphics are drawn from the most reputable and reliable sources, such as from the various branches of the U.S. government and from private organizations and associations. Every effort has been made to secure the most recent information available. Readers should bear in mind that many major studies take years to conduct and that additional years often pass before the data from these studies are made available to the public. Therefore, in many cases the most recent information available in 2012 is dated from 2009 or 2010. Older statistics are sometimes presented as well, if they are landmark studies or of particular interest and no more-recent information exists.

Even though statistics are a major focus of the *Information Plus Reference Series*, they are by no means its only content. Each book also presents the widely held positions and important ideas that shape how the book's subject is discussed in the United States. These positions are explained in detail and, where possible, in the words of their proponents. Some of the other material to be found in these books includes historical background, descriptions of major events related to the subject, relevant laws and court cases, and examples of how these issues play out in American life. Some books also feature primary documents or have pro and con debate sections that provide the words and opinions of prominent Americans on both sides of a controversial topic. All material is presented in an evenhanded and unbiased manner; readers will never be encouraged to accept one view of an issue over another.

## HOW TO USE THIS BOOK

Race and ethnicity have acted as some of the most divisive factors in U.S. history. Many people, from all racial and ethnic backgrounds, have struggled, sometimes at great peril to themselves, to provide equality for all people in the United States. Nevertheless, it is an undeniable fact that African-Americans, Hispanics, Native Americans, Asian-Americans, and other minority groups have a different experience living in the United States than do whites. This book reports on and examines the differences between minority groups and white Americans across the economic, political, and social spectrums.

*Minorities: Race and Ethnicity in America* consists of eight chapters and three appendixes. Each chapter is devoted to a particular aspect of minorities. For a summary of the information that is covered in each chapter, please see the synopses that are provided in the Table of Contents. Chapters generally begin with an overview of the basic facts and background information on the chapter's topic, then proceed to examine subtopics of particular interest. For example, Chapter 3: Education begins with an overview of enrollment of minority students in public schools and addresses risk factors in education. Next, it examines minority groups in detail, including specific factors that promote or stand in the way of academic performance. Attempts to reform the public school system and promote equality in education are discussed. The chapter concludes with a look at racial and ethnic minority students in higher education. Readers can find their way through a chapter by looking for the section and subsection headings, which are clearly set off from the text. They can also refer to the book's extensive Index if they already know what they are looking for.

## Statistical Information

The tables and figures featured throughout *Minorities: Race and Ethnicity in America* will be of particular use to readers in learning about this issue. These tables and figures represent an extensive collection of the most recent and important statistics on minorities, as well as related issues—for example, graphics cover the number of different minority peoples living in the United States overall and in specific regions, their average earnings as compared to whites, the rates at which they are the victims of various crimes, and the health problems that disproportionately afflict certain minority groups. Gale, Cengage Learning believes that making this information available to readers is the most important way to fulfill the goal of this book: to help readers understand the issues and controversies surrounding minorities and reach their own conclusions about them.

Each table or figure has a unique identifier appearing above it, for ease of identification and reference. Titles for the tables and figures explain their purpose. At the end of each table or figure, the original source of the data is provided.

To help readers understand these often complicated statistics, all tables and figures are explained in the text. References in the text direct readers to the relevant statistics. Furthermore, the contents of all tables and figures are fully indexed. Please see the opening section of the Index at the back of this volume for a description of how to find tables and figures within it.

## Appendixes

Besides the main body text and images, *Minorities: Race and Ethnicity in America* has three appendixes. The first is the Important Names and Addresses directory. Here, readers will find contact information for a number

of government and private organizations that can provide further information on aspects of minorities. The second appendix is the Resources section, which can also assist readers in conducting their own research. In this section, the author and editors of *Minorities: Race and Ethnicity in America* describe some of the sources that were most useful during the compilation of this book. The final appendix is the detailed Index. It has been greatly expanded from previous editions and should make it even easier to find specific topics in this book.

## ADVISORY BOARD CONTRIBUTIONS

The staff of Information Plus would like to extend its heartfelt appreciation to the Information Plus Advisory Board. This dedicated group of media professionals provides feedback on the series on an ongoing basis. Their comments allow the editorial staff who work on the project to continually make the series better and more user-friendly. The staff's top priority is to produce the highest-quality and most useful books possible, and the Information Plus Advisory Board's contributions to this process are invaluable.

The members of the Information Plus Advisory Board are:

- Kathleen R. Bonn, Librarian, Newbury Park High School, Newbury Park, California

- Madelyn Garner, Librarian, San Jacinto College, North Campus, Houston, Texas

- Anne Oxenrider, Media Specialist, Dundee High School, Dundee, Michigan

- Charles R. Rodgers, Director of Libraries, Pasco-Hernando Community College, Dade City, Florida

- James N. Zitzelsberger, Library Media Department Chairman, Oshkosh West High School, Oshkosh, Wisconsin

## COMMENTS AND SUGGESTIONS

The editors of the *Information Plus Reference Series* welcome your feedback on *Minorities: Race and Ethnicity in America*. Please direct all correspondence to:

Editors
*Information Plus Reference Series*
27500 Drake Rd.
Farmington Hills, MI 48331-3535

# CHAPTER 1
# WHO ARE MINORITIES?

## MINORITIES ARE A GROWING PERCENTAGE OF THE NATION

The U.S. Census Bureau reports that in 2010 the U.S. population totaled 308.7 million people. (See Table 1.1.) Of that number, 196.8 million (63.7%) people identified themselves as non-Hispanic white alone, down from 69.1% in 2000. The other 36.3% were members of one or more minority racial or ethnic groups. Even though Lindsay M. Howden and Julie A. Meyer of the Census Bureau report in *Age and Sex Composition: 2010* (May 2011, http://www .census.gov/prod/cen2010/briefs/c2010br-03.pdf) that women were a majority of the nation's population in 2010 (157 million women versus 151.8 million men), women are often considered to be a "minority" in social issues because they have been historically discriminated against in American society. In this publication, however, women are treated only in relation to racial or ethnic minority groups.

Minority populations are growing faster than is the non-Hispanic white population. The Census Bureau projects that between 2000 and 2050 the non-Hispanic white population will grow by only 4%, whereas the non-Hispanic African-American population will grow by 51%, the Asian-American population will grow by 220%, and the Hispanic population will grow by 273%. (See Table 1.2.) The nation is increasingly diverse due to the growth in immigration and interracial marriages. In some areas of the United States, particularly the South and the West, many areas have minority populations of 50% or more. (See Figure 1.1.)

## CHANGING RACIAL AND ETHNIC ORIGIN CLASSIFICATIONS

For the 1980 and 1990 censuses the Census Bureau divided the U.S. population into the four racial categories that were identified by the Office of Management and Budget—White, Black, American Indian/Alaskan Native, and Asian/Pacific Islander—and added the category "Some Other Race." The U.S. government uses these race and ethnic origin data to make decisions, among other things, about funding and making laws. For example, federal programs use the race information to monitor and ensure that the civil rights of African-Americans and other minority groups are not being violated, and states use the data to ensure compliance with political redistricting requirements.

As ethnic identity becomes more complex because of immigration and interracial marriages and births, a growing number of people object to categories that are based on race. It is no longer unusual to find Americans whose backgrounds include two or more races.

Katherine K. Wallman explains in "Data on Race and Ethnicity: Revising the Federal Standard" (*American Statistician*, vol. 52, no. 1, 1998) that these standards came under attack because many Americans believed they did not accurately reflect the diversity of the nation's population. Between 1993 and 1995 the Census Bureau conducted hearings and invited public comment on the proposal under consideration to add new choices to the categories that had been used during the 1990 census. Among the Census Bureau's findings were that Arab-Americans were unhappy with their official designation as "white, non-European." This group included people from the Middle East, Turkey, and North Africa. In addition, many indigenous Hawaiians wanted to be recategorized from Pacific Islander to Native American, reflecting historical accuracy and giving them access to greater minority benefits.

Some Hispanics wanted the Census Bureau to identify them as a race and not as an ethnic origin, and to replace the word *Hispanic* with *Latino*. They asserted that *Hispanic* recalled the colonization of Latin America by Spain and Portugal and argued that the term was as offensive as the term *Negro* was for African-Americans. However, when Hispanics were surveyed, the results showed they preferred to be identified by their families' country of origin, such as Puerto Rican, Colombian, Cuban, or sometimes just American.

**TABLE 1.1**

### Population by Hispanic origin and by race, 2000 and 2010

| Hispanic or Latino origin and race | 2000 Number | 2000 Percentage of total population | 2010 Number | 2010 Percentage of total population | Change, 2000 to 2010 Number | Change, 2000 to 2010 Percent |
|---|---|---|---|---|---|---|
| **Hispanic or Latino origin or race** | | | | | | |
| Total population | 281,421,906 | 100.0 | 308,745,538 | 100.0 | 27,323,632 | 9.7 |
| Hispanic or Latino | 35,305,818 | 12.5 | 50,477,594 | 16.3 | 15,171,776 | 43.0 |
| Not Hispanic or Latino | 246,116,088 | 87.5 | 258,267,944 | 83.7 | 12,151,856 | 4.9 |
| White alone | 194,552,774 | 69.1 | 196,817,552 | 63.7 | 2,264,778 | 1.2 |
| **Race** | | | | | | |
| Total population | 281,421,906 | 100.0 | 308,745,538 | 100.0 | 27,323,632 | 9.7 |
| One race | 274,595,678 | 97.6 | 299,736,465 | 97.1 | 25,140,787 | 9.2 |
| White | 211,460,626 | 75.1 | 223,553,265 | 72.4 | 12,092,639 | 5.7 |
| Black or African American | 34,658,190 | 12.3 | 38,929,319 | 12.6 | 4,271,129 | 12.3 |
| American Indian and Alaska Native | 2,475,956 | 0.9 | 2,932,248 | 0.9 | 456,292 | 18.4 |
| Asian | 10,242,998 | 3.6 | 14,674,252 | 4.8 | 4,431,254 | 43.3 |
| Native Hawaiian and other Pacific Islander | 398,835 | 0.1 | 540,013 | 0.2 | 141,178 | 35.4 |
| Some other race | 15,359,073 | 5.5 | 19,107,368 | 6.2 | 3,748,295 | 24.4 |
| Two or more races* | 6,826,228 | 2.4 | 9,009,073 | 2.9 | 2,182,845 | 32.0 |

*In Census 2000, an error in data processing resulted in an overstatement of the two or more races population by about 1 million people (about 15 percent) nationally, which almost entirely affected race combinations involving some other race. Therefore, data users should assess observed changes in the two or more races population and race combinations involving some other race between Census 2000 and the 2010 Census with caution. Changes in specific race combinations not involving some other race, such as white and black or African American or white and Asian, generally should be more comparable.

SOURCE: Karen R. Humes, Nicholas A. Jones, and Robert R. Ramirez, "Table 1. Population by Hispanic or Latino Origin and by Race for the United States: 2000 and 2010," in *Overview of Race and Hispanic Origin: 2010*, U.S. Census Bureau, March 2011, http://www.census.gov/prod/cen2010/briefs/c2010br-02 .pdf (accessed October 30, 2011)

A number of African-Americans wanted the Census Bureau to retire the term *Black*. Nevertheless, there was some difference of opinion. For example, people from the Caribbean preferred to be labeled by their families' country of origin, such as Jamaican-American or Haitian-American. Africans who were not American also found the term inaccurate. Even though the term *African-American* has become more prominent in spoken English in recent years, lack of agreement and the length of the term have been significant factors in preventing its adoption by the government.

## The 2000 Census

Conforming to revised standards that were issued by the Office of Management and Budget, the 2000 census recategorized the races into White, Black/African-American/ Negro, American Indian/Alaskan Native, Native Hawaiian/ Other Pacific Islander, and Asian. The Census Bureau also added a sixth category: Some Other Race. In addition, the Census Bureau included two ethnic categories: Hispanic/ Latino and Not Hispanic/Not Latino. To provide an accurate count of multiracial Americans, the 2000 census allowed Americans to select more than one race. Write-in spaces allowed Native Americans to record their tribal affiliation, and individuals of Hispanic origin could write in a national affiliation other than the major groups of Mexican, Cuban, and Puerto Rican.

In "Impact of Census' Race Data Debated" (*USA Today*, March 12, 2001), Martin Kasindorf and Haya El Nasser explain that many Americans thought that the

official recognition of multiracial Americans would profoundly change how Americans think about race in the long term. Some believed that racial lines would blur until racial differences no longer became so important in American life. Others took a more pessimistic view, arguing that because African-Americans marry outside their racial categories less than other minorities, the difference between an "expanded majority" of whites and the African-American minority group would harden even further.

## The 2010 Census

For the 2010 census, the U.S. government announced the inclusion of even more specific racial categories. The Population Reference Bureau notes in "The 2010 Census Questionnaire: Seven Questions for Everyone" (April 2009, http://www.prb.org/Articles/2009/questionnaire.aspx) that there were 15 racial categories: White; Black, African-American, or Negro; American Indian or Alaskan Native; Asian Indian; Japanese; Native Hawaiian; Chinese; Korean; Guamanian or Chamorro; Filipino; Vietnamese; Samoan; other Asian; other Pacific Islander; and "Some Other Race." The 2010 census also considered Hispanic origin separately from race, with Hispanics able to identify with any race. The census also allowed respondents to choose more than one race.

Stephanie Sy reports in "2010 Census Offends Some Americans with Handling of Race" (ABC News, April 1, 2010) that despite its attempt to be more inclusive, the

**TABLE 1.2**

**Projected change in population size by race and Hispanic origin, 2000–50**

[Resident population as of July 1. Numbers in thousands.]

| Race and Hispanic origin[a] | 2000–2050 | | 2000–2025 | | 2025–2050 | |
|---|---|---|---|---|---|---|
| | Numerical | Percent | Numerical | Percent | Numerical | Percent |
| **Total population** | **156,852** | **56** | **75,294** | **27** | **81,558** | **23** |
| One race | 144,602 | 52 | 70,605 | 25 | 73,997 | 21 |
| White | 96,202 | 42 | 47,683 | 21 | 48,519 | 18 |
| Black | 21,127 | 59 | 10,777 | 30 | 10,350 | 22 |
| AIAN | 2,786 | 104 | 1,363 | 51 | 1,423 | 35 |
| Asian | 23,729 | 222 | 10,439 | 98 | 13,290 | 63 |
| NHPI | 757 | 163 | 343 | 74 | 414 | 51 |
| Two or more races | 12,250 | 311 | 4,687 | 119 | 7,563 | 88 |
| Race alone or in combination:[b] | | | | | | |
| White | 107,482 | 46 | 51,931 | 22 | 55,551 | 20 |
| Black | 28,468 | 76 | 13,391 | 36 | 15,077 | 30 |
| AIAN | 4,349 | 102 | 2,099 | 49 | 2,250 | 35 |
| Asian | 28,484 | 235 | 12,283 | 101 | 16,201 | 66 |
| NHPI | 1,664 | 182 | 730 | 80 | 934 | 57 |
| **Not Hispanic** | **59,689** | **24** | **35,151** | **14** | **24,538** | **9** |
| One race | 49,783 | 20 | 31,278 | 13 | 18,505 | 7 |
| White | 7,576 | 4 | 10,891 | 6 | −3,315 | −2 |
| Black | 17,535 | 51 | 9,289 | 27 | 8,246 | 19 |
| AIAN | 1,254 | 60 | 726 | 35 | 528 | 19 |
| Asian | 22,982 | 220 | 10,155 | 97 | 12,827 | 62 |
| NHPI | 434 | 118 | 216 | 59 | 218 | 37 |
| Two or more races | 9,906 | 288 | 3,873 | 113 | 6,033 | 83 |
| Race alone or in combination:[b] | | | | | | |
| White | 16,714 | 8 | 14,404 | 7 | 2,310 | 1 |
| Black | 23,703 | 67 | 11,506 | 32 | 12,197 | 26 |
| AIAN | 2,166 | 62 | 1,204 | 35 | 962 | 21 |
| Asian | 26,921 | 230 | 11,736 | 100 | 15,185 | 65 |
| NHPI | 1,071 | 142 | 510 | 67 | 561 | 44 |
| **Hispanic** | **97,163** | **273** | **40,143** | **113** | **57,020** | **75** |
| One race | 94,819 | 270 | 39,328 | 112 | 55,491 | 75 |
| White | 88,626 | 270 | 36,793 | 112 | 51,833 | 74 |
| Black | 3,592 | 256 | 1,488 | 106 | 2,104 | 73 |
| AIAN | 1,533 | 268 | 638 | 112 | 895 | 74 |
| Asian | 746 | 317 | 283 | 120 | 463 | 89 |
| NHPI | 323 | 336 | 127 | 132 | 196 | 88 |
| Two or more races | 2,344 | 472 | 814 | 164 | 1,530 | 117 |
| Race alone or in combination:[b] | | | | | | |
| White | 90,768 | 273 | 37,527 | 113 | 53,241 | 75 |
| Black | 4,764 | 294 | 1,884 | 116 | 2,880 | 82 |
| AIAN | 2,183 | 281 | 895 | 115 | 1,288 | 77 |
| Asian | 1,563 | 412 | 547 | 144 | 1,016 | 110 |
| NHPI | 593 | 378 | 220 | 140 | 373 | 99 |

[a]Hispanics may be of any race.
[b]In combination' means in combination with one or more other races. The sum of the five race groups adds to more than the total change because individuals may report more than one race.
Black = Black or African American; AIAN = American Indian and Alaska Native; NHPI = Native Hawaiian and other Pacific Islander.
Note: The original race data from Census 2000 are modified to eliminate the "some other race" category. This modification is used for all Census Bureau projections products.

SOURCE: "Table 7. Projected Change in Population Size by Race and Hispanic Origin for the United States: 2000 to 2050," in *National Population Projections: 2008 National Population Projections*, U.S. Census Bureau, August 14, 2008, http://www.census.gov/population/www/projections/summarytables.html (accessed October 30, 2011)

Census Bureau still came under criticism for its handling of racial and ethnic categories during the 2010 census. For example, the Census Bureau included "Negro" on the 2010 form, a historically offensive term. In addition, even though the ninth question included 15 racial categories, it did not include a way for Arabs to mark either their race or ethnicity, and mixed-race people were forced to choose "other."

A more in-depth discussion of the major race and ethnic groups follows.

## HISPANICS AND LATINOS

*Hispanic* is a broad term that is used to describe a varied ethnic group of individuals who trace their cultural heritage to Spain or to Spanish-speaking countries in Latin America. The term can also refer to people whose Spanish ancestors were residents of the southwestern region of the United States that was formerly under Spanish or Mexican control. Even though some Americans with origins in Latin America have asked the Census Bureau to refer to them as Latinos, for the purposes of

**FIGURE 1.1**

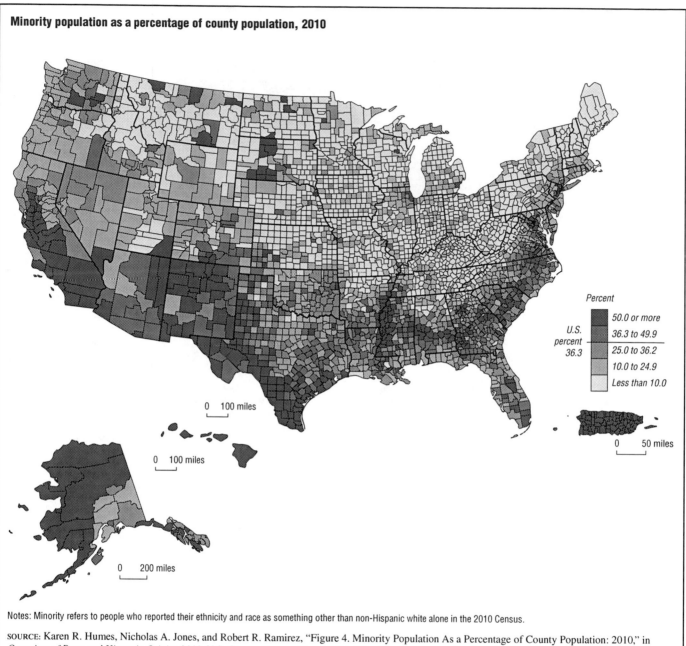

**Minority population as a percentage of county population, 2010**

Percent

U.S. percent 36.3

| | |
|---|---|
| | 50.0 or more |
| | 36.3 to 49.9 |
| | 25.0 to 36.2 |
| | 10.0 to 24.9 |
| | Less than 10.0 |

0   100 miles

0   100 miles

0   200 miles

0   50 miles

Notes: Minority refers to people who reported their ethnicity and race as something other than non-Hispanic white alone in the 2010 Census.

SOURCE: Karen R. Humes, Nicholas A. Jones, and Robert R. Ramirez, "Figure 4. Minority Population As a Percentage of County Population: 2010," in *Overview of Race and Hispanic Origin: 2010,* U.S. Census Bureau, March 2011, http://www.census.gov/prod/cen2010/briefs/c2010br-02.pdf (accessed October 30, 2011)

this book the term *Hispanic* will be used to refer to all minority populations of Hispanic or Latino descent.

The Census Bureau indicates that in 2010 nearly 50.5 million Hispanics lived in the United States. (See Table 1.1.) As 16.3% of the population, they were the largest minority group in the nation. Frank Hobbs and Nicole Stoops of the Census Bureau indicate in *Demographic Trends in the 20th Century* (November 2002, http://www.census.gov/prod/2002pubs/censr-4.pdf) that in 1980 Hispanics represented 14.6 million people (6.4% of the total U.S. population). In 1990 Hispanics totaled about 22.4 million people (9% of the total U.S. population). The 2000 census counted

35.3 million Hispanics (12.5% of the total U.S. population) living in the United States. The Hispanic population, within the country, increased by 141.7% between 1980 and 2000. The Census Bureau predicts in National Population Projections (2008, http://www.census.gov/population/www/projections/summarytables.html) that by 2050 there will be 132.8 million Hispanics (30.2% of the total U.S. population) living in the United States.

Immigration and high birthrates are two major reasons for the large growth of the Hispanic population. In *Estimates of the Unauthorized Immigrant Population Residing in the United States: January 2011* (March 2012, http://www.dhs.gov/xlibrary/assets/statistics/publications/ois_ill_pe_2011.pdf), Michael Hoefer, Nancy Rytina, and Bryan Baker of the U.S. Department of Homeland Security (DHS) estimate that as of January 2011 approximately 11.5 million unauthorized immigrants lived in the United States. The researchers explain that the unauthorized immigrant population did not increase significantly after 2007 because of high U.S. unemployment, an improving economy in Mexico, and stepped-up U.S. border patrols and enforcement. The majority of unauthorized immigrants were from Mexico; in January 2011, 6.8 million (59%) unauthorized immigrants were from that country. El Salvador and Guatemala were the next leading source countries of unauthorized immigrants, with 660,000 (6%) and 520,000 (5%), respectively.

The Census Bureau collected information on the Hispanic population in the 2010 Current Population Survey and published its findings in *The Hispanic Population in the United States: 2010* (June 2011, http://www.census.gov/population/www/socdemo/hispanic/cps2010.html). It found that 12.7 million (70.2%) of the 18.1 million foreign-born Hispanics were not citizens as of 2010. About 63% of all Hispanics had been born in the United States, and another 11% had become naturalized citizens. This varied by country of origin, however. Almost all Puerto Ricans (99.7%) had been born in the United States, because Puerto Rico is a U.S. territory. As of 2010 more Mexicans than any other foreign group had been born in the United States: 64.7% of Mexicans, 37.4% of Cubans, 35.8% of Central Americans, and 34.6% of South Americans had been born in the United States. Cubans had the highest proportion of those who had become naturalized citizens: 37.4% of Cubans, 28.2% of South Americans, 16.7% of Central Americans, and only 8.4% of Mexicans had become naturalized citizens. Central Americans had the highest percentage of residents who were not citizens (47.5%), followed by South Americans (37.2%), Mexicans (26.9%), and Cubans (25.2%).

## Hispanic Origins

Hispanic-Americans trace their origins to a number of countries. The Census Bureau reports that in 2010 nearly 32 million (63%) of the 50.5 million Hispanics living in the United States were of Mexican heritage. (See Table 1.3.) Another 4.6 million (9.2%) were of Puerto Rican heritage; 4 million (7.9%) were of Central American heritage; 2.8 million (5.5%) were of South American heritage; and 1.8 million (3.5%) were of Cuban heritage. The differences in origin can often mean significant variations in where Hispanics live in the United States and in their educational attainment, income, and living conditions.

## Geographic Distribution

Different areas of the United States have more Hispanics living in them. According to Sharon R. Ennis, Merarys

Ríos-Vargas, and Nora G. Albert of the Census Bureau, in *The Hispanic Population: 2010* (May 2011, http://www.census.gov/prod/cen2010/briefs/c2010br-04.pdf), in 2010 more Hispanics lived in the West (40.8%) than in any other region, followed by the South (36.1%), the Northeast (13.9%), and the Midwest (9.2%). (See Table 1.4.) In 2010 more than a quarter (27.8%) of the Hispanic population of the nation lived in California and 18.7% lived in Texas. (See Figure 1.2.) Less than 10% of the national Hispanic population lived in Florida (8.4%), New York (6.8%), Illinois (4%), Arizona (3.8%), New Jersey (3.1%), and Colorado (2.1%). The remaining 25.4% of the national Hispanic population lived in all the other states combined. Figure 1.3 shows Hispanics as a percentage of the total U.S. population at the county-level; areas of southern Texas, Southern California, New Mexico, and southern Florida consisted of more than 50% Hispanic people.

Hispanics from different countries of origin tend to live in different areas of the country as well. Ennis, Ríos-Vargas, and Albert note that in 2010 the largest Hispanic origin group in most of the country was Mexican. However, in many states in the Northeast, including Connecticut, Delaware, Massachusetts, New Hampshire, New York, and Pennsylvania, Puerto Ricans were the dominant Hispanic origin group. In Florida, Cubans were the dominant origin group, while in Virginia and the District of Columbia Salvadorans were the dominant group. In Rhode Island Dominicans were the dominant origin group.

## Mexican-Americans

Many Hispanic-Americans are descendants of the Spanish and Mexican people who lived in the West and Southwest when these regions were controlled by Spain (starting in the 1500s) and later by Mexico (after Mexico gained its independence from Spain in 1821). Their forebears were absorbed into the United States when Texas revolted, broke away from Mexico, became a republic, and then finally joined the United States during the 1840s. The Mexican-American War (1846–1848) added Arizona, California, Colorado, New Mexico, Utah, and territories north of the Rio Grande to the United States with the signing of the Treaty of Guadalupe Hidalgo in 1848. As a result, Hispanics living in these areas became Americans.

The Mexican-origin population, which more than doubled during the last two decades of the 20th century, continues to grow in the 21st century. According to the Census Bureau, 31.8 million people (10.3% of the U.S. population) were of Mexican origin in 2010. (See Table 1.3.) Mexican-Americans represented 63% of the Hispanic population in the United States in 2010. The DHS indicates in *2010 Yearbook of Immigration Statistics* (August 2011, http://www.dhs.gov/xlibrary/assets/statistics/yearbook/2010/ois_yb_2010.pdf) that by far the largest number of legal immigrants comes from Mexico each year. In 2010,

TABLE 1.3

**Hispanic origin population by type, 2000 and 2010**

| Origin and type | 2000 | | 2010 | | Change, 2000 to 2010[a] | |
|---|---|---|---|---|---|---|
| | Number | Percent of total | Number | Percent of total | Number | Percent |
| **Hispanic or Latino origin** | | | | | | |
| Total | 281,421,906 | 100.0 | 308,745,538 | 100.0 | 27,323,632 | 9.7 |
| Hispanic or Latino | 35,305,818 | 12.5 | 50,477,594 | 16.3 | 15,171,776 | 43.0 |
| Not Hispanic or Latino | 246,116,088 | 87.5 | 258,267,944 | 83.7 | 12,151,856 | 4.9 |
| **Hispanic or Latino by type** | | | | | | |
| Total | 35,305,818 | 100.0 | 50,477,594 | 100.0 | 15,171,776 | 43.0 |
| Mexican | 20,640,711 | 58.5 | 31,798,258 | 63.0 | 11,157,547 | 54.1 |
| Puerto Rican | 3,406,178 | 9.6 | 4,623,716 | 9.2 | 1,217,538 | 35.7 |
| Cuban | 1,241,685 | 3.5 | 1,785,547 | 3.5 | 543,862 | 43.8 |
| Other Hispanic or Latino | 10,017,244 | 28.4 | 12,270,073 | 24.3 | 2,252,829 | 22.5 |
| Dominican (Dominican Republic) | 764,945 | 2.2 | 1,414,703 | 2.8 | 649,758 | 84.9 |
| Central American (excludes Mexican) | 1,686,937 | 4.8 | 3,998,280 | 7.9 | 2,311,343 | 137.0 |
| Costa Rican | 68,588 | 0.2 | 126,418 | 0.3 | 57,830 | 84.3 |
| Guatemalan | 372,487 | 1.1 | 1,044,209 | 2.1 | 671,722 | 180.3 |
| Honduran | 217,569 | 0.6 | 633,401 | 1.3 | 415,832 | 191.1 |
| Nicaraguan | 177,684 | 0.5 | 348,202 | 0.7 | 170,518 | 96.0 |
| Panamanian | 91,723 | 0.3 | 165,456 | 0.3 | 73,733 | 80.4 |
| Salvadoran | 655,165 | 1.9 | 1,648,968 | 3.3 | 993,803 | 151.7 |
| Other Central American[b] | 103,721 | 0.3 | 31,626 | 0.1 | −72,095 | −69.5 |
| South American | 1,353,562 | 3.8 | 2,769,434 | 5.5 | 1,415,872 | 104.6 |
| Argentinean | 100,864 | 0.3 | 224,952 | 0.4 | 124,088 | 123.0 |
| Bolivian | 42,068 | 0.1 | 99,210 | 0.2 | 57,142 | 135.8 |
| Chilean | 68,849 | 0.2 | 126,810 | 0.3 | 57,961 | 84.2 |
| Colombian | 470,684 | 1.3 | 908,734 | 1.8 | 438,050 | 93.1 |
| Ecuadorian | 260,559 | 0.7 | 564,631 | 1.1 | 304,072 | 116.7 |
| Paraguayan | 8,769 | — | 20,023 | — | 11,254 | 128.3 |
| Peruvian | 233,926 | 0.7 | 531,358 | 1.1 | 297,432 | 127.1 |
| Uruguayan | 18,804 | 0.1 | 56,884 | 0.1 | 38,080 | 202.5 |
| Venezuelan | 91,507 | 0.3 | 215,023 | 0.4 | 123,516 | 135.0 |
| Other South American[c] | 57,532 | 0.2 | 21,809 | — | −35,723 | −62.1 |
| Spaniard | 100,135 | 0.3 | 635,253 | 1.3 | 535,118 | 534.4 |
| All other Hispanic or Latino[d] | 6,111,665 | 17.3 | 3,452,403 | 6.8 | −2,659,262 | −43.5 |

—Percentage rounds to 0.0.

[a]The observed changes in Hispanic origin counts between Census 2000 and the 2010 Census could be attributed to a number of factors. Demographic change since 2000, which includes births and deaths in a geographic area and migration in and out of a geographic area, will have an impact on the resulting 2010 Census counts. Some changes in the Hispanic origin question's wording and format since Census 2000 could have influenced reporting patterns in the 2010 Census. Additionally, changes to the Hispanic origin edit and coding procedures could have impacted the 2010 counts. These factors should especially be considered when observing changes for detailed Hispanic groups.
[b]This category includes people who reported Central American Indian groups, "Canal Zone," and "Central American."
[c]This category includes people who reported South American Indian groups and "South American."
[d]This category includes people who reported "Hispanic" or "Latino" and other general terms.

SOURCE: Sharon R. Ennis, Merarys Rios-Vargas, and Nora G. Albert, "Table 1. Hispanic or Latino Origin Population by Type: 2000 and 2010," in *The Hispanic Population: 2010*, U.S. Census Bureau, May 2011, http://www.census.gov/prod/cen2010/briefs/c2010br-04.pdf (accessed October 30, 2011)

139,120 Mexicans legally immigrated to the United States, with many more coming illegally. Daniel Dockterman of the Pew Hispanic Center notes in the fact sheet "Hispanics of Mexican Origin in the United States, 2009" (May 26, 2011, http://www.pewhispanic.org/files/2011/07/71.pdf) that most Mexicans live either in California (36.4%) or in Texas (25.4%).

## Puerto Ricans

The situation of Puerto Ricans is unique in American society. The Caribbean island of Puerto Rico, formerly a Spanish colony, became a U.S. commonwealth after it was ceded to the United States by the Treaty of Paris in 1898, which ended the Spanish-American War (1898). In 1917 the Revised Organic Act (the Jones Act) granted the island a bill of rights and its own legislature. It also conferred U.S. citizenship to all Puerto Ricans.

Ruth Glasser explains in "Tobacco Valley: Puerto Rican Farm Workers in Connecticut" (*Hog River Journal*, vol. 1, no. 1, 2002) that following World War II (1939–1945) an industrialization program was launched in Puerto Rico. Even though the program benefited many, it sharply reduced the number of agricultural jobs on the island, driving many rural residents to the cities. Combined with a high birthrate, this led to unemployment, overcrowding, and poverty. These conditions forced many Puerto Ricans to move to the mainland United States, particularly New York City, New York. Since 1993, when President Bill Clinton (1946–) eliminated tax exemptions for manufacturing firms in Puerto Rico, industries have moved away from the island in search of cheaper labor, further compounding the economic problems of Puerto Rico. According to Virginia E. Sánchez Korrol, in *From Colonia to Community: The*

TABLE 1.4

**Detailed Hispanic origin groups with a population size of one million or more by region, 2010**

| Origin | United States Number | United States Percent | Northeast Number | Northeast Percent | Midwest Number | Midwest Percent | South Number | South Percent | West Number | West Percent |
|---|---|---|---|---|---|---|---|---|---|---|
| Total Hispanic | 50,477,594 | 100.0 | 6,991,969 | 13.9 | 4,661,678 | 9.2 | 18,227,508 | 36.1 | 20,596,439 | 40.8 |
| Central American | 35,796,538 | 100.0 | 1,644,749 | 4.6 | 3,700,814 | 10.3 | 12,642,799 | 35.3 | 17,808,176 | 49.7 |
| Mexican | 31,798,258 | 100.0 | 918,188 | 2.9 | 3,470,726 | 10.9 | 10,945,244 | 34.4 | 16,464,100 | 51.8 |
| Guatemalan | 1,044,209 | 100.0 | 203,931 | 19.5 | 95,588 | 9.2 | 348,287 | 33.4 | 396,403 | 38.0 |
| Salvadoran | 1,648,968 | 100.0 | 270,509 | 16.4 | 61,894 | 3.8 | 655,184 | 39.7 | 661,381 | 40.1 |
| Other Central American[a] | 1,305,103 | 100.0 | 252,121 | 19.3 | 72,606 | 5.6 | 694,084 | 53.2 | 286,292 | 21.9 |
| South American[b] | 2,769,434 | 100.0 | 1,033,473 | 37.3 | 158,768 | 5.7 | 1,150,536 | 41.5 | 426,657 | 15.4 |
| Caribbean | 7,823,966 | 100.0 | 3,745,150 | 47.9 | 523,524 | 6.7 | 3,008,377 | 38.5 | 546,915 | 7.0 |
| Cuban | 1,785,547 | 100.0 | 197,173 | 11.0 | 62,990 | 3.5 | 1,376,453 | 77.1 | 148,931 | 8.3 |
| Dominican | 1,414,703 | 100.0 | 1,104,802 | 78.1 | 25,799 | 1.8 | 258,383 | 18.3 | 25,719 | 1.8 |
| Puerto Rican | 4,623,716 | 100.0 | 2,443,175 | 52.8 | 434,735 | 9.4 | 1,373,541 | 29.7 | 372,265 | 8.1 |
| All other Hispanic[c] | 4,087,656 | 100.0 | 568,597 | 13.9 | 278,572 | 6.8 | 1,425,796 | 34.9 | 1,814,691 | 44.4 |

[a]This category includes people who reported "Costa Rican," "Honduran," "Nicaraguan," "Panamanian," Central American Indian groups, "Canal Zone," and "Central American."
[b]This category includes people who reported "Argentinean," "Bolivian," "Chilean," "Colombian," "Ecuadorian," "Paraguayan," "Peruvian," "Uruguayan," "Venezuelan," South American Indian groups, and "South American."
[c]This category includes people who reported "Spaniard," as well as "Hispanic" or "Latino" and other general terms.

SOURCE: Sharon R. Ennis, Merarys Rios-Vargas, and Nora G. Albert, "Table 3. Detailed Hispanic or Latino Origin Groups with a Population Size of One Million or More for the United States and Regions: 2010," in *The Hispanic Population: 2010*, U.S. Census Bureau, May 2011, http://www.census.gov/prod/cen2010/briefs/c2010br-04.pdf (accessed October 30, 2011)

**FIGURE 1.2**

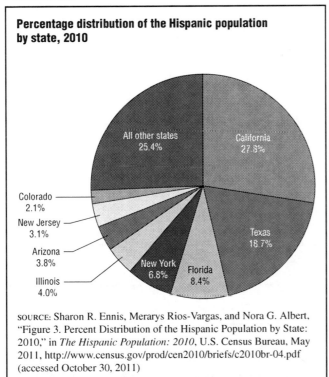

**Percentage distribution of the Hispanic population by state, 2010**

All other states 25.4%
California 27.8%
Texas 18.7%
Florida 8.4%
New York 6.8%
Illinois 4.0%
Arizona 3.8%
New Jersey 3.1%
Colorado 2.1%

SOURCE: Sharon R. Ennis, Merarys Rios-Vargas, and Nora G. Albert, "Figure 3. Percent Distribution of the Hispanic Population by State: 2010," in *The Hispanic Population: 2010*, U.S. Census Bureau, May 2011, http://www.census.gov/prod/cen2010/briefs/c2010br-04.pdf (accessed October 30, 2011)

*History of Puerto Ricans in New York City* (1994), in 1940 fewer than 70,000 Puerto Ricans lived in the contiguous United States. The Census Bureau notes that by 2010, over 4.6 million Puerto Ricans called the United States home. (See Table 1.3.) Partly because of the ease with which Puerto Ricans can travel in the United States, many move freely back and forth between the United States and Puerto Rico.

In "A Puerto Rican Rebirth in El Barrio; After Exodus, Gentrification Changes Face of East Harlem" (*New York Times*, December 10, 2002), Joseph Berger explains that most of the first Puerto Ricans who arrived in the United States settled in New York City in the Manhattan neighborhood of East Harlem, which came to be known as El Barrio (the Neighborhood). Eventually, Puerto Rican immigrants moved in greater numbers to other boroughs of the city and into New Jersey.

According to Dockterman, in the fact sheet "Hispanics of Puerto Rican Origin in the United States, 2009" (May 26, 2011, http://pewhispanic.org/files/factsheets/72.pdf), by 2009 more Puerto Ricans lived in the United States than in Puerto Rico. In 2010 Puerto Ricans represented 9.2% of the Hispanic population living in the United States. (See Table 1.3.) The Pew Hispanic Center finds that Puerto Ricans were concentrated in New York and Florida.

**Cuban-Americans**

According to the Pew Hispanic Center, in the fact sheet "Cubans in the United States" (August 25, 2006, http://pewhispanic.org/files/factsheets/23.pdf), many Cubans fled Cuba during the early 1960s after the Fulgencio Batista (1901–1973) regime was overthrown by Fidel Castro (1926–). Cuban immigrants tended to settle in Miami, Florida, and in the surrounding Dade County. Most of these political refugees were older, middle class, and educated. Many fled to maintain a capitalist way of life, and many succeeded in achieving economic prosperity in the United States. A second phase of Cuban immigration took place from about 1965 to 1974, legally bringing middle- and working-class Cubans to the United States through Cuban and U.S. government programs.

FIGURE 1.3

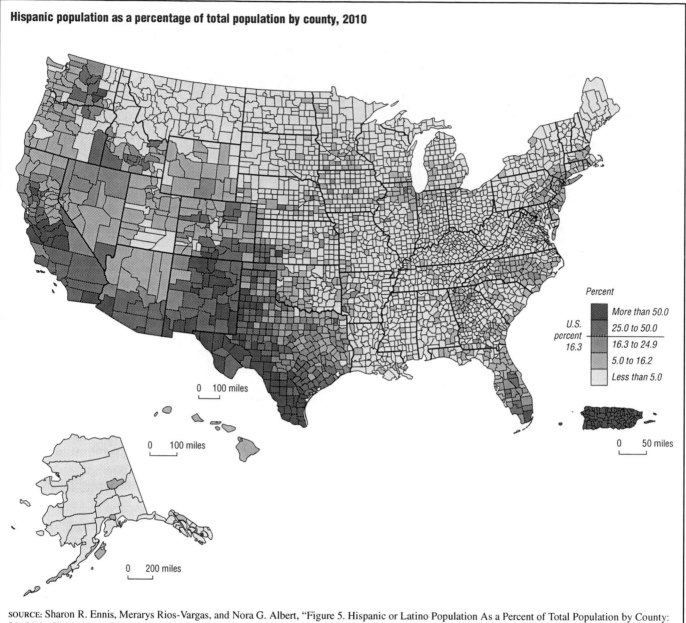

**Hispanic population as a percentage of total population by county, 2010**

Percent

U.S.
percent
16.3

More than 50.0
25.0 to 50.0
16.3 to 24.9
5.0 to 16.2
Less than 5.0

0   100 miles

0   100 miles

0   200 miles

0   50 miles

SOURCE: Sharon R. Ennis, Merarys Rios-Vargas, and Nora G. Albert, "Figure 5. Hispanic or Latino Population As a Percent of Total Population by County: 2010," in *The Hispanic Population: 2010*, U.S. Census Bureau, May 2011, http://www.census.gov/prod/cen2010/briefs/c2010br-04.pdf (accessed October 30, 2011)

In "Mariel Boatlift" (May 7, 2011, http://www.global security.org/military/ops/mariel-boatlift.htm), John Pike reports that in 1980, 125,000 people seeking refuge from Castro's government fled Cuba in what became known as the Mariel Boatlift, named after the town in Cuba from which they sailed. Because most of these new immigrants were from less wealthy and less educated backgrounds than their predecessors, and some were actually criminals or people who were mentally ill, many had difficulty fitting into the existing Cuban communities in the United States. Also, unlike the Cubans who came before them, they had spent 20 years living under a dictatorship that was vastly different from the democratic government they encountered in the United States.

This difference led to further difficulties in adjustment to their new home.

Mireya Navarro reports in "Last of Refugees from Cuba in '94 Flight Now Enter U.S." (*New York Times*, February 1, 1996) that in 1994 more than 29,000 Cubans tried to enter the United States after fleeing a severe economic crisis in their own country. Most attempted the trip by boats and rafts but were intercepted by the U.S. Coast Guard and taken back to Cuba, where they were detained at Guantánamo Bay, the U.S. naval base. By January 1996 most detainees had been allowed to enter the United States, and the detention camps were closed. The Pew Hispanic Center notes that under current U.S. policy, Cubans who are able to reach the United

States are allowed to stay, whereas those who are intercepted at sea are returned to Cuba.

Even though language differences cause initial difficulties for Cuban immigrants, Dockterman explains in the fact sheet "Hispanics of Cuban Origin in the United States, 2009" (May 26, 2011, http://pewhispanic.org/files/factsheets/73 .pdf) that most adapt well. Cubans have a higher level of educational attainment and are the most economically successful of the Hispanic ethnic groups. Unlike Americans of Mexican and Puerto Rican backgrounds, who began migrating throughout the country during the 1990s, the Cuban population has generally remained concentrated in Florida, even though large numbers also live in New Jersey, New York, and California. Cubans continue to come to the United States. In *2010 Yearbook of Immigration Statistics*, the DHS notes that 33,573 Cubans immigrated to the United States in 2010.

## AFRICAN-AMERICANS

In 1619 the first Africans arrived in colonial North America. Subsequently, their numbers increased rapidly to fill the growing demand for slave labor in the new land. The first slaves were brought into this country by way of the West Indies, but as demand increased, they were soon brought directly to the English colonies on the mainland in North America. Most were delivered to the South and worked on plantations, where they supplied cheap labor.

The vast majority of African-Americans in the United States were kept as slaves until the Civil War (1861–1865). According to the 1860 census (http://www2.census.gov/ prod2/decennial/documents/1860a-02.pdf), the states that made up the Confederacy in the South at the outbreak of hostilities had a slave population of 3.5 million, compared with a white population of nearly 5.5 million. By contrast, the Union states and territories in the North had a white population of 21.5 million, with slaves numbering 432,650.

In 1863 President Abraham Lincoln (1809–1865) issued the Emancipation Proclamation, which technically freed slaves in the Confederate states, although those states did not recognize the legality of the proclamation. In 1865 the 13th Amendment to the U.S. Constitution abolished slavery throughout the United States. In 1868 the 14th Amendment afforded former slaves and other African-Americans equal protection under the law, and in 1870 the 15th Amendment granted them the right to vote. The present population of African-Americans in the United States includes not only those who have descended from former slaves but also those who have since emigrated from Africa, the West Indies, and Central and South America.

According to the Census Bureau, in 2010, 38.9 million people who identified their race as non-Hispanic black alone lived in the United States. (See Table 1.1.) Generally, even mixed-race individuals in the United States identify as African-American due to the rigid politics of race in the nation. In 2010 African-Americans made up 12.6% of the population, up from 12.3% in 2000.

## Geographic Distribution

Few African-Americans voluntarily migrated from the southern farms and plantations that had been their homes during the first decades after the abolition of slavery. As a result, at the beginning of the 20th century a large majority of African-Americans still lived in the South. However, when World War I (1914–1918) interrupted the flow of migrant labor from Europe, large numbers of African-Americans migrated from the rural South to northern industrial cities to take advantage of new work opportunities there. Compared with the oppressive system of segregation in the South, economic and social conditions were better in the North for many African-Americans, thereby encouraging a continuous flow of migrants. According to the article "North by South: The African American Great Migration" (August 28, 2005, http://northbysouth.kenyon.edu/), between 1900 and 1960, 4.8 million African-Americans left the South and settled in northern cities such as Chicago, Illinois; Detroit, Michigan; Cleveland, Ohio; Pittsburgh, Pennsylvania; and New York City. The African-American migrations following World War I and World War II are among the largest voluntary internal migrations in U.S. history.

Most African-Americans moved to the Northeast and Midwest, although after 1940 significant numbers also moved West. The traditional migration from the South to the North dwindled dramatically during the 1970s. In fact, after 1975, largely due to the favorable economic conditions that were developing in the booming Sunbelt cities, African-Americans started migrating in droves to the South. Sonya Rastogi et al. of the Census Bureau indicate in *The Black Population: 2010* (September 2011, http:// www.census.gov/prod/cen2010/briefs/c2010br-06.pdf) that in 2010 all six states whose populations were more than 25% African-American were in the South: Mississippi (37.6%), Louisiana (32.8%), Georgia (31.5%), Maryland (30.9%), South Carolina (28.8%), and Alabama (26.8%). As Figure 1.4 shows, more than half (55%) of all African-Americans lived in the South in 2010; 18.1% lived in the Midwest, 17.1% lived in the Northeast, and 9.8% lived in the West.

## White Flight

African-Americans and other minorities are significantly more likely than whites to live in metropolitan areas, inside of central cities. According to Rastogi et al., in *Black Population*, African-Americans are concentrated in counties near metropolitan areas, especially in the Northeast, Midwest, and West. Figure 1.5 shows that in most of the 20 largest metropolitan statistical areas in 2010, non-Hispanic African-Americans made up a greater share of the population than did non-Hispanic whites.

FIGURE 1.4

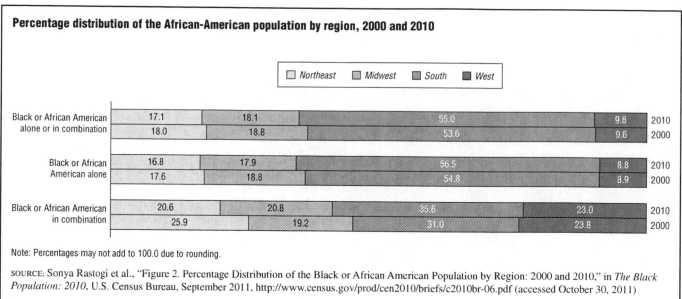

Percentage distribution of the African-American population by region, 2000 and 2010

☐ Northeast   ▨ Midwest   ▨ South   ■ West

Note: Percentages may not add to 100.0 due to rounding.

SOURCE: Sonya Rastogi et al., "Figure 2. Percentage Distribution of the Black or African American Population by Region: 2000 and 2010," in *The Black Population: 2010*, U.S. Census Bureau, September 2011, http://www.census.gov/prod/cen2010/briefs/c2010br-06.pdf (accessed October 30, 2011)

Eric Bickford of the University of California, Berkeley, explains in "White Flight: The Effect of Minority Presence on Post World War II Suburbanization" (September 1999, http://www.cliometrics.org/publications/flight.htm) that a primary reason for the high proportion of African-Americans in central cities has been "white flight." Beginning in the 1950s, as African-Americans moved to northeastern and midwestern cities, whites who were economically able to do so moved to suburban areas. Before the Civil Rights Act of 1964, which prohibited discrimination in housing, African-Americans were not given the same opportunities to move away from cities, whether or not they were economically able to do so. As wealthier whites abandoned city neighborhoods, taking their tax dollars with them, city neighborhoods rapidly deteriorated, leaving poor and nonwhite residents to deal with increasing crime and neighborhood deterioration.

In 2010 the 10 cities with the largest number of African-Americans included New York City (2.2 million), Chicago (913,000), Philadelphia, Pennsylvania (687,000), Detroit (602,000), and Houston, Texas (514,000). (See Table 1.5.) Table 1.6 lists the 10 cities with 100,000 or more total population that had the highest percentage of African-Americans in 2010: Detroit (84.3%), Jackson, Mississippi (80.1%), Miami Gardens, Florida (77.9%), Birmingham, Alabama (74%), Baltimore, Maryland (65.1%), Memphis, Tennessee (64.1%), New Orleans, Louisiana (61.2%), Flint, Michigan (59.5%), Montgomery, Alabama (57.4%), and Savannah, Georgia (56.7%). Eight of these cities were in the South; the other two were in the economically depressed state of Michigan.

## ASIAN-AMERICANS

The term *Asian-American* is a catchall term that did not gain currency until the late 1960s and early 1970s. It was not until 1980 that the Census Bureau created the "Asian and Pacific Islander" category, a departure from the previous practice of counting several Asian groups separately. Even though seemingly a geographic description, "Asian and Pacific Islander" contains racial overtones, given that natives of Australia and New Zealand are not included, nor are whites born in the Asian region of the former Soviet Union. In 2010 nearly 14.7 million Asian-Americans lived in the United States, making up 4.8% of the country's population. (See Table 1.1.) Native Hawaiians and other Pacific Islanders had a population of 540,013, making up 0.2% of the total U.S. population.

### Chinese Immigration during the 1800s

In "Chinese Immigration" (2012, http://www.loc.gov/teachers/classroommaterials/presentationsandactivities/presentations/immigration/chinese.html), the Library of Congress explains that the first major immigration of people from Asia to the United States involved the Chinese. From the time of the California gold rush of 1849 until the early 1880s, it is estimated that as many as 250,000 Chinese immigrated to the United States, with the vast majority coming from the Pearl River delta of Guangdong Province. Many hoped to strike it rich in California, the "Golden Mountain," and then return home. A few fulfilled that dream, but most stayed in the United States, two-thirds in California, where they faced intense discrimination. They became the object of political posturing that portrayed "cheap Chinese labor" as a threat to U.S. workers.

After the Civil War, when most African-Americans were able to gain citizenship with the adoption of the 14th Amendment in 1868, an exception was carved out for Asian immigrants. They were designated "aliens ineligible to citizenship." The Chinese Exclusion Act of 1882 then stopped

**FIGURE 1.5**

**Proportion of race and ethnic groups living inside the largest principal city of the 20 largest metropolitan statistical areas, 2010**

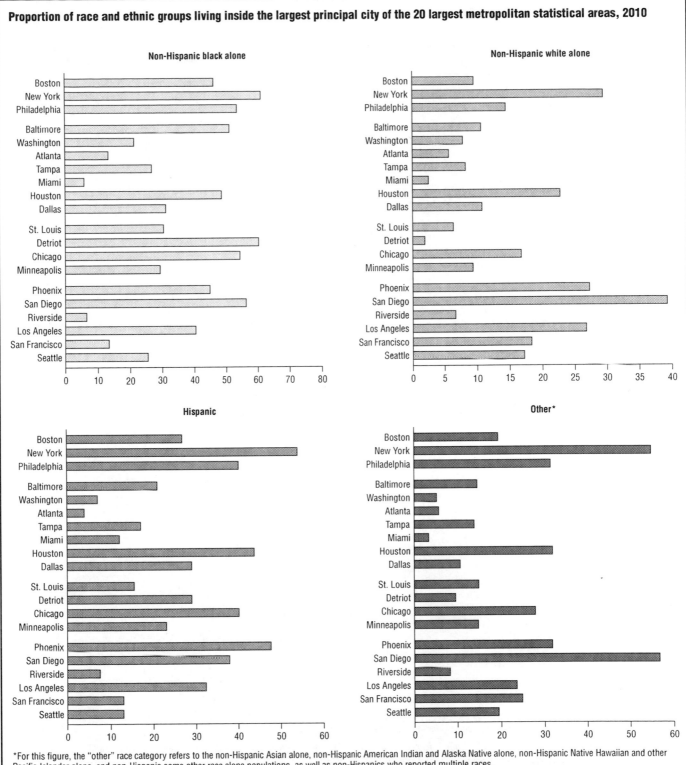

*For this figure, the "other" race category refers to the non-Hispanic Asian alone, non-Hispanic American Indian and Alaska Native alone, non-Hispanic Native Hawaiian and other Pacific Islander alone, and non-Hispanic some other race alone populations, as well as non-Hispanics who reported multiple races.

Notes: Principal cities within regions are organized based on proximity to each other. Boston, New York, and Philadelphia are located in the Northeast census region. Baltimore, Washington, Atlanta, Tampa, Miami, Houston, and Dallas are located in the South census region. St. Louis, Detroit, Chicago, and Minneapolis are located in the Midwest census region. Phoenix, San Diego, Riverside, Los Angeles, San Francisco, and Seattle are located in the West census region.

SOURCE: Sonya Rastogi et al., "Figure 7. Proportion of Race and Ethnic Groups Living inside the Largest Principal City of the 20 Largest Metropolitan Statistical Areas: 2010," in *The Black Population: 2010*, U.S. Census Bureau, September 2011, http://www.census.gov/prod/cen2010/briefs/c2010br-06.pdf (accessed October 30, 2011).

## TABLE 1.5

**Places with the largest number of African-Americans, 2010**

| Place* | Total population | Black or African American alone or in combination | | Black or African American alone | | Black or African American in combination | |
|---|---|---|---|---|---|---|---|
| | | Rank | Number | Rank | Number | Rank | Number |
| New York, NY | 8,175,133 | 1 | 2,228,145 | 1 | 2,088,510 | 1 | 139,635 |
| Chicago, IL | 2,695,598 | 2 | 913,009 | 2 | 887,608 | 3 | 25,401 |
| Philadelphia, PA | 1,526,006 | 3 | 686,870 | 3 | 661,839 | 4 | 25,031 |
| Detroit, MI | 713,777 | 4 | 601,988 | 4 | 590,226 | 13 | 11,762 |
| Houston, TX | 2,099,451 | 5 | 514,217 | 5 | 498,466 | 8 | 15,751 |
| Memphis, TN | 646,889 | 6 | 414,928 | 6 | 409,687 | 58 | 5,241 |
| Baltimore, MD | 620,961 | 7 | 403,998 | 7 | 395,781 | 29 | 8,217 |
| Los Angeles, CA | 3,792,621 | 8 | 402,448 | 8 | 365,118 | 2 | 37,330 |
| Washington, DC | 601,723 | 9 | 314,352 | 9 | 305,125 | 22 | 9,227 |
| Dallas, TX | 1,197,816 | 10 | 308,087 | 10 | 298,993 | 23 | 9,094 |
| Columbus, OH | 787,033 | 15 | 237,077 | 16 | 220,241 | 5 | 16,836 |
| San Diego, CA | 1,307,402 | 40 | 104,374 | 43 | 87,949 | 6 | 16,425 |
| Phoenix, AZ | 1,445,632 | 37 | 109,544 | 40 | 93,608 | 7 | 15,936 |
| Indianapolis, IN | 829,718 | 14 | 240,789 | 15 | 226,671 | 9 | 14,118 |
| Boston, MA | 617,594 | 21 | 163,629 | 23 | 150,437 | 10 | 13,192 |

*Places of 100,000 or more total population. The 2010 Census showed 282 places in the United States with 100,000 or more population. They included 273 incorporated places (including 5 city-county consolidations) and 9 census designated places that were not legally incorporated.

SOURCE: Sonya Rastogi et al., "Table 6. Ten Places with the Largest Number of Blacks or African Americans: 2010," in *The Black Population: 2010*, U.S. Census Bureau, September 2011, http://www.census.gov/prod/cen2010/briefs/c2010br-06.pdf (accessed October 30, 2011)

## TABLE 1.6

**Places with the highest percentage of African-Americans, 2010**

| Place* | Total population | Black or African American alone or in combination | | Black or African American alone | | Black or African American in combination | |
|---|---|---|---|---|---|---|---|
| | | Rank | Percent of total population | Rank | Percent of total population | Rank | Percent of total population |
| Detroit, MI | 713,777 | 1 | 84.3 | 1 | 82.7 | 83 | 1.6 |
| Jackson, MS | 173,514 | 2 | 80.1 | 2 | 79.4 | 242 | 0.7 |
| Miami Gardens, FL | 107,167 | 3 | 77.9 | 3 | 76.3 | 91 | 1.6 |
| Birmingham, AL | 212,237 | 4 | 74.0 | 4 | 73.4 | 257 | 0.6 |
| Baltimore, MD | 620,961 | 5 | 65.1 | 5 | 63.7 | 134 | 1.3 |
| Memphis, TN | 646,889 | 6 | 64.1 | 6 | 63.3 | 225 | 0.8 |
| New Orleans, LA | 343,829 | 7 | 61.2 | 7 | 60.2 | 184 | 1.0 |
| Flint, MI | 102,434 | 8 | 59.5 | 9 | 56.6 | 9 | 2.9 |
| Montgomery, AL | 205,764 | 9 | 57.4 | 8 | 56.6 | 231 | 0.8 |
| Savannah, GA | 136,286 | 10 | 56.7 | 10 | 55.4 | 139 | 1.3 |
| Lansing, MI | 114,297 | 69 | 27.8 | 78 | 23.7 | 1 | 4.1 |
| Tacoma, WA | 198,397 | 132 | 15.0 | 145 | 11.2 | 2 | 3.8 |
| Killeen, TX | 127,921 | 40 | 37.9 | 46 | 34.1 | 3 | 3.8 |
| Syracuse, NY | 145,170 | 51 | 33.1 | 57 | 29.5 | 4 | 3.6 |
| Providence, RI | 178,042 | 109 | 19.4 | 114 | 16.0 | 5 | 3.3 |
| Fairfield, CA | 105,321 | 111 | 19.0 | 118 | 15.7 | 6 | 3.3 |
| Rochester, NY | 210,565 | 29 | 44.9 | 33 | 41.7 | 7 | 3.2 |
| Fayetteville, NC | 200,564 | 31 | 44.8 | 32 | 41.9 | 8 | 2.9 |
| Vallejo, CA | 115,942 | 81 | 24.9 | 83 | 22.1 | 10 | 2.9 |

*Places of 100,000 or more total population. The 2010 Census showed 282 places in the United States with 100,000 or more population. They included 273 incorporated places (including 5 city-county consolidations) and 9 census designated places that were not legally incorporated.

SOURCE: Sonya Rastogi et al., "Table 7. Ten Places with the Highest Percentage of Blacks or African Americans: 2010," in *The Black Population: 2010*, U.S. Census Bureau, September 2011, http://www.census.gov/prod/cen2010/briefs/c2010br-06.pdf (accessed October 30, 2011)

the entry of Chinese into the country altogether, except for a few merchants and students. As a result, China became the source of the United States' first illegal aliens. Claire Lui states in "How Illegal Immigration Was Born" (May 7, 2007, http://www.americanheritage.com/) that besides jumping ship or illegally crossing borders, many Chinese immigrants took advantage of the 1906 earthquake in San Francisco, which destroyed the city's vital statistics records, to gain legal status by forging U.S. birth certificates. By law, any male of Chinese heritage born in the United States had the right to return to China for any children he fathered (although he could not bring back the alien mother). As a result, many of these fraudulent U.S. citizens escorted to the United States a host of "paper sons." Despite this traffic and other means of illegal entry, the Chinese-American population declined from the 1880s to the 1920s. Laws regulating Chinese immigration to the United States did not change until World War II, when China became an ally. President Franklin D. Roosevelt (1882–1945) persuaded Congress to repeal the Chinese Exclusion Act in 1943.

People of other nationalities that make up the Asian-American category also began immigrating to the United States before World War II. The Japanese first came to the United States in significant numbers during the 1890s, although many laborers had previously settled in Hawaii. Like the Chinese, the Japanese mostly lived in the western United States. There was some call for a "Japanese Exclusion Act," but because Japan was an emerging Pacific power, such legislation was never passed. Overall, Japanese immigrants fared better than their Chinese counterparts and soon outpaced them in population. However, the Library of Congress notes in "Japanese Immigration" (2012, http://www.loc.gov/teachers/classroommaterials/presentationsandactivities/presentations/immigration/japanese.html) that when Japan and the United States went to war in 1941, over 100,000 Americans of Japanese descent, including many who were native-born U.S. citizens, were removed from their homes and confined in detention camps. By 1945 approximately 125,000 people of Japanese descent had been sent to these camps. It is noteworthy that even though the United States was also at war with Germany and Italy, citizens of German and Italian descent or birth were not subject to incarceration due to their heritage.

Before World War II Filipinos, Asian-Indians, and Koreans represented a negligible share of the Asian-American population. In *Historical Census Statistics on Population Totals by Race, 1790 to 1990, and by Hispanic Origin, 1970 to 1990, for the United States, Regions, Divisions, and States* (September 2002, http://www.census.gov/population/www/documentation/twps0056/twps0056.html), Campbell Gibson and Kay Jung of the Census Bureau indicate that in 1940 there were 254,918 Asian-Americans living in the United States; 126,947 were Japanese, 77,504 were Chinese, and 45,563 were Filipino. Asian-Indians totaled 2,405, and Koreans numbered even fewer, at 1,711. As was the case with Puerto Ricans, Filipinos began immigrating to the United States in the years following the Spanish-American War, when their country was annexed and eventually granted commonwealth status. Designated "American nationals," Filipinos held a unique position: They were not eligible for citizenship, but they also could not be prevented from entering the United States. Many Filipinos immigrated during the 1920s looking for work, but the Great Depression of the 1930s stemmed this flow.

Asian-Indians had come to the United States in small numbers, generally settling in New York City and other eastern ports, but it was not until the early years of the 20th century that they began immigrating to the West Coast, generally entering through western Canada. Koreans came to the United States from Hawaii, where several thousand had immigrated between 1903 and 1905. Both Asian-Indians and Koreans lost their eligibility to enter the United States following the Immigration Act of 1917, which accounted for their small populations before World War II. Once the Chinese Exclusion Act was repealed, however, the door was also open for Filipinos and Asian-Indians to gain entry to the United States as well as to earn citizenship during the postwar years. The Korean War (1950–1953) led to a long-term U.S. military presence in Korea, resulting in a number of Korean-born wives of military personnel relocating to the United States. In addition, many Korean-born children were adopted and brought to the United States. A larger influx of Korean families immigrated during the mid-1960s.

## Sharp Rise in Immigration

Asian immigration during the 1980s can be divided into two so-called streams. The first stream came from Asian countries that already had large populations in the United States (such as China, the Philippines, and South Korea). These immigrants, many of whom were highly educated, came primarily for family reunification and through employment provisions of the immigration laws. The second stream consisted primarily of immigrants and refugees from the war-torn countries of Southeast Asia (Cambodia, Laos, and Vietnam). They were admitted under U.S. policies that supported political refugees after the Vietnam War (1954–1975), as well as those escaping unstable economic and political conditions in neighboring countries. The Office of Refugee Settlement notes in *Annual ORR Reports to Congress—1999* (1999, http://www.acf.hhs.gov/programs/orr/data/arc_99.htm) that between fiscal years 1975 and 1999, 1.3 million refugees from Southeast Asia had arrived in the United States.

According to the DHS, in *2010 Yearbook of Immigration Statistics*, China was the top Asian country of origin for Asian immigrants in 2010—in that year 70,863 immigrants from China made their way to the United States. India was second, with 69,162 immigrants; 30,632 Vietnamese immigrants and 22,227 South Korean immigrants made their way to the United States that same year.

## Geographic Distribution

According to Elizabeth M. Hoeffel et al. of the Census Bureau, in *The Asian Population: 2010* (March 2012, http://www.census.gov/prod/cen2010/briefs/c2010br-11.pdf), Asian-Americans were heavily concentrated in the West—46.2% of Asian-Americans lived in the West in 2010, while 22.1% lived in the South, 19.8% lived in the Northeast, and 11.9% lived in the Midwest. Three-fourths of all Asian-Americans lived in 10 states: California (5.6 million), New York (1.6 million), Texas

(1.1 million), Hawaii (800,000), New Jersey (800,000), Illinois (700,000), Florida (600,000), Washington (600,000), Virginia (500,000), and Pennsylvania (400,000). In 2010 California had the highest proportion of Asian-Americans in the continental United States, at 14.9%. Nevada (9%), New Jersey (9%), Washington (9%), and New York (8.2%) also had high proportions of Asian-Americans in their populations.

According to Hoeffel et al., eight of the 10 cities of 100,000 or more total population with the highest proportion of Asian-Americans were in California, including Daly City (58.4%) and Fremont (54.5%), which both had Asian-American populations of over 50%. The largest numbers of Asian-Americans lived in New York (1.1 million), Los Angeles, California (484,000), San Jose, Texas (327,000), San Francisco (289,000), and San Diego, California (241,000).

## NATIVE AMERICANS

Most archaeologists agree that the people known as Native Americans and Alaskan Natives arrived in North America from northeast Asia at least 30,000 years ago during the last of the Ice Age glaciations (coverings of large areas of the earth with ice). At that time the two continents were connected by a land bridge over what is currently the Bering Strait. However, according to Charles W. Petit, in "Rediscovering America: The New World May Be 20,000 Years Older Than Experts Thought" (*U.S. News and World Report*, October 12, 1998), some archaeologists dispute this theory by citing evidence that indicates that migrants may have actually arrived many thousands of years earlier, perhaps by boat. For example, the article "New Evidence Puts Man in North America 50,000 Years Ago" (*Science-Daily*, November 18, 2004) notes that artifacts have been discovered along the Savannah River in Allendale County, South Carolina, that date back to at least 50,000 years ago. The article indicates that "the findings are significant because they suggest that humans inhabited North America well before the last ice age more than 20,000 years ago, a potentially explosive revelation in American archaeology."

Migrants who settled on the northern coast of Alaska and the Yukon River valley, which were free of ice barriers, became known as Eskimos and Aleuts. Those who ventured farther south followed the eastern slope of the Rocky Mountains and continued along the mountainous spine of North America into South America. They eventually moved east throughout the central plains and eastern highlands of both continents and were later erroneously named Indians by exploring Spaniards. The misnomer is attributed to Christopher Columbus (1451–1506), who, on landing in the Bahamas in 1492, thought he had reached the islands off the eastern region of Asia, called the Indies. He therefore greeted the inhabitants as "Indians." In the 21st century many descendants of the original settlers prefer to be called Native Americans.

Most Native American groups had a close relationship with the earth. Some specialized in farming, whereas others focused on hunting and/or fishing. The arrival of the Europeans eventually changed the Native Americans' way of life. Devastating wars, diseases, the annihilation of the buffalo, and the loss of land fit for cultivation to Europeans led to the elimination of much of their population.

In 2010, 2.9 million Native Americans and Alaskan Natives lived in the United States, making up approximately 0.9% of the population. (See Table 1.1.) According to Tina Norris, Paula L. Vines, and Elizabeth M. Hoeffel of the Census Bureau, in *The American Indian and Alaska Native Population: 2010* (January 2012, http://www.census.gov/prod/cen2010/briefs/c2010br-10.pdf), another 2.3 million people reported being Native American or Alaskan Native in combination with one or more other races.

### Geographic Distribution

In *American Indian and Alaska Native Population*, Norris, Vines, and Hoeffel report that in 2010 the five cities of 100,000 or more total population with the highest proportion of Native Americans and Alaskan Natives included Anchorage, Alaska (12.4%), Tulsa, Oklahoma (9.2%), Norman, Oklahoma (8.1%), Oklahoma City, Oklahoma (6.3%), and Billings, Montana (6%). New York City had the largest Native American and Alaskan Native population (112,000), followed by Los Angeles (54,000).

Many Native Americans and Alaskan Natives live on or near reservations and are members of groupings called tribes. Norris, Vines, and Hoeffel note that about one out of five (20.5%) Native Americans and Alaskan Natives lived in Native American areas in 2010, 1.5% lived in Alaskan Native village statistical areas, and 78% lived outside of Native American and Alaskan Native areas. The largest tribal groupings were the Cherokee, with 819,105 members, followed by the Navajo, with 332,129 members, and the Choctaw, with 195,764 members. Many Alaskan Natives are also members of such groups. The largest tribal groupings of Alaskan Natives in 2010 were the Yup'ik, with 33,889 members, followed by the Inupiat, with 33,360 members, and the Tlingit-Haida, with 26,080 members.

## A MULTIRACIAL SOCIETY

In the 2010 census about 3% of respondents, or 9 million Americans, reported that they were more than one race. Most of these respondents reported that they were white in combination with another race (7.5 million). (See Table 1.7.) However, large percentages of Native Hawaiians and other Pacific Islanders (55.9%) and Native Americans and Alaskan Natives (43.8%) reported multiple races, compared with much smaller percentages of Asian-Americans (15.3%), African-Americans (7.4%), and whites (3.2%).

TABLE 1.7

**Race by the alone-or-in-combination, alone, and in-combination categories, 2010**

| Race | Number | Percentage of total population | Percentage of alone or in combination |
|---|---|---|---|
| **Total population** | 308,745,538 | 100.0 | (X) |
| **White** | | | |
| Alone or in combination | 231,040,398 | 74.8 | (X) |
| Alone | 223,553,265 | 72.4 | 96.8 |
| In combination | 7,487,133 | 2.4 | 3.2 |
| **Black or African American** | | | |
| Alone or in combination | 42,020,743 | 13.6 | (X) |
| Alone | 38,929,319 | 12.6 | 92.6 |
| In combination | 3,091,424 | 1.0 | 7.4 |
| **American Indian or Alaska Native** | | | |
| Alone or in combination | 5,220,579 | 1.7 | (X) |
| Alone | 2,932,248 | 0.9 | 56.2 |
| In combination | 2,288,331 | 0.7 | 43.8 |
| **Asian** | | | |
| Alone or in combination | 17,320,856 | 5.6 | (X) |
| Alone | 14,674,252 | 4.8 | 84.7 |
| In combination | 2,646,604 | 0.9 | 15.3 |
| **Native Hawaiian and other Pacific Islander** | | | |
| Alone or in combination | 1,225,195 | 0.4 | (X) |
| Alone | 540,013 | 0.2 | 44.1 |
| In combination | 685,182 | 0.2 | 55.9 |
| **Some other race** | | | |
| Alone or in combination | 21,748,084 | 7.0 | (X) |
| Alone | 19,107,368 | 6.2 | 87.9 |
| In combination | 2,640,716 | 0.9 | 12.1 |

(X) Not applicable.
Note: The total population is equal to the number of respondents. In the 2010 Census, there were 308,745,538 respondents. The total of all race categories alone or in combination with one or more other races is equal to the number of responses; therefore, it adds to more than the total population.

SOURCE: Karen R. Humes, Nicholas A. Jones, and Robert R. Ramirez, "Table 3. Race by the Alone-or-In-Combination, Alone, and In-Combination Categories for the United States: 2010," in *Overview of Race and Hispanic Origin: 2010*, U.S. Census Bureau, March 2011, http://www.census.gov/prod/cen2010/briefs/c2010br-02.pdf (accessed October 30, 2011)

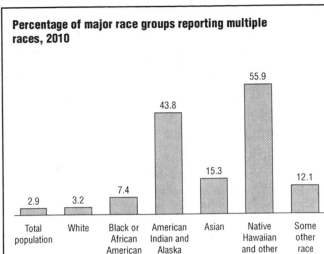

**FIGURE 1.6**

**Percentage of major race groups reporting multiple races, 2010**

Note: Specified race group refers to the alone or in-combination population.

SOURCE: Karen R. Humes, Nicholas A. Jones, and Robert R. Ramirez, "Figure 2. Percentage of Major Race Groups Reporting Multiple Races: 2010," in *Overview of Race and Hispanic Origin: 2010*, U.S. Census Bureau, March 2011, http://www.census.gov/prod/cen2010/briefs/c2010br-02.pdf (accessed October 30, 2011)

**TABLE 1.8**

**Public opinion on the impact of Barack Obama's presidency on race relations, by race, political affiliation, and age, August 2011**

Impact of Barack Obama's presidency on U.S. race relations

| | Better | Not changed | Worse | Net better |
|---|---|---|---|---|
| | % | % | % | +/− |
| National adults | 35 | 41 | 23 | +12 |
| Blacks | 48 | 27 | 24 | +24 |
| Whites | 31 | 45 | 22 | +9 |
| Democrats | 46 | 38 | 15 | +31 |
| Independents | 34 | 40 | 25 | +9 |
| Republicans | 19 | 48 | 32 | −13 |
| 18 to 34 years | 42 | 34 | 24 | +18 |
| 35 to 54 years | 33 | 45 | 21 | +12 |
| 55 and older | 32 | 42 | 24 | +8 |

SOURCE: Lydia Saad, "Impact of Barack Obama's Presidency on U.S. Race Relations," in *One-Third in U.S. See Improved Race Relations under Obama*, August 24, 2011, http://www.gallup.com/poll/149141/One-Third-Improved-Race-Relations-Obama.aspx (accessed October 30, 2011). Copyright © 2011 by The Gallup Organization. Reproduced by Permission of The Gallup Organization.

(See Figure 1.6.) Rigid black-white racial politics in the United States may have led whites and African-Americans to underreport their multiracial origins.

## RELATIONS BETWEEN WHITES AND MINORITY GROUPS

In *One-Third in U.S. See Improved Race Relations under Obama* (August 24, 2011, http://www.gallup.com/poll/149141/One-Third-Improved-Race-Relations-Obama.aspx), Lydia Saad of the Gallup Organization reports on a 2011 poll about whether relations between racial and ethnic groups have improved under Barack Obama (1961–), the United States' first African-American president. Overall, 35% of Americans said race relations have improved under the Obama administration, which was down from 41% in 2009. Almost half (48%) of African-Americans and 31% of whites said race relations have improved. (See Table 1.8.) About a quarter (27%) of African-Americans and 45% of whites said race relations have not changed, and 24% of African-Americans and 22% of whites said race relations have gotten worse since Obama's election. Nevertheless, Saad notes that 52% of all Americans "are still optimistic that race relations will get better in the years ahead as a result of Obama's presidency."

Saad notes in *Whites May Exaggerate Black-Hispanic Tensions* (July 17, 2008, http://www.gallup.com/poll/108868/

Whites-May-Exaggerate-BlackHispanic-Tensions.aspx) that in 2008, 81% of Americans said they believe relations between whites and Asian-Americans are "very/somewhat good," 68% believed relations between whites and African-Americans are "very/somewhat good," and 65% believed relations between whites and Hispanics are "very/somewhat good." Non-Hispanic whites were significantly more likely than non-Hispanic African-Americans to perceive relations between whites and African-Americans as being good (70% and 61%, respectively).

In *Americans Divided on Whether King's Dream Has Been Realized* (August 26, 2011, http://www.gallup.com/poll/149201/Americans-Divided-Whether-King-Dream-Realized.aspx), Jeffrey M. Jones of the Gallup Organization reports on a 2011 poll in which Americans were asked whether Martin Luther King Jr.'s (1929–1968) dream of U.S. racial equality has been realized. A larger proportion of African-Americans (54%) than whites (49%) responded that racial equality has been achieved. (See Table 1.9.)

**TABLE 1.9**

**Public opinion on whether Martin Luther King Jr.'s dream of racial equality has been realized, August 2011**

HAS MARTIN LUTHER KING'S DREAM BEEN REALIZED?

Thinking back to Dr. Martin Luther King and his dream of racial equality, do you think that dream has now been realized in the United States, or not?

(Asked of those who say Dr. King's dream has not been realized) Do you think the United States has made major progress toward realizing that dream, minor progress, or no progress at all?

| | All Americans | Whites | Blacks |
|---|---|---|---|
| | % | % | % |
| Yes, realized | 51 | 49 | 54 |
| No, not realized | 49 | 51 | 45 |
| (Made major progress) | (23) | (26) | (13) |
| (Made minor progress) | (3) | (23) | (28) |
| (Made no progress) | (3) | (2) | (4) |

SOURCE:: Jeffrey M. Jones, "Has Martin Luther King Jr.'s Dream Been Realized?" in *Americans Divided on Whether King's Dream Has Been Realized*, August 26, 2011, http://www.gallup.com/poll/149201/Americans-Divided-Whether-King-Dream-Realized.aspx (accessed October 30, 2011). Copyright © 2011 by The Gallup Organization. Reproduced by Permission of The Gallup Organization.

# CHAPTER 2
# FAMILY LIFE AND LIVING ARRANGEMENTS

The family has been historically regarded as the cornerstone of society in the United States. For many years, particularly when the nation was primarily an agricultural society, extended families (multiple generations living in the same household) were common. As the culture became more urban and mobile, nuclear families (two parents and their children) became the American norm.

However, the makeup of families and their role in society have been undergoing a massive change. Shifts in economics, employment, moral values, and social conditions have led to an increasing number of single men and women living alone, cohabitations without marriage, and single-parent families. A growing number of children, especially minority children, are being raised by one parent or by neither parent, as in the case of children being raised by grandparents or foster parents. How these changes affect minorities in the United States can be best understood through a detailed look at minority families.

## MARITAL STATUS

The U.S. Census Bureau reports in *America's Families and Living Arrangements: 2011* (November 2011, http://www.census.gov/population/www/socdemo/hh-fam/cps2011.html) that in 2011, 123.9 million Americans (aged 15 years and older) were married, up from 95.3 million in 1970 and 112.6 million in 1990 but down from 127.1 million in 2005. This figure includes both people who did and people who did not live with their spouses. However, the proportion of people of marriage age who were married has decreased steadily since 1960, even though the absolute numbers of married people have increased until quite recently. According to the Census Bureau, in "Marital Status of the Population 15 Years Old and Over, by Sex, Race, and Hispanic Origin: 1950 to Present" (November 2011, http://www.census.gov/population/www/socdemo/hh-fam.html#history), in 1960, 67.6% of the population aged 15 years and older was married, dropping to 64.2%

in 1970, 61% in 1980, 58.7% in 1990, 56.2% in 2000, and to a low of 50.8% in 2011. (See Table 2.1.)

The proportion of African-Americans who were married has been lower than the proportion of married adults in the general population since 1960 and has dropped faster as well. According to the Census Bureau, of all African-Americans aged 15 years and older, 60.3% in 1960, 55.4% in 1970, 46.5% in 1980, 42.4% in 1990, and 39.2% in 2000 were married. By 2011 only 31.4% of African-Americans aged 15 years and older were married. (See Table 2.1.) That same year 60.5% of Asian-Americans, 54.9% of non-Hispanic whites, and 45.3% of Hispanics aged 15 years and older were married.

### Never Married

Racial differences among never-married people are also significant. Among those over the age of 15 years, African-Americans are far more likely than non-Hispanic whites, Hispanics, or Asian-Americans to have never married. In 2011, 47.4% of African-Americans had never been married, compared with 40% of Hispanics, 29% of Asian-Americans, and 26.2% of non-Hispanic whites. (See Table 2.1.)

One reason that the proportion of never-married individuals aged 15 years and older has increased over time is that the age at first marriage has steadily risen since 1970 for all races and ethnic groups. The median age (half of all people below the median value and half of all people above the median value) of first marriage for women rose from 20.8 in 1970 to 26.5 in 2011. (See Figure 2.1.) The median age of first marriage for men rose from 23.2 in 1970 to 28.7 in 2011. This rise in the age at first marriage accounts for some of the decreases in the proportion of adults who have ever married.

Another reason that the proportion of never-married individuals has increased is the rise in cohabitation. The Census Bureau reports in *Families and Living Arrangements* (November 2011, http://www.census.gov/population/www/

# TABLE 2.1

## Marital status of people 15 years and over, by sex, race, and Hispanic origin, 2011

[Numbers in thousands, except for percentages]

| | Total Number | Married spouse present Number | Married spouse absent Number | Widowed Number | Divorced Number | Separated Number | Never married Number | Total Percent | Married spouse present Percent | Married spouse absent Percent | Widowed Percent | Divorced Percent | Separated Percent | Never married Percent |
|---|---|---|---|---|---|---|---|---|---|---|---|---|---|---|
| **All races** | | | | | | | | | | | | | | |
| Total 15+ | 243,858 | 120,309 | 3,570 | 14,236 | 24,432 | 5,501 | 75,810 | 100.0 | 49.3 | 1.5 | 5.8 | 10.0 | 2.3 | 31.1 |
| Male Total 15+ | 118,828 | 60,155 | 1,816 | 2,929 | 10,670 | 2,410 | 40,847 | 100.0 | 50.6 | 1.5 | 2.5 | 9.0 | 2.0 | 34.4 |
| Female Total 15+ | 125,030 | 60,155 | 1,754 | 11,306 | 13,762 | 3,091 | 34,963 | 100.0 | 48.1 | 1.4 | 9.0 | 11.0 | 2.5 | 28.0 |
| **White, Non-Hispanic** | | | | | | | | | | | | | | |
| Total 15+ | 164,071 | 88,677 | 1,543 | 10,549 | 17,583 | 2,695 | 43,024 | 100.0 | 54.0 | 0.9 | 6.4 | 10.7 | 1.6 | 26.2 |
| Male Total 15+ | 80,079 | 44,413 | 731 | 2,160 | 7,921 | 1,266 | 23,589 | 100.0 | 55.5 | 0.9 | 2.7 | 9.9 | 1.6 | 29.5 |
| Female Total 15+ | 83,992 | 44,265 | 812 | 8,389 | 9,662 | 1,429 | 19,435 | 100.0 | 52.7 | 1.0 | 10.0 | 11.5 | 1.7 | 23.1 |
| **Black alone** | | | | | | | | | | | | | | |
| Total 15+ | 29,752 | 8,679 | 642 | 1,704 | 3,334 | 1,288 | 14,104 | 100.0 | 29.2 | 2.2 | 5.7 | 11.2 | 4.3 | 47.4 |
| Male Total 15+ | 13,529 | 4,461 | 271 | 324 | 1,301 | 522 | 6,651 | 100.0 | 33.0 | 2.0 | 2.4 | 9.6 | 3.9 | 49.2 |
| Female Total 15+ | 16,223 | 4,218 | 372 | 1,381 | 2,033 | 766 | 7,454 | 100.0 | 26.0 | 2.3 | 8.5 | 12.5 | 4.7 | 45.9 |
| **Asian alone** | | | | | | | | | | | | | | |
| Total 15+ | 11,498 | 6,615 | 342 | 534 | 519 | 150 | 3,338 | 100.0 | 57.5 | 3.0 | 4.6 | 4.5 | 1.3 | 29.0 |
| Male Total 15+ | 5,423 | 3,128 | 168 | 84 | 184 | 48 | 1,812 | 100.0 | 57.7 | 3.1 | 1.5 | 3.4 | 0.9 | 33.4 |
| Female Total 15+ | 6,076 | 3,487 | 174 | 450 | 335 | 102 | 1,527 | 100.0 | 57.4 | 2.9 | 7.4 | 5.5 | 1.7 | 25.1 |
| **Hispanic** | | | | | | | | | | | | | | |
| Total 15+ | 35,052 | 14,874 | 1,026 | 1,244 | 2,586 | 1,295 | 14,027 | 100.0 | 42.4 | 2.9 | 3.5 | 7.4 | 3.7 | 40.0 |
| Male Total 15+ | 18,097 | 7,382 | 652 | 302 | 1,090 | 553 | 8,118 | 100.0 | 40.8 | 3.6 | 1.7 | 6.0 | 3.1 | 44.9 |
| Female Total 15+ | 16,954 | 7,491 | 374 | 942 | 1,495 | 742 | 5,909 | 100.0 | 44.2 | 2.2 | 5.6 | 8.8 | 4.4 | 34.9 |

—Represents or rounds to zero.
Note: Prior to 2001, this table included group quarters people. Hispanics may be of any race.

SOURCE: Adapted from "Table A1. Marital Status of People 15 Years and over, by Age, Sex, Personal Earnings, Race, and Hispanic Origin, 2011," in *America's Families and Living Arrangements: 2011*, U.S. Census Bureau, November 2011, http://www.census.gov/population/www/socdemo/hh-fam/cps2011.html (accessed November 2, 2011)

**FIGURE 2.1**

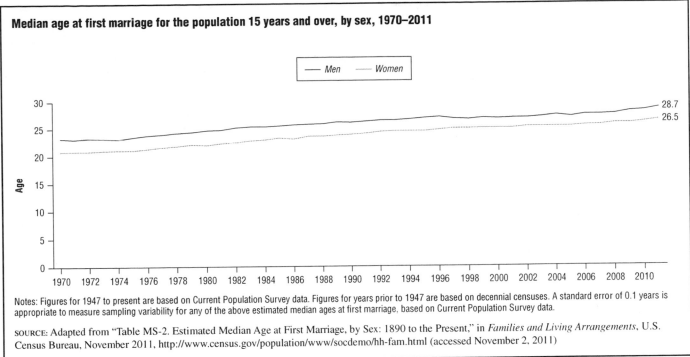

Median age at first marriage for the population 15 years and over, by sex, 1970–2011

Notes: Figures for 1947 to present are based on Current Population Survey data. Figures for years prior to 1947 are based on decennial censuses. A standard error of 0.1 years is appropriate to measure sampling variability for any of the above estimated median ages at first marriage, based on Current Population Survey data.

SOURCE: Adapted from "Table MS-2. Estimated Median Age at First Marriage, by Sex: 1890 to the Present," in *Families and Living Arrangements*, U.S. Census Bureau, November 2011, http://www.census.gov/population/www/socdemo/hh-fam.html (accessed November 2, 2011)

socdemo/hh-fam.html) that in 2011, 7.6 million unmarried couples cohabitated in the United States, up from 4.1 million in 2001 and 2.9 million in 1996. Unlike in the past, the birth of children does not necessarily lead to parents marrying. In 2011, 3 million cohabitating couples, or 39.9%, had children.

**Interracial Marriage**

Laws that prohibited interracial marriage were on the books in many states until 1967. In that year the U.S. Supreme Court unanimously decided in *Loving v. Virginia* (388 U.S. 1) that prohibitions against interracial marriage were unconstitutional. Nevertheless, interracial marriages were rare even into the 1970s. After 1980 interracial marriages became much more common. The Census Bureau reports that the number of interracial married couples nearly quadrupled between 1980 and 2010. (See Table 2.2.) For example, in 1980 there were 167,000 African-American–white interracial married couples; by 2010 there were 558,000 African-American–white interracial married couples. In 1980 there were 450,000 married couples with one white spouse and one spouse of a race other than white or African-American, such as Native American or Asian and Pacific Islander; in 2010 over 1.7 million married couples fit this description. Even though the proportion of interracial married couples is rising, the vast majority of married couples continue to be made up of two spouses of the same race. In 1980, 651,000 married couples were interracial; by 2010 there were 2.4 million.

Why is the number of interracial and interethnic marriage rising? Michael J. Rosenfeld of Stanford University argues in "The Steady Rise of Non-traditional Romantic Unions" (March 8, 2007, http://www.contemporaryfamilies.org/marriage-partnership-divorce/unions.html) that the rise in immigration from Asian and Hispanic countries is partially responsible, because neither of these groups is as segregated from white society as African-Americans have historically been in the United States. He also cites a rising marriage age, greater acceptance of diversity, and improving race relations as reasons marriages between whites and African-Americans have increased.

In fact, considerable progress has been made in the public acceptance of interracial marriage. According to Joseph Carroll of the Gallup Organization, in *Most Americans Approve of Interracial Marriages* (August 16, 2007, http://www.gallup.com/poll/28417/Most-Americans-Approve-Interracial-Marriages.aspx), in 1958 only 4% of Americans were accepting of marriage between couples of different races, and as late as 1994, 48% of all Americans approved. By 2007, however, 77% of Americans said they approved of marriages between African-Americans and whites. Support for interracial marriages was higher among African-Americans (85%) than among whites (75%). Younger Americans were more accepting of interracial marriages than older Americans—85% of people between the ages of 18 and 49 years approved, whereas among adults over the age of 50 years only 67% approved.

In *Record-High 86% Approve of Black-White Marriages* (September 12, 2011, http://www.gallup.com/poll/149390/Record-High-Approve-Black-White-Marriages.aspx), Jeffrey M. Jones of the Gallup Organization indicates that in just four years the approval rating for African-American–white marriages had jumped by

**TABLE 2.2**

**Interracially married couples by race and Hispanic origin of spouses, selected years 1980–2010**

[In thousands.]

| Race and origin of spouses | 1980 | 1990 | 2000 | 2008 | 2009 | 2010 |
|---|---|---|---|---|---|---|
| **Married couples, total**[a] | 49,714 | 53,256 | 56,497 | 60,129 | 60,844 | 60,384 |
| Interracial married couples, total | 651 | 964 | 1,464 | 2,340 | 2,437 | 2,413 |
| White/black | 167 | 211 | 363 | 481 | 550 | 558 |
| Black husband/white wife | 122 | 150 | 268 | 317 | 354 | 390 |
| White husband/black wife | 45 | 61 | 95 | 164 | 196 | 168 |
| White/other race[b] | 450 | 720 | 1,051 | 1,737 | 1,759 | 1,723 |
| Black/other race[b] | 34 | 33 | 50 | 122 | 128 | 132 |
| **Hispanic origin** | | | | | | |
| Hispanic/Hispanic | 1,906 | 3,085 | 4,739 | 6,390 | 6,317 | 6,166 |
| Hispanic/other origin (not Hispanic) | 891 | 1,193 | 1,743 | 2,222 | 2,421 | 2,289 |
| All other couples (not of Hispanic origin) | 46,917 | 48,979 | 50,015 | 51,517 | 52,107 | 51,928 |

[a]Includes other married couples not shown separately.
[b]"Other race," is any race other than white or black, such as American Indian, Japanese, Chinese, etc. This total excludes combinations of other races by other races.
Notes: Persons 15 years old and over. Persons of Hispanic origin may be of any race.

SOURCE:: "Table 60. Interracially Married Couples by Race and Hispanic Origin of Spouses: 1980 to 2010," in *Statistical Abstract of the United States: 2012*, 131st ed., U.S. Census Bureau, September 2011, http://www.census.gov/compendia/statab/2012/tables/12s0060.pdf (accessed November 3, 2011)

seven percentage points, from 79% in 2007 to 86% in 2011. Overall, 96% of African-Americans and 84% of whites approved of interracial marriages in 2011. Support of interracial marriages was particularly high among 18- to 29-year-olds (97%), people residing in the West (91%) and the East (90%), people with a college degree (92%) or postgraduate degree (94%), and among people who described themselves as "liberal" (95%). These data suggest that within a generation or two, almost all Americans will approve of interracial marriages.

## Divorce

The Census Bureau reports that in 2011, 24.4 million adults aged 15 years and older were divorced. (See Table 2.1.) In other words, 10% of all people aged 15 years and older were divorced and had not remarried at the time of the survey—thus, the proportion of ever-divorced people is much higher. A similar proportion of African-Americans (11.2%) and non-Hispanic whites (10.7%) were divorced, whereas a much lower proportion of Hispanics (7.4%) and Asian-Americans (4.5%) were divorced. In *Marital Status and Living Arrangements: March 1994* (February 1996, http://www.census.gov/prod/1/pop/p20-484.pdf), Arlene F. Saluter of the Census Bureau reports that divorce for most groups rose sharply from 1970 to the 1990s, when 4.4% of African-Americans, 3.9% of Hispanics, and 3.1% of whites were divorced. The divorce rate leveled off during the 1990s, according to Jason Fields of the Census Bureau, in *America's Families and Living Arrangements: 2003* (November 2004, http://www.census.gov/prod/2004pubs/p20-553.pdf).

Because men are considerably more likely than women to remarry following a divorce, there are significantly higher proportions of currently divorced women than currently divorced men. In 2011, 1.3 million (9.6%) African-American men were currently divorced, compared with 2 million (12.5%) African-American women; and 7.9 million (9.9%) non-Hispanic white men were divorced, compared with 9.7 million (11.5%) non-Hispanic white women. (See Table 2.1.) Among those of Hispanic origin, 1.1 million (6%) men and 1.5 million (8.8%) women were divorced. In the Asian-American community, 184,000 (3.4%) men and 335,000 (5.5%) women were divorced. Many more women of each race and ethnicity remained divorced than men.

## Death of a Spouse

In 2011, 14.2 million (5.8%) people aged 15 years and older in the United States were widowed. (See Table 2.1.) Across all racial and ethnic groups, more women than men were widowed because of the shorter average life span of men, the tendency of wives to be younger than their husbands, and the greater likelihood that men will remarry. This was particularly pronounced in the non-Hispanic white and African-American communities. Nearly 8.4 million (10%) non-Hispanic white women were widowed, compared with only 2.2 million (2.7%) non-Hispanic white men. A similar proportion of African-American women (1.4 million, or 8.5%) were widowed, compared with 324,000 (2.4%) African-American men. Among Asian-Americans, 450,000 (7.4%) women were widowed, compared with only 84,000 (1.5%) men. Among Hispanics, 942,000 (5.6%) women were widowed, compared with 302,000 (1.7%) men.

## TEENAGE PREGNANCY

Over the generations, a major change in American attitudes has removed much of the social stigma from unwed motherhood. Unmarried women of all ages are having children openly and with a regularity that was unheard of just a few generations ago. Many women do not feel the need to marry immediately when they become pregnant. Joyce A. Martin et al. of the Centers for Disease Control and Prevention (CDC) indicate in "Births: Final Data for 2009" (*National Vital Statistics Reports*, vol. 60, no. 1, November 3, 2011) that in 2009 nearly 1.7 million babies were born to single mothers—the highest number ever recorded; 41% of all births were to unmarried mothers in that year. (See Table 2.3.) However, even though the proportion of all births to unmarried mothers has risen, between 1990 and 2009 the birthrate to unmarried teenagers decreased. For example, Martin et al. note that among 15- to 17-year-olds the birthrate decreased from 29.6 births per 1,000 women in 1990 to 19.3 births per 1,000 women in 2009. However, Brady E. Hamilton, Joyce A. Martin, and Stephanie J. Ventura of the CDC note in "Births: Preliminary Data for 2010" (*National Vital Statistics Reports*, vol. 60, no. 2, November 17, 2011) that the birthrate for teenagers rose markedly between 2005 and

**TABLE 2.3**

**Births and birth rates to unmarried women, by age, race, and Hispanic origin of mother, 2009**

| Measure and age of mother | All races[a] | White | | Black | | American Indian or Alaska Native[b] | Asian or Pacific Islander[b] | Hispanic[c] |
|---|---|---|---|---|---|---|---|---|
| | | Total[b] | Non-Hispanic | Total[b] | Non-Hispanic | | | |
| **Number** | | | | | | | | |
| All ages | 1,693,658 | 1,142,871 | 641,252 | 475,718 | 444,044 | 31,812 | 43,257 | 531,445 |
| Under 15 years | 4,980 | 2,981 | 1,035 | 1,821 | 1,703 | 105 | 73 | 2,048 |
| 15–19 years | 357,474 | 241,568 | 132,030 | 102,664 | 95,973 | 7,519 | 5,723 | 116,011 |
| 15 years | 15,398 | 9,949 | 3,812 | 4,802 | 4,486 | 379 | 268 | 6,481 |
| 16 years | 36,101 | 24,249 | 10,567 | 10,507 | 9,766 | 766 | 579 | 14,390 |
| 17 years | 65,595 | 44,818 | 22,558 | 18,360 | 17,098 | 1,425 | 992 | 23,507 |
| 18 years | 103,092 | 69,836 | 39,188 | 29,501 | 27,626 | 2,145 | 1,610 | 32,426 |
| 19 years | 137,288 | 92,716 | 55,905 | 39,494 | 36,997 | 2,804 | 2,274 | 39,207 |
| 20–24 years | 624,293 | 419,174 | 253,757 | 180,128 | 168,818 | 11,902 | 13,089 | 176,486 |
| 25–29 years | 394,556 | 266,157 | 147,026 | 109,131 | 101,690 | 7,141 | 12,127 | 126,112 |
| 30–34 years | 198,168 | 134,133 | 66,761 | 53,532 | 49,620 | 3,445 | 7,058 | 70,993 |
| 35–39 years | 89,854 | 61,737 | 31,048 | 22,681 | 20,971 | 1,399 | 4,037 | 32,017 |
| 40 years and over | 24,333 | 17,121 | 9,595 | 5,761 | 5,269 | 301 | 1,150 | 7,778 |
| **Rate per 1,000 unmarried women in specified group** | | | | | | | | |
| 15–44 years[d] | 50.5 | 46.3 | 33.0 | 69.9 | — | — | 27.4 | 96.8 |
| 15–19 years | 35.0 | 30.8 | 21.7 | 58.9 | — | — | 12.4 | 62.5 |
| 15–17 years | 19.3 | 16.9 | 10.3 | 32.6 | — | — | 6.7 | 38.8 |
| 18–19 years | 58.2 | 51.1 | 38.1 | 96.8 | — | — | 21.1 | 100.3 |
| 20–24 years | 74.6 | 66.1 | 49.8 | 120.2 | — | — | 31.4 | 135.3 |
| 25–29 years | 72.7 | 68.0 | 47.2 | 94.3 | — | — | 42.2 | 150.5 |
| 30–34 years | 57.5 | 57.1 | 37.0 | 60.8 | — | — | 42.0 | 120.8 |
| 35–39 years | 30.2 | 30.6 | 19.8 | 29.0 | — | — | 29.2 | 68.2 |
| 40–44 years[e] | 7.9 | 7.8 | 5.5 | 7.8 | — | — | 10.4 | 18.1 |
| **Percent of births to unmarried women** | | | | | | | | |
| All ages | 41.0 | 36.0 | 29.0 | 72.3 | 72.8 | 65.4 | 17.2 | 53.2 |
| Under 15 years | 99.0 | 98.6 | 98.3 | 99.9 | 99.9 | 97.2 | 96.1 | 98.8 |
| 15–19 years | 87.2 | 83.7 | 82.7 | 97.1 | 97.5 | 90.4 | 81.1 | 85.1 |
| 15 years | 98.4 | 97.9 | 98.2 | 99.7 | 99.8 | 97.2 | 98.2 | 97.6 |
| 16 years | 95.5 | 93.9 | 94.5 | 99.4 | 99.6 | 96.8 | 92.1 | 93.6 |
| 17 years | 92.6 | 90.3 | 90.6 | 98.9 | 99.1 | 95.1 | 88.1 | 90.4 |
| 18 years | 87.8 | 84.3 | 84.3 | 97.4 | 97.8 | 90.5 | 81.6 | 84.6 |
| 19 years | 81.7 | 77.1 | 76.5 | 95.2 | 95.7 | 85.9 | 74.5 | 78.5 |
| 20–24 years | 62.1 | 55.8 | 51.7 | 86.2 | 87.0 | 73.3 | 44.5 | 64.2 |
| 25–29 years | 33.8 | 29.0 | 22.4 | 65.8 | 66.4 | 56.5 | 17.2 | 46.6 |
| 30–34 years | 20.7 | 17.8 | 11.8 | 50.0 | 50.2 | 46.5 | 8.3 | 36.3 |
| 35–39 years | 19.0 | 16.7 | 11.4 | 42.0 | 41.9 | 43.5 | 8.4 | 32.9 |
| 40 years and over | 21.4 | 19.4 | 14.7 | 40.3 | 40.0 | 39.5 | 10.9 | 34.0 |

—Data not available.
[a]Includes races other than white and black and origin not stated.
[b]Race and Hispanic origin are reported separately on birth certificates. Race categories are consistent with 1977 Office of Management and Budget standards. Data for persons of Hispanic origin are included in the data for each race group according to the mother's reported race.
Thirty-three states and the District of Columbia reported multiple-race data for 2009 that were bridged to single-race categories for comparability with other states.
[c]Includes all persons of Hispanic origin of any race.
[d]Birth rates computed by relating total births to unmarried mothers, regardless of age of mother, to unmarried women aged 15–44 years.
[e]Birth rates computed by relating births to unmarried mothers aged 40 and over to unmarried women aged 40–44.
Notes: For 49 states and the District of Columbia, marital status is reported in the birth registration process.
Rates cannot be computed for unmarried non-Hispanic black women or for American Indian or Alaska Native women due to population size.

SOURCE: Joyce A. Martin et al., "Table 15. Births and Birth Rates to Unmarried Women, by Age, Race, and Hispanic Origin of Mother: United States, 2009," in "Births: Final Data for 2009," *National Vital Statistics Reports*, vol. 60, no. 1, November 2011, http://www.cdc.gov/nchs/data/nvsr/nvsr60/nvsr60_01.pdf (accessed November 3, 2011)

FIGURE 2.2

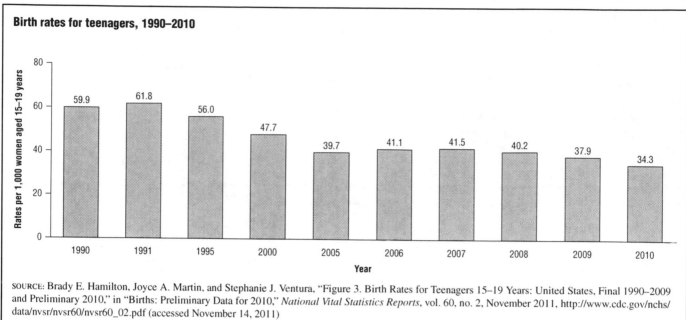

**Birth rates for teenagers, 1990–2010**

SOURCE: Brady E. Hamilton, Joyce A. Martin, and Stephanie J. Ventura, "Figure 3. Birth Rates for Teenagers 15–19 Years: United States, Final 1990–2009 and Preliminary 2010," in "Births: Preliminary Data for 2010," *National Vital Statistics Reports*, vol. 60, no. 2, November 2011, http://www.cdc.gov/nchs/data/nvsr/nvsr60/nvsr60_02.pdf (accessed November 14, 2011)

2007, the first increase since 1991. Even so, after 2007 the birthrate for teens began declining again, from 41.5 births per 1,000 women aged 15 to 19 years in 2007 to 34.3 per 1,000 in 2010. (See Figure 2.2.)

Experts offer many possible explanations for the high rates of teenage motherhood. Among them are lack of access to birth control, lack of education, and little hope for the future, including absence of educational goals. What is certain is that the health of the babies born to teenagers is at risk. According to Xi-Kuan Chen et al., in "Teenage Pregnancy and Adverse Birth Outcomes: A Large Population Based Retrospective Cohort Study" (*International Journal of Epidemiology*, vol. 36, no. 2, April 2007), teenage pregnancy is associated with higher rates of preterm delivery, low birth weight, and neonatal mortality regardless of the socioeconomic status of the mother, adequate prenatal care, amount of education, or other known risk factors. These adverse outcomes are even more pronounced among minority teens. Shih-Chen Chang et al. note in "Characteristics and Risk Factors for Adverse Birth Outcomes in Pregnant Black Adolescents" (*Journal of Pediatrics*, vol. 143, no. 2, August 2003) that African-American teenagers are twice as likely as white teenagers to deliver low birth weight babies and 1.5 times more likely to have premature babies. Both low birth weight and premature babies experience a number of serious health and developmental problems. In general, babies born to teenage mothers of all races suffer a higher risk of low birth weight, preterm delivery, and infant mortality when compared with babies born to older mothers.

In addition, teen pregnancy is linked to adverse outcomes for the mother. In "Unpredicted Trajectories: The Relationship between Race/Ethnicity, Pregnancy during Adolescence, and Young Women's Outcomes" (*Journal of Adolescent Health*, vol. 47, no. 2, August 2010), Whitney N. Casares et al. find that adolescent pregnancy increases the risk that the mother will use public assistance programs as a result of poverty and decreases the odds of high educational attainment. However, the researchers note that young African-American women who become pregnant are more likely to continue with their education than are young white women.

The largest decline in teen birthrates between 1991 and 2009 was among non-Hispanic African-American teens; the birthrate for this group fell from 118.2 to 56.7 births per 1,000 women aged 15 to 19 years. (See Figure 2.3 and Table 2.4.) Non-Hispanic African-American teens had the highest birthrate in 1991, but by 2009 they had the second-highest birthrate. Even though the teen Hispanic birthrate had fallen from 104.6 births per 1,000 women aged 15 to 19 years in 1991 to 63.6 births per 1,000 women in 2009, these teens had the highest birthrate in 2009. In 2009 Native American or Alaskan Native teens had a birthrate of 43.8, non-Hispanic white teens had a birthrate of 25.7, and Asian or Pacific Islander teens had a birthrate of 12.6. Preliminary data for 2010 suggest that birthrates among all teenagers aged 15 to 19 years old fell from 2009 to 2010.

## MINORITY FAMILY STRUCTURE

### Married-Couple Families

The Census Bureau defines a family as two or more people living together who are related by birth, marriage, or adoption. A household, however, can be family or nonfamily and is simply all people who occupy a housing unit. The

FIGURE 2.3

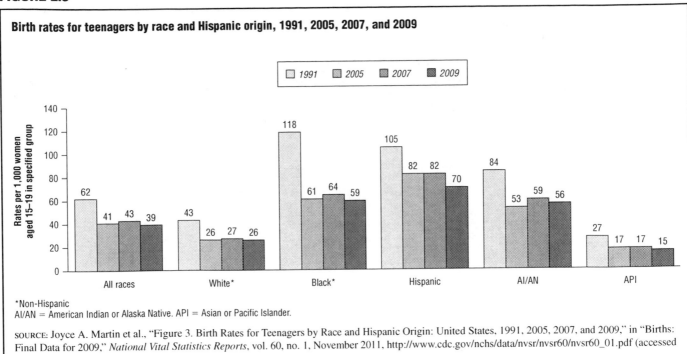

**Birth rates for teenagers by race and Hispanic origin, 1991, 2005, 2007, and 2009**

*Non-Hispanic
AI/AN = American Indian or Alaska Native. API = Asian or Pacific Islander.

SOURCE: Joyce A. Martin et al., "Figure 3. Birth Rates for Teenagers by Race and Hispanic Origin: United States, 1991, 2005, 2007, and 2009," in "Births: Final Data for 2009," *National Vital Statistics Reports*, vol. 60, no. 1, November 2011, http://www.cdc.gov/nchs/data/nvsr60/nvsr60_01.pdf (accessed November 3, 2011)

proportion of married-couple families among all households declined between 1970 and 2011. According to Fields, 70.6% of all households in 1970 were married-couple families. By 2011 the Census Bureau (2011, http://www.census.gov/population/www/socdemo/hh-fam/cps2011.html) reports that the proportion of households that were married-couple families had dropped to 48.9%.

The proportion of married-couple families among all family households declined between 1970 and 2011 for all races and ethnicities. In *Household and Family Characteristics: March 1994* (September 1995, http://www.census.gov/prod/1/pop/p20-483.pdf), Steve Rawlings and Arlene F. Saluter of the Census Bureau report numbers from 1970 and 1980, which here are compared with numbers from 2011 reported by the Census Bureau in *America's Families and Living Arrangements: 2011*. In 1970, 86.9% of non-Hispanic white families were married-couple families, compared with 80.8% in 2011. Asian-Americans also maintained a proportion of married-couple families comparable to that among the non-Hispanic white community. In 1980, 84.5% of Asian-American family households were headed by married couples; by 2011 this proportion had decreased to 79.7%. A high proportion of Hispanic families were headed by a married couple in 1970 (80.6%), but by 2011 this proportion had decreased more significantly (to 63.1%) than had the proportion of married-couple families among either non-Hispanic whites or Asian-Americans. However, the percentage of married-couple families was the lowest, and had decreased the most dramatically, among African-Americans between 1970 and 2011. In 1970, 68.3% of African-American families were headed by a married couple; by 2011 this proportion had dropped to 44.4%.

By 2011 only 49.3% of all people aged 15 years and older lived with a spouse. (See Table 2.1.) In comparison to this average, 57.5% of all adult Asian-Americans and 54% of all adult non-Hispanic whites lived with a spouse. In contrast, 42.4% of all Hispanic adults and only 29.2% of all African-American adults lived with a spouse.

**Single-Parent Households**

In 1970 there were 3 million families headed by a single mother, accounting for 10.3% of all family households with children. (See Table 2.5.) By 2011 there were 8.6 million single-mother families, 24.7% of all families with children. Single-father families increased from 345,000 in 1970 to 2.2 million in 2011, increasing from 1.2% to 6.4% of families with children. Most single-parent households in the United States continue to be headed by women. The proportion of family households headed by women with no husband present has grown among all racial and ethnic groups.

In 2010 Asian-Americans and non-Hispanic whites had the lowest proportion of family households headed by single women. Among Asian-American family households, 447,000 (12.4%) were headed by a female, and 7.3 million (13.4%) non-Hispanic white family households were headed by a female. (See Table 2.6.) Hispanic women were about twice as likely to head family households as

**TABLE 2.4**

## Births for women aged 10–19 years, by age, race, and Hispanic origin, selected years 1991–2010

| Age and race and Hispanic origin of mother | Year | | | | | | Percent change, 2009–2010 | Percent change, 2007–2010 | Percent change, 2005–2007 | Percent change, 1991–2010 |
|---|---|---|---|---|---|---|---|---|---|---|
| | 2010 | 2009 | 2008 | 2007 | 2005 | 1991 | | | | |
| **10–14 years** | | | | | | | | | | |
| All races and origins[a] | 0.4 | 0.5 | 0.6 | 0.6 | 0.6 | 1.4 | −20 | −33 | † | −71 |
| Non-Hispanic white[b] | 0.2 | 0.2 | 0.2 | 0.2 | 0.2 | 0.5 | † | † | † | −60 |
| Non-Hispanic black[b] | 1.0 | 1.1 | 1.4 | 1.4 | 1.6 | 4.9 | −9 | −29 | −13 | −80 |
| American Indian or Alaska Native total[b, c] | 0.5 | 0.6 | 0.7 | 0.7 | 0.8 | 1.6 | † | −29 | † | −69 |
| Asian or Pacific Islander total[b, c] | 0.1 | 0.1 | 0.2 | 0.2 | 0.2 | 0.8 | † | −50 | † | −88 |
| Hispanic[d] | 0.8 | 1.0 | 1.1 | 1.2 | 1.3 | 2.4 | −20 | −33 | −8 | −67 |
| **15–19 years** | | | | | | | | | | |
| All races and origins[a] | 34.3 | 37.9 | 40.2 | 41.5 | 39.7 | 61.8 | −9 | −17 | 5 | −44 |
| Non-Hispanic white[b] | 23.5 | 25.7 | 26.7 | 27.2 | 26.0 | 43.4 | −9 | −14 | 5 | −46 |
| Non-Hispanic black[b] | 51.5 | 56.7 | 60.4 | 62.0 | 59.4 | 118.2 | −9 | −17 | 4 | −56 |
| American Indian or Alaska Native total[b, c] | 38.7 | 43.8 | 47.4 | 49.4 | 46.0 | 84.1 | −12 | −22 | 7 | −54 |
| Asian or Pacific Islander total[b, c] | 10.9 | 12.6 | 13.8 | 14.8 | 15.4 | 27.3 | −13 | −26 | −4 | −60 |
| Hispanic[d] | 55.7 | 63.6 | 70.3 | 75.3 | 76.5 | 104.6 | −12 | −26 | −2 | −47 |
| **15–17 years** | | | | | | | | | | |
| All races and origins[a] | 17.3 | 19.6 | 21.1 | 21.7 | 21.1 | 38.6 | −12 | −20 | 3 | −55 |
| Non-Hispanic white[b] | 10.0 | 11.0 | 11.6 | 11.9 | 11.5 | 23.6 | −9 | −16 | 3 | −58 |
| Non-Hispanic black[b] | 27.4 | 31.0 | 33.6 | 34.6 | 34.1 | 86.1 | −12 | −21 | † | −68 |
| American Indian or Alaska Native total[b, c] | 20.1 | 23.7 | 25.9 | 26.2 | 26.3 | 51.9 | −15 | −23 | † | −61 |
| Asian or Pacific Islander total[b, c] | 5.1 | 6.3 | 7.0 | 7.4 | 7.7 | 16.3 | −19 | −31 | † | −69 |
| Hispanic[d] | 32.3 | 37.3 | 42.2 | 44.4 | 45.8 | 69.2 | −13 | −27 | −3 | −53 |
| **18–19 years** | | | | | | | | | | |
| All races and origins[a] | 58.3 | 64.0 | 68.2 | 71.7 | 68.4 | 94.0 | −9 | −19 | 5 | −38 |
| Non-Hispanic white[b] | 42.6 | 46.2 | 48.6 | 50.4 | 48.0 | 70.6 | −8 | −15 | 5 | −40 |
| Non-Hispanic black[b] | 85.6 | 93.5 | 100.0 | 105.2 | 100.2 | 162.2 | −8 | −19 | 5 | −47 |
| American Indian or Alaska Native total[b, c] | 66.1 | 73.6 | 80.4 | 86.4 | 78.1 | 134.2 | −10 | −23 | 11 | −51 |
| Asian or Pacific Islander total[b, c] | 18.7 | 20.9 | 22.9 | 24.9 | 26.4 | 42.2 | −11 | −25 | −6 | −56 |
| Hispanic[d] | 90.7 | 103.3 | 114.0 | 124.7 | 124.4 | 155.5 | −12 | −27 | † | −42 |

Notes: Data for 2010 are based on continuous files of records received from the states. Rates per 1,000 women in specified age and race and Hispanic origin group. Population enumerated as of April 1 for 2010 and estimated as of July 1 for all other years. Rates for 2005–2009 have been revised using (intercensal) population estimates based on the 2000 and 2010 census and may differ from rates previously published.

†Difference not statistically significant.

[a]Includes births to white Hispanic and black Hispanic women and births with origin not stated, not shown separately.

[b]Race and Hispanic origin are reported separately on birth certificates. Persons of Hispanic origin may be of any race. Race categories are consistent with the 1977 Office of Management and Budget (OMB) standards. In 2010, thirty-eight states and the District of Columbia reported multiple-race data that were bridged to the single-race categories for comparability with other states. Multiple-race reporting areas vary for 2005–2010.

[c]Includes persons of Hispanic origin according to the mother's reported race.

[d]Includes all persons of Hispanic origin of any race.

SOURCE: Brady E. Hamilton, Joyce A. Martin, and Stephanie J. Ventura, "Table 5. Births for Women Aged 10–19 Years, by Age, Race, and Hispanic Origin of Mother: United States, Final 1991, 2005, and 2007–2009 and Preliminary 2010," in "Births: Preliminary Data for 2010," *National Vital Statistics Reports*, vol. 60, no. 2, November 2011, http://www.cdc.gov/nchs/data/nvsr/nvsr60/nvsr60_02.pdf (accessed November 14, 2011)

were non-Hispanic white women, and single African-American women were more than three times as likely as non-Hispanic white women to head family households. In 2010 there were 2.7 million (26.4%) Hispanic families headed by a female and 4.1 million (44.3%) African-American families headed by a female. Hispanic and African-American female-headed families were also more likely to contain children than female-headed families of other races and ethnic groups. Nearly two-thirds of Hispanic female-headed families (63.4%) and African-American female-headed families (61.3%) contained children under the age of 18 years, compared with 53.1% of non-Hispanic white and 40.7% of Asian-American female-headed families.

## Living Arrangements of Children

Changes in the marital circumstances of adults naturally affect the living arrangements of children. High divorce rates, an increased delay in first marriages, and more out-of-wedlock births have resulted in fewer children living with two parents. In 2011, 51.5 million (68.9%) children under the age of 18 years were living with two parents (not necessarily both birth parents), meaning that three out of 10

**TABLE 2.5**

**Families with children, by type, 1950–2011**

| Year | Mother only | Father only | Married couple |
|------|-------------|-------------|----------------|
| 1950 | 1,272 | 229 | 18,824 |
| 1951 | 1,659 | 231 | 19,389 |
| 1952 | 1,514 | 233 | 19,606 |
| 1953 | 1,521 | 277 | 19,920 |
| 1954 | 1,615 | 283 | 20,645 |
| 1955 | 1,870 | 256 | 21,064 |
| 1956 | 1,814 | 298 | 21,631 |
| 1957 | 1,855 | 265 | 22,139 |
| 1958 | 1,822 | 293 | 22,426 |
| 1959 | 1,943 | 232 | 22,894 |
| 1960 | 2,099 | 232 | 23,358 |
| 1961 | 2,185 | 190 | 23,514 |
| 1962 | 2,229 | 254 | 23,788 |
| 1963 | 2,229 | 361 | 24,321 |
| 1964 | 2,361 | 268 | 24,439 |
| 1965 | 2,485 | 249 | 24,406 |
| 1966 | 2,450 | 278 | 24,276 |
| 1967 | 2,584 | 331 | 24,646 |
| 1968 | 2,772 | 297 | 24,895 |
| 1969 | 2,888 | 323 | 25,136 |
| 1970 | 2,971 | 345 | 25,541 |
| 1971 | 3,365 | 331 | 25,091 |
| 1972 | 3,598 | 365 | 25,482 |
| 1973 | 3,798 | 386 | 25,387 |
| 1974 | 4,081 | 391 | 25,278 |
| 1975 | 4,404 | 484 | 25,169 |
| 1976 | 4,621 | 446 | 25,110 |
| 1977 | 4,784 | 486 | 24,875 |
| 1978 | 5,206 | 539 | 24,625 |
| 1979 | 5,288 | 569 | 24,514 |
| 1980 | 5,445 | 616 | 24,961 |
| 1981 | 5,634 | 666 | 24,927 |
| 1982 | 5,868 | 679 | 24,465 |
| 1983 | 5,718 | 737 | 24,363 |
| 1984 | 5,907 | 799 | 24,340 |
| 1985 | 6,006 | 896 | 24,210 |
| 1986 | 6,105 | 935 | 24,630 |
| 1987 | 6,297 | 955 | 24,646 |
| 1988 | 6,273 | 1,047 | 24,600 |
| 1989 | 6,519 | 1,068 | 24,735 |
| 1990 | 6,599 | 1,153 | 24,537 |
| 1991 | 6,823 | 1,181 | 24,397 |
| 1992 | 7,043 | 1,283 | 24,420 |
| 1993 | 7,226 | 1,324 | 24,707 |
| 1994 | 7,647 | 1,314 | 25,058 |
| 1995 | 7,615 | 1,440 | 25,241 |
| 1996 | 7,656 | 1,628 | 24,920 |
| 1997 | 7,874 | 1,709 | 25,083 |
| 1998 | 7,693 | 1,798 | 25,269 |
| 1999 | 7,841 | 1,706 | 25,066 |
| 2000 | 7,571 | 1,786 | 25,248 |
| 2001 | 7,538 | 1,836 | 25,980 |
| 2002 | 8,010 | 1,903 | 25,792 |
| 2003 | 8,139 | 1,915 | 25,914 |
| 2004 | 8,221 | 1,931 | 25,793 |
| 2005 | 8,270 | 2,021 | 25,919 |
| 2006 | 8,389 | 2,095 | 25,982 |
| 2007 | 8,585 | 2,015 | 26,158 |
| 2008 | 8,374 | 2,162 | 25,173 |
| 2009 | 8,394 | 2,111 | 25,129 |
| 2010 | 8,419 | 2,224 | 24,575 |
| 2011 | 8,597 | 2,225 | 23,938 |

SOURCE: Adapted from "Table FM-1. Families by Presence of Own Children under 18: 1950 to Present," in *Families and Living Arrangements*, U.S. Census Bureau, November 2011, http://www.census.gov/population/www/socdemo/hh-fam.html (accessed November 2, 2011)

(31.1%) children were living with either a single parent or no parents. (See Table 2.7.) African-American children and, to a lesser extent, Hispanic children have been particularly affected by these changes; 54.7% of African-American children and 29.2% of Hispanic children lived with one parent in 2011, compared with 19.9% of non-Hispanic white children and 10.3% of Asian-American children. (See Figure 2.4.)

**AFRICAN-AMERICAN CHILDREN.** In 2011, 4.2 million (37.7%) African-American children under the age of 18 years lived with two parents, whereas 5.7 million (51.3%) lived with their mothers only. (See Table 2.7.) A higher proportion of African-American children lived with neither parent (843,000, or 7.6%) than lived with their fathers only (387,000, or 3.5%). The Census Bureau (September 21, 2006, http://www.census.gov/population/socdemo/hh-fam/ch3.pdf) reports that in 1970 the proportions of African-American children who lived with one parent (31.7%) or two parents (58.6%) were virtually the reverse of their living arrangements in 2011.

A large number of African-American children live with neither parent. A disproportionate number of them are in foster care. In *AFCARS Report* (June 2011, http://www.acf.hhs.gov/programs/cb/stats_research/afcars/tar/report18.pdf), the U.S. Department of Health and Human Services reports that on September 30, 2010, 29% of children in foster care were African-American. According to the Census Bureau, in *America's Families and Living Arrangements: 2011*, if the number of African-American children in foster care reflected their proportion in the general population, only 14.9% of children in foster care would be African-American.

**HISPANIC CHILDREN.** In 2011 a higher proportion of Hispanic children (11.6 million, or 66.9%) than African-American children were living with two parents, but this proportion was still lower than the proportion of non-Hispanic white children who lived with two parents (31.3 million, or 77.2%). (See Table 2.7.) Over 4.6 million (26.5%) Hispanic children lived with a single mother and 479,000 (2.8%) lived with a single father. This proportion was considerably higher than among non-Hispanic whites—6.4 million (15.9%) non-Hispanic white children lived with a single mother and 1.6 million (4%) lived with a single father—but well below the proportion of African-American children living with a single parent. Approximately 677,000 (3.9%) Hispanic children lived with neither parent. Some of these children likely lived with other relatives, such as grandparents, or with foster parents.

**ASIAN-AMERICAN CHILDREN.** The Asian-American family is typically a close-knit unit, and members are traditionally respectful of the authority of the elder members of the family. As the younger generation becomes more assimilated into American culture, however, the unchallenged role of elders may not remain as strong. Even so, family tradition and honor are still held in high regard. In 2011, 2.9 million (87.4%) Asian-American children were living with both parents, a proportion higher than that of non-Hispanic whites. (See Table 2.7.) About 299,000 (9.1%) Asian-American children lived with a single mother and 42,000

**TABLE 2.6**

## Families by number of own children under 18 years old, by race and Hispanic origin, 2000, 2005, and 2010

| Race, Hispanic origin, and year | Number of families (1,000) | | | | | Percent distribution | | | | |
|---|---|---|---|---|---|---|---|---|---|---|
| | Total | No children | One child | Two children | Three or more children | Total | No children | One child | Two children | Three or more children |
| **All families[a]** | | | | | | | | | | |
| 2000 | 72,025 | 37,420 | 14,311 | 13,215 | 7,080 | 100 | 52 | 20 | 18 | 10 |
| 2005 | 76,858 | 40,647 | 15,069 | 13,741 | 7,400 | 100 | 53 | 20 | 18 | 10 |
| 2010, total | 78,833 | 43,615 | 15,149 | 12,947 | 7,122 | 100 | 55 | 19 | 16 | 9 |
| Married couple | 58,410 | 33,835 | 9,567 | 9,658 | 5,351 | 100 | 58 | 16 | 17 | 9 |
| Male householder[b] | 5,580 | 3,356 | 1,375 | 576 | 273 | 100 | 60 | 25 | 10 | 5 |
| Female householder[b] | 14,843 | 6,424 | 4,207 | 2,714 | 1,499 | 100 | 43 | 28 | 18 | 10 |
| **White families[c]** | | | | | | | | | | |
| 2000 | 60,251 | 32,144 | 11,496 | 10,918 | 5,693 | 100 | 53 | 19 | 18 | 9 |
| 2005 | 63,079 | 34,255 | 11,872 | 11,127 | 5,825 | 100 | 54 | 19 | 18 | 9 |
| 2010, total | 64,120 | 36,464 | 11,856 | 10,275 | 5,525 | 100 | 57 | 18 | 16 | 9 |
| Married couple | 50,163 | 29,616 | 7,982 | 8,092 | 4,473 | 100 | 59 | 16 | 16 | 9 |
| Male householder[b] | 4,194 | 2,518 | 1,045 | 436 | 196 | 100 | 60 | 25 | 10 | 5 |
| Female householder[b] | 9,762 | 4,331 | 2,829 | 1,747 | 856 | 100 | 44 | 29 | 18 | 9 |
| **Black families[c]** | | | | | | | | | | |
| 2000 | 8,664 | 3,882 | 2,101 | 1,624 | 1,058 | 100 | 45 | 24 | 19 | 12 |
| 2005 | 8,902 | 4,077 | 2,059 | 1,641 | 1,125 | 100 | 46 | 23 | 18 | 13 |
| 2010, total | 9,358 | 4,502 | 2,142 | 1,608 | 1,106 | 100 | 48 | 23 | 17 | 12 |
| Married couple | 4,274 | 2,357 | 733 | 695 | 489 | 100 | 55 | 17 | 16 | 12 |
| Male householder[b] | 939 | 541 | 235 | 104 | 59 | 100 | 58 | 25 | 11 | 6 |
| Female householder[b] | 4,145 | 1,604 | 1,174 | 809 | 557 | 100 | 39 | 28 | 20 | 13 |
| **Asian families[c]** | | | | | | | | | | |
| 2005 | 3,142 | 1,535 | 730 | 646 | 230 | 100 | 49 | 23 | 21 | 7 |
| 2010, total | 3,592 | 1,794 | 777 | 754 | 267 | 100 | 50 | 22 | 21 | 7 |
| Married couple | 2,888 | 1,327 | 638 | 678 | 246 | 100 | 46 | 22 | 23 | 8 |
| Male householder[b] | 257 | 202 | 40 | 13 | 2 | 100 | 79 | 16 | 5 | 1 |
| Female householder[b] | 447 | 265 | 99 | 63 | 19 | 100 | 59 | 22 | 14 | 4 |
| **Hispanic families[d]** | | | | | | | | | | |
| 2000 | 7,561 | 2,747 | 1,791 | 1,693 | 1,330 | 100 | 36 | 24 | 22 | 18 |
| 2005 | 9,521 | 3,528 | 2,130 | 2,163 | 1,699 | 100 | 37 | 22 | 23 | 18 |
| 2010, total | 10,412 | 4,173 | 2,344 | 2,269 | 1,626 | 100 | 40 | 23 | 22 | 16 |
| Married couple | 6,589 | 2,497 | 1,366 | 1,576 | 1,149 | 100 | 38 | 21 | 24 | 17 |
| Male householder[b] | 1,079 | 670 | 210 | 124 | 75 | 100 | 62 | 19 | 11 | 7 |
| Female householder[b] | 2,745 | 1,005 | 768 | 569 | 402 | 100 | 37 | 28 | 21 | 15 |
| **Non-Hispanic white families[c]** | | | | | | | | | | |
| 2005 | 54,257 | 30,965 | 9,924 | 9,151 | 4,217 | 100 | 57 | 18 | 17 | 8 |
| 2010, total | 54,445 | 32,569 | 9,691 | 8,173 | 4,012 | 100 | 60 | 18 | 15 | 7 |
| Married couple | 43,954 | 27,254 | 6,689 | 6,627 | 3,385 | 100 | 62 | 15 | 15 | 7 |
| Male householder[b] | 3,200 | 1,897 | 851 | 322 | 130 | 100 | 59 | 27 | 10 | 4 |
| Female householder[b] | 7,291 | 3,418 | 2,152 | 1,224 | 497 | 100 | 47 | 29 | 17 | 7 |

[a]Includes other races and non-Hispanic groups, not shown separately.
[b]No spouse present.
[c]Beginning with the 2003 Current Population Survey (CPS), respondents could choose more than one race. 2005 and 2010 data represent persons who selected this race group only and exclude persons reporting more than one race. The CPS prior to 2003 only allowed respondents to report one race group.
[d]Hispanic persons may be any race.

SOURCE: "Table 64. Family Households by Number of Own Children under 18 Years of Age: 2000 to 2010," in *Statistical Abstract of the United States: 2012*, 131st ed., U.S. Census Bureau, September 2011, http://www.census.gov/compendia/statab/2012/tables/12s0064.pdf (accessed November 3, 2011)

---

(1.3%) lived with a single father. Approximately 75,000 (2.3%) lived with neither parent.

**HOUSING GRANDCHILDREN.** Because of many factors, including the high cost of housing, substance abuse, and the inability of some parents to care for their children, many children are living with their grandparents. It is especially common in the African-American community for children to live with their grandparents, with or without one or both of their parents present. In *America's Families and Living Arrangements: 2011*, the Census Bureau indicates that in 2011, 534,000 (4.8%) African-

American children lived in a grandparent's home without either of their parents present. The proportion of children who lived in a grandparent's home is significantly higher when children who lived with one or both parents in the home of a grandparent are added to this total. More than one out of 10 (1.2 million, or 10.9%) African-American children lived in the home of a grandparent, with or without a parent present, in 2011. In other words, more than one out of 10 African-American children were living in the home of a grandparent in 2011, and about one out of 20 were being raised exclusively by a grandparent.

# TABLE 2.7

## Living arrangements of children and marital status of parents, by age, race, and Hispanic origin, 2011

[Numbers in thousands]

| | Total | Living with both parents | | Living with mother only | | | | | Living with father only | | | | | Living with neither parent |
| --- | --- | --- | --- | --- | --- | --- | --- | --- | --- | --- | --- | --- | --- | --- |
| | | Married to each other | Not married to each other | Married spouse absent | Widowed | Divorced | Separated | Never married | Married spouse absent | Widowed | Divorced | Separated | Never married | No parent present |
| **All children** | 74,630 | 48,516 | 2,940 | 1,029 | 651 | 5,388 | 2,487 | 8,080 | 130 | 145 | 1,236 | 398 | 719 | 2,910 |
| **Age of child** | | | | | | | | | | | | | | |
| Under 1 year | 4,105 | 2,612 | 512 | 46 | 14 | 45 | 49 | 661 | — | — | 9 | 3 | 39 | 115 |
| 1–2 years | 8,433 | 5,463 | 735 | 85 | 13 | 242 | 214 | 1,237 | 2 | — | 22 | 31 | 117 | 271 |
| 3–5 years | 13,008 | 3,524 | 656 | 198 | 36 | 561 | 408 | 1,794 | 16 | 10 | 123 | 57 | 192 | 432 |
| 6–8 years | 12,473 | 8,256 | 404 | 210 | 93 | 851 | 426 | 1,367 | 13 | 17 | 228 | 65 | 127 | 416 |
| 9–11 years | 12,217 | 8,027 | 299 | 177 | 103 | 1,071 | 465 | 1,111 | 29 | 31 | 241 | 70 | 81 | 510 |
| 12–14 years | 11,897 | 7,710 | 179 | 142 | 169 | 1,239 | 465 | 1,006 | 38 | 34 | 258 | 65 | 89 | 503 |
| 15–17 years | 12,499 | 7,925 | 155 | 172 | 222 | 1,378 | 461 | 904 | 31 | 52 | 354 | 107 | 73 | 664 |
| **Race** | | | | | | | | | | | | | | |
| White alone | 56,319 | 39,940 | 2,046 | 630 | 486 | 4,010 | 1,673 | 3,706 | 98 | 115 | 1,048 | 316 | 475 | 1,776 |
| Black alone | 11,155 | 3,680 | 528 | 289 | 111 | 961 | 624 | 3,732 | 21 | 24 | 104 | 59 | 179 | 843 |
| Asian alone | 3,297 | 2,811 | 72 | 43 | 20 | 116 | 50 | 70 | 7 | — | 24 | 2 | 9 | 75 |
| All remaining single races and all race combinations | 3,859 | 2,085 | 295 | 67 | 35 | 301 | 140 | 573 | 4 | 6 | 61 | 20 | 56 | 216 |
| **Race** | | | | | | | | | | | | | | |
| Hispanic* | 17,418 | 10,484 | 1,165 | 349 | 130 | 1084 | 817 | 2,233 | 40 | 34 | 126 | 88 | 191 | 677 |
| White alone, Non-Hispanic | 40,616 | 30,311 | 1,037 | 321 | 367 | 3,071 | 930 | 1,749 | 59 | 84 | 941 | 230 | 313 | 1,203 |
| All remaining single races and all race combinations, non-hispanic | 16,596 | 7,721 | 738 | 359 | 155 | 1,233 | 740 | 4,098 | 30 | 28 | 170 | 80 | 215 | 1,030 |

—Represents or rounds to zero.
*Hispanics may be of any race.
Note: Excludes children in group quarters, and those who are a family reference person or spouse.

SOURCE: Adapted from "Table C3. Living Arrangements of Children under 18 Years and Marital Status of Parents, by Age, Sex, Race, and Hispanic Origin and Selected Characteristics of the Child for All Children: 2011," in *America's Families and Living Arrangements: 2011*, U.S. Census Bureau, November 2011, http://www.census.gov/population/www/socdemo/hh-fam/cps2011.html (accessed November 2, 2011)

FIGURE 2.4

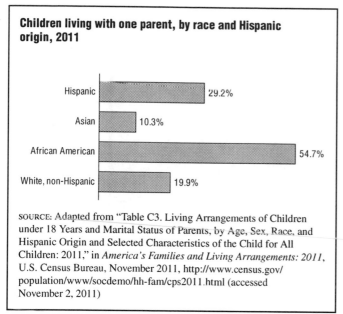

**Children living with one parent, by race and Hispanic origin, 2011**

SOURCE: Adapted from "Table C3. Living Arrangements of Children under 18 Years and Marital Status of Parents, by Age, Sex, Race, and Hispanic Origin and Selected Characteristics of the Child for All Children: 2011," in *America's Families and Living Arrangements: 2011*, U.S. Census Bureau, November 2011, http://www.census.gov/population/www/socdemo/hh-fam/cps2011.html (accessed November 2, 2011)

About 342,000 (2%) Hispanic children lived in the home of a grandparent with neither parent present in 2011. This number jumps to 1.4 million (7.8%) when children who lived with one or both parents in the home of a grandparent are added. Among Asian-Americans, 20,000 (0.6%) children under the age of 18 years lived in the home of a grandparent with neither parent present in 2011. This number climbs to 120,000 (3.6%) when children who lived with one or both parents in the home of a grandparent are counted. Among non-Hispanic whites, only 699,000 (1.7%) children lived in the home of a grandparent with neither parent present in 2011; 2.1 million (5.1%) white children lived in the home of a grandparent with or without a parent present. African-American children, then, were the most likely to be living in the home of a grandparent, with or without a parent present, whereas Asian-American children were the least likely to be living with a grandparent. Children of all races and ethnicities were significantly more likely to be living with their mother in their grandparents' home rather than with the father in their grandparents' home.

## HOMEOWNERSHIP

Owning one's home has traditionally been the American dream. However, for many Americans, especially minorities, purchasing a home can be difficult or impossible. The Census Bureau's Housing Vacancy Survey calculates homeownership rates by race and ethnicity of householder (the rate is computed by dividing the number of owner households by the total number of households). In 2010 the rate for non-Hispanic white householders who owned their home was 74.4%, for Asian or Pacific Islander householders it was 58.9%, for Native American or Alaskan Native householders it was 52.3%, for Hispanic householders it was

47.5%, and for African-American householders it was 45.4%. (See Table 2.8.)

### Subprime Mortgage Crisis

Even though compared with non-Hispanic white homeownership the proportion of minority homeownership is low, these numbers actually reflect significant growth in the purchase of homes by minorities. Homeownership rates rose for all groups between 1994 and 2007, but they rose faster among minority groups. (See Table 2.8.) A number of factors were responsible for the growth of minority homeownership during the 1990s. The administration of President Bill Clinton (1946–) provided more lending opportunities for minorities by revitalizing the Federal Housing Administration and improving enforcement of the Community Reinvestment Act, which was passed by Congress in 1977 to encourage banks and other lending institutions to invest in the communities in which they operate. Furthermore, the U.S. Department of Housing and Urban Development pressured the Federal National Mortgage Association (Fannie Mae) and the Federal Home Loan Mortgage Corporation (Freddie Mac) to initiate programs to help minority and low-income borrowers in securing mortgages. Fannie Mae is a private company that was created by Congress in 1938 to improve the housing industry during the Great Depression. Its smaller counterpart, Freddie Mac, is a shareholder-owned company created by Congress in 1970 to support homeownership. Both Fannie Mae and Freddie Mac buy mortgages, package them into bonds backed by the government, and sell them to investors, thereby freeing up money for additional mortgage lending. Besides these efforts, minority homeownership was also helped by a considerably strong economy and a robust stock market during the 1990s and by low mortgage rates during the first few years of the first decade of the 21st century.

President George W. Bush (1946–) also made minority homeownership a priority of his administration. His administration announced several initiatives to help minority and low-income Americans buy homes. Arguing that many Americans could afford a monthly mortgage payment but lacked the funds for a down payment, in 2003 Bush signed the American Dream Downpayment Assistance Act, authorizing $200 million per year in down payment assistance to at least 40,000 low-income families.

However, expanding mortgages to low and moderate income borrowers at high interest rates—called the "subprime market"—seriously undermined the American economy by the end of the first decade of the 21st century. Fannie Mae and Freddie Mac took on increasingly risky mortgage loans during this period. By 2007 an increasing number of borrowers were unable to meet their mortgage payments and home foreclosures skyrocketed. As foreclosures added to the available housing stock and credit tightened, home prices

# TABLE 2.8

**Homeownership rates by race and Hispanic origin of householder, 1994–2010**

| | 1994 | 1995 | 1996ᵃ | 1997 | 1998 | 1999 | 2000 | 2001 | 2002 | 2003 | 2004 | 2005 | 2006 | 2007 | 2008 | 2009 | 2010 |
|---|---|---|---|---|---|---|---|---|---|---|---|---|---|---|---|---|---|
| **U.S. total** | **64.0** | **64.7** | **65.4** | **65.7** | **66.3** | **66.8** | **67.4** | **67.8** | **67.9** | **68.3** | **69.0** | **68.9** | **68.8** | **68.1** | **67.8** | **67.4** | **66.9** |
| White, total | 67.7 | 68.7 | 69.1 | 69.3 | 70.0 | 70.5 | 71.1 | 71.6 | 71.7 | 72.1 | 72.8 | 72.7 | 72.6 | 72.0 | 71.7 | 71.4 | 71.0 |
| Non-Hispanic white | 70.0 | 70.9 | 71.7 | 72.0 | 72.6 | 73.2 | 73.8 | 74.3 | 74.7 | 75.4 | 76.0 | 75.8 | 75.8 | 75.2 | 75.0 | 74.8 | 74.4 |
| Black, total | 42.3 | 42.7 | 44.1 | 44.8 | 45.6 | 46.3 | 47.2 | 47.7 | 47.4 | 48.1 | 49.1 | 48.2 | 47.9 | 47.2 | 47.4 | 46.2 | 45.4 |
| All other races, total | 47.7 | 47.2 | 51.0 | 52.5 | 53.0 | 53.7 | 53.5 | 54.2 | 54.5 | 56.0 | 58.6 | 59.2 | 59.9 | 59.2 | 58.5 | 57.8 | 57.0 |
| American Indian or Alaskan Native | 51.7 | 55.8 | 51.6 | 51.7 | 54.3 | 56.1 | 56.2 | 55.4 | 54.0 | 54.3 | 55.6 | 58.2 | 58.2 | 56.9 | 56.5 | 56.2 | 52.3 |
| Asian or Native Hawaiian/Pacific Islander | 51.3 | 50.8 | 50.8 | 52.8 | 52.6 | 53.1 | 52.8 | 53.9 | 54.6 | 56.3 | 59.8 | 60.1 | 60.8 | 60.0 | 59.5 | 59.3 | 58.9 |
| Other | 36.1 | 37.4 | NA | NA | NA | NA | NA | NA | NA | | | | | | | | |
| Hispanic or Latino | 41.2 | 42.1 | 42.8 | 43.3 | 44.7 | 45.5 | 46.3 | 47.3 | 47.0 | 46.7 | 48.1 | 49.5 | 49.7 | 49.7 | 49.1 | 48.4 | 47.5 |
| Non-Hispanic | 65.9 | 66.7 | 67.4 | 67.8 | 68.3 | 68.9 | 69.5 | 69.9 | 70.2 | 70.8 | 71.5 | 71.2 | 71.2 | 70.5 | 70.3 | 69.8 | 69.4 |

NA = Not applicable.

ᵃBeginning in 1996 to 2002, those answering 'other' for race were allocated to one of the 4 race categories—white, black, American Indian, Aleut, or Eskimo (one category), or Asian or Native Hawaiian.

ᵇAsian, Native Hawaiian or other Pacific Islander, American Indian or Alaska Native (only one race reported) and two or more races.

SOURCE: Adapted from "Table 22. Homeownership Rates by Race and Ethnicity of Householder: 1994 to 2010," in *Housing Vacancies and Homeownership Annual Statistics: 2010*, U.S. Census Bureau, 2011, http://www.census.gov/hhes/www/housing/hvs/annual10/ann10ind.html (accessed November 4, 2011)

declined. Securities backed by subprime mortgages, which were widely owned by financial firms, lost their value, leading to a precipitous decline in the capital of banks as well as to a worldwide credit crisis and plunging the nation into a deep recession.

By mid-2008 Fannie Mae and Freddie Mac were nearly in ruins. In September 2008 the director of the Federal Housing Finance Agency announced that Fannie Mae and Freddie Mac, which together guaranteed about half of the U.S. mortgage market, would be put into a conservatorship of the agency. Dawn Kopecki and Alison Vekshin note in "Frank to Recommend Replacing Fannie Mae, Freddie Mac" (*Bloomberg News*, January 22, 2010) that the companies, which were essentially bailed out by the federal government, received $110.6 billion in taxpayer-funded aid between 2008 and 2009.

The article "Foreclosures (2012 Robosigning and Mortgage Servicing Settlement)" (*New York Times*, April 2, 2012) notes that the housing crisis continued into 2012. Between 2007 and early 2012 approximately 4 million families lost their homes to foreclosure. Continued high unemployment meant that many homeowners who had lost their jobs also lost their homes.

Other Americans retained their homes, which were now worth less than what they owed on their mortgages. In February 2012 the U.S. government came to a settlement agreement with five of the country's largest banks: Bank of America, JP Morgan Chase, Wells Fargo, Citigroup, and Ally Financial. These banks were accused of foreclosure processes that were unethical, abusive, and fraudulent. The settlement provided $26 million to help current "underwater" homeowners and former homeowners. The lenders agreed to restructure debt and refinance homes at lower interest rates. About 750,000 former owners of foreclosed homes would receive payments of about $2,000. However, Shaila Dewan reports in "Pressure Grows on Fannie and Freddie to Cut Principal on Loans" (*New York Times*, February 27, 2012) that more than half of all outstanding mortgage loans were held by Fannie Mae and Freddie Mac and were not eligible for relief under the settlement. Furthermore, many observers, such as Gretchen Morgenson in "The Deal Is Done, but Hold the Applause" (*New York Times*, February 11, 2012) and Joe Nocera in "Two Cheers for the Settlement" (*New York Times*, February 17, 2012), questioned how much relief the settlement would actually provide to struggling homeowners.

# CHAPTER 3
# EDUCATION

In *The Condition of Education 2005* (June 2005, http://nces.ed.gov/pubs2005/2005094.pdf), the National Center for Education Statistics (NCES) reports that two factors—rising immigration and the baby boom echo—boosted public school enrollment from the latter part of the 1980s to the first few years of the first decade of the 21st century. According to Susan Aud et al., in *The Condition of Education 2011* (May 2011, http://nces.ed.gov/pubs2011/2011033.pdf), enrollment was projected to reach 49.3 million students during the 2010–11 academic year and then set new public school enrollment records each year through 2020–21, with a projected enrollment of 52.7 million students in that year.

Along with this increase in enrollment came an increase in the proportion of public school students who were considered to be part of a minority group, due largely to the growth in the Hispanic public school population. In 2009, 45.2% of public school students enrolled in prekindergarten through 12th grade belonged to a minority group. (See Table 3.1.) Hispanics (22.3%) and African-Americans (15.3%) accounted for the largest number of minority students in public schools. These figures represented a significant increase since 1989, when white students made up 67.9% and minority students only 32.1% of the public school population. However, minority enrollment in public schools differed from region to region. Between 1989 and 2009 the number of white students remained about the same in the West, decreased in the Northeast and the Mideast, and increased in the South. (See Figure 3.1.) According to Aud et al., in 2009 the Midwest had the lowest proportion of minority students (28.8%) and the West had the highest (56.5%). Nearly four out of 10 (39.8%) students in the West were Hispanic, whereas nearly a quarter (23.4%) of students in the South was African-American.

## RISK FACTORS IN EDUCATION

In the United States education is often viewed as a way out of poverty to a better life. Many observers believe edu-cation is the key to narrowing the economic gap between the races. Even though many individual minority students strive for, and achieve, great educational success, on average minority students perform less well than white students in school and are generally more likely than their white counterparts to drop out of school. Asian-Americans are the exception to this rule. Many Asian-American students accomplish stunning academic achievements. Educators point with pride to these high-achieving students, who have often overcome both language and cultural barriers. Why are some groups more at risk of failure, and other groups more likely to succeed in school?

The Early Childhood Longitudinal Study, Birth Cohort, a study by the NCES, attempts to begin answering this question by assessing preschoolers' readiness for school. The study collected information on a cohort (a group of individuals with several characteristics in common) of children born in 2001 and followed them through 2007, focusing on the children's early development and how parents prepared their children for school. Even though at nine months of age little variation in mental and motor skills was found by race or ethnic group, several demographic characteristics were related to the likelihood of families engaging in activities that help prepare children for school. These characteristics include reading or telling children stories, singing to them, taking them on errands, playing peek-a-boo, and allowing them to play outside. The NCES indicates in *Condition of Education 2005* that in 2001–02 Asian-American families were more likely than other minority groups to read to their children (26%), tell them stories (25%), and play peek-a-boo (73%), although they were less likely to facilitate outside playing (43%) and significantly less likely to take their children on errands (38%) than were other minority families.

In contrast, both African-American and Hispanic families were less likely to read to (23% and 21%, respectively) and tell their children stories (24% and 21%, respectively),

**TABLE 3.1**

**Number and percentage distribution of the race and Hispanic origin of public school students in prekindergarten through 12th grade, 1989–2009**

[Numbers in thousands]

| October of year | Total | White | Black | Hispanic | Asian | Pacific Islander | American Indian/ Alaska Native | Two or more races |
|---|---|---|---|---|---|---|---|---|
| | | | | | **Enrollment** | | | |
| 1989 | 42,248 | 28,689 | 7,061 | 4,792 | 1,243* | * | 402 | — |
| 1990 | 43,086 | 28,991 | 7,202 | 5,054 | 1,304* | * | 407 | — |
| 1991 | 43,463 | 29,103 | 7,373 | 5,159 | 1,374* | * | 367 | — |
| 1992 | 44,041 | 29,304 | 7,524 | 5,310 | 1,455* | * | 351 | — |
| 1993 | 45,079 | 30,094 | 7,576 | 5,457 | 1,480* | * | 360 | — |
| 1994 | 46,887 | 30,656 | 8,039 | 6,423 | 1,141* | * | 390 | — |
| 1995 | 47,320 | 30,788 | 8,132 | 6,751 | 1,065* | * | 309 | — |
| 1996 | 47,487 | 29,960 | 8,002 | 7,025 | 1,936* | * | 563 | — |
| 1997 | 49,467 | 30,896 | 8,560 | 7,487 | 1,920* | * | 604 | — |
| 1998 | 48,817 | 30,164 | 8,505 | 7,647 | 1,946* | * | 555 | — |
| 1999 | 49,338 | 30,259 | 8,304 | 8,080 | 2,193* | * | 501 | — |
| 2000 | 49,198 | 29,963 | 8,337 | 8,214 | 2,044* | * | 641 | — |
| 2001 | 50,005 | 30,427 | 8,391 | 8,400 | 2,125* | * | 662 | — |
| 2002 | 50,443 | 30,426 | 8,434 | 8,981 | 1,980* | * | 622 | — |
| 2003 | 50,653 | 29,395 | 8,232 | 9,513 | 1,829 | 163 | 314 | 1,208 |
| 2004 | 50,568 | 28,738 | 8,289 | 9,870 | 1,967 | 102 | 403 | 1,200 |
| 2005 | 50,835 | 29,047 | 8,056 | 10,141 | 1,883 | 89 | 351 | 1,269 |
| 2006 | 50,663 | 28,486 | 7,977 | 10,470 | 1,900 | 117 | 336 | 1,376 |
| 2007 | 51,082 | 28,357 | 7,903 | 10,865 | 2,080 | 134 | 398 | 1,345 |
| 2008 | 50,768 | 27,923 | 8,002 | 11,093 | 1,903 | 86 | 440 | 1,322 |
| 2009 | 51,144 | 28,030 | 7,839 | 11,418 | 1,903 | 154 | 444 | 1,356 |
| | | | | | **Percentage distribution** | | | |
| 1989 | 100.0 | 67.9 | 16.7 | 11.3 | 2.9* | * | 1.0 | — |
| 1990 | 100.0 | 67.3 | 16.7 | 11.7 | 3.0* | * | 0.9 | — |
| 1991 | 100.0 | 67.0 | 17.0 | 11.9 | 3.2* | * | 0.8 | — |
| 1992 | 100.0 | 66.5 | 17.1 | 12.1 | 3.3* | * | 0.8 | — |
| 1993 | 100.0 | 66.8 | 16.8 | 12.1 | 3.3* | * | 0.8 | — |
| 1994 | 100.0 | 65.4 | 17.1 | 13.7 | 2.4* | * | 0.8 | — |
| 1995 | 100.0 | 65.1 | 17.2 | 14.3 | 2.3* | * | 0.7 | — |
| 1996 | 100.0 | 63.1 | 16.9 | 14.8 | 4.1* | * | 1.2 | — |
| 1997 | 100.0 | 62.5 | 17.3 | 15.1 | 3.9* | * | 1.2 | — |
| 1998 | 100.0 | 61.8 | 17.4 | 15.7 | 4.0* | * | 1.1 | — |
| 1999 | 100.0 | 61.3 | 16.8 | 16.4 | 4.4* | * | 1.0 | — |
| 2000 | 100.0 | 60.9 | 16.9 | 16.7 | 4.2* | * | 1.3 | — |
| 2001 | 100.0 | 60.8 | 16.8 | 16.8 | 4.2* | * | 1.3 | — |
| 2002 | 100.0 | 60.3 | 16.7 | 17.8 | 3.9* | * | 1.2 | — |
| 2003 | 100.0 | 58.0 | 16.3 | 18.8 | 3.6 | 0.3 | 0.6 | 2.4 |
| 2004 | 100.0 | 56.8 | 16.4 | 19.5 | 3.9 | 0.2 | 0.8 | 2.4 |
| 2005 | 100.0 | 57.1 | 15.8 | 19.9 | 3.7 | 0.2 | 0.7 | 2.5 |
| 2006 | 100.0 | 56.2 | 15.7 | 20.7 | 3.8 | 0.2 | 0.7 | 2.7 |
| 2007 | 100.0 | 55.5 | 15.5 | 21.3 | 4.1 | 0.3 | 0.8 | 2.6 |
| 2008 | 100.0 | 55.0 | 15.8 | 21.9 | 3.7 | 0.2 | 0.9 | 2.6 |
| 2009 | 100.0 | 54.8 | 15.3 | 22.3 | 3.7 | 0.3 | 0.9 | 2.7 |

—Not available.

*From 1989 through 2002, data on Asian and Pacific Islander students were not reported separately; therefore, Pacific Islander students are included with Asian students during this period.

Notes: Estimates include all public school students enrolled in prekindergarten through 12th grade. Over time, the Current Population Survey (CPS) has had different response options for race/ethnicity. Race categories exclude persons of Hispanic ethnicity. Totals include other race/ethnicity categories not separately shown. Detail may not sum to totals because of rounding.

SOURCE: Susan Aud et al., "Table A-5-1. Number and Percentage Distribution of Public School Students Enrolled in Prekindergarten through 12th Grade by Race/Ethnicity: October 1989–October 2009," in *The Condition of Education 2011*, U.S. Department of Education, National Center for Education Statistics, May 2011, http://nces.ed.gov/pubs2011/2011033.pdf (accessed November 30, 2011)

and more likely to sing to them (73% and 70%, respectively) and play peek-a-boo (61% and 64%, respectively) than were white families in 2001–02. This may be partly because poor families are much less likely to read to their children or tell them stories than are nonpoor families, and African-American and Hispanic families are disproportionately poor. African-American families, white families, and Hispanic families were about equally likely to take their children on errands and facilitate outside playing.

In its third wave, the Early Childhood Longitudinal Study, Birth Cohort, collected more specific information about the readiness of preschoolers for school. Researchers assessed children between the ages of 48 and 57 months. In

FIGURE 3.1

**Number of public school students in prekindergarten through 12th grade by region, race, and Hispanic origin, 1989–2009**

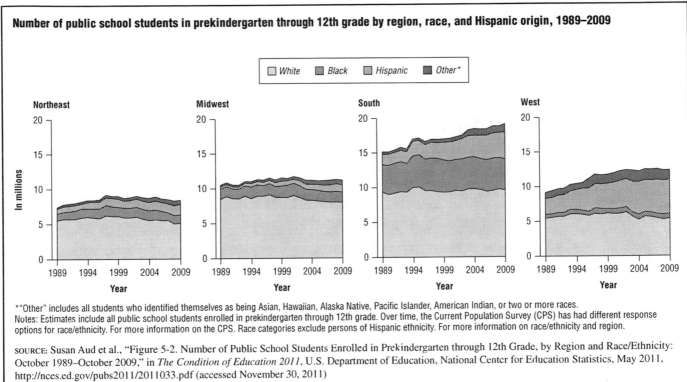

*"Other" includes all students who identified themselves as being Asian, Hawaiian, Alaska Native, Pacific Islander, American Indian, or two or more races.
Notes: Estimates include all public school students enrolled in prekindergarten through 12th grade. Over time, the Current Population Survey (CPS) has had different response options for race/ethnicity. For more information on the CPS. Race categories exclude persons of Hispanic ethnicity. For more information on race/ethnicity and region.

SOURCE: Susan Aud et al., "Figure 5-2. Number of Public School Students Enrolled in Prekindergarten through 12th Grade, by Region and Race/Ethnicity: October 1989–October 2009," in *The Condition of Education 2011*, U.S. Department of Education, National Center for Education Statistics, May 2011, http://nces.ed.gov/pubs2011/2011033.pdf (accessed November 30, 2011)

---

*Preschool: First Findings from the Preschool Follow-up of the Early Childhood Longitudinal Study, Birth Cohort* (October 2007, http://nces.ed.gov/pubs2008/2008025.pdf), Jodi Jacobson Chernoff et al. note that children's language knowledge—or ability to understand words or retell a story—varied by race and ethnicity, with non-Hispanic white children (9.2) scoring the highest, followed by non-Hispanic African-American children (8), Asian-American children (7.9), Native American and Alaskan Native children (7.9), and Hispanic children (7.4). Overall literacy, such as letter recognition and understanding aspects of reading such as reading from left to right, also varied by race and ethnicity. Asian-American children (17.5) scored the highest on overall literacy, followed by non-Hispanic white children (14.2), non-Hispanic African-American children (12), Hispanic children (10.7), and Native American and Alaskan Native children (9.6). Asian-American preschoolers (26.3) also scored the highest on mathematics knowledge and skills, followed by non-Hispanic white preschoolers (24.2), non-Hispanic African-American preschoolers (20.6), Hispanic preschoolers (20.1), and Native American and Alaskan Native preschoolers (17.6). Therefore, overall, Native American and Alaskan Native, Hispanic, and non-Hispanic African-American children were less prepared for school than were either non-Hispanic white or Asian-American children.

Kristin Denton Flanagan and Cameron McPhee note in *The Children Born in 2001 at Kindergarten Entry: First Findings from the Kindergarten Data Collections* of the *Early Childhood Longitudinal Study, Birth Cohort* (October 2009, http://nces.ed.gov/pubs2010/2010005.pdf) that by the time these children entered school, the average early reading scale scores varied considerably by race and ethnicity. Asian-American children (51.9) scored the highest, followed by non-Hispanic white children (46.4), non-Hispanic African-American children (41.1), Hispanic children (39.4), and Native American and Alaskan Native children (37.1). Mathematics scale scores also varied by race and ethnic group, although less dramatically. Asian-American children (48.7) scored the highest and non-Hispanic white children (46.5) scored the second highest. Non-Hispanic African-American children (40.4), Hispanic children (40.3), and Native American and Alaskan Native children (37.3) scored substantially lower.

**Preprimary Education**

One activity that can help preschoolers prepare for elementary school is attending center-based early childhood programs. Angelina KewalRamani et al. state in *Status and Trends in the Education of Racial and Ethnic Minorities* (September 2007, http://nces.ed.gov/pubs2007/2007039.pdf) that "research has suggested that intensive, high-quality preschool programs can have positive effects on the cognitive and academic development of low-income minority children, both in the short- and long-term." In 2005–06, 57.5% of all four-year-olds who were not yet enrolled in kindergarten were enrolled in center-based preschools. However, Asian-American preschoolers were the most likely to be enrolled in these high-quality private

FIGURE 3.2

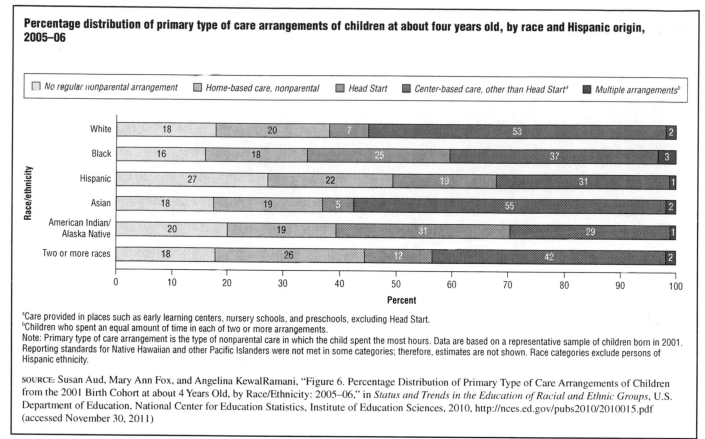

**Percentage distribution of primary type of care arrangements of children at about four years old, by race and Hispanic origin, 2005–06**

Legend: No regular nonparental arrangement | Home-based care, nonparental | Head Start | Center-based care, other than Head Start[a] | Multiple arrangements[b]

| Race/ethnicity | No regular nonparental arrangement | Home-based care, nonparental | Head Start | Center-based care, other than Head Start | Multiple arrangements |
|---|---|---|---|---|---|
| White | 18 | 20 | 7 | 53 | 2 |
| Black | 16 | 18 | 25 | 37 | 3 |
| Hispanic | 27 | 22 | 19 | 31 | 1 |
| Asian | 18 | 19 | 5 | 55 | 2 |
| American Indian/Alaska Native | 20 | 19 | 31 | 29 | 1 |
| Two or more races | 18 | 26 | 12 | 42 | 2 |

[a]Care provided in places such as early learning centers, nursery schools, and preschools, excluding Head Start.
[b]Children who spent an equal amount of time in each of two or more arrangements.
Note: Primary type of care arrangement is the type of nonparental care in which the child spent the most hours. Data are based on a representative sample of children born in 2001. Reporting standards for Native Hawaiian and other Pacific Islanders were not met in some categories; therefore, estimates are not shown. Race categories exclude persons of Hispanic ethnicity.

SOURCE: Susan Aud, Mary Ann Fox, and Angelina KewalRamani, "Figure 6. Percentage Distribution of Primary Type of Care Arrangements of Children from the 2001 Birth Cohort at about 4 Years Old, by Race/Ethnicity: 2005–06," in *Status and Trends in the Education of Racial and Ethnic Groups*, U.S. Department of Education, National Center for Education Statistics, Institute of Education Sciences, 2010, http://nces.ed.gov/pubs2010/2010015.pdf (accessed November 30, 2011)

programs (55%), followed by white preschoolers (53%). (See Figure 3.2.) Large proportions of Native American and Alaskan Native (31%), African-American (25%), and Hispanic students (19%) attended Head Start programs.

In *Digest of Education Statistics, 2010* (April 2011, http://nces.ed.gov/pubs2011/2011015.pdf), Thomas D. Snyder and Sally A. Dillow report data on the distribution of children in low-, medium-, and high-quality child care arrangements. During the 2005–06 school year Hispanic children were the most likely to be enrolled in a high-quality center-based program (39.8%), followed by whites (36%) and Asian-Americans (32.8%). (See Table 3.2.) African-American children were the most likely to be enrolled in a low-quality center-based program (14.8%). Among children in home-based care that was provided by a relative or a nonrelative, Hispanic children (62.5%) and African-American children (52.8%) were significantly more likely than white children (29.9%) to be enrolled in low-quality care.

## Educational Progress

The Early Childhood Longitudinal Study, Kindergarten Class of 1998–99, another research study conducted by the NCES, collected information on a cohort of children who began kindergarten during the fall of 1998 and followed them through the spring of 2004. The study specifically looked at children's achievement in mathe-

matics and reading as they progressed through school. The study found that several family risk factors (such as poverty, non-English primary home language, mother's lack of a high school diploma/general education diploma, or a single-parent household) were inversely related to gains in mathematics and reading through third grade. Minority children had higher numbers of risk factors than did white children. However, even when controlling for family risk factors, African-American children had lower average achievement scores than other racial and ethnic groups when they began kindergarten, and the gap in these achievement scores widened from the start of kindergarten through the end of third grade. Researchers have not yet proposed an explanation for this difference, but it may be due to entrenched racism within American culture and the school system—if children of a particular group are expected to perform poorly, they may in fact do so.

According to the NCES, in *The Condition of Education 2004* (June 2004, http://nces.ed.gov/pubs2004/2004077.pdf), researchers found that by the end of third grade the mean (average) scale scores for reading achievement were highest for non-Hispanic whites (112) and Asians and Pacific Islanders (111), followed by Hispanics (105) and non-Hispanic African-Americans (98). The same pattern held true in mathematics. The mean scale scores for mathematics achievement were highest for non-Hispanic whites (89) and

# TABLE 3.2

**Percentage distribution of quality rating of child care arrangements of children at about 4 years of age, by type of arrangement and selected child and family characteristics, 2005–06**

| | Quality rating of primary type of child care arrangement[a] | | | | | | | | | | | |
|---|---|---|---|---|---|---|---|---|---|---|---|---|
| | Home-based relative and nonrelative care[b, c] | | | All center-based programs | | | | | | | | |
| | | | | Head Start and other center-based programs[d] | | | Head Start[d] | | | Center-based care other than Head Start[d, e] | | |
| Selected characteristic | Low | Medium | High | Low | Medium | High | Low | Medium | High | Low | Medium | High |
| Total | 42.6 | 47.9 | 9.5 | 9.5 | 55.9 | 34.6 | 3.2 | 56.7 | 40.1 | 11.6 | 55.6 | 32.8 |
| **Sex of child** | | | | | | | | | | | | |
| Male | 45.5 | 44.1 | 10.4 | 6.3 | 53.5 | 40.2 | 2.2 | 56.5 | 41.2 | 7.7 | 52.4 | 39.8 |
| Female | 39.3 | 52.2 | 8.5 | 12.7 | 58.2 | 29.1 | 4.3 | 56.8 | 38.9 | 15.2 | 58.7 | 26.2 |
| **Race/ethnicity of child** | | | | | | | | | | | | |
| White | 29.9 | 55.3 | 14.9 | 9.3 | 54.7 | 36.0 | 4.0 | 47.5 | 48.5 | 10.2 | 55.8 | 34.0 |
| Black | 52.8 | 47.2 | ‡ | 14.8 | 59.9 | 25.3 | 6.9 | 67.0 | 26.1 | 20.8 | 54.6 | 24.6 |
| Hispanic | 62.5 | 33.4 | 4.1 | 7.2 | 52.9 | 39.8 | ‡ | 56.2 | 43.4 | 11.7 | 50.8 | 37.6 |
| Asian | ‡ | ‡ | ‡ | 5.5 | 61.7 | 32.8 | ‡ | ‡ | ‡ | 5.9 | 64.8 | 29.3 |
| Pacific Islander | ‡ | ‡ | ‡ | ‡ | ‡ | ‡ | ‡ | ‡ | ‡ | ‡ | ‡ | ‡ |
| American Indian/Alaska Native | ‡ | ‡ | ‡ | ‡ | 73.5 | 23.5 | ‡ | ‡ | ‡ | ‡ | ‡ | ‡ |
| Two or more races | ‡ | ‡ | ‡ | 8.5 | 66.0 | 25.5 | ‡ | 59.7 | 40.3 | 11.9 | 68.4 | 19.7 |
| **Age of child** | | | | | | | | | | | | |
| Less than 48 months | 31.8 | 64.3 | 3.9 | 9.8 | 57.1 | 33.1 | ‡ | 62.3 | 35.3 | 12.5 | 55.2 | 32.3 |
| 48 to 52 months | 40.3 | 47.2 | 12.5 | 12.3 | 54.9 | 32.8 | 0.9 | 55.5 | 43.6 | 16.2 | 54.7 | 29.1 |
| 53 to 57 months | 46.6 | 42.5 | 10.9 | 7.3 | 56.5 | 36.2 | 3.8 | 57.5 | 38.7 | 8.4 | 56.2 | 35.4 |
| 58 or more months | ‡ | ‡ | ‡ | 7.2 | 55.1 | 37.7 | 14.9 | 46.7 | 38.4 | 5.0 | 57.5 | 37.5 |
| **Mother's employment status** | | | | | | | | | | | | |
| Full-time (35 hours or more) | 36.6 | 56.6 | 6.9 | 14.9 | 55.5 | 29.6 | 4.9 | 47.7 | 47.4 | 17.6 | 57.6 | 24.8 |
| Part-time (less than 35 hours) | 48.9 | 35.1 | 16.0 | 5.7 | 60.9 | 33.4 | 3.2 | 59.8 | 37.0 | 6.5 | 61.2 | 32.3 |
| Looking for work | ‡ | ‡ | ‡ | 14.0 | 53.4 | 32.5 | ‡ | 73.1 | 24.5 | 22.4 | 39.2 | 38.4 |
| Not in labor force | ‡ | ‡ | ‡ | 3.5 | 53.3 | 43.2 | 1.7 | 59.0 | 39.2 | 4.2 | 51.2 | 44.7 |
| No mother in household | ‡ | ‡ | ‡ | ‡ | ‡ | ‡ | ‡ | ‡ | ‡ | ‡ | ‡ | ‡ |
| **Parents' highest level of education** | | | | | | | | | | | | |
| Less than high school | ‡ | ‡ | ‡ | 12.6 | 59.6 | 27.8 | ‡ | 57.4 | 40.4 | 20.8 | 61.3 | 17.9 |
| High school completion | 62.0 | 32.8 | 5.3 | 6.3 | 49.2 | 44.5 | 5.4 | 51.8 | 42.9 | 6.7 | 47.9 | 45.4 |
| Some college/vocational | 41.7 | 50.9 | 7.4 | 15.3 | 59.0 | 25.7 | 2.6 | 62.0 | 35.3 | 21.5 | 57.5 | 21.0 |
| Bachelor's degree | 29.9 | 62.1 | 8.0 | 6.7 | 59.8 | 33.4 | ‡ | ‡ | ‡ | 7.3 | 60.2 | 32.6 |
| Any graduate education | 10.3 | 61.3 | 28.3 | 5.0 | 53.6 | 41.4 | ‡ | ‡ | ‡ | 5.3 | 54.5 | 40.2 |
| **Poverty status[f]** | | | | | | | | | | | | |
| Below poverty threshold | 68.1 | 28.3 | 3.6 | 9.0 | 59.2 | 31.8 | 2.6 | 57.8 | 39.7 | 15.0 | 60.6 | 24.4 |
| At or above poverty threshold | 35.8 | 53.2 | 11.1 | 9.7 | 54.8 | 35.6 | 3.8 | 55.6 | 40.5 | 10.8 | 54.6 | 34.6 |
| **Socioeconomic status[g]** | | | | | | | | | | | | |
| Lowest 20 percent | 71.2 | 26.4 | 2.4 | 6.7 | 58.6 | 34.7 | 3.5 | 53.0 | 43.6 | 9.8 | 63.9 | 26.4 |
| Middle 60 percent | 43.3 | 49.7 | 7.0 | 11.2 | 56.5 | 32.3 | 3.2 | 59.7 | 37.1 | 14.0 | 55.4 | 30.6 |
| Highest 20 percent | 7.8 | 66.3 | 25.9 | 7.3 | 52.2 | 40.5 | ‡ | ‡ | ‡ | 7.5 | 52.7 | 39.8 |

‡Reporting standards not met.
[a]Primary type of care arrangement is the type of nonparental care in which the child spent the most hours.
[b]Care provided in the child's home or in another private home by a relative (excluding parents) or by a person unrelated to the child.
[c]Quality rating based on the Family Day Care Rating Scale (FDCRS). Low quality = score of 1 but less than 3. Medium quality = score of 3 but less than 5. High quality = score of 5 to 7.
[d]Quality rating based on the Early Childhood Environment Rating Scale (ECERS). Low quality = score of 1 but less than 3. Medium quality = score of 3 but less than 5. High quality = score of 5 to 7.
[e]Care provided in places such as early learning centers, nursery schools, and preschools, not classified as Head Start.
[f]Poverty status based on Census Bureau guidelines from 2002, which identify a dollar amount determined to meet a household's needs, given its size and composition. In 2002, a family of four was considered to live below the poverty threshold if its income was less than or equal to $18,392.
[g]Socioeconomic status (SES) was measured by a composite score based on parental education and occupations, and family income.
Notes: Estimates weighted by W33P0. Estimates pertain to children assessed between 44 months and 65 months of age. Rating is for child's primary type of care arrangement, which was the type of nonparental care in which the child spent the most hours. Children who were primarily cared for by parents or in multiple arrangements are not included in this table. Ratings of care arrangement quality using both the FDCRS and ECERS scales were based on interviewer observations of children's interactions with adults and peers, children's exposure to materials and activities, the extent to which and the manner in which routine care needs were met, and the furnishings and displays in the classroom. The FDCRS and ECERS metrics are designed to be equivalent. Race categories exclude persons of Hispanic ethnicity. Detail may not sum to totals because of rounding and suppression of cells that do not meet standards. Some data have been revised from previously published figures.

SOURCE: Thomas D. Snyder and Sally A. Dillow, "Table 56. Percentage Distribution of Quality Rating of Child Care Arrangements of Children at about 4 Years of Age, by Type of Arrangement and Selected Child and Family Characteristics: 2005–06," in *Digest of Education Statistics, 2010*, U.S. Department of Education, National Center for Education Statistics, April 2011, http://nces.ed.gov/pubs2011/2011015.pdf (accessed November 30, 2011)

Asians and Pacific Islanders (88), followed by Hispanics (82) and non-Hispanic African-Americans (73). From the start of kindergarten through third grade, non-Hispanic whites, Asians and Pacific Islanders, and Hispanics made similar gains in both reading and mathematics; however, non-Hispanic African-Americans lagged behind in both areas.

**READING PERFORMANCE.** The ability to read is fundamental to most aspects of education. When students cannot read well, they usually cannot succeed in other subject areas and will eventually have additional problems in a society that requires increasingly sophisticated job skills.

The National Assessment of Educational Progress (NAEP) measures reading and mathematics proficiency at four levels. Basic indicates that students have achieved partial mastery of fundamental knowledge and skills at their grade level; below level indicates less than this level. Proficient indicates solid mastery of knowledge and skills, and advanced indicates superior achievement and performance.

The NAEP finds that in 2007 students of certain minority groups were more likely to be below basic in reading achievement at all grade levels. At fourth grade only 22% of whites and 23% of Asians and Pacific Islanders were below basic, whereas 50% of Hispanics, 51% of Native Americans and Alaskan Natives, and 54% of African-Americans were. (See Figure 3.3.) At eighth grade 16% of whites and 20% of Asians and Pacific Islanders were below basic in reading achievement, whereas 42% of Hispanics, 44% of Native Americans and Alaskan Natives, and 45% of African-Americans were. (See Figure 3.4.) At 12th grade 21% of whites and 26% of Asians and Pacific Islanders were below basic in reading achievement, whereas 33% of Native Americans and Alaskan Natives, 40% of Hispanics, and 46% of African-Americans were. (See Figure 3.5.) At each grade level whites and Asians and Pacific Islanders were more likely to be at an advanced reading achievement level than were students from other racial and ethnic backgrounds.

**SCIENCE AND MATHEMATICS PERFORMANCE.** In a time when science and technology are considered to be vital to the nation's economy and position in the international community, education observers are concerned about the generally poor American performance in mathematics and science. Since 1971 the NAEP has tested students to determine their mathematical knowledge, skills, and aptitudes. The measurement assesses students in five content areas: number sense, properties, and operations; measurement; geometry and spatial sense; data analysis, statistics, and probability; and algebra and functions. The NAEP also tests students on their knowledge of facts, understanding of concepts, and ability to reason in the life, physical, and earth sciences.

In 2009 Asians and Pacific Islanders outperformed all other racial and ethnic groups in mathematics for each grade reported, consistently showing a lower proportion below basic and a higher proportion at advanced than all other groups. Among fourth graders, 8% of Asians and Pacific Islanders and 9% of whites were below basic achievement in math, whereas 29% of Hispanics, 34% of Native Americans and Alaskan Natives, and 36% of

**FIGURE 3.3**

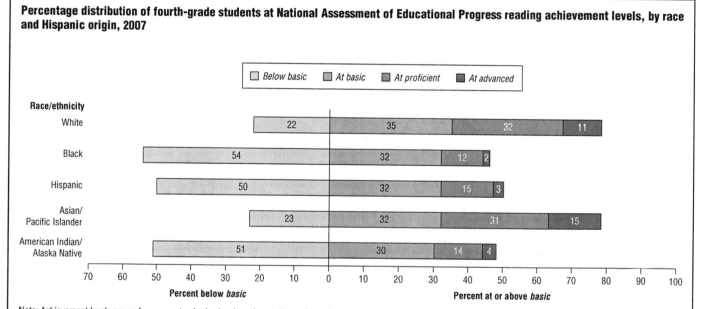

Percentage distribution of fourth-grade students at National Assessment of Educational Progress reading achievement levels, by race and Hispanic origin, 2007

Note: Achievement levels are performance standards showing what students should know and be able to do. *Basic* denotes partial mastery of knowledge and skills that are fundamental for proficient work at a given grade. (Below *Basic*, therefore, denotes less than this level of achievement.) *Proficient* represents solid academic performance. Students reaching this level have demonstrated competency over challenging subject matter. *Advanced* signifies superior performance. National Assessment of Educational Progress reports data on student race/ethnicity based on informaton obtained from school rosters. Race categories exclude persons of Hispanic ethnicity.

SOURCE: Susan Aud, Mary Ann Fox, and Angelina KewalRamani, "Figure 11.1a. Percentage Distribution of 4th-Grade Students at National Assessment of Educational Progress (NAEP) Reading Achievement Levels, by Race/Ethnicity: 2007," in *Status and Trends in the Education of Racial and Ethnic Groups*, U.S. Department of Education, National Center for Education Statistics, Institute of Education Sciences, 2010, http://nces.ed.gov/pubs2010/2010015.pdf (accessed November 30, 2011)

FIGURE 3.4

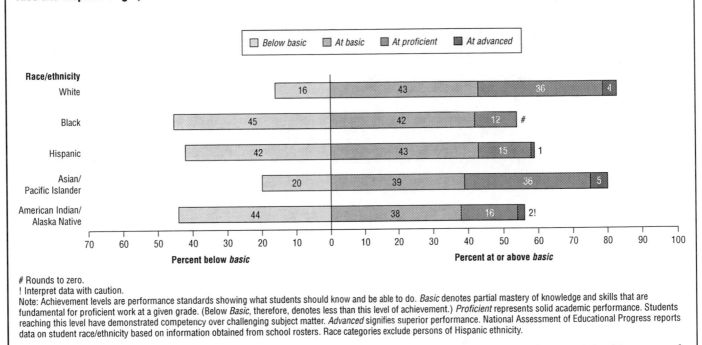

Percentage distribution of eighth-grade students at National Assessment of Educational Progress reading achievement levels, by race and Hispanic origin, 2007

# Rounds to zero.
! Interpret data with caution.
Note: Achievement levels are performance standards showing what students should know and be able to do. *Basic* denotes partial mastery of knowledge and skills that are fundamental for proficient work at a given grade. (Below *Basic*, therefore, denotes less than this level of achievement.) *Proficient* represents solid academic performance. Students reaching this level have demonstrated competency over challenging subject matter. *Advanced* signifies superior performance. National Assessment of Educational Progress reports data on student race/ethnicity based on information obtained from school rosters. Race categories exclude persons of Hispanic ethnicity.

SOURCE: Susan Aud, Mary Ann Fox, and Angelina KewalRamani, "Figure 11.1b. Percentage Distribution of 8th-Grade Students at National Assessment of Educational Progress (NAEP) Reading Achievement Levels, by Race/Ethnicity: 2007," in *Status and Trends in the Education of Racial and Ethnic Groups*, U.S. Department of Education, National Center for Education Statistics, Institute of Education Sciences, 2010, http://nces.ed.gov/pubs2010/2010015.pdf (accessed November 30, 2011)

African-Americans were. (See Figure 3.6.) Among eighth graders, 11% of whites and 20% of Asians and Pacific Islanders were at advanced proficiency in math, compared with 1% of African-Americans, 2% of Hispanics, and 3% of Native Americans and Alaskan Natives. (See Figure 3.7.) The differences in average mathematics scale scores persisted among 12th graders. (See Figure 3.8.)

Results were similar in the NAEP science assessment, although white students consistently scored slightly higher than did Asian and Pacific Islander students. The NAEP measures science proficiency on a scale from 0 to 500. The NAEP finds that in 2005 white fourth graders averaged the highest scale score of 162, followed by Asian and Pacific Islander fourth graders, who averaged 158. (See Table 3.3.) Native Americans averaged 138, Hispanics averaged 133, and African-Americans averaged 129. These differences persisted through the 12th grade.

## Dropping Out

When students drop out or fail to complete high school, both the individual and society suffer. Dropping out of school often results in limited occupational and economic opportunities for these individuals. KewalRamani et al. note in *Status and Trends in the Education of Racial and Ethnic Minorities* that individuals who drop out of school have higher unemployment rates and lower earnings than individuals who graduate from high school. For society, high dropout rates may result in increased costs of government assistance programs for these individuals and their families, costly public training programs, and higher crime rates.

In 2009, 8.1% of all 16- to 24-year-olds had dropped out of high school. (See Table 3.4.) The dropout rate was highest among Hispanics (17.6%), followed by African-Americans (9.3%) and whites (5.2%). However, since 1995 the percentage of dropouts in this age group has decreased for all race and ethnic groups, especially among Hispanics. (See Figure 3.9.)

More detailed statistics are available for 2007. In that year, Asian-Americans were the least likely to drop out (3%), followed by whites (6.1%), Native Hawaiians and Pacific Islanders (7.6%), African-Americans (11.5%), Native Americans and Alaskan Natives (15.3%), and Hispanics (19.9%). (See Table 3.5.) However, the dropout rate varied greatly depending on the place of birth. Overall, only 7.7% of native-born 16- to 24-year-olds had dropped out of high school, whereas 21.2% of foreign-born individuals of that age group had.

This discrepancy was particularly true among Hispanic students; 34.3% of foreign-born Hispanic students dropped out of school in 2007, three times more than any other

**FIGURE 3.5**

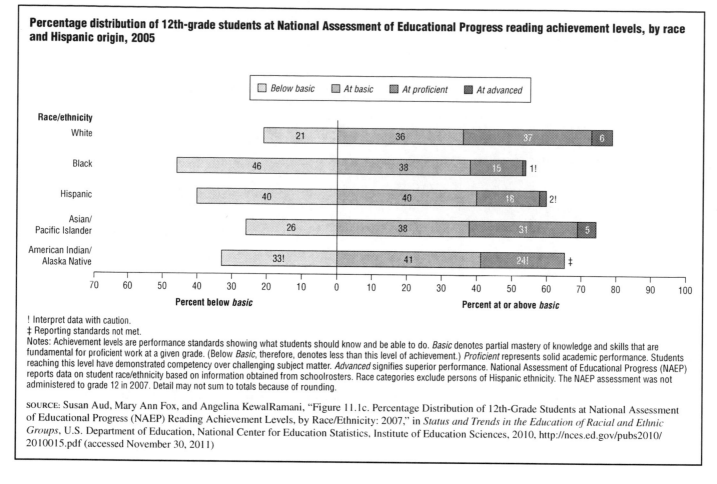

**Percentage distribution of 12th-grade students at National Assessment of Educational Progress reading achievement levels, by race and Hispanic origin, 2005**

☐ *Below basic*  ▨ *At basic*  ▨ *At proficient*  ▨ *At advanced*

Race/ethnicity

| | Below basic | At basic | At proficient | At advanced |
|---|---|---|---|---|
| White | 21 | 36 | 37 | 6 |
| Black | 46 | 38 | 15 | 1! |
| Hispanic | 40 | 40 | 18 | 2! |
| Asian/Pacific Islander | 26 | 38 | 31 | 5 |
| American Indian/Alaska Native | 33! | 41 | 24! | ‡ |

70 60 50 40 30 20 10 0 10 20 30 40 50 60 70 80 90 100

**Percent below *basic***    **Percent at or above *basic***

! Interpret data with caution.
‡ Reporting standards not met.
Notes: Achievement levels are performance standards showing what students should know and be able to do. *Basic* denotes partial mastery of knowledge and skills that are fundamental for proficient work at a given grade. (Below *Basic*, therefore, denotes less than this level of achievement.) *Proficient* represents solid academic performance. Students reaching this level have demonstrated competency over challenging subject matter. *Advanced* signifies superior performance. National Assessment of Educational Progress (NAEP) reports data on student race/ethnicity based on information obtained from schoolrosters. Race categories exclude persons of Hispanic ethnicity. The NAEP assessment was not administered to grade 12 in 2007. Detail may not sum to totals because of rounding.

SOURCE: Susan Aud, Mary Ann Fox, and Angelina KewalRamani, "Figure 11.1c. Percentage Distribution of 12th-Grade Students at National Assessment of Educational Progress (NAEP) Reading Achievement Levels, by Race/Ethnicity: 2007," in *Status and Trends in the Education of Racial and Ethnic Groups*, U.S. Department of Education, National Center for Education Statistics, Institute of Education Sciences, 2010, http://nces.ed.gov/pubs2010/2010015.pdf (accessed November 30, 2011)

group. (See Table 3.5.) In addition, among Hispanics, individuals from some countries were more likely to drop out when compared with others. Nearly three out of 10 (29.2%) individuals with Central American ancestry had dropped out, as had nearly a quarter (22.2%) of individuals with Mexican roots, although the dropout rate was much lower among those born in the United States than among immigrants. By contrast, individuals with Cuban or a South American ancestry had a dropout rate of only 6% and 8%, respectively.

One reason for the high dropout rate among foreign-born Hispanic young adults may be their undocumented immigration status. Some Hispanic youth who were brought to the United States as children see little benefit in graduating from high school as "illegal" residents. Beginning in 2001 advocacy groups urged Congress to pass the Development, Relief, and Education for Alien Minors (DREAM) Act. The act would have allowed students to remain in the United States for up to six years after high school graduation, as long as they either attended college or joined the military. The act would also have allowed these students to pay in-state tuition rates for college in the state in which they had resided for at least five years. At the end of this period, students who completed the two-year college or military requirement would be allowed to become permanent residents. In 2006 the act passed the U.S. Senate as part of the Comprehensive Immigration Reform Act of 2006; however, in October 2007 it fell eight votes short of the 60 votes necessary to bring the bill up for full debate. The act was introduced again in the 110th Congress, where it died in committee, and in the 111th Congress, where it was again referred to committee. The administration of President Barack Obama (1961–) promoted passage of the DREAM Act as part of the National Defense Authorization Act in 2010; however, the bill was filibustered in the Senate and died without a 60-vote majority in December of that year.

## MINORITY STUDENTS IN SCHOOL
### Asian-American Students Often Excel

Jamie Lew of Rutgers University, in "Burden of Acting Neither White nor Black: Asian American Identities and Achievement in Urban Schools" (*Urban Review*, vol. 38, no. 5, December 2006), and Stacey J. Lee of the University of Wisconsin, Madison, in "Additional Complexities: Social Class, Ethnicity, Generation, and Gender in Asian American Student Experiences" (*Race, Ethnicity and Education*, vol. 9, no. 1, March 2006), indicate that Asian-American students often excel at school, sometimes performing better than their

**FIGURE 3.6**

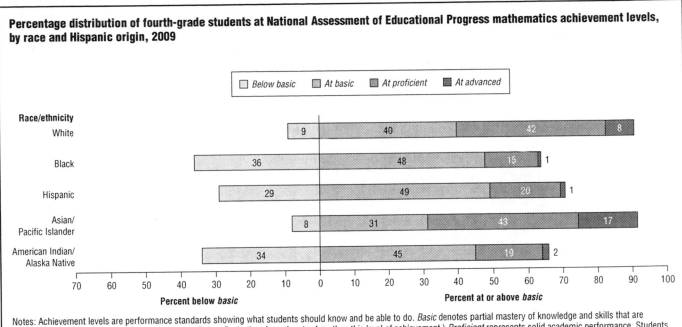

Percentage distribution of fourth-grade students at National Assessment of Educational Progress mathematics achievement levels, by race and Hispanic origin, 2009

Notes: Achievement levels are performance standards showing what students should know and be able to do. *Basic* denotes partial mastery of knowledge and skills that are fundamental for proficient work at a given grade. (Below *Basic*, therefore, denotes less than this level of achievement.) *Proficient* represents solid academic performance. Students reaching this level have demonstrated competency over challenging subject matter. *Advanced* signifies superior performance. National Assessment of Educational Progress (NAEP) reports data on student race/ethnicity based on information obtained from school rosters. Race categories exclude persons of Hispanic ethnicity. Detail may not sum to totals because of rounding.

SOURCE: Susan Aud, Mary Ann Fox, and Angelina KewalRamani, "Figure 11.2a. Percentage Distribution of 4th-Grade Students at National Assessment of Educational Progress (NAEP) Mathematics Achievement Levels, by Race/Ethnicity: 2009," in *Status and Trends in the Education of Racial and Ethnic Groups*, U.S. Department of Education, National Center for Education Statistics, Institute of Education Sciences, 2010, http://nces.ed.gov/pubs2010/2010015.pdf (accessed November 30, 2011)

**FIGURE 3.7**

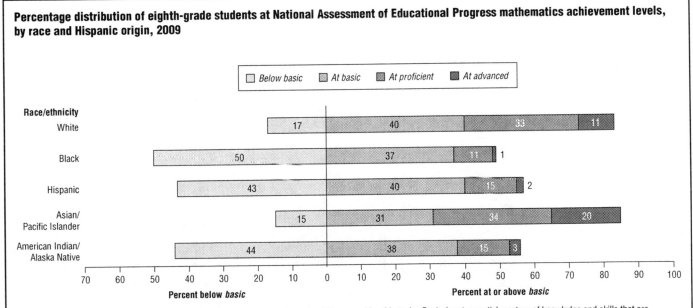

Percentage distribution of eighth-grade students at National Assessment of Educational Progress mathematics achievement levels, by race and Hispanic origin, 2009

Notes: Achievement levels are performance standards showing what students should know and be able to do. *Basic* denotes partial mastery of knowledge and skills that are fundamental for proficient work at a given grade. (Below *Basic*, therefore, denotes less than this level of achievement.) *Proficient* represents solid academic performance. Students reaching this level have demonstrated competency over challenging subject matter. *Advanced* signifies superior performance. National Assessment of Educational Progress (NAEP) reports data on student race/ethnicity based on information obtained from school rosters. Race categories exclude persons of Hispanic ethnicity. Detail may not sum to totals because of rounding.

SOURCE: Susan Aud, Mary Ann Fox, and Angelina KewalRamani, "Figure 11.2b. Percentage Distribution of 8th-Grade Students at National Assessment of Educational Progress (NAEP) Mathematics Achievement Levels, by Race/Ethnicity: 2009," in *Status and Trends in the Education of Racial and Ethnic Groups*, U.S. Department of Education, National Center for Education Statistics, Institute of Education Sciences, 2010, http://nces.ed.gov/pubs2010/2010015.pdf (accessed November 30, 2011)

**FIGURE 3.8**

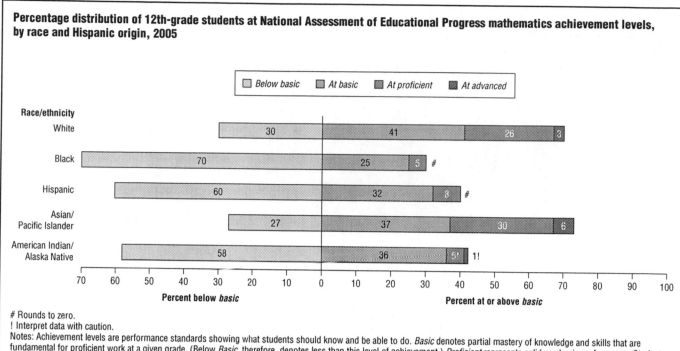

Percentage distribution of 12th-grade students at National Assessment of Educational Progress mathematics achievement levels, by race and Hispanic origin, 2005

# Rounds to zero.
! Interpret data with caution.
Notes: Achievement levels are performance standards showing what students should know and be able to do. *Basic* denotes partial mastery of knowledge and skills that are fundamental for proficient work at a given grade. (Below *Basic*, therefore, denotes less than this level of achievement.) *Proficient* represents solid academic performance. Students reaching this level have demonstrated competency over challenging subject matter. *Advanced* signifies superior performance. National Assessment of Educational Progress (NAEP) reports data on student race/ethnicity based on information obtained from school rosters. Race categories exclude persons of Hispanic ethnicity. The NAEP assessment was not administered to grade 12 in 2007. Detail may not sum to totals because of rounding.

SOURCE: Susan Aud, Mary Ann Fox, and Angelina KewalRamani, "Figure 11.2c. Percentage Distribution of 12th-Grade Students at National Assessment of Educational Progress (NAEP) Mathematics Achievement Levels, by Race/Ethnicity: 2005," in *Status and Trends in the Education of Racial and Ethnic Groups*, U.S. Department of Education, National Center for Education Statistics, Institute of Education Sciences, 2010, http://nces.ed.gov/pubs2010/2010015.pdf (accessed November 30, 2011)

**TABLE 3.3**

Average science scale scores by sex, grade, race and Hispanic origin, 1996, 2000, and 2005

| Selected characteristic, percentile, and achievement level | 4th-graders | | | 8th-graders | | | 12th-graders | | |
|---|---|---|---|---|---|---|---|---|---|
| | 1996[a] | 2000 | 2005 | 1996[a] | 2000 | 2005 | 1996[a] | 2000 | 2005 |
| **All students** | 147 | 147 | 151 | 149 | 149 | 149 | 150 | 146 | 147 |
| **Sex** | | | | | | | | | |
| Male | 148 | 149 | 153 | 150 | 153 | 150 | 154 | 148 | 149 |
| Female | 146 | 145 | 149 | 148 | 146 | 147 | 147 | 145 | 145 |
| **Race/ethnicity** | | | | | | | | | |
| White | 158 | 159 | 162 | 159 | 161 | 160 | 159 | 153 | 156 |
| Black | 120 | 122 | 129 | 121 | 121 | 124 | 123 | 122 | 120 |
| Hispanic | 124 | 122 | 133 | 128 | 127 | 129 | 131 | 128 | 128 |
| Asian/Pacific Islander | 144 | ‡ | 158 | 151 | 153 | 156 | 147 | 149 | 153 |
| American Indian | 129 | 135 | 138 | 148 | 147 | 128 | 144 | 151 | 139 |
| **Achievement level** | | | | Percent attaining science achievement levels | | | | | |
| Below basic | 37 | 37 | 32 | 40 | 41 | 41 | 43 | 48 | 46 |
| At or above basic[b] | 63 | 63 | 68 | 60 | 59 | 59 | 57 | 52 | 54 |
| At or above proficient[c] | 28 | 27 | 29 | 29 | 30 | 29 | 21 | 18 | 18 |
| At advanced[d] | 3 | 3 | 3 | 3 | 4 | 3 | 3 | 2 | 2 |

‡Reporting standards not met.
[a]Testing accommodations (e.g., extended time, small group testing) for children with disabilities and limited-English-proficient students were not permitted on the 1996 science assessment.
[b]Basic denotes partial mastery of the knowledge and skills that are fundamental for proficient work.
[c]Proficient represents solid academic performance. Students reaching this level have demonstrated competency over challenging subject matter.
[d]Advanced signifies superior performance.
Note: The National Assessment of Education Progress (NAEP) science scale ranges from 0 to 300. Race categories exclude persons of Hispanic ethnicity.

SOURCE: Adapted from Thomas D. Snyder and Sally A. Dillow, "Table 148. Average Science Scale Scores and Percentage of 4th-, 8th-, and 12th-Graders Attaining Science Achievement Levels, by Selected Student Characteristics and Percentile: 1996, 2000, and 2005," in *Digest of Education Statistics, 2010*, U.S. Department of Education, National Center for Education Statistics, April 2011, http://nces.ed.gov/pubs2011/2011015.pdf (accessed November 30, 2011)

TABLE 3.4

**Percentage of 16- to 24-year-olds who were high school dropouts, by sex, race, and Hispanic origin, selected years 1970–2009**

| Year | Total status dropout rate | | | | Male status dropout rate | | | | Female status dropout rate | | | |
|------|-----------|-------|-------|----------|-----------|-------|-------|----------|-----------|-------|-------|----------|
| | All races[a] | White | Black | Hispanic | All races[a] | White | Black | Hispanic | All races[a] | White | Black | Hispanic |
| 1970[b] | 15.0 | 13.2 | 27.9 | — | 14.2 | 12.2 | 29.4 | — | 15.7 | 14.1 | 26.6 | — |
| 1975 | 13.9 | 11.4 | 22.9 | 29.2 | 13.3 | 11.0 | 23.0 | 26.7 | 14.5 | 11.8 | 22.9 | 31.6 |
| 1980 | 14.1 | 11.4 | 19.1 | 35.2 | 15.1 | 12.3 | 20.8 | 37.2 | 13.1 | 10.5 | 17.7 | 33.2 |
| 1985 | 12.6 | 10.4 | 15.2 | 27.6 | 13.4 | 11.1 | 16.1 | 29.9 | 11.8 | 9.8 | 14.3 | 25.2 |
| 1990 | 12.1 | 9.0 | 13.2 | 32.4 | 12.3 | 9.3 | 11.9 | 34.3 | 11.8 | 8.7 | 14.4 | 30.3 |
| 1995[c] | 12.0 | 8.6 | 12.1 | 30.0 | 12.2 | 9.0 | 11.1 | 30.0 | 11.7 | 8.2 | 12.9 | 30.0 |
| 2000[c] | 10.9 | 6.9 | 13.1 | 27.8 | 12.0 | 7.0 | 15.3 | 31.8 | 9.9 | 6.9 | 11.1 | 23.5 |
| 2005[c, d] | 9.4 | 6.0 | 10.4 | 22.4 | 10.8 | 6.6 | 12.0 | 26.4 | 8.0 | 5.3 | 9.0 | 18.1 |
| 2006[c, d] | 9.3 | 5.8 | 10.7 | 22.1 | 10.3 | 6.4 | 9.7 | 25.7 | 8.3 | 5.3 | 11.7 | 18.1 |
| 2007[c, d] | 8.7 | 5.3 | 8.4 | 21.4 | 9.8 | 6.0 | 8.0 | 24.7 | 7.7 | 4.5 | 8.8 | 18.0 |
| 2008[c, d] | 8.0 | 4.8 | 9.9 | 18.3 | 8.5 | 5.4 | 8.7 | 19.9 | 7.5 | 4.2 | 11.1 | 16.7 |
| 2009[c, d] | 8.1 | 5.2 | 9.3 | 17.6 | 9.1 | 6.3 | 10.6 | 19.0 | 7.0 | 4.1 | 8.1 | 16.1 |

—Not available.

[a]Includes other racial/ethnic categories not separately shown.

[b]White and black include persons of Hispanic ethnicity.

[c]Because of changes in data collection procedures, data may not be comparable with figures for years prior to 1992.

[d]White and black exclude persons identifying themselves as two or more races.

Notes: "Status" dropouts are 16- to 24-year-olds who are not enrolled in school and who have not completed a high school program, regardless of when they left school. People who have received General Equivalency Diploma (GED) credentials are counted as high school completers. All data are based on October counts. Data are based on sample surveys of the civilian nonin-stitutionalized population, which excludes persons in prisons, persons in the military, and other persons not living in households. Race categories exclude persons of Hispanic ethnicity except where otherwise noted.

SOURCE: Adapted from Thomas D. Snyder and Sally A. Dillow, "Table 115. Percentage of High School Dropouts among Persons 16 through 24 Years Old (Status Dropout Rate), by Sex and Race/Ethnicity: Selected Years, 1960 through 2009," in *Digest of Education Statistics, 2010*, U.S. Department of Education, National Center for Education Statistics, April 2011, http://nces.ed.gov/pubs2011/2011015.pdf (accessed November 30, 2011)

**FIGURE 3.9**

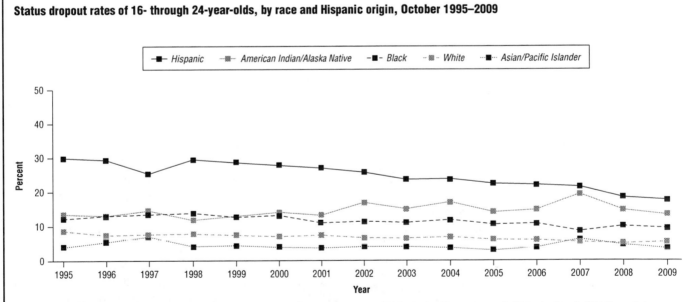

**Status dropout rates of 16- through 24-year-olds, by race and Hispanic origin, October 1995–2009**

Notes: The status dropout rate is the percentage of 16- through 24-year-olds who are not enrolled in high school and have not earned a high school credential (either a diploma or an equivalency credential such as a General Educational Development [GED] certificate). The status dropout rate includes all dropouts regardless of when they last attended school. Data for American Indians/Alaska Natives in 1999 have been suppressed due to unstable estimates. Race categories exclude persons of Hispanic ethnicity. One should use caution when making comparisons between data for 1995 and later years because of differing response options for race/ethnicity.

SOURCE: Susan Aud et al., "Figure 20-2. Status Dropout Rates of 16- through 24-Year-Olds in the Civilian, Noninstitutionalized Population, by Race/Ethnicity: October Current Population Survey (CPS) 1995–2009," in *The Condition of Education 2011*, U.S. Department of Education, National Center for Education Statistics, May 2011, http://nces.ed.gov/pubs2011/2011033.pdf (accessed November 30, 2011)

white peers. Joyce Beiyu Tan and Shirley Yates note in "Academic Expectations as Sources of Stress in Asian Students" (*Social Psychology of Education: An International Journal*, vol. 14, no. 3, September 2011) that education is highly valued in Asian cultures with a Confucian heritage; Asian parents often have high educational aspirations and expectations of their children. According to Weihua Fan, Cathy M. Williams, and Christopher A. Wolters, in

**TABLE 3.5**

Percentage of 16- to 24-year-olds who were high school dropouts, by nativity, race, and Hispanic origin, with Hispanic and Asian subgroups, 2007

| Race/ethnicity | Population | Number of status dropouts | Status dropout rate (percent) | Dropout rate for born within the United States[a] (percent) | Dropout rate for born outside the United States[a] (percent) |
|---|---|---|---|---|---|
| Total[b] | 38,491,300 | 3,582,600 | 9.3 | 7.7 | 21.2 |
| White | 23,350,100 | 1,425,900 | 6.1 | 6.1 | 5.4 |
| Black | 5,535,400 | 634,600 | 11.5 | 11.8 | 7.6 |
| Hispanic | 6,766,000 | 1,349,500 | 19.9 | 11.5 | 34.3 |
| Mexican | 4,459,300 | 991,100 | 22.2 | 12.1 | 38.8 |
| Puerto Rican | 604,100 | 89,200 | 14.8 | 12.8 | 23.0 |
| Cuban | 180,200 | 10,900 | 6.0 | 5.3 | 8.0 |
| Dominican | 192,500 | 25,100 | 13.0 | 8.7 | 18.1 |
| Salvadoran | 215,300 | 55,600 | 25.8 | 10.1 | 41.1 |
| Other Central American | 323,600 | 94,500 | 29.2 | 8.6 | 40.8 |
| South American | 319,900 | 25,500 | 8.0 | 5.4 | 9.8 |
| Other Hispanic or Latino | 471,200 | 57,500 | 12.2 | 11.3 | 18.8 |
| Asian | 1,565,400 | 46,600 | 3.0 | 2.2 | 3.7 |
| Asian Indian | 286,200 | 3,900 | 1.4 | 0.8! | 1.8 |
| Chinese[c] | 356,700 | 10,100 | 2.8 | 1.0! | 4.6 |
| Filipino | 192,900 | 2,300 | 1.2 | 0.4! | 1.7 |
| Japanese | 266,900 | 6,900 | 2.6 | 2.6 | 2.6 |
| Korean | 63,200 | 800! | 1.3! | 1.3! | 1.4! |
| Vietnamese | 164,600 | 6,600 | 4.0 | 3.9 | 4.1 |
| Other Asian | 234,900 | 16,000 | 6.8 | 4.8 | 9.7 |
| Native Hawaiian/Pacific Islander | 72,400 | 5,500 | 7.6 | 5.5 | 12.0 |
| American Indian/Alaska Native | 317,700 | 48,600 | 15.3 | 15.4 | 1.8! |

!Interpret data with caution.
[a]United States refers to the 50 states and the District of Columbia.
[b]Total includes other race/ethnicity categories not separately shown.
[c]Excludes Taiwanese. Taiwanese is included in the "Other Asian" category.

Notes: The data presented here represent status dropout rates. The status dropout rate is defined for this table as the percentage of 16- to 24-year-olds who are not in high school and who have not earned a high school credential (either a diploma or equivalency credential such as a General Equivalency Diploma [GED]). It includes all dropouts, regardless of when they last attended school, as well as individuals who may have never attended school in the United States, such as immigrants who did not complete a high school diploma in their home country. This table includes institutionalized persons and noninstitutionalized persons. Therefore, estimates are not directly comparable to the 2007 estimates. Race categories exclude persons of Hispanic ethnicity.

SOURCE: Susan Aud, Mary Ann Fox, and Angelina KewalRamani, "Table 18.1b. Percentage of 16- to 24-Year-Olds Who Were High School Status Dropouts, by Nativity and Race/Ethnicity with Hispanic and Asian Subgroups: 2007," in *Status and Trends in the Education of Racial and Ethnic Groups*, U.S. Department of Education, National Center for Education Statistics, Institute of Education Sciences, 2010, http://nces.ed.gov/pubs2010/2010015.pdf (accessed November 30, 2011)

"Parental Involvement in Predicting School Motivation: Similar and Differential Effects across Ethnic Groups" (*Journal of Educational Research*, vol. 105, no. 1, 2012), parental advising and other involvement in their children's education is highly related to student school motivation. As a result, Asian parents tend to be particularly involved in their children's education.

In addition, Asian-American students generally have fewer family risk factors than do other minority children, including living below the poverty level, living in a household where the primary language is not English, having a mother whose highest education is less than a high school diploma or equivalent, and living in a single-parent household. When these risk factors are present, they affect the performance of Asian-American students as well as students from all racial and ethnic backgrounds.

## Progress for African-American Students

Even though the average academic performance of African-American students, in general, remains below that of white students, high school graduation rates among African-Americans rose considerably during the second half of the 20th century. Snyder and Dillow indicate in *Digest of Education Statistics, 2010* that 42.6% of African-American students and 38.5% of Hispanic students graduated from high school in 1975. The graduation rate has increased more dramatically for African-American students since 1975 than it has for Hispanic students. In 2010 African-Americans aged 25 years and older were less likely than whites to have earned a high school diploma, but they were more likely than Hispanics to have received a diploma. More than four out of five (84.6%) African-Americans of this age group had received a high school diploma.

Snyder and Dillow note that the percentage of African-American high school graduates who enrolled in college within 12 months after graduation fluctuated throughout the period between 1972 and 2007, from a low of 32.5% in 1973 to a high of 69.5% in 2009. The 2009 percentage represented the largest proportion ever of recent African-American high school graduates to attend college.

FIGURE 3.10

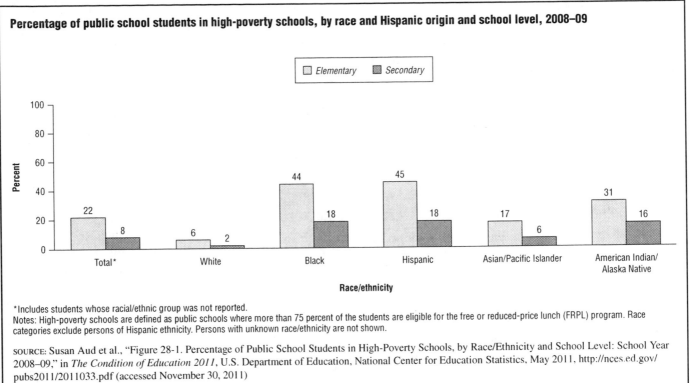

**Percentage of public school students in high-poverty schools, by race and Hispanic origin and school level, 2008–09**

*Includes students whose racial/ethnic group was not reported.
Notes: High-poverty schools are defined as public schools where more than 75 percent of the students are eligible for the free or reduced-price lunch (FRPL) program. Race categories exclude persons of Hispanic ethnicity. Persons with unknown race/ethnicity are not shown.

SOURCE: Susan Aud et al., "Figure 28-1. Percentage of Public School Students in High-Poverty Schools, by Race/Ethnicity and School Level: School Year 2008–09," in *The Condition of Education 2011*, U.S. Department of Education, National Center for Education Statistics, May 2011, http://nces.ed.gov/pubs2011/2011033.pdf (accessed November 30, 2011)

**SCHOOL SEGREGATION.** One reason African-American children have historically lagged behind white children in educational achievement has been the separate and inferior schools that they have been forced to attend. In 1954, in *Brown v. Board of Education of Topeka, Kansas* (347 U.S. 483), the U.S. Supreme Court declared that separate schools for African-American children were inherently unequal and that schools had to desegregate. Nearly 60 years later, more and more school districts are questioning whether the federal courts need to continue supervising desegregation. However, despite regulations and busing, many inner-city schools are still not integrated, and academic achievement for African-American children is still lagging. Many white students have moved (with their family's tax dollars) to the suburbs or transferred to private schools to avoid inner-city schools with high populations of minority students.

For example, Susan Aud, Mary Ann Fox, and Angelina KewalRamani indicate in *Status and Trends in the Education of Racial and Ethnic Groups* (July 2010, http://nces.ed.gov/pubs2010/2010015.pdf) that between 1993 and 2008 the percentage of central city public school students who were white decreased from 44.3% to 32.7%, whereas the proportion of minority students increased from 55.7% to 67.3%. During the 2008–09 academic year 45% of Hispanic elementary school students, 44% of African-American elementary school students, and 31% of Native American and Alaskan Native elementary school students were in high-poverty schools, compared with 17% of Asian and Pacific Islander elementary school

students and just 6% of white elementary school students. (See Figure 3.10.) Even though a lower proportion of secondary school students were in high-poverty schools, a greater than average proportion of those students were African-American, Hispanic, and Native American and Alaskan Native. In fact, in *The Condition of Education 2009* (June 2009, http://nces.ed.gov/pubs2009/2009081.pdf), Michael Planty et al. explain that segregation increased between the 1990–91 school year and the 2006–07 school year. In 1990–91, 45% of African-American students attended schools with a 75% minority enrollment; by 2006–07, 52% attended such schools.

Half a century after *Brown*, the Supreme Court restricted the use of plans that use race as a factor in assigning students to schools in an effort to promote racial diversity. The two cases, decided in a joint ruling in June 2007, were: *Parents Involved in Community Schools v. Seattle School District* (No. 05-908) and *Meredith v. Jefferson County* (No. 05-915). The court did not, however, declare that race could never be used to achieve diversity. Regardless, Robert Barnes reports in "Divided Court Limits Use of Race by School Districts" (*Washington Post*, June 29, 2007) that experts observe that many school districts will abandon policies designed to achieve racial diversity as a result of this ruling.

Resegregation began during the 1990s and most likely will accelerate as a result of the Supreme Court decision. In *Reviving the Goal of an Integrated Society: A 21st Century*

*Challenge* (January 2009, http://civilrightsproject.ucla.edu/research/k-12-education/integration-and-diversity/reviving-the-goal-of-an-integrated-society-a-21st-century-challenge/orfield-reviving-the-goal-mlk-2009.pdf), Gary Orfield of the Civil Rights Project at Harvard University notes that the June 2007 Supreme Court decision was a dramatic reversal of the gains that had been made during the civil rights era. He suggests that African-Americans and Hispanics were more segregated in 2009 than they had been during the last 40 years. More specifically, he states that "millions of nonwhite students are locked into 'dropout factory' high schools, where huge percentages do not graduate, have little future in the American economy, and almost none are well prepared for college."

During the 2007–08 school year 87% of white students attended public elementary or secondary schools where the percentage of minority enrollment was less than 50%. (See Figure 3.11.) By contrast, 51% of Native American and Alaskan Native students, 43% of Asian and Pacific Islander students, 26% of African-American students, and 22% of Hispanic students attended these schools. Conversely, 59% of Hispanic students and 53% of African-American students attended schools where minorities made up 75% or more of the student population. A third (34%) of Asian and Pacific Islander students and 30% of Native American and Alaskan Native students attended schools with such high minority enrollment. However, only 4% of white students attended schools where minorities made up 75% or more of the student population. These percentages attest to the continued segregation of minority students in the U.S. public school system.

CRITICAL RACE THEORY. Bree Picower of New York University argues in "The Unexamined Whiteness of Teaching: How White Teachers Maintain and Enact Dominant Racial Ideologies" (*Race Ethnicity and Education*, vol. 12, no. 2, July 2009) that the ideas about race brought into the classroom by white teachers are entrenched and difficult to change and that these ideas negatively affect students of color. In fact, the idea that racism is pervasive and permanent is a basic premise of critical race theory; racism's pervasiveness and permanency translates into achievement gaps in the classroom.

Structural racism works against African-American students in the classroom. In "The Song Remains the Same: Transposition and the Disproportionate Representation of Minority Students in Special Education" (*Race Ethnicity and Education*, vol. 11, no. 4, December 2008), Gregg Beratan of the University of London posits that such ideas have resulted in the "legal" segregation of students of color into special education classrooms in the aftermath of the *Brown* decision. He writes, "The disproportionate representation of minority students in special education is as clear an example of a racist outcome as one can find." According to Sabina E. Vaught and

Angelina E. Castagno, in "'I Don't Think I'm a Racist': Critical Race Theory, Teacher Attitudes, and Structural Racism" (*Race Ethnicity and Education*, vol. 11, no. 2, July 2008), achievement gaps are structural—not individual—and remedying these gaps will therefore require systemic, rather than individual, change.

## Hispanic Educational Attainment Holds Steady

Even though Hispanics made modest gains in education during the 1990s, low educational attainment has been a major hindrance to their economic advancement in the United States. Snyder and Dillow find in *Digest of Education Statistics, 2010* that Hispanics continued to trail behind other groups in high school graduation rates in 2010. Only 69.4% of Hispanics aged 25 to 29 years had received high school diplomas, compared with 94.5% of whites, 94% of Asians and Pacific Islanders, and 89.6% of African-Americans. Not surprisingly, in 2010 Asians and Pacific Islanders, whites, and African-Americans were more likely to have graduated from college than were Hispanics. (See Figure 3.12.)

Why do Hispanics trail other racial and ethnic groups in educational attainment? A language barrier may be one reason. In 2009, 7.4 million (65.8%) out of 11.3 million Hispanic students in kindergarten through 12th grade spoke Spanish at home. (See Table 3.6.) One out of six (16.2%) Hispanic students spoke English with difficulty.

However, there are some signs that the Hispanic population is making slow but steady progress in educational attainment in the United States. Snyder and Dillow indicate that the proportion of Hispanic adults aged 25 to 29 years with a high school diploma rose from 57.1% in 1995 to 69.4% in 2010. Likewise, the proportion of Hispanics with a bachelor's degree also rose, from 8.9% in 1995 to 13.5% in 2010.

## Native American Educational Attainment Remains Low

Native Americans have the lowest educational attainment of all minority groups, which is attributable in part to a high dropout rate. According to Jill Fleury DeVoe and Kristen E. Darling-Churchill, in *Status and Trends in the Education of American Indians and Alaska Natives: 2008* (September 2008, http://nces.ed.gov/pubs2008/2008084.pdf), 48,500 students attended Bureau of Indian Education schools and tribal schools during the 2006–07 academic year. In 2005–06, 644,000 Native American and Alaskan Native students attended public schools.

Kristin Denton Flanagan and Jen Park indicate in *American Indian and Alaska Native Children: Findings from the Base Year of the Early Childhood Longitudinal Study, Birth Cohort* (August 2005, http://nces.ed.gov/pubs2005/2005116.pdf) that a high proportion of Native American children have certain risk factors that may affect

FIGURE 3.11

**Percentage distribution of public elementary and secondary school students of each racial/ethnic group, by percentage enrollment in school of selected racial/ethnic group, 2007–08**

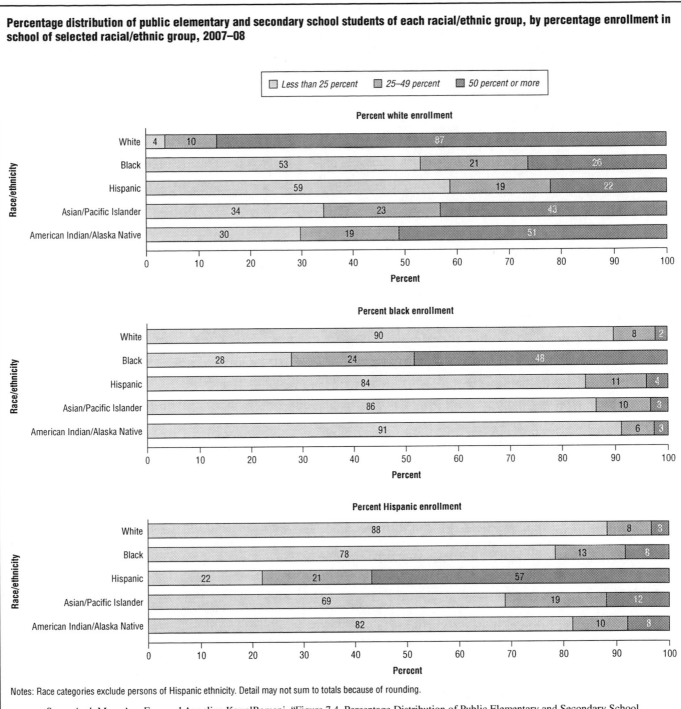

Notes: Race categories exclude persons of Hispanic ethnicity. Detail may not sum to totals because of rounding.

SOURCE: Susan Aud, Mary Ann Fox, and Angelina KewalRamani, "Figure 7.4. Percentage Distribution of Public Elementary and Secondary School Students of Each Racial/Ethnic Group, by Percent Enrollment in School of Selected Racial/Ethnic Group: 2007–08," in *Status and Trends in the Education of Racial and Ethnic Groups*, U.S. Department of Education, National Center for Education Statistics, Institute of Education Sciences, http://nces.ed.gov/pubs2010/2010015.pdf (accessed November 30, 2011)

their educational attainment. The Early Childhood Longitudinal Study, Birth Cohort, oversampled Native American children to better study their educational experiences. Fully a third (34%) of Native American children lived below the poverty line, compared with 23% of all children. A quarter (24%) of all Native American children lived with a single parent, compared with 20% of all children. In addition,

Native American parents had low educational attainment. A third (34%) of the mothers and 27% of the fathers had not completed high school, compared with 27% of all mothers and 17% of all fathers. Furthermore, only 9% of Native American mothers and 6% of Native American fathers had earned a bachelor's degree or higher, compared with 24% of all mothers and 24% of all fathers.

FIGURE 3.12

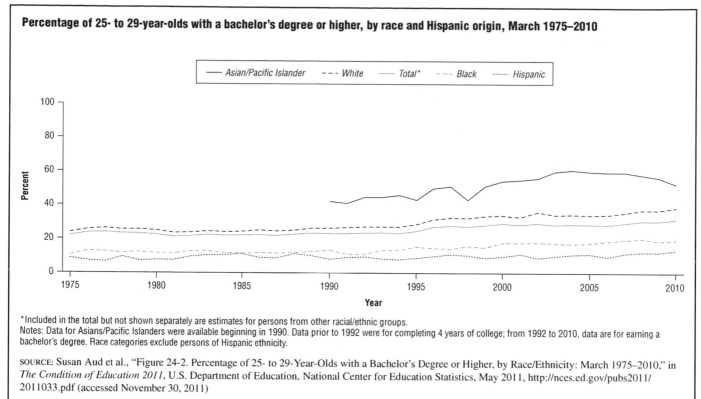

**Percentage of 25- to 29-year-olds with a bachelor's degree or higher, by race and Hispanic origin, March 1975–2010**

*Included in the total but not shown separately are estimates for persons from other racial/ethnic groups.
Notes: Data for Asians/Pacific Islanders were available beginning in 1990. Data prior to 1992 were for completing 4 years of college; from 1992 to 2010, data are for earning a bachelor's degree. Race categories exclude persons of Hispanic ethnicity.

SOURCE: Susan Aud et al., "Figure 24-2. Percentage of 25- to 29-Year-Olds with a Bachelor's Degree or Higher, by Race/Ethnicity: March 1975–2010," in *The Condition of Education 2011*, U.S. Department of Education, National Center for Education Statistics, May 2011, http://nces.ed.gov/pubs2011/2011033.pdf (accessed November 30, 2011)

In 2009 Native American and Alaskan Native eighth graders had the highest rate of absences of any race or ethnic group in the month preceding the study—64% of Native American and Alaskan Native students had been absent, and 28% had been absent three or more times in the past month. (See Table 3.7.) A smaller proportion of Hispanic students (56%), white students (56%), African-American students (55%), and Asian and Pacific Islander students (37%) had been absent in the past month, whereas only 23% of African-American students, 22% of Hispanic students, 19% of white students, and 11% of Asian and Pacific Islander students had been absent three or more times in the past month. High rates of absenteeism were associated with lower rates of achieving at least a "Basic" level of achievement on the NAEP mathematics assessment. Only 43% of Native American and Alaskan Native students who had been absent three or more times achieved Basic or above, compared with 59% of students who had been absent one or two times and 64% of students who had not been absent at all.

## REFORMING THE PUBLIC SCHOOL SYSTEM
### No Child Left Behind

In January 2002 President George W. Bush (1946–) signed into law the No Child Left Behind (NCLB) Act, which was intended to improve the U.S. public school system and provide educational choice, especially for minority families. The law mandated that all public school students be proficient in reading and math by 2014, with progress measured by the administration of annual stand-ardized tests. In addition, all subgroups (those with certain racial backgrounds, limited English proficiency, or disabilities or from low-income families) must meet the same performance standards as all students. Failure to make adequate yearly progress may result in escalating sanctions against the school, including the payment of transportation costs for students who wish to transfer to better-performing schools, extra tutoring for low-income students, replacement of the school staff, and potentially converting the school to a charter school or even turning to a private company to operate the school.

Even though the NCLB was passed with bipartisan support, critics quickly emerged, including those who charged that the mandate was underfinanced by the Bush administration. Another problem was that because of the strict testing requirements, many schools that were regarded as successful by almost all objective measures found themselves designated as failed schools. In some cases a school failed to meet its goal simply because two or three students in a subgroup failed to take a standardized test. A further problem was that minority students who attended schools that were unquestionably substandard found that even if by law they had the right to transfer to another school, there were few places to go. In *Holding NCLB Accountable: Achieving Accountability, Equity, and School Reform* (2008), a multipart study that was conducted by the Civil Rights Project at Harvard University and edited by Gail L. Sunderman, the researchers find that no districts are able to approve

TABLE 3.6

**Number and percentage of children ages 5–17 who spoke a language other than English at home and who spoke English with difficulty, by selected characteristics, 2009**

[Numbers in thousands]

| Characteristic | Total, ages 5–17 | Spoke a language other than English at home | | Spoke English with difficulty | | | | | | | |
| | | | | Total, ages 5–17 | | Ages 5–9 | | Ages 10–13 | | Ages 14–17 | |
| | | Number | Percent | Number | Percent | Number | Percent | Number | Percent | Number | Percent |
|---|---|---|---|---|---|---|---|---|---|---|---|
| Total | 53,300 | 11,204 | 21.0 | 2,654 | 5.0 | 1,373 | 6.8 | 632 | 3.9 | 649 | 3.9 |
| **Language spoken at home** | | | | | | | | | | | |
| Spanish | 8,043 | 8,043 | 100.0 | 1,950 | 24.2 | 1,031 | 32.9 | 455 | 19.0 | 464 | 18.4 |
| Other Indo-European[a] | 1,484 | 1,484 | 100.0 | 279 | 18.8 | 134 | 23.8 | 66 | 15.7 | 79 | 15.7 |
| Asian/Pacific Islander[b] | 1,244 | 1,244 | 100.0 | 333 | 26.8 | 167 | 33.9 | 83 | 22.2 | 83 | 22.1 |
| Other | 433 | 433 | 100.0 | 92 | 21.3 | 42 | 24.6 | 27 | 20.1 | 23 | 18.1 |
| **Race/ethnicity[c]** | | | | | | | | | | | |
| White | 30,090 | 1,724 | 5.7 | 339 | 1.1 | 141 | 1.3 | 74 | 0.8 | 124 | 1.3 |
| Black | 7,448 | 425 | 5.7 | 98 | 1.3 | 33 | 1.2 | 27 | 1.2 | 38 | 1.5 |
| Hispanic | 11,258 | 7,403 | 65.8 | 1,819 | 16.2 | 998 | 21.8 | 432 | 12.5 | 389 | 12.0 |
| Mexican | 7,942 | 5,398 | 68.0 | 1,422 | 17.9 | 815 | 24.9 | 331 | 13.6 | 276 | 12.3 |
| Puerto Rican | 1,029 | 458 | 44.5 | 68 | 6.6 | 29 | 7.1 | 17 | 5.6 | 22 | 7.0 |
| Cuban | 254 | 164 | 64.5 | 31 | 12.4 | 14 | 15.1 | 8 | 8.9 | 10 | 12.8 |
| Dominican | 286 | 245 | 85.5 | 56 | 19.5 | 20 | 18.8 | 16 | 18.6 | 20 | 21.0 |
| Central American | 756 | 607 | 80.3 | 147 | 19.4 | 75 | 24.5 | 37 | 15.8 | 35 | 16.2 |
| South American | 478 | 351 | 73.4 | 59 | 12.3 | 26 | 14.7 | 15 | 9.9 | 18 | 11.8 |
| Other Hispanic | 512 | 179 | 35.0 | 36 | 7.0 | 19 | 9.1 | 8 | 5.4 | 9 | 5.7 |
| Asian | 2,163 | 1,384 | 64.0 | 350 | 16.2 | 179 | 20.5 | 86 | 13.1 | 85 | 13.5 |
| Asian Indian | 415 | 272 | 65.5 | 39 | 9.5 | 24 | 12.3 | 9 | 7.3 | 7 | 6.9 |
| Chinese | 483 | 340 | 70.4 | 89 | 18.4 | 45 | 23.5 | 22 | 14.6 | 22 | 15.5 |
| Filipino | 341 | 128 | 37.6 | 26 | 7.5 | 12 | 9.2 | 7 | 6.4 | 7 | 6.6 |
| Japanese | 57 | 30 | 53.4 | 13 | 22.8 | 8 | 35.2 | 4 | 20.3 | 2 | 8.9 |
| Korean | 197 | 139 | 70.5 | 40 | 20.0 | 17 | 24.7 | 9 | 15.4 | 13 | 19.4 |
| Vietnamese | 271 | 216 | 79.5 | 69 | 25.4 | 37 | 33.0 | 16 | 19.3 | 16 | 21.1 |
| Other Asian | 399 | 259 | 65.0 | 75 | 18.7 | 36 | 23.6 | 20 | 16.2 | 18 | 15.2 |
| Pacific Islander | 77 | 23 | 29.3 | 5 | 6.0 | 2 | 6.1 | 1! | 5.8 | 1! | 5.9! |
| American Indian/Alaska Native | 392 | 59 | 15.1 | 10 | 2.6 | 3 | 2.4 | 3 | 2.5 | 4 | 2.9 |
| Two or more races | 1,708 | 129 | 7.5 | 24 | 1.4 | 12 | 1.7 | 5 | 1.1 | 6 | 1.3 |
| **Citizenship** | | | | | | | | | | | |
| U.S.-born citizen | 50,801 | 9,144 | 18.0 | 1,892 | 3.7 | 1,136 | 5.8 | 399 | 2.6 | 357 | 2.3 |
| Naturalized U.S. citizen | 514 | 286 | 55.7 | 58 | 11.2 | 15 | 11.3 | 16 | 9.8 | 27 | 12.2 |
| Non-U.S. citizen | 1,985 | 1,773 | 89.3 | 704 | 35.5 | 223 | 44.7 | 217 | 31.8 | 265 | 32.9 |
| **Poverty status[d]** | | | | | | | | | | | |
| Poor | 9,780 | 3,112 | 31.8 | 956 | 9.8 | 517 | 12.8 | 232 | 7.9 | 207 | 7.4 |
| Near-poor | 11,237 | 3,341 | 29.7 | 827 | 7.4 | 439 | 9.9 | 195 | 5.7 | 194 | 5.7 |
| Nonpoor | 31,451 | 4,619 | 14.7 | 824 | 2.6 | 394 | 3.5 | 192 | 2.0 | 238 | 2.3 |

!Interpret with caution.

[a]An Indo-European language other than Spanish (e.g., French, German, Portuguese, etc.).

[b]Any native spoken language that linguists classify variously as a Sino-Tibetan, Austroasiatic, or Austronesian language.

[c]Race categories exclude persons of Hispanic ethnicity. Totals may include some racial/ethnic categories not shown separately.

[d]Children in families whose incomes are below the poverty threshold are classified as poor, those in families with incomes at 100–199 percent of the poverty threshold are classified as near-poor, and those in families with incomes at 200 percent or more of the poverty threshold are classified as nonpoor. Detail may not sum to totals because of missing values for poverty.

Notes: Respondents were asked whether each child in the household spoke a language other than English at home. Those who answered "yes" were asked how well each child could speak English using the following categories: "very well," "well," "not well," and "not at all." All children who were reported to speak English less than "very well" were considered to have difficulty speaking English. A Spanish-language version of the American Community Survey (ACS) was available to respondents. Detail may not sum to totals because of rounding.

SOURCE: Susan Aud et al., "Table A-6-2. Number and Percentage of Children Ages 5–17 Who Spoke a Language Other Than English at Home and Who Spoke English with Difficulty, by Selected Characteristics: 2009," in *The Condition of Education 2011*, U.S. Department of Education, National Center for Education Statistics, May 2011, http://nces.ed.gov/pubs2011/2011033.pdf (accessed November 30, 2011)

all transfer requests. However well intentioned, the NCLB is proving difficult to implement, demonstrating once again that there are no easy answers to improving the U.S. educational system, especially for minority and low-income students.

In the meantime, students performing at the highest levels have suffered under the act. Sam Dillon, in "Schools Cut Back Subjects to Push Reading and Math" (*New York Times*, March 26, 2006), and Jennifer Booher-Jennings of Columbia University, in "Below the Bubble: 'Educational Triage' and the Texas Accountability System" (*American Educational Research Journal*, vol. 42, no. 2, June 20, 2005), report that many critics consider the law inflexible and so flawed that it actually undercuts the very goals it seeks to achieve. Some question the reliance on high-stakes standardized tests, which force schools to spend a

**TABLE 3.7**

Percentage distribution of 8th-graders and percentage at or above *Basic* on the National Assessment of Educational Progress mathematics assessment, by race and Hispanic origin and number of days absent from school in the past month, 2009

| Race/ethnicity | Total | No absences | 1–2 absences | 3 or more absences |
|---|---|---|---|---|
| | | Percentage distribution | | |
| **Total\*** | **100** | **45** | **35** | **20** |
| White | 100 | 44 | 37 | 19 |
| Black | 100 | 45 | 32 | 23 |
| Hispanic | 100 | 45 | 34 | 22 |
| Asian/Pacific Islander | 100 | 63 | 26 | 11 |
| American Indian/Alaska Native | 100 | 35 | 36 | 28 |
| | | Percentage at or above *Basic* | | |
| **Total\*** | **73** | **78** | **74** | **60** |
| White | 83 | 87 | 84 | 73 |
| Black | 50 | 56 | 50 | 38 |
| Hispanic | 57 | 63 | 58 | 44 |
| Asian/Pacific Islander | 85 | 89 | 84 | 68 |
| American Indian/Alaska Native | 56 | 64 | 59 | 43 |

\*Total includes other race/ethnicity categories not separately shown.
Notes: Race categories exclude persons of Hispanic ethnicity. Detail may not sum to totals because of rounding.

SOURCE: Susan Aud, Mary Ann Fox, and Angelina KewalRamani, "Table 16. Percentage Distribution of 8th-Graders and Percentage at or above *Basic* on the National Assessment of Educational Progress (NAEP) Mathematics Assessment, by the Number of Days Absent from School in the Past Month and Race/Ethnicity: 2009," in *Status and Trends in the Education of Racial and Ethnic Groups*, U.S. Department of Education, National Center for Education Statistics, Institute of Education Sciences, 2010, http://nces.ed.gov/pubs2010/2010015.pdf (accessed November 30, 2011)

considerable amount of time preparing students to take the tests, an effort that produces no lasting educational benefit and requires a reallocation of resources. In many cases gifted students' programs have been cut back. Because low-income, minority gifted students lack the options of their white counterparts, they are left to languish in classes that fail to stimulate them.

Even the law's own accountability systems show little progress since its implementation. The NCES indicates in *The Nation's Report Card: Reading 2011* (November 2011, http://nces.ed.gov/nationsreportcard/pdf/main2011/2012457.pdf) that despite small gains in reading scores of fourth and eighth graders between 1992 and 2011, the achievement gap between white and minority students had not narrowed. Only one state saw African-American–white score gaps narrow at grade eight, and only two states saw Hispanic-white score gaps narrow between 1998 and 2011. The NCES notes in *The Nation's Report Card: Mathematics 2011* (November 2011, http://nces.ed.gov/nationsreportcard/pdf/main2011/2012458.pdf) that the same was true in mathematics. Even though the achievement gap between African-American and white fourth graders had narrowed somewhat between 1990 and 2011, among eighth graders the gap had not narrowed at all. In addition, Bobby D. Rampey, Gloria S. Dion, and Patricia L. Donahue find in *The Nation's Report Card: Trends in Academic Progress in Reading and Math-*

*ematics 2008* (April 2009, http://nces.ed.gov/nationsreport card/pdf/main2008/2009479.pdf) that the NCLB had no effect on closing the gap between the performance of white students and African-American and Hispanic students between 2004 and 2008 in either math or reading.

The Forum on Educational Accountability was formed by several organizations that oppose certain provisions of the NCLB and that want changes in the law's pending reauthorization. Among the changes the forum advocates are those proposed in "Joint Organizational Statement on No Child Left Behind Act" (October 21, 2004, http://www.edaccount ability.org/Joint_Statement.html), which as of December 2011 had 156 organizational signers:

- Replace arbitrary proficiency targets with achievement targets based on the success rates in the best public schools

- Measure progress by students' progress rather than by point-in-time tests

- Increase accountability of school districts and state governments to the federal government

- Use a variety of measures of student performance, not only standardized testing

- Institute funding for research into effective accountability systems

- Develop effective accountability systems

- Decrease testing burden by testing only selected grades

- Train teachers better and encourage ongoing professional development

- Reform the system of sanctioning underperforming schools to better support the goal of improved student achievement

- Increase funding

Critics of the NCLB found an ally in the Obama administration. Under President Obama's direction, the U.S. Department of Education released *A Blueprint for Reform: The Reauthorization of the Elementary and Secondary Education Act* (March 2010, http://www2.ed.gov/policy/elsec/leg/blueprint/blueprint.pdf). The blueprint proposed increasing funding for states to broaden the assessments used to evaluate academic skills above basic levels, expanding requirements to include subjects other than reading and mathematics, relaxing the stringent accountability punishments, providing incentives to keep students in school, and narrowing the achievement gap. Cameron Brenchley reports in "We Can't Wait: 10 States Approved for NCLB Flexibility" (February 9, 2012, http://www.ed.gov/blog/2012/02/we-cant-wait-10-states-approved-for-nclb-flexibility/) that in early February 2012 President Obama announced that 10 states had been granted greater flexibility in exchange for implementing plans for comprehensive school reforms, including teacher and principal development, assessments and evaluations independent of test schools, and higher educational standards. In the press release "26 More States and D.C. Seek Flexibility from NCLB to Drive Education Reforms in Second Round of Requests" (February 29, 2012, http://www.ed.gov/news/press-releases/26-more-states-and-dc-seek-flexibility-nclb-drive-education-reforms-second-round), the Department of Education indicates that by late February 2012 another 26 states and the District of Columbia had submitted requests for flexible plans.

## School "Choice"

Planty et al. find in *Condition of Education 2009* that the percentage of parents who enrolled their children in chosen public schools, rather than in their assigned public schools, increased from 11% in 1993 to 15.5% in 2007. Nearly half (46.2%) the parents surveyed reported that they had the option to send their children to a chosen public school. Among those parents, 66.8% sent their children to their assigned public school, whereas 24.5% sent their children to a chosen public school. In 2007 African-American students (36.2%) were the most likely to attend a chosen public school and white students (20.3%) were the least likely to attend one, probably because white students were less likely to be assigned to schools in high-poverty areas and were more likely to attend chosen private schools.

SCHOOL VOUCHERS. Despite the Supreme Court's rejection of segregated schools, many minority students have been relegated to failing neighborhood public schools with little diversity. One proposed solution to this problem is the school voucher, a concept that was pioneered by the Nobel Prize–winning economist Milton Friedman (1912–2006) in 1955. The Friedman Foundation for Educational Choice explains in "School Choice" (2012, http://www.friedmanfoundation.org/friedman/schoolchoice/) that the voucher program provides parents with a predetermined amount of money—in essence the tax dollars already collected by a community to be used for education—and allows parents to present that voucher to the public or private school of their choice. Proponents for vouchers believe that not only will minority children benefit but also that public schools, fearful of losing tax revenues, will gain an incentive to improve. Opponents of vouchers, such as the National Educational Association (NEA), in "Vouchers" (2012, http://www.nea.org/home/16378.htm), maintain that choice will simply drain money from the public schools and worsen their condition, while not providing real choice for students from impoverished or low-income families.

Vouchers have been used on an experimental basis around the country. The main programs are in Milwaukee, Wisconsin, enacted in 1990, and in Cleveland, Ohio, enacted in 1995; also, a program for children with disabil-

ities was enacted in Florida in 1999. More recent programs have been established on a smaller scale, including a special education voucher program in Georgia, enacted in 2007, and programs in Arizona, enacted in 2006 but under court challenge, and in New Orleans, Louisiana, enacted in 2008. The article "Topic A: Obama's Compromise on D.C.'s School Vouchers Program" (*Washington Post*, May 10, 2009) indicates that President Obama essentially ended the District of Columbia voucher program, established in 2004, when he signed a spending bill in 2009 that prevented new students from entering the program.

These programs have produced mixed results. Even though some minority children have been able to use vouchers to escape inferior schools, many families still lack the money that is necessary to educate their children outside of the public school system. The value of the vouchers, ranging from $1,250 to $3,700, is simply too small to cover the tuition for most traditional private schools, leading a number of parents to opt for Catholic schools, which can be less expensive. However, the funding of religious education may not hold up to constitutional scrutiny. In "Vouchers Are Constitutionally Suspect" (2001, http://www.adl.org/vouchers/vouchers_constit_suspect.asp), the Anti-Defamation League states that "voucher programs . . . would force citizens—Christians, Jews, Muslims and atheists—to pay for the religious indoctrination of school children at schools with narrow parochial agendas. In many areas, 80 percent of vouchers would be used in schools whose central mission is religious training."

Moreover, parents using vouchers incur additional costs, such as transportation and school lunches, that many have found they cannot afford. According to Andrew Stephen, in "America—Andrew Stephen on Magic Solutions for US Schools" (*New Statesman*, December 9, 2002), in Florida "a quarter of the kids who were signed up for vouchers this school year have already found themselves back in the public system." In these cases, voucher programs end up not helping low-income children at all but segregating them further in neighborhood public schools while children from higher-income families who can afford the additional costs use the vouchers to attend private schools.

The voucher movement suffered a serious setback in January 2006, when the Florida Supreme Court struck down that state's Opportunity Scholarship voucher system, saying that it violated the constitutional requirement of a uniform system of free public schools. With this argument, the court avoided the controversial issue of whether public school dollars could be used to fund parochial education. The NEA reports in "Florida High Court Rules against Vouchers" (January 2006, http://www.nea.org/home/16987.htm) that even supporters of the voucher system in Florida admitted that the court's decision most likely threatened the two other voucher programs in use in the state. In "Utah Voters Resoundingly

Defeat School Voucher Ballot Issue" (December 7, 2007, http://www.nsba.org/), the National School Boards Association notes that a further setback occurred in Utah in November 2007, when voters rejected a statewide voucher program. In general, taxpayers do not support voucher programs.

Even so, limited voucher programs have been enacted in some states. The National School Boards Association explains in "Voucher Strategy Center" (2012, http://www.nsba.org/Advocacy/Key-Issues/SchoolVouchers/VoucherStrategyCenter) that in July 2011 Arizona created an "Empowerment Scholarship Account" that would allow parents of children with disabilities to get vouchers to pay for tuition and fees at private schools. Indiana enacted an income-based voucher program in May 2011 that would offset private school fees for students in grades first to eighth. Utah and Oklahoma have enacted scholarship programs for students with disabilities that pay private school tuition for some students.

**CHARTER SCHOOLS.** Like vouchers, the idea of charter schools has also found proponents in the minority community. A charter school is publicly financed but operates independent of school districts, thereby combining the advantages of a private school with the free tuition of a public school. Parents, teachers, and other groups receive a charter from a state legislature to operate these schools, which in effect exist as independent school districts. They receive public funds and are accountable for both their financing and educational standards.

According to Robin J. Lake and Paul T. Hill, in *Hopes, Fears, and Reality: A Balanced Look at American Charter Schools in 2005* (November 2005, http://www.ncsrp.org/downloads/HopesandFears2005_report.pdf), the charter school experiment started in Minnesota in 1992. Aud et al. report in *Condition of Education 2011* that by the 2008–09 school year, 4,694 charter schools taught over 1.4 million students in 40 states and the District of Columbia. As with vouchers, results have been uneven, with a number of successes offset by charter schools that failed to improve student achievement. Overall, however, the charter school movement has stood the test of time, and these schools have provided some parents with real options for their children's education. In "Charter Schools and Achievement" (October 2011, http://www.crpe.org/cs/crpe/download/csr_files/brief_NCRSP_Betts Tang_Oct11.pdf), Julian R. Betts and Y. Emily Tang of the National Charter School Research Project find that charter elementary school students perform better in math and reading than their traditional public school counterparts and that charter middle school students perform better in math. However, the researchers note that there is no significant effect on achievement at the high school level. In 2009 the charter school movement gained even more momentum with the support of the Obama admin-

istration, which pressured states to lift restrictions on the establishment and growth of charter schools by using discretionary education funds contained in the American Recovery and Reinvestment Act, which was signed into law in February 2009.

However, one unintended consequence of charter schools is that they are more segregated than public schools. Aud et al. note that during the 2008–09 academic year 31% of charter school students were African-American, compared with 15.3% of conventional public school students; 25.1% of charter school students were Hispanic, compared with 22.3% of conventional public school students; and 37.9% of charter school students were white, compared with 54.8% of conventional public school students. In "Charter Schools and Race: A Lost Opportunity for Integrated Education" (*Education Policy Analysis Archives*, vol. 11, no. 32, September 5, 2003), Erica Frankenberg and Chungmei Lee of Harvard University state that "seventy percent of all black charter school students attend intensely segregated minority schools compared with 34% of black public school students.... The pattern for Latino segregation is mixed; on the whole, Latino charter school students are less segregated than their black counterparts." Amy Stambach and Natalie Crow Becker note in "Finding the Old in the New: On Race and Class in US Charter School Debates" (*Race Ethnicity and Education*, vol. 9, no. 2, July 2006) that the "political and social processes surrounding charter school formation can promote racial exclusion and class stratification" rather than overcome socioeconomic stratification within the public school system, as their founders often intend.

## HIGHER EDUCATION
### Preparation for College

**HIGH SCHOOL COURSE-TAKING.** High school students are better prepared for college-level coursework if they take advanced courses while still in high school. Asian-American students are more likely than other students to take advanced math and science courses in high school. White students, while less likely to take these courses than Asian-American students, are significantly more likely than most minority students to take these courses. According to the College Board (August 18, 2009, http://professionals.collegeboard.com/profdownload/cbs-2009-Graph-8_2009-Seniors-Taking-Physics-Precalc-Calc-Race-Ethnicity.pdf), the most recent detailed data that were available as of April 2012, 53% of all college-bound seniors in 2009 had taken physics, 53% had taken precalculus, and 28% had taken calculus. Among Asian-American students, 66% took physics, 69% took precalculus, and 48% took calculus. More than half (54%) of white students took physics, while 55% took precalculus and 30% took calculus. However, only 44% of African-American students took physics, 36% took precalculus, and 14% took calculus. Even though higher proportions of Hispanic and Native American students took these upper-level courses than did African-American students, white students were more likely to have taken them.

According to Snyder and Dillow, in *Digest of Education Statistics, 2010,* Asian and Pacific Islander students were more likely to achieve the highest academic levels in science and mathematics in 2005. More than four out of 10 (42.8%) completed biology, chemistry, and physics, compared with 29% of white students, 21.3% of African-American students, 18.9% of Hispanic students, and 14.1% of Native American and Alaskan Native students. Nearly three out of 10 (29.8%) Asian and Pacific Islander students completed a calculus course, compared with 15.3% of white students, 7.9% of Native American and Alaskan Native students, 6.3% of Hispanic students, and 5.5% of African-American students.

However, Snyder and Dillow report that Hispanic students earned more credits in English, on average, than did other students, perhaps because they were the most likely to speak English as a second language. In 2005 Hispanic students earned, on average, 4.8 credits in English, African-American and Asian and Pacific Islander students each earned 4.5 credits, Native American and Alaskan Native students earned 4.4 credits, and white students earned 4.3 credits. By contrast, Hispanic students earned the fewest history credits, on average, with 3.8 credits, whereas Asian and Pacific Islander students earned 3.9 credits, African-American and white students each earned 4 credits, and Native American and Alaskan Native students earned 4.1 credits. Asian and Pacific Islander students earned far more foreign language credits, on average, than did other students (2.4), compared with 2 credits for white students, 1.9 credits for Hispanic students, 1.7 credits for African-American students, and 1.4 credits for Native American and Alaskan Native students.

According to Snyder and Dillow, Asian and Pacific Islander students were the most likely to take the toughest course load in high school in 2005. More than four out of 10 (42.9%) Asian and Pacific Islander students took the toughest load of four English courses, three social science courses, three science courses, three math courses, half a year of computer science, and two language courses. African-American students (39.9%) were the next most likely to take this course load, followed by white students (35.8%), Hispanic students (33%), and Native American and Alaskan Native students (24.5%).

Advanced placement courses are college-level courses that are offered to students in high school. The College Board developed 37 courses in 20 subjects; college credit can be awarded for a qualifying score of 3.0 or better on a five-point scale. According to Aud, Fox, and KewalRamani, in *Status and Trends in the Education of Racial and Ethnic Groups,* between 1999 and 2008 the number of students taking advanced placement examinations increased by 125.4%. The participation of minority students increased more than the participation of white students. For example,

the participation of African-American students increased by 249.9%, the participation of Hispanic students increased by 233.7%, the participation of Native American and Alaskan Native students increased by 147.1%, and the participation of Asian-American students increased by 133.5%, whereas the participation of white students increased by 113.1%. However, Michael Planty, Stephen Provasnik, and Bruce Daniel explain in *High School Coursetaking: Findings from the Condition of Education 2007* (June 2007, http://nces .ed.gov/pubs2007/2007065.pdf) that even though the average scores of white and Asian-American students remained relatively stable during this period, at 3 and 3.1, respectively, the scores of other minority students declined. This lack of preparation for college coursework could affect these students' acceptance to and success in college.

**GRADE POINT AVERAGE.** Most groups of minority students, except for Asian-American students, are at a disadvantage when applying to college because of low grades in high school. According to the College Board, in "2011 SAT Trends" (2012, http://professionals.collegeboard.com/data-reports-research/sat/cb-seniors-2011/tables), in 2011 the average grade point average (GPA) of most minority groups who took the Scholastic Assessment Test (SAT) was lower than 3.34, which was the average GPA of all students who took the SAT. The average GPA of African-American students was 0.32 lower than the average GPA, the average of Hispanic students was 0.13 lower, and the average of Native American students was 0.07 lower. Asian-American students outperformed white students, however, with an average of a 3.5 GPA compared with 3.43 for white students.

## SAT and ACT Scores

Students wishing to enter most colleges and universities in the United States must take the SAT or the ACT Assessment (formerly the American College Test). These are standardized tests that are intended to measure verbal and mathematical ability to determine readiness for college-level work. Most students take the SAT. Performance on the SAT is measured in three areas, each on a scale of 200 to 800: critical reading, mathematics, and a written essay portion that was added to the SAT in 2005.

Historically, minority students have not scored as well on the SAT as white students, but gains have been made by some groups since 2001. The College Board indicates in *2011 College-Bound Seniors: Total Group Profile Report* (August 2011, http://professionals.collegeboard.com/prof download/cbs2011_total_group_report.pdf) that in 2011 the average score for the critical reading portion of the SAT among whites was 528, compared with 517 for Asians or Pacific Islanders, 484 for Native Americans or Alaskan Natives, and 428 for African-Americans. Among Hispanic subgroups, Mexican-Americans averaged 451 on the critical reading portion of the test, Puerto Ricans averaged 452, and the rest of the Hispanic subgroups combined for an average of 451. In "2011 SAT Trends," the College Board states that the average critical reading scores for minority groups generally declined between 2001 and 2011. Asians or Pacific Islanders were the only group that experienced a large increase, from 501 to 517. The average scores of Native Americans or Alaskan Natives also improved marginally, from 481 to 484. Hispanic students' average score declined from 456 to 451; as did African-Americans' average score, which decreased from 433 to 428. White students also experienced a slight decline, from 529 to 528.

According to the College Board, mathematics scores were better in 2011 than they were in 2001 for all minority groups. In 2011 Asians or Pacific Islanders scored the highest by far on the math portion of the test, with an average score of 595, up from 566 in 2001. Other groups' scores improved only marginally over the decade. Whites scored an average of 535, up from 531 in 2001. Native Americans or Alaskan Natives scored 488, up from 479 in 2001. Hispanics scored 463, up from 460 in 2001. African-Americans scored 427, up from 426 in 2001.

The writing portion of the SAT was a relatively new part of the test in 2011, having only been added by the College Board in 2005. In 2011 Asians or Pacific Islanders and whites did the best on this portion of the test, at 528 and 516, respectively. Native Americans or Alaskan Natives averaged 465, Hispanics averaged 444, and African-Americans scored an average of 417.

## Minority College Attendance

Generally, minority enrollment in colleges and universities has grown ever since racial and ethnic enrollment

statistics were first reported in 1975. Even though these gains are encouraging, they must be viewed in the context of overall participation rates in higher education and degree completion rates.

In *Digest of Education Statistics, 2010*, Snyder and Dillow note that in 2009, 45% of whites aged 18 to 24 years were enrolled in colleges and universities, compared with 37.7% of African-Americans and 27.5% of Hispanics in this age group. (See Table 3.8.) However, Aud, Fox, and KewalRamani note in *Status and Trends in the Education of Racial and Ethnic Groups* that Asians and Pacific Islanders have the highest percentage of young people enrolled in colleges and universities. In 2008, 57.6% of all Asians and Pacific Islanders aged 18 to 24 years were enrolled in higher education.

## Earning a Bachelor's Degree

College participation rates are telling, but so, too, are college completion rates. A number of students begin college, only to drop out before receiving a bachelor's degree. Aud et al. indicate in *Condition of Education 2011* that in 2010 only 19.4% of African-Americans between the ages of 25 and 29 years had earned a bachelor's degree or higher. (See Figure 3.12.) Among Hispanics in this age group, only 13.5% had received a bachelor's degree or higher. Among Asians and Pacific Islanders in this age group, 52.5% had received a bachelor's degree or higher—the highest completion rate of any race or ethnic group.

College completion rates among Asian-Americans and Hispanics vary according to their country of origin. In *Status and Trends in the Education of Racial and Ethnic*

**TABLE 3.8**

**Enrollment rates of 18- to 24-year-olds in degree-granting institutions, by type of institution, sex, and race and Hispanic origin of student, selected years 1975–2009**

| Year | Total, all students | Enrollment as a percent of all 18- to 24-year-olds | | | | | | | Total, all students | Enrollment as a percent of all 18- to 24-year-olds high school completers[a] | | | | | | |
| | | Type of institution | | Sex | | Race/ethnicity | | | | Type of institution | | Sex | | Race/ethnicity | | |
| | | 2-year | 4-year | Male | Female | White | Black | Hispanic | | 2-year | 4-year | Male | Female | White | Black | Hispanic |
|------|------|------|------|------|------|------|------|------|------|------|------|------|------|------|------|------|
| 1975 | 26.3 | 9.0 | 17.3 | 29.0 | 23.7 | 27.4 | 20.4 | 20.4 | 32.5 | 11.1 | 21.4 | 36.2 | 29.2 | 32.3 | 31.5 | 35.5 |
| 1980 | 25.7 | 7.1 | 18.6 | 26.4 | 25.0 | 27.3 | 19.4 | 16.1 | 31.8 | 8.8 | 23.0 | 33.5 | 30.3 | 32.1 | 27.6 | 29.9 |
| 1985 | 27.8 | 7.4 | 20.4 | 28.4 | 27.2 | 30.0 | 19.6 | 16.9 | 33.7 | 8.9 | 24.8 | 35.3 | 32.3 | 34.9 | 26.0 | 26.8 |
| 1990 | 32.0 | 8.7 | 23.3 | 32.3 | 31.8 | 35.1 | 25.4 | 15.8 | 39.1 | 10.6 | 28.5 | 40.0 | 38.3 | 40.4 | 32.7 | 28.7 |
| 1995 | 34.3 | 8.9 | 25.4 | 33.1 | 35.5 | 37.9 | 27.5 | 20.7 | 42.3 | 11.0 | 31.3 | 41.7 | 43.0 | 44.0 | 35.4 | 35.2 |
| 2000 | 35.5 | 9.4 | 26.0 | 32.6 | 38.4 | 38.7 | 30.5 | 21.7 | 43.2 | 11.5 | 31.8 | 40.8 | 45.6 | 44.1 | 39.3 | 36.2 |
| 2005[b] | 38.9 | 9.6 | 29.2 | 35.3 | 42.5 | 42.8 | 33.1 | 24.8 | 46.8 | 11.6 | 35.2 | 44.3 | 49.1 | 48.6 | 41.4 | 37.4 |
| 2006[b] | 37.3 | 9.6 | 27.8 | 34.1 | 40.6 | 41.0 | 32.6 | 23.6 | 45.0 | 11.5 | 33.5 | 42.2 | 47.7 | 46.5 | 42.0 | 35.5 |
| 2007[b] | 38.8 | 10.9 | 27.9 | 35.5 | 42.1 | 42.6 | 33.1 | 26.6 | 46.1 | 13.0 | 33.1 | 43.4 | 48.6 | 47.8 | 40.1 | 39.2 |
| 2008[b] | 35.6 | 9.1 | 26.5 | 34.1 | 37.0 | 39.4 | 30.4 | 18.7 | 43.7 | 11.2 | 32.5 | 42.9 | 44.4 | 45.3 | 39.2 | 31.6 |
| 2009[b] | 41.3 | 11.7 | 29.6 | 38.4 | 44.2 | 45.0 | 37.7 | 27.5 | 48.8 | 13.9 | 35.0 | 46.4 | 51.2 | 50.3 | 46.7 | 38.7 |

[a]All students who enrolled in college are counted as high school completers, including students who enrolled in college but did not report high school completion.
[b]After 2002, white and black data exclude persons identifying themselves as two or more races.
Notes: Data are based on sample surveys of the civilian noninstitutional population. Percentages based on 18- to 24-year-olds high school completers for 1992 and later years use a slightly different definition of completion and may not be precisely comparable with figures for other years. Totals include other racial/ethnic groups not separately shown. Race categories exclude persons of Hispanic ethnicity except where otherwise noted.

SOURCE: Adapted from Thomas D. Snyder and Sally A. Dillow, "Table 212. Enrollment Rates of 18- to 24-Year-Olds in Degree-Granting Institutions, by Type of Institution and Sex and Race/Ethnicity of Student: 1967 through 2009," in *Digest of Education Statistics, 2010*, U.S. Department of Education, National Center for Education Statistics, April 2011, http://nces.ed.gov/pubs2011/2011015.pdf (accessed November 30, 2011)

*Groups*, Aud, Fox, and KewalRamani report that among Hispanics aged 25 to 29 years in 2007, those who traced their roots to Cuba or South America had the highest completion rates, at 29.7% and 28.2%, respectively. About 15.5% of Dominicans in this age group had a bachelor's degree, and 15.7% of Puerto Ricans had a bachelor's degree. A much lower proportion of Hispanics who traced their roots to Mexico (8.5%) or Central America (10.2%) had earned a bachelor's degree by the age of 29 years.

Among those of Asian origin, 25- to 29-year-olds who traced their roots to India had the highest percentage of bachelor's degrees, whereas those who traced their roots to Japan had the lowest percentage. Four out of five (80%) Indians in this age group had bachelor's degrees, compared with 70.3% of Chinese, 59.6% of Filipinos, 54% of Koreans, 44.6% of Vietnamese, and 40.8% of Japanese. It should be noted that the percentage of those who traced their roots to Japan and held bachelor's degrees was still more than twice as high as the percentage of African-Americans (17.2%) in the same age group with bachelor's degrees.

## Affirmative Action in Higher Education

In the landmark 1978 affirmative action case *Regents of the University of California v. Bakke* (438 U.S. 265), the Supreme Court allowed race and ethnicity to be considered in college admissions in the interest of racial and ethnic diversity on U.S. college campuses. This led many schools to take special steps to boost the number of minorities that they admitted, a process commonly called affirmative action.

Over time, many people came to see affirmative action as a negative policy. Their reasons varied, but a common complaint was that affirmative action allowed some minority students to get into colleges even when their test scores and high school grades were below what those colleges would accept from white students. In June 1996 Pete Wilson (1933–), the governor of California, urged California voters to support the California Civil Rights Initiative (Proposition 209), a proposal to eliminate affirmative action in higher-education enrollment. In November 1996 California voters approved Proposition 209, which prohibited public universities from considering race and ethnicity when deciding on admissions. Sheila O'Rourke of the University of California (UC) reports in "Strategies for Achieving Faculty Diversity at the University of California in a Post-Proposition 209 Legal Climate" (2002) that in 1997, the last year that UC considered race and ethnicity in its admissions process, 17.9% of the students who were admitted were from underrepresented minority groups (Native Americans, African-Americans, and Hispanics). In 1998, the first year of admissions after Proposition 209 went into effect, the proportion of underrepresented minorities dropped to 15.5%.

In *Hopwood v. Texas* (78 F.3d 932 [1996]), the U.S. Court of Appeals for the Fifth Circuit unanimously ruled that the University of Texas (UT) School of Law was discrim-

inating against white students by using race and ethnicity as a factor in admissions. Four white applicants charged that less-qualified African-American and Hispanic students had been accepted instead of them because of racial preference on the part of UT. The appeals court ruled that colleges could not give preferences to minority students—even for what it called "the wholesome practice of correcting perceived racial imbalance in the student body." In the opinion of the appeals court, "any consideration of race or ethnicity by the law school for the purpose of achieving a diverse student body is not a compelling interest under the Fourteenth Amendment." The *Hopwood* decision applied to all public universities in Texas, Louisiana, and Mississippi. In Texas, Dan Morales (1956–), the attorney general of Texas, applied the admissions ruling to include financial aid and scholarships.

This decision negatively affected the number of underrepresented minority students at the UT School of Law. According to Lydia Lum, in "Minority Rolls Cut by Hopwood" (*Houston Chronicle*, September 16, 1997), in 1997, following the decision affecting the law school, out of 500 incoming students, only four African-American students and 26 Mexican-Americans were enrolled, down from 31 African-American students and 42 Mexican-American students the previous year. At the undergraduate level, public universities throughout Texas also saw a drop in minority applications. Texas A&M University registered nearly 15% fewer Hispanics and 23% fewer African-Americans that year.

**PUBLIC UNIVERSITIES RESPOND.** In 1998 the UT system became the first public university to grant automatic admission to first-time freshmen based on class rank. Under Texas Education Code 51.803, students who graduate in the top 10% of their class from an accredited Texas high school are guaranteed admission to UT. Because some high schools have large minority populations, state officials hoped that more minority students would be admitted to state universities. After initial declines in minority enrollment, UT announced in early 2003 that Hispanic enrollment had returned to the pre-*Hopwood* level and that African-American enrollment was nearing its 1996 level. However, James C. McKinley Jr. reports in "Texas Vote Curbs a College Admission Guarantee Meant to Bolster Diversity" (*New York Times*, May 30, 2009) that in 2009 Texas legislators limited automatic college admissions to 75% of the incoming freshman class, even though some state senators argued that such a limit would again depress minority enrollment. McKinley explains that this limit was put in place to give admissions officials more "latitude in putting together a class" and to lessen the so-called brain drain of students attending colleges and universities outside of the state.

In March 1999 UC regents approved a similar admissions policy called Eligibility in the Local Context (ELC).

According to the article "Freshman Eligibility in the Local Context (ELC)" (November 17, 2003, http://www.universityofcalifornia.edu/news/compreview/freshmanelc.pdf), under the ELC students graduating in the top 4% of their class in California high schools are eligible for admission to one of UC's undergraduate campuses. The ELC was implemented starting with freshmen applicants during the fall of 2001. According to Rebecca Trounson, in "Admissions Studies Find Flaws" (*Los Angeles Times*, February 11, 2003), early reports did not find evidence, however, that the program boosted minority enrollment.

Catherine L. Horn and Stella M. Flores of Harvard University note in *Percent Plans in College Admissions: A Comparative Analysis of Three States' Experiences* (2003, http://civilrightsproject.ucla.edu/) that in November 1999 Florida implemented a similar plan called the Talented 20. Horn and Flores review the three admissions plans by Texas, California, and Florida and conclude that "any increases in racial/ethnic diversity on these campuses cannot be singularly attributed to percent plans because they have happened in the context of the extensive race-attentive efforts made by these schools."

## Supreme Court Affirms Racial Preferences

In June 2003 the Supreme Court made two separate rulings on the admissions practices at the University of Michigan's undergraduate college and law school. In an effort to achieve diversity in the student body, the undergraduate college used a point system by awarding points on a scale of 150 to African-American, Hispanic, and Native American applicants. In *Gratz v. Bollinger* (539 U.S. 244), the court rejected this system, maintaining that it was too broad and too much like a quota, and ruled that it violated the equal protection clause in the 14th Amendment of the U.S. Constitution. By contrast, the University of Michigan law school weighed race and ethnicity along with a number of other admissions factors. In *Grutter v. Bollinger* (539 U.S. 306), the court deemed this approach legal because it furthered "a compelling interest in obtaining the educational benefits that flow from a diverse student body." As a result, the court upheld the concept of race-conscious admissions, but the nuanced approach to admissions that the court found acceptable left the door open for further lawsuits. Even though smaller schools can devote more time and attention to individual applicants, larger institutions still face the problem of how to use race and ethnicity as a factor in screening many applications without assigning a numerical value to an individual's minority status.

Adam Liptak reports in "Justices Take up Race as a Factor in College Entry" (*New York Times*, February 21, 2012) that in 2012 the Supreme Court agreed to hear a new challenge to affirmative action policies in higher education. After the 2003 Michigan rulings, education officials in Texas announced they would again use race as a factor

for historically underrepresented minority groups. In 2008 Abigail Fisher, a white student from Sugar Land, Texas, was refused admission; she sued, alleging racial discrimination. After her claim was rejected by a federal judge and the U.S. Court of Appeals for the Fifth Circuit, the Supreme Court agreed to hear the case. The case was expected to come before the court in October 2012. Liptak notes that the court is likely to rule against the practice of using limited racial preferences to achieve diversity on college and university campuses.

## Views of Educational Opportunities for African-Americans

African-Americans are less likely than whites to say that their children have the same opportunity as white children to get a good education. A Gallup Organization poll (http://www.gallup.com/poll/1687/Race-Relations.aspx#2) that was conducted in June 2008 found that 49% of African-Americans said their children "have as good a chance as white children" of receiving a good education. This figure had declined from a high of 68% in 1990. Nevertheless, a large majority of non-Hispanic whites (80%) and Hispanics (74%) believed that African-American children "have as good a chance" as their white peers to get a good education.

This racial divide in perceptions of educational opportunities for African-American children continued into discussions of higher education. In *Blacks Convinced Discrimination Still Exists in College Admission Process* (August 24, 2007, http://www.gallup.com/poll/28507/Blacks-Convinced-Discrimination-Still-Exists-College-Admission-Process.aspx), Frank Newport of the Gallup Organization reports on a 2007 poll, in which respondents were asked: "If two equally qualified students, one white and one black, applied to a major U.S. college or university, who do you think would have the better chance of being accepted to the college—the white student, the black student—or would they have the same chance?" Nearly half (48%) of non-Hispanic white respondents believed the two students would have the same chance, another quarter (26%) believed the African-American student would have the better chance, and one out of five (20%) believed the white student would have the better chance. African-Americans responded differently. Only 28% believed the two students would have the same chance, whereas 61% believed the white student would have the better chance. One out of 20 (5%) African-American respondents believed the African-American student would have the better chance for college admission. Newport notes that African-Americans who themselves had a college education felt most strongly that the white student would have the advantage.

## Tribal Colleges

Special postsecondary institutions, collectively known as tribal colleges, were established to prepare Native American and Alaskan Native students with the skills most needed on reservations, while at the same time preserving their culture. Usually situated in areas where the students cannot otherwise pursue education beyond high school without leaving the community, these colleges all offer associate's degrees. In addition, some offer bachelor's and master's degrees. Tribal colleges are located in Alaska, Arizona, Kansas, Michigan, Minnesota, Montana, Nebraska, New Mexico, North Dakota, Oklahoma, South Dakota, Washington, Wisconsin, and Wyoming.

Tribal colleges offer courses ranging from teaching and nursing to secretarial skills and computer science that meet the needs of specific communities. Besides tribal languages, traditional subjects are a part of the curricula. For example, in *Salish Kootenai College Course Catalog, 2010–2012* (2010, http://ecampus.skc.edu/ICS/icsfs/1%29_2010-12 _SKC_Catalog.pdf?target=8f255109-4a8b-4df6-b272-e08 fa111d94f), Salish Kootenai College in Montana indicates that a variety of tribal language and culture courses are offered, including "Coyote Stories," which covers morality tales that have important lessons of Indian life. These stories can only be told during the winter. "Tipi Setup" teaches students various techniques that are used by Montana tribes to erect tepees; "Hide Tanning" teaches students how to tan a fresh deer, elk, moose, or buffalo hide and turn it into buckskin; and "Stickgame" introduces students to the rules and techniques of this Native American game.

In "Fall 2005 Enrollment" (April 2, 2007, http://www .aihec.org/colleges/documents/fall05enrollment.pdf), the most recent publication on this topic as of April 2012, the American Indian Higher Education Consortium reports that 16,986 students were enrolled in tribal colleges during the fall of 2005. Approximately four out of five (80%) students enrolled in tribal colleges were Native American or Alaskan Native.

## Historically Black Colleges and Universities

According to the Department of Education, in "List of HBCUs—White House Initiative on Historically Black Colleges and Universities" (September 15, 2011, http://www2 .ed.gov/about/inits/list/whhbcu/edlite-list.html), there were 105 historically black colleges and universities located in the United States in 2011. Alabama had the largest number of historically black colleges, at 15, North Carolina had 11 institutions, Georgia had 10, Texas had 8, and South Carolina had 8. Snyder and Dillow report that 322,789 students, 264,090 of them African-American, were enrolled in these institutions during the fall of 2009.

Historically black colleges and universities often offer unique courses and programs of study to students. For example, Howard University (2012, http://www.coas.howard.edu/ afroamerican/courses.html), a traditional black college that was founded in the District of Columbia in 1867, has an African-American studies department that offers a major and a minor. Courses include "Black Philosophies of Education," which explores historical and contemporary theories of education of African-American students; "Commercial Exploitation of the Third World," which examines colonial and imperialistic economies and explores the political and economic forces that influence people of color around the world; and both 19th- and 20th-century "Black Social and Political Thought," which examines influential political and social ideas that were supported by African-American leaders in U.S. history. Florida A&M University (2007, http:// www.famu.edu/histpol/African%20American%20Studies% 20BS%20-%20Evaluation%20Form.pdf), which was founded in Tallahassee in 1887, also has an African-American studies program. Majors are required to take two African-American history courses, two African history courses, "Blacks and the Political Process," "African-American Novel," and "Psychology of Race and Prejudice," among other courses.

# CHAPTER 4
# MINORITIES IN THE LABOR FORCE

## A HISTORICAL PERSPECTIVE

Members of minority groups have always been an important part of the U.S. labor force. In many instances groups were allowed and encouraged or even forced to immigrate to the United States (or, what would eventually become the United States) to fill specific labor needs. Perhaps the most obvious example is the involuntary immigration of Africans, who provided slave labor for southern plantations as early as the 17th century. Later, Asians and Hispanics were employed to mine resources, farm land, and build railroads.

### African-Americans

Since 1619, with the arrival of the first slave ships to North American shores, African-Americans have been part of the labor force. Even though most worked as unpaid slaves on southern plantations, a few were allowed to work for pay to purchase their freedom and that of their family, an effort that often took many years. Besides laboring on farms and in households, some enslaved people developed talents in masonry, music, or other skills and were hired out by their owners.

On January 1, 1863, during the Civil War (1861–1865), President Abraham Lincoln (1809–1865) issued the Emancipation Proclamation. This freed all slaves in the Confederacy, although the Confederate states did not recognize the authority of the Union government and blacks in the South remained enslaved. The proclamation did not free slaves who were being held in Northern states, where slavery remained legal unless it was abolished by state law. On January 31, 1865, Congress passed the 13th Amendment, which abolished slavery in the entire United States; it was ratified after the war. Then, on July 9, 1868, the 14th Amendment was ratified by three-fourths of the U.S. states, providing citizenship to African-Americans, as it did to all immigrants born or naturalized in the United States. However, when the period of Reconstruction (1865–1877) came

to an end, many Southern states enacted so-called black codes, which were new laws that restricted the freedom of African-Americans living in the South. These codes included provisions that forbade African-Americans from leaving their jobs without permission. African-Americans in the South labored under these codes for decades.

The Library of Congress (LOC) explains in "African Immigration" (2012, http://www.loc.gov/teachers/class roommaterials/presentationsandactivities/presentations/ immigration/african.html) that because the best job prospects were in urban areas in the North and because the obstacles created by racial discrimination were the least burdensome there, hundreds of thousands of African-Americans left their rural southern homes and migrated north and west before and during World War I (1914–1918) in search of unskilled work in factories and homes. During the 1940s arms production for World War II (1939–1945) again attracted hundreds of thousands of African-Americans to the North, bringing about a moderate increase in the number of African-American workers in these factories. These migrations of African-Americans from the South to the North following both world wars were the largest movements of people within the United States in the country's history and did much to influence its future.

### Asian-Americans

In "Chinese and Westward Expansion" (2012, http:// memory.loc.gov/ammem/award99/cubhtml/theme1.html), the LOC notes that Chinese immigrants came to the United States not only because of the California gold rush but also to work on railroads, on farms, and in construction and manufacturing. The LOC states in "Japanese Immigration" (2012, http:// www.loc.gov/teachers/classroommaterials/presentation sandactivities/presentations/immigration/japanese.html) that between 1886 and 1911 more than 400,000 Japanese immigrants came to the United States, often to work on the rapidly expanding sugarcane plantations in Hawaii or on the fruit and vegetable farms in California. However, the Gentleman's Agreement of 1907 between President Theodore Roosevelt (1858–1919) and the Japanese government stopped the flow of Japanese workers to the United States by withholding passports, thus cutting the flow to a trickle.

The most recent wave of Asians came to the United States during the 1970s and 1980s, when hundreds of thousands of refugees were admitted from Vietnam, Laos, and Cambodia following the Vietnam War (1954–1975). The first wave of refugees came from Vietnam when Saigon fell to the North Vietnamese communists in April 1975. Over 100,000 Vietnamese who had worked for the U.S. military during the war fled Vietnam for the United States, where they were resettled in communities around the nation. Subsequent waves of refugees fled Vietnam legally and illegally over the decades. According to the Southeast Asia Resource Action Center, in *Southeast Asian Americans at a Glance: Statistics on Southeast Asians adapted from the American Community Survey* (October 6 2011, http://www.searac.org/sites/default/files/STATISTICAL%20PROFILE%202010.pdf), as of 2010 the largest number of Vietnamese lived in California (647,589), Texas (227,968), Washington (75,843), Florida (65,772), and Virginia (59,984). When the Laotian government was toppled by a communist regime after the fall of South Vietnam in 1975, Laotian and Hmong refugees fled to Thailand and were then resettled in the United States. Likewise, when Cambodia was taken over by the Khmer Rouge in 1976, Cambodian refugees fled to Thailand and were then resettled in other countries, including the United States.

## Hispanics

Many Hispanics can trace their roots to the time when the southwestern states were still a part of Mexico. However, the ancestors of most Hispanics arrived after Mexico surrendered much of its territory following its defeat in the Mexican-American War (1846–1848). The U.S. policy toward Hispanic workers (mainly from Mexico) has alternately encouraged and discouraged immigration, reflecting the nation's changing needs for labor. In "Mexican Immigration" (2012, http://www.loc.gov/teachers/classroommaterials/presentationsandactivities/presentations/immigration/mexican.html), the LOC notes that before the 20th century, when there was little demand in the Southwest for Mexican labor, Mexicans moved back and forth across completely open borders to work in mines, on ranches, and on railroads.

However, as the Southwest began to develop and as Asian immigration slowed, the demand for Mexican labor increased. According to the LOC, "Between 1910 and 1930, the number of Mexican immigrants counted by the U.S. census tripled from 200,000 to 600,000." The need for Mexican labor was so great that during World War I the Immigration and Naturalization Service exempted many Mexicans from meeting most immigration conditions, such as head taxes (paying a small amount to enter the country) and literacy requirements. Even though legal immigration rose, a large amount of illegal immigration also occurred. Historians estimate that during the 1920s there were as many illegal as legal Mexican immigrants in the country.

The LOC explains that during the Great Depression of the 1930s, when jobs became scarce, many Americans believed the nation's unemployment situation was significantly compounded by illegal aliens working in the United States. As a result, hundreds of thousands of Mexican immigrants, both legal immigrants and illegal aliens, were repatriated (sent back) to Mexico.

Following the outbreak of World War II, the United States needed workers to help in its role as a supplier to the Allied countries. When the lure of better-paying factory jobs brought many rural workers to the city, the nation looked to Mexico to fill the need for agricultural workers. The Bracero Program (1942–1964) permitted the entry of Mexican farm workers on a temporary contractual basis with U.S. employers. Even though the program was considered to be an alternative to illegal immigration, it likely contributed to it because there were more workers who wanted to participate in the program than there were openings. According to the LOC, more than 5 million Mexican immigrants came to the United States during and after the war as part of the Bracero Program, and hundreds of thousands stayed.

Marc Perry et al. of the U.S. Census Bureau estimate in *Evaluating Components of International Migration: Legal Migrants* (December 2001, http://www.census.gov/population/www/documentation/twps0059/twps0059.html) that over 1 million undocumented Hispanics entered the United States during the early 1980s. A major downturn in the Mexican economy led to a surge in Mexican immigrants, and hundreds of thousands of other Hispanics arrived from Central America, most notably from El Salvador and Guatemala, to escape bloody civil wars and repressive regimes. Overall, Hispanics accounted for approximately one out of every three legal immigrants to the United States during this period. In 1986 the Immigration Reform and Control Act gave more than 2 million Mexicans legal status in the United States. Since that time, Hispanics from Cuba, Central and South America, and Mexico have continued to enter the United States, legally and illegally.

**"GET TOUGH" POLICY.** To stem the flow of undocumented workers, a "get tough" policy was initiated in 1994, but many critics believed that the money spent on installing infrared sensors, cameras, and stadium-level lighting along the U.S.-Mexican border was essentially wasted. Instead of crossing at more populated and better-secured areas, illegal immigrants crossed into the United States through mountains and deserts, facing dangerous conditions, and many died as a result.

In September 2006 Congress passed a bill that authorized the construction of a 700-mile (1,100-km) fence along the U.S.-Mexican border in California, Arizona, New Mexico, and Texas and the installation of a high-tech surveillance system to keep illegal Mexican immigrants from crossing into the United States. Jonathan Weisman reports in "With Senate Vote, Congress Passes Border Fence Bill" (*Washington Post*, September 30, 2006) that the fence would cost $6 billion to construct. Critics charged that the fence, as planned, would be impossible to construct across the rugged terrain and the borders of the Tohono O'odham Nation, which opposed the bill.

According to the U.S. Government Accountability Office (GAO), in *Secure Border Initiative: Technology Deployment Delays Persist and the Impact of Border Fencing Has Not Been Assessed* (September 2009, http://www.gao.gov/new.items/d09896.pdf), by June 2009, 661 miles (1,064 km) of the still-unfinished fence had been completed at a cost of $2.4 billion. The new fencing had been breached 3,363 times, requiring an average $1,300 repair for each breach, and the GAO estimated that the new fencing would cost $6.5 billion to maintain through 2029. In *Briefing on U.S. Customs and Border Protection's Border Security Fencing, Infrastructure, and Technology Fiscal Year 2011 Expenditure Plan* (November 16, 2011, http://www.gao.gov/new.items/d12106r.pdf), the GAO notes that the administration of President Barack Obama (1961–), in responding to escalating costs, actually decreased funding for the border security program from its high of $1.3 billion in 2008 to just $573 million in 2011.

Even though arrests of illegal aliens along the southwestern border increased after 1994, enforcement in the workplace was rare. In fact, the U.S. economy became so dependent on a pool of low-wage workers that mass deportation of undocumented workers was not a realistic option. In "Temporary Worker Program Is Explained" (*Washington Post*, October 19, 2005), Darryl Fears and Michael A. Fletcher state that in January 2004 President George W. Bush (1946–) proposed a guest-worker program that would grant a three-year work permit to millions of undocumented workers. This permit would be renewable for at least three more years, with a chance to apply for a green card to gain permanent residency. In addition, workers in other countries could apply for work permits to take jobs that no U.S. citizen wanted. That program was not approved, and since then various types of guest-worker programs have been introduced by many lawmakers.

Guest-worker programs have come under criticism because opponents argue they leave foreign workers vulnerable to exploitation. For example, the article "Broad Opposition to Guest Worker Program" (Associated Press, October 21, 2009) notes that a 2009 lawsuit alleged that a Tennessee company, Cumberland Environmental Resources Company, abused the nonagricultural guest-worker program by lying about the availability of U.S. workers and failing to pay immigrants the prevailing wage required by law. The article also reports that a survey undertaken by the Economic Policy Institute in 2008 found that 98% of temporary workers "were paid less than the prevailing wage in occupations they commonly filled." According to Julia Preston, in "Suit Points to Guest Worker Program Flaws" (*New York Times*, February 1, 2010), a 2007 lawsuit against a marine oil-rig company located in Mississippi alleged that Indian workers had been abused and discriminated against.

Barb Howe of Farmworker Justice reports in "Labor Department Reverses Bush Administration Changes to Guestworker Program" (February 11, 2010, http://www.harvestingjustice.org/index.php?option=com_content&view=article&id=470&Itemid=68) that the Bush administration, having failed to expand the guest-worker programs already in place while in office, issued rules during its final days that reversed regulations, which had somewhat protected foreign workers in the H-2A program. These rules slashed minimum wages and reduced government oversight of the program. One year later, however, the Obama administration restored the older minimum wage formula, restored the requirement that employers pay employees' transportation costs, and reinstated several government oversight regulations. In "Labor Dept. Issues New Rules for Guest Workers" (*New York Times*, February 10, 2012), Preston notes that in February 2012 the U.S. Department of Labor issued important changes in the H-2B program that require businesses to hire qualified local workers if possible and that make it more difficult for businesses to exploit foreign workers by paying low wages.

STATE IMMIGRATION LAWS. In 2010 Arizona adopted the nation's harshest immigration law in the country, known as SB1070. This bill allowed police officers to ask about individuals' immigration status in the course of any contact with police. It also required officers to detain individuals who they suspected were illegal immigrants. Several of the law's most contentious provisions were blocked by federal courts, including provisions that required officers to check immigration status and required immigrants to carry their immigration papers at all times. In April 2012 the U.S. Supreme Court heard arguments about whether to uphold the law or declare it unconstitutional. A final ruling was expected in June 2012.

Regardless, SB1070's provisions hurt industries that faced labor shortages as immigrants, both legal and illegal, left the state. Garin Groff explains in "Costly SB 1070 Brought Businesses to the Table" (*East Valley Tribune* [Tempe, Arizona], April 24, 2011) that crops were not being tended due to a shortage of farm workers. Construction companies reported not being able to bid for projects because of shortages of workers. In addition, many companies and tourists canceled travel plans to Arizona in protest to the new law's provisions.

## LABOR FORCE PARTICIPATION AND UNEMPLOYMENT

Participation in the labor force means that a person is either employed or actively seeking employment. Those who are not looking for work because they are "going to school" or "unable to work" are not considered to be part of the labor force. The labor force increases with the long-term growth of the population. It responds to economic forces and social trends, and its size changes with the seasons.

To be classified as unemployed, a person must:

- Not have worked in the week specified for the survey

- Have actively sought work sometime during the four weeks preceding the survey

- Be currently available to take a suitable job

Due to a global economic recession that began in 2007, unemployment rates hit double digits in October 2009 for the first time since 1983. According to the U.S. Bureau of Labor Statistics (BLS), in *The Employment Situation— March 2012* (April 6, 2012, http://www.bls.gov/news .release/pdf/empsit.pdf), in March 2011 the unemployment rate was 8.9%, even though the recession had officially ended in mid-2009. The unemployment rate in March 2012 remained high, at 8.2%. Even though all ethnic and racial groups were affected by the recession and its lingering impacts, some groups were harder hit than others.

For example, in December 2011 nearly 2.9 million (15.8%) African-Americans in the civilian labor force were unemployed. (See Table 4.1.) Their unemployment rate was 53% higher than that of the white population, at 7.5% (9.3 million). Nearly 2.6 million (11%) Hispanics in the civilian labor force were unemployed in December 2011. (See Table 4.2.) The lowest unemployment rate was among Asian-Americans. Seasonally adjusted figures were not available, but in December 2011 approximately 514,000 Asian-Americans in the civilian labor force were unemployed, with an unemployment rate of 6.8%. (See Table 4.1.)

### African-Americans

Historically, African-American workers have participated in the labor force in larger proportions than whites, primarily because African-American women were more likely to be working than their white counterparts. However, the increased entry of white women into the labor force since the 1970s has narrowed the gap between the two races. The BLS (February 5, 2010, http://www.bls.gov/ webapps/legacy/cpsatab2.htm) reports that in December 1972, 26.2 million (42.7%) white women over the age of 20 years participated in the labor force, compared with

3.6 million (51.5%) African-American women of the same age. By December 2011, 54.5 million (59%) white women over the age of 20 years were in the civilian labor force, which was still proportionately lower than the 9.2 million (62.2%) African-American women of the same age who participated in the labor force. (See Table 4.1.)

Conversely, the labor force participation rate of African-American men aged 20 years and older has declined since the 1970s. The BLS notes that in December 1972, 4.4 million (78%) African-American men aged 20 years and older were in the civilian labor force; in December 2011, 8.3 million (69%) were in the labor force. (See Table 4.1.) In comparison, 44.4 million (81.8%) white men were employed in December 1972; in December 2011, 65.4 million (73.8%) white men aged 20 years and older were in the civilian labor force. The overall participation rate for all African-Americans (men and women) was 61.8% (18.1 million) in December 2011, compared with a participation rate of 64.3% (124.5 million) for all whites.

Even though unemployment rates rise and fall with the strength of the economy, for several decades the unemployment rates for African-Americans have been nearly twice the rates for whites. Often having fewer marketable skills and less education than do whites, in addition to facing long-standing discrimination in the labor force, African-Americans are more likely to remain unemployed for longer periods, especially during a recession. As a result, they are more likely to be labeled as "long-term unemployed" (those without work for at least 27 weeks).

In December 2011 the unemployment rate for African-American men aged 20 years and older was 15.7% (1.3 million), which was 54.7% higher than that of white men of the same age, 7.1% (4.6 million). (See Table 4.1.) African-American women aged 20 years and older had an unemployment rate of 13.9% (1.3 million), which was 51.1% higher than the unemployment rate of white women of the same age, 6.8% (3.7 million).

### Hispanics

The BLS began maintaining annual employment data on Hispanics in 1973. In December 2011, 23.3 million (66.7%) Hispanics were employed or actively looking for work. (See Table 4.2.) However, the labor force participation rate among Hispanic subgroups varies. In 2010 Mexican-Americans had the highest overall participation rate among the three largest Hispanic groups in the United States. More than two out of three Mexican-Americans (14.4 million, or 67.7%) participated in the civilian labor force, followed by Cuban-Americans (970,000, or 62.6%) and Puerto Ricans (1.9 million, or 61.3%). (See Table 4.3.)

Men aged 20 years and older in all three groups had a much higher labor force participation rate than did women of the same age. This difference in rates of labor force participation was especially pronounced for Mexican-Americans.

TABLE 4.1

## Employment status of the civilian population, by race, sex, and age, 2010–11

[Numbers in thousands]

| Employment status, race, sex, and age | Not seasonally adjusted | | | Seasonally adjusted* | | | | | |
|---|---|---|---|---|---|---|---|---|---|
| | Dec. 2010 | Nov. 2011 | Dec. 2011 | Dec. 2010 | Aug. 2011 | Sept. 2011 | Oct. 2011 | Nov. 2011 | Dec. 2011 |
| **White** | | | | | | | | | |
| Civilian noninstitutional population | 192,749 | 193,598 | 193,682 | 192,749 | 193,236 | 193,365 | 193,493 | 193,598 | 193,682 |
| Civilian labor force | 124,309 | 124,565 | 124,114 | 124,719 | 124,604 | 124,701 | 124,804 | 124,652 | 124,543 |
| Participation rate | 64.5 | 64.3 | 64.1 | 64.7 | 64.5 | 64.5 | 64.5 | 64.4 | 64.3 |
| Employed | 114,035 | 115,584 | 115,117 | 114,150 | 114,704 | 114,818 | 114,837 | 115,130 | 115,254 |
| Employment-population ratio | 59.2 | 59.7 | 59.4 | 59.2 | 59.4 | 59.4 | 59.3 | 59.5 | 59.5 |
| Unemployed | 10,274 | 8,981 | 8,998 | 10,569 | 9,901 | 9,883 | 9,967 | 9,522 | 9,288 |
| Unemployment rate | 8.3 | 7.2 | 7.2 | 8.5 | 7.9 | 7.9 | 8.0 | 7.6 | 7.5 |
| Not in labor force | 68,439 | 69,033 | 69,567 | 68,030 | 68,631 | 68,664 | 68,689 | 68,945 | 69,139 |
| **Men, 20 years and over** | | | | | | | | | |
| Civilian labor force | 64,978 | 65,407 | 65,248 | 65,063 | 65,139 | 65,280 | 65,318 | 65,366 | 65,373 |
| Participation rate | 73.9 | 73.9 | 73.7 | 74.0 | 73.8 | 73.9 | 73.9 | 73.9 | 73.8 |
| Employed | 59,280 | 60,938 | 60,484 | 59,537 | 60,155 | 60,283 | 60,195 | 60,605 | 60,751 |
| Employment-population ratio | 67.4 | 68.9 | 68.3 | 67.7 | 68.1 | 68.2 | 68.1 | 68.5 | 68.6 |
| Unemployed | 5,698 | 4,469 | 4,764 | 5,525 | 4,984 | 4,998 | 5,123 | 4,761 | 4,623 |
| Unemployment rate | 8.8 | 6.8 | 7.3 | 8.5 | 7.7 | 7.7 | 7.8 | 7.3 | 7.1 |
| **Women, 20 years and over** | | | | | | | | | |
| Civilian labor force | 54,927 | 54,659 | 54,516 | 54,905 | 54,649 | 54,691 | 54,685 | 54,520 | 54,481 |
| Participation rate | 59.7 | 59.2 | 59.0 | 59.7 | 59.3 | 59.3 | 59.3 | 59.1 | 59.0 |
| Employed | 51,261 | 51,091 | 51,080 | 50,941 | 50,829 | 50,807 | 50,880 | 50,774 | 50,768 |
| Employment-population ratio | 55.7 | 55.3 | 55.3 | 55.3 | 55.2 | 55.1 | 55.1 | 55.0 | 55.0 |
| Unemployed | 3,667 | 3,568 | 3,435 | 3,964 | 3,820 | 3,884 | 3,805 | 3,746 | 3,713 |
| Unemployment rate | 6.7 | 6.5 | 6.3 | 7.2 | 7.0 | 7.1 | 7.0 | 6.9 | 6.8 |
| **Both sexes, 16 to 19 years** | | | | | | | | | |
| Civilian labor force | 4,404 | 4,499 | 4,350 | 4,751 | 4,816 | 4,730 | 4,801 | 4,766 | 4,688 |
| Participation rate | 34.4 | 35.2 | 34.1 | 37.1 | 37.6 | 37.0 | 37.6 | 37.3 | 36.8 |
| Employed | 3,494 | 3,555 | 3,552 | 3,671 | 3,720 | 3,728 | 3,761 | 3,751 | 3,736 |
| Employment-population ratio | 27.3 | 27.8 | 27.8 | 28.7 | 29.1 | 29.1 | 29.4 | 29.4 | 29.3 |
| Unemployed | 910 | 944 | 798 | 1,079 | 1,097 | 1,002 | 1,040 | 1,015 | 952 |
| Unemployment rate | 20.7 | 21.0 | 18.3 | 22.7 | 22.8 | 21.2 | 21.7 | 21.3 | 20.3 |
| **Black or African American** | | | | | | | | | |
| Civilian noninstitutional population | 28,896 | 29,259 | 29,286 | 28,896 | 29,158 | 29,193 | 29,228 | 29,259 | 29,286 |
| Civilian labor force | 17,835 | 17,900 | 18,024 | 17,933 | 17,957 | 18,096 | 18,067 | 17,934 | 18,110 |
| Participation rate | 61.7 | 61.2 | 61.5 | 62.1 | 61.6 | 62.0 | 61.8 | 61.3 | 61.8 |
| Employed | 15,120 | 15,236 | 15,285 | 15,098 | 14,965 | 15,224 | 15,351 | 15,151 | 15,248 |
| Employment-population ratio | 52.3 | 52.1 | 52.2 | 52.2 | 51.3 | 52.1 | 52.5 | 51.8 | 52.1 |
| Unemployed | 2,715 | 2,664 | 2,739 | 2,836 | 2,992 | 2,872 | 2,716 | 2,783 | 2,862 |
| Unemployment rate | 15.2 | 14.9 | 15.2 | 15.8 | 16.7 | 15.9 | 15.0 | 15.5 | 15.8 |
| Not in labor force | 11,061 | 11,359 | 11,262 | 10,963 | 11,202 | 11,097 | 11,161 | 11,325 | 11,176 |
| **Men, 20 years and over** | | | | | | | | | |
| Civilian labor force | 8,079 | 8,185 | 8,264 | 8,089 | 8,178 | 8,151 | 8,180 | 8,195 | 8,272 |
| Participation rate | 68.8 | 68.4 | 69.0 | 68.9 | 68.7 | 68.3 | 68.5 | 68.5 | 69.0 |
| Employed | 6,758 | 6,917 | 7,006 | 6,732 | 6,703 | 6,796 | 6,867 | 6,851 | 6,969 |
| Employment-population ratio | 57.6 | 57.8 | 58.5 | 57.4 | 56.3 | 57.0 | 57.5 | 57.3 | 58.2 |
| Unemployed | 1,321 | 1,268 | 1,258 | 1,358 | 1,475 | 1,355 | 1,313 | 1,344 | 1,302 |
| Unemployment rate | 16.4 | 15.5 | 15.2 | 16.8 | 18.0 | 16.6 | 16.0 | 16.4 | 15.7 |
| **Women, 20 years and over** | | | | | | | | | |
| Civilian labor force | 9,141 | 9,106 | 9,113 | 9,195 | 9,154 | 9,277 | 9,262 | 9,095 | 9,160 |
| Participation rate | 62.9 | 61.9 | 61.8 | 63.3 | 62.4 | 63.2 | 63.0 | 61.8 | 62.2 |
| Employed | 7,998 | 7,948 | 7,886 | 8,002 | 7,926 | 8,051 | 8,093 | 7,911 | 7,885 |
| Employment-population ratio | 55.0 | 54.0 | 53.5 | 55.1 | 54.1 | 54.8 | 55.0 | 53.7 | 53.5 |
| Unemployed | 1,143 | 1,158 | 1,227 | 1,192 | 1,228 | 1,226 | 1,169 | 1,184 | 1,275 |
| Unemployment rate | 12.5 | 12.7 | 13.5 | 13.0 | 13.4 | 13.2 | 12.6 | 13.0 | 13.9 |
| **Both sexes, 16 to 19 years** | | | | | | | | | |
| Civilian labor force | 615 | 608 | 647 | 649 | 625 | 667 | 625 | 643 | 679 |
| Participation rate | 23.4 | 23.7 | 25.3 | 24.7 | 24.2 | 25.8 | 24.3 | 25.0 | 26.5 |
| Employed | 365 | 370 | 394 | 363 | 335 | 377 | 390 | 388 | 393 |
| Employment-population ratio | 13.9 | 14.4 | 15.4 | 13.8 | 13.0 | 14.6 | 15.2 | 15.1 | 15.3 |
| Unemployed | 250 | 238 | 254 | 286 | 289 | 291 | 234 | 255 | 286 |
| Unemployment rate | 40.7 | 39.1 | 39.2 | 44.0 | 46.3 | 43.6 | 37.5 | 39.6 | 42.1 |

Among Mexican-Americans, 8.5 million (84.4%) men and 5.2 million (57.8%) women participated in the labor force. (See Table 4.3.) Among Cuban-Americans, 524,000 (73.7%) men and 419,000 (55.9%) women participated in the labor force. Among Puerto Ricans, 958,000 (71.1%) men and 853,000 (59.5%) women participated in the labor force.

## TABLE 4.1

### Employment status of the civilian population, by race, sex, and age, 2010–11 [CONTINUED]

[Numbers in thousands]

| Employment status, race, sex, and age | Not seasonally adjusted | | | Seasonally adjusted* | | | | | |
|---|---|---|---|---|---|---|---|---|---|
| | Dec. 2010 | Nov. 2011 | Dec. 2011 | Dec. 2010 | Aug. 2011 | Sept. 2011 | Oct. 2011 | Nov. 2011 | Dec. 2011 |
| **Asian** | | | | | | | | | |
| Civilian noninstitutional population | 11,387 | 11,589 | 11,580 | — | — | — | — | — | — |
| Civilian labor force | 7,355 | 7,419 | 7,505 | — | — | — | — | — | — |
| Participation rate | 64.6 | 64.0 | 64.8 | — | — | — | — | — | — |
| Employed | 6,829 | 6,939 | 6,991 | — | — | — | — | — | — |
| Employment-population ratio | 60.0 | 59.9 | 60.4 | — | — | — | — | — | — |
| Unemployed | 526 | 480 | 514 | — | — | — | — | — | — |
| Unemployment rate | 7.2 | 6.5 | 6.8 | — | — | — | — | — | — |
| Not in labor force | 4,032 | 4,170 | 4,075 | — | — | — | — | — | — |

*The population figures are not adjusted for seasonal variation; therefore, identical numbers appear in the unadjusted and seasonally adjusted columns.
—Data not available.
Notes: Estimates for the above race groups will not sum to totals because data are not presented for all races. Updated population controls are introduced annually with the release of January data.

SOURCE: "Table A-2. Employment Status of the Civilian Population by Race, Sex, and Age," in *The Employment Situation—December 2011*, U.S. Department of Labor, Bureau of Labor Statistics, January 6, 2012, http://www.bls.gov/news.release/pdf/empsit.pdf (accessed January 15, 2012)


## TABLE 4.2

### Employment status of the Hispanic population, by sex and age, 2010–11

[Numbers in thousands]

| Employment status, sex, and age | Not seasonally adjusted | | | Seasonally adjusted* | | | | | |
|---|---|---|---|---|---|---|---|---|---|
| | Dec. 2010 | Nov. 2011 | Dec. 2011 | Dec. 2010 | Aug. 2011 | Sept. 2011 | Oct. 2011 | Nov. 2011 | Dec. 2011 |
| **Hispanic or Latino ethnicity** | | | | | | | | | |
| Civilian noninstitutional population | 34,188 | 34,808 | 34,885 | 34,188 | 34,555 | 34,640 | 34,724 | 34,808 | 34,885 |
| Civilian labor force | 22,929 | 23,255 | 23,309 | 22,873 | 22,938 | 23,014 | 23,253 | 23,222 | 23,270 |
| Participation rate | 67.1 | 66.8 | 66.8 | 66.9 | 66.4 | 66.4 | 67.0 | 66.7 | 66.7 |
| Employed | 19,957 | 20,684 | 20,731 | 19,916 | 20,353 | 20,411 | 20,601 | 20,574 | 20,699 |
| Employment-population ratio | 58.4 | 59.4 | 59.4 | 58.3 | 58.9 | 58.9 | 59.3 | 59.1 | 59.3 |
| Unemployed | 2,972 | 2,571 | 2,579 | 2,957 | 2,585 | 2,603 | 2,652 | 2,648 | 2,571 |
| Unemployment rate | 13.0 | 11.1 | 11.1 | 12.9 | 11.3 | 11.3 | 11.4 | 11.4 | 11.0 |
| Not in labor force | 11,259 | 11,553 | 11,575 | 11,315 | 11,617 | 11,626 | 11,471 | 11,586 | 11,615 |
| **Men, 20 years and over** | | | | | | | | | |
| Civilian labor force | 13,115 | 13,169 | 13,256 | — | — | — | — | — | — |
| Participation rate | 82.3 | 81.7 | 82.0 | — | — | — | — | — | — |
| Employed | 11,431 | 11,884 | 11,868 | — | — | — | — | — | — |
| Employment-population ratio | 71.7 | 73.7 | 73.4 | — | — | — | — | — | — |
| Unemployed | 1,684 | 1,285 | 1,387 | — | — | — | — | — | — |
| Unemployment rate | 12.8 | 9.8 | 10.5 | — | — | — | — | — | — |
| **Women, 20 years and over** | | | | | | | | | |
| Civilian labor force | 8,880 | 9,085 | 9,082 | — | — | — | — | — | — |
| Participation rate | 59.2 | 59.6 | 59.4 | — | — | — | — | — | — |
| Employed | 7,892 | 8,118 | 8,146 | — | — | — | — | — | — |
| Employment-population ratio | 52.7 | 53.2 | 53.3 | — | — | — | — | — | — |
| Unemployed | 988 | 967 | 936 | — | — | — | — | — | — |
| Unemployment rate | 11.1 | 10.6 | 10.3 | — | — | — | — | — | — |
| **Both sexes, 16 to 19 years** | | | | | | | | | |
| Civilian labor force | 934 | 1,000 | 972 | — | — | — | — | — | — |
| Participation rate | 28.6 | 29.2 | 28.3 | — | — | — | — | — | — |
| Employed | 633 | 682 | 716 | — | — | — | — | — | — |
| Employment-population ratio | 19.4 | 19.9 | 20.9 | — | — | — | — | — | — |
| Unemployed | 300 | 319 | 256 | — | — | — | — | — | — |
| Unemployment rate | 32.2 | 31.8 | 26.3 | — | — | — | — | — | — |

*The population figures are not adjusted for seasonal variation; therefore, identical numbers appear in the unadjusted and seasonally adjusted columns.
—Data not available.
Notes: Persons whose ethnicity is identified as Hispanic or Latino may be of any race. Updated population controls are introduced annually with the release of January data.

SOURCE: "Table A-3. Employment Status of the Hispanic or Latino Population by Sex and Age," in *The Employment Situation—December 2011*, U.S. Department of Labor, Bureau of Labor Statistics, January 6, 2012, http://www.bls.gov/news.release/pdf/empsit.pdf (accessed January 15, 2012)

**TABLE 4.3**

## Employment status of the Mexican, Puerto Rican, and Cuban populations in the United States, by sex and age, 2009–10

[Numbers in thousands]

| | Hispanic or Latino ethnicity | | | | | | | |
|---|---|---|---|---|---|---|---|---|
| | Total[a] | | Mexican origin | | Puerto Rican origin | | Cuban origin | |
| Employment status, sex, and age | 2009 | 2010 | 2009 | 2010 | 2009 | 2010 | 2009 | 2010 |
| **Total** | | | | | | | | |
| Civilian noninstitutional population | 32,891 | 33,713 | 20,923 | 21,267 | 2,962 | 3,110 | 1,442 | 1,549 |
| Civilian labor force | 22,352 | 22,748 | 14,210 | 14,403 | 1,850 | 1,906 | 877 | 970 |
| Percent of population | 68.0 | 67.5 | 67.9 | 67.7 | 62.4 | 61.3 | 60.8 | 62.6 |
| Employed | 19,647 | 19,906 | 12,478 | 12,622 | 1,594 | 1,612 | 795 | 850 |
| Unemployed | 2,706 | 2,843 | 1,732 | 1,781 | 256 | 293 | 82 | 120 |
| Unemployment rate | 12.1 | 12.5 | 12.2 | 12.4 | 13.8 | 15.4 | 9.4 | 12.4 |
| Not in labor force | 10,539 | 10,964 | 6,713 | 6,864 | 1,113 | 1,204 | 565 | 579 |
| **Men, 16 years and over** | | | | | | | | |
| Civilian noninstitutional population | 16,897 | 17,359 | 11,008 | 11,208 | 1,421 | 1,522 | 725 | 759 |
| Civilian labor force | 13,310 | 13,511 | 8,807 | 8,896 | 970 | 1,009 | 503 | 540 |
| Percent of population | 78.8 | 77.8 | 80.0 | 79.4 | 68.3 | 66.3 | 69.4 | 71.2 |
| Employed | 11,640 | 11,800 | 7,704 | 7,800 | 825 | 835 | 461 | 470 |
| Unemployed | 1,670 | 1,711 | 1,103 | 1,096 | 145 | 174 | 42 | 70 |
| Unemployment rate | 12.5 | 12.7 | 12.5 | 12.3 | 15.0 | 17.3 | 8.4 | 12.9 |
| Not in labor force | 3,588 | 3,849 | 2,201 | 2,312 | 451 | 513 | 222 | 219 |
| **Men, 20 years and over** | | | | | | | | |
| Civilian noninstitutional population | 15,305 | 15,693 | 9,934 | 10,087 | 1,254 | 1,346 | 687 | 711 |
| Civilian labor force | 12,730 | 12,958 | 8,411 | 8,513 | 918 | 958 | 487 | 524 |
| Percent of population | 83.2 | 82.6 | 84.7 | 84.4 | 73.2 | 71.1 | 70.9 | 73.7 |
| Employed | 11,256 | 11,438 | 7,447 | 7,547 | 791 | 803 | 448 | 458 |
| Unemployed | 1,474 | 1,519 | 965 | 967 | 127 | 154 | 39 | 66 |
| Unemployment rate | 11.6 | 11.7 | 11.5 | 11.4 | 13.9 | 16.1 | 8.0 | 12.5 |
| Not in labor force | 2,575 | 2,735 | 1,523 | 1,573 | 336 | 389 | 200 | 187 |
| **Women, 16 years and over** | | | | | | | | |
| Civilian noninstitutional population | 15,993 | 16,354 | 9,915 | 10,059 | 1,542 | 1,588 | 717 | 790 |
| Civilian labor force | 9,043 | 9,238 | 5,403 | 5,507 | 880 | 896 | 374 | 430 |
| Percent of population | 56.5 | 56.5 | 54.5 | 54.7 | 57.1 | 56.4 | 52.1 | 54.4 |
| Employed | 8,007 | 8,106 | 4,774 | 4,822 | 769 | 777 | 334 | 379 |
| Unemployed | 1,036 | 1,132 | 629 | 685 | 110 | 119 | 40 | 50 |
| Unemployment rate | 11.5 | 12.3 | 11.6 | 12.4 | 12.5 | 13.3 | 10.7 | 11.7 |
| Not in labor force | 6,951 | 7,116 | 4,512 | 4,552 | 662 | 692 | 343 | 360 |
| **Women, 20 years and over** | | | | | | | | |
| Civilian noninstitutional population | 14,463 | 14,776 | 8,882 | 9,008 | 1,383 | 1,434 | 677 | 749 |
| Civilian labor force | 8,560 | 8,789 | 5,080 | 5,207 | 827 | 853 | 364 | 419 |
| Percent of population | 59.2 | 59.5 | 57.2 | 57.8 | 59.8 | 59.5 | 53.8 | 55.9 |
| Employed | 7,649 | 7,788 | 4,535 | 4,609 | 730 | 747 | 327 | 370 |
| Unemployed | 911 | 1,001 | 545 | 597 | 97 | 106 | 37 | 49 |
| Unemployment rate | 10.6 | 11.4 | 10.7 | 11.5 | 11.7 | 12.4 | 10.2 | 11.6 |
| Not in labor force | 5,903 | 5,987 | 3,802 | 3,802 | 557 | 581 | 313 | 331 |
| **Both sexes, 16 to 19 years** | | | | | | | | |
| Civilian noninstitutional population | 3,123 | 3,243 | 2,107 | 2,173 | 325 | 329 | 79 | 88 |
| Civilian labor force | 1,063 | 1,002 | 719 | 684 | 105 | 95 | 26 | 27 |
| Percent of population | 34.0 | 30.9 | 34.1 | 31.5 | 32.4 | 28.8 | 33.6 | 30.4 |
| Employed | 742 | 680 | 497 | 466 | 74 | 62 | 20 | 21 |
| Unemployed | 321 | 322 | 222 | 217 | 32 | 33 | 6 | 6 |
| Unemployment rate | 30.2 | 32.2 | 30.9 | 31.8 | 30.2 | 35.2 | [b] | [b] |
| Not in labor force | 2,061 | 2,242 | 1,388 | 1,489 | 220 | 234 | 52 | 61 |

[a]Includes persons of Central or South American origin and of other Hispanic or Latino ethnicity, not shown separately.
[b]Data not shown where base is less than 35,000.
Notes: Persons whose ethnicity is identified as Hispanic or Latino may be of any race. Updated population controls are introduced annually with the release of January data.

SOURCE: "6. Employment Status of the Hispanic or Latino Population by Sex, Age, and Detailed Ethnic Group," in *Employment and Earnings*, U.S. Department of Labor, Bureau of Labor Statistics, 2011, http://www.bls.gov/cps/cpsaat6.pdf (accessed January 15, 2012)

The unemployment rate for Hispanics in December 2011 was 11% (2.6 million). (See Table 4.2.) According to the BLS (February 5, 2010, http://www.bls.gov/webapps/legacy/cpsatab3.htm), this rate had nearly doubled from the rate of 5.8% (1.3 million) in November 2007 because of the global economic recession. The unemployment rate varies among Hispanic people depending on the country of origin. In 2010 the Puerto Rican–origin population had the highest rate of unemployment at 15.4% (293,000). (See Table 4.3.) Cuban-Americans and Mexican-Americans had the lowest unemployment rate of the Hispanic subgroups at 12.4% (120,000 and 1.8 million, respectively).

## Asian-Americans

In December 2011, 7.5 million (64.8%) Asian-Americans aged 16 years and older were in the civilian labor force. (See Table 4.1.) In 2010, 3.3 million (59%) Asian-American women and 3.8 million (76.6%) Asian-American men aged 20 years and older were in the labor force. (See Table 4.4.) In that year, a higher percentage of Asian-American men aged 20 years and older was participating in the labor force than either white men (65.3 million, or 74.6%) or African-American men (8.1 million, or 69.5%). Among women aged 20 years and older, a higher percentage of African-American women (9.1 million, or 63.2%) and white women (55 million, or 59.9%)

## TABLE 4.4

### Employment status of the civilian noninstitutional population, by sex, age, and race, 2009–10

[Numbers in thousand]

| Employment status, sex, and age | Total 2009 | Total 2010 | White 2009 | White 2010 | Black or African American 2009 | Black or African American 2010 | Asian 2009 | Asian 2010 |
|---|---|---|---|---|---|---|---|---|
| **Total** | | | | | | | | |
| Civilian noninstitutional population | 235,801 | 237,830 | 190,902 | 192,075 | 28,241 | 28,708 | 10,842 | 11,199 |
| Civilian labor force | 154,142 | 153,889 | 125,644 | 125,084 | 17,632 | 17,862 | 7,156 | 7,248 |
| Percent of population | 65.4 | 64.7 | 65.8 | 65.1 | 62.4 | 62.2 | 66.0 | 64.7 |
| Employed | 139,877 | 139,064 | 114,996 | 114,168 | 15,025 | 15,010 | 6,635 | 6,705 |
| Unemployed | 14,265 | 14,825 | 10,648 | 10,916 | 2,606 | 2,852 | 522 | 543 |
| Unemployment rate | 9.3 | 9.6 | 8.5 | 8.7 | 14.8 | 16.0 | 7.3 | 7.5 |
| Not in labor force | 81,659 | 83,941 | 65,258 | 66,991 | 10,609 | 10,846 | 3,685 | 3,951 |
| **Men, 16 years and over** | | | | | | | | |
| Civilian noninstitutional population | 114,136 | 115,174 | 93,433 | 94,082 | 12,705 | 12,939 | 5,170 | 5,315 |
| Civilian labor force | 82,123 | 81,985 | 68,051 | 67,728 | 8,265 | 8,415 | 3,857 | 3,893 |
| Percent of population | 72.0 | 71.2 | 72.8 | 72.0 | 65.0 | 65.0 | 74.6 | 73.2 |
| Employed | 73,670 | 73,359 | 61,630 | 61,252 | 6,817 | 6,865 | 3,551 | 3,588 |
| Unemployed | 8,453 | 8,626 | 6,421 | 6,476 | 1,448 | 1,550 | 306 | 305 |
| Unemployment rate | 10.3 | 10.5 | 9.4 | 9.6 | 17.5 | 18.4 | 7.9 | 7.8 |
| Not in labor force | 32,013 | 33,189 | 25,382 | 26,353 | 4,441 | 4,524 | 1,314 | 1,422 |
| **Men, 20 years and over** | | | | | | | | |
| Civilian noninstitutional population | 105,493 | 106,596 | 86,789 | 87,502 | 11,379 | 11,626 | 4,837 | 4,984 |
| Civilian labor force | 78,897 | 78,994 | 65,372 | 65,265 | 7,914 | 8,076 | 3,777 | 3,820 |
| Percent of population | 74.8 | 74.1 | 75.3 | 74.6 | 69.6 | 69.5 | 78.1 | 76.6 |
| Employed | 71,341 | 71,230 | 59,626 | 59,438 | 6,628 | 6,680 | 3,493 | 3,534 |
| Unemployed | 7,555 | 7,763 | 5,746 | 5,828 | 1,286 | 1,396 | 284 | 286 |
| Unemployment rate | 9.6 | 9.8 | 8.8 | 8.9 | 16.3 | 17.3 | 7.5 | 7.5 |
| Not in labor force | 26,596 | 27,603 | 21,417 | 22,236 | 3,465 | 3,550 | 1,060 | 1,164 |
| **Women, 16 years and over** | | | | | | | | |
| Civilian noninstitutional population | 121,665 | 122,656 | 97,469 | 97,993 | 15,536 | 15,769 | 5,671 | 5,884 |
| Civilian labor force | 72,019 | 71,904 | 57,593 | 57,356 | 9,367 | 9,447 | 3,300 | 3,355 |
| Percent of population | 59.2 | 58.6 | 59.1 | 58.5 | 60.3 | 59.9 | 58.2 | 57.0 |
| Employed | 66,208 | 65,705 | 53,366 | 52,916 | 8,208 | 8,145 | 3,084 | 3,117 |
| Unemployed | 5,811 | 6,199 | 4,227 | 4,440 | 1,159 | 1,302 | 216 | 238 |
| Unemployment rate | 8.1 | 8.6 | 7.3 | 7.7 | 12.4 | 13.8 | 6.6 | 7.1 |
| Not in labor force | 49,646 | 50,752 | 39,876 | 40,638 | 6,169 | 6,322 | 2,371 | 2,529 |
| **Women, 20 years and over** | | | | | | | | |
| Civilian noninstitutional population | 113,265 | 114,333 | 91,078 | 91,683 | 14,178 | 14,425 | 5,372 | 5,566 |
| Civilian labor force | 68,856 | 68,990 | 54,976 | 54,957 | 8,988 | 9,110 | 3,248 | 3,285 |
| Percent of population | 60.8 | 60.3 | 60.4 | 59.9 | 63.4 | 63.2 | 60.5 | 59.0 |
| Employed | 63,699 | 63,456 | 51,231 | 50,997 | 7,956 | 7,944 | 3,045 | 3,064 |
| Unemployed | 5,157 | 5,534 | 3,745 | 3,960 | 1,032 | 1,165 | 203 | 221 |
| Unemployment rate | 7.5 | 8.0 | 6.8 | 7.2 | 11.5 | 12.8 | 6.2 | 6.7 |
| Not in labor force | 44,409 | 45,343 | 36,101 | 36,725 | 5,190 | 5,315 | 2,124 | 2,281 |
| **Both sexes, 16 to 19 years** | | | | | | | | |
| Civilian noninstitutional population | 17,043 | 16,901 | 13,035 | 12,891 | 2,684 | 2,657 | 632 | 649 |
| Civilian labor force | 6,390 | 5,906 | 5,295 | 4,861 | 729 | 677 | 131 | 143 |
| Percent of population | 37.5 | 34.9 | 40.6 | 37.7 | 27.2 | 25.5 | 20.8 | 22.0 |
| Employed | 4,837 | 4,378 | 4,138 | 3,733 | 442 | 386 | 97 | 108 |
| Unemployed | 1,552 | 1,528 | 1,157 | 1,128 | 288 | 291 | 35 | 35 |
| Unemployment rate | 24.3 | 25.9 | 21.8 | 23.2 | 39.5 | 43.0 | 26.4 | 24.8 |
| Not in labor force | 10,654 | 10,995 | 7,740 | 8,030 | 1,954 | 1,980 | 501 | 506 |

Notes: Estimates for the above race groups will not sum to totals because data are not presented for all races. Updated population controls are introduced annually with the release of January data.

SOURCE: "5. Employment Status of the Civilian Noninstitutional Population by Sex, Age, and Race," in *Employment and Earnings*, U.S. Department of Labor, Bureau of Labor Statistics, 2011, http://www.bls.gov/cps/cpsaat5.pdf (accessed January 15, 2012)

were participating in the labor force than were Asian-American women (3.3 million, or 59%).

The unemployment rate for Asian-Americans is similar to the rate for whites. In December 2011 the unemployment rate for Asian-Americans was 6.8% (514,000). (See Table 4.1.) The low rate of unemployment among Asian-Americans can be attributed, in part, to their high educational attainment and their commitment to small family businesses.

Older Asian-Americans tend to work longer because of the strong work ethic in Asian cultures and frequently because of economic need. Often, they are employed in family businesses that do not offer retirement benefits. Depending on the time of their immigration and their work history, Asian-Americans aged 65 years and older may not be entitled to adequate Social Security benefits. Also, some may have immigrated under circumstances that prevented them from retaining any wealth they might have accumulated in their native lands.

### Native Americans and Alaskan Natives

Gathering accurate statistical data on the labor force participation rates of Native Americans is difficult. They are often counted as "other" in BLS and Census Bureau data, making specific information hard to obtain. In addition, the concepts that guide the assessment of labor force participation nationally are considered to be inappropriate for Native American population groups. For example, because few jobs are available on many reservations, many adults do not actively seek work—but to exclude these individuals from the statistics on the labor force results in a serious underestimation of unemployment of Native Americans.

Tina Norris, Paula L. Vines, and Elizabeth M. Hoeffel of the Census Bureau indicate in *The American Indian and Alaska Native Population: 2010* (January 2012, http://www.census.gov/prod/cen2010/briefs/c2010br-10.pdf) that in 2010, 32.9% of Native Americans and Alaskan Natives lived in "American Indian areas"—that is, reservations or trust lands. In *American Indian Population and Labor Force Report, 2005* (September 2008, http://www.bia.gov/cs/groups/public/documents/text/idc-001719.pdf), the most recent report on this topic as of April 2012, the Bureau of Indian Affairs notes that in 2005 the unemployment rates on reservations averaged 49%, but varied greatly among reservations. On some reservations nine out of 10 people in the labor force or more were out of work, such as in Arctic Village (90%), Pechanga Band of Luigero Mission (91%), Beaver Village (93%), the Native Village of Tyonek (93%), Nooryik Native Community (93%), Sokaogon Chippewa Community (93%), the Native Village of Unga (94%), Soboba Band of Luiseno Mission Indians (94%), the Native Village of Elim (95%), the Native Village of Kanatak (96%), as well as the tiny villages of the Ramona Band, the Village of Chuilla, and Telida Village,

where 100% of the workforce was unemployed. In contrast, a few villages had a 0% unemployment rate, such as Blue Lake Rancheria, the Baskenta Band of Nomiaki Indians, Buena Vista Rancheria of Me-Wuk, the California Valley Miwok Tribe, the Coeur D'Alene Tribe, the Iowa Tribe, the Mescolero Apache Tribe, the Native Village of Chignik Lagoon, the Paiute Indian Tribe, the Potter Valley Rancheria, the Pueblo of Taos, the Pueblo of Zia, the San Pasqual Band of Diegueno Mission Indians, and the Seneca Nation. Regardless, many tribes had unemployment rates well over 50%.

In many cases reservations do not generate the jobs that are necessary to support Native American families. Even when Native Americans are employed, the Bureau of Indian Affairs notes that fully a third (32%) of employed individuals earns wages below the poverty guidelines. This fact helps explain why Native American tribes have been so willing to introduce or expand casino gambling on their reservations. The National Indian Gaming Association finds in *The Economic Impact of Indian Gaming* (March 2010, http://www.indiangaming.org/info/NIGA_2009 _Economic_Impact_Report.pdf) that in 2009, 237 Native American tribes engaged in gaming in 28 states and generated 628,000 jobs and $26.2 billion in revenue from gaming, $3.2 billion of which came from related hospitality services. In "Lands of Opportunity: Social and Economic Effects of Tribal Gaming on Localities" (*Policy Matters*, vol. 1, no. 4, Summer 2007), Mindy Marks and Kate Spilde Contreras of the University of California, Riverside, note that the economic benefits often help the people most in need. The researchers state that "tribal governments with gaming are concentrating employment opportunity in areas that are economically worse off than areas without gaming reservations."

## DISCRIMINATORY EMPLOYMENT PRACTICES

Under Title VII of the Civil Rights Act of 1964, employers may not intentionally use race, skin color, age, gender, religious beliefs, or national origin as the basis for decisions relating to almost any aspect of the employment relationship, including hiring. Despite this law, African-Americans, Hispanics, and other minority groups continue to suffer from discriminatory hiring practices as well as from other race- and ethnicity-based obstacles to finding employment.

In one of the highest profile workplace discrimination cases in recent years, civil rights attorneys filed a class action lawsuit in June 2003 against Abercrombie & Fitch, one of the nation's largest clothing retailers, for discriminating against people of Hispanic, Asian-American, and African-American descent. The young adults were represented by the Mexican American Legal Defense and Educational Fund, the Asian Pacific American Legal Center, the National Association for the Advancement of Colored People's Legal

Defense and Educational Fund, and the law firm of Lieff Cabraser Heimann & Bernstein LLP. According to Lieff Cabraser Heimann & Bernstein, in the press release "Lieff Cabraser and Civil Rights Organizations Announce Abercrombie & Fitch Charged with Employment Discrimination in Federal Class Action Lawsuit" (June 17, 2003, http://www.afjustice.com/press_release_01.htm), Thomas A. Saenz of the Mexican American Legal Defense and Educational Fund said, "Through means both subtle and direct, Abercrombie has consistently reinforced to its store managers that they must recruit and maintain an overwhelmingly white workforce." In the press release "$40 Million Payment, Detailed Plan for Diversity in Employment Discrimination Suit against Retail Giant Abercrombie & Fitch" (November 16, 2004, http://www.afjustice.com/press_release _02.htm), Lieff Cabraser Heimann & Bernstein states that the lawsuit was settled in November 2004. The company agreed to pay $40 million to the applicants and employees who charged the company with discrimination and to comply with provisions related to the recruitment, hiring, job assignment, training, and promotion of minority employees. This was a prominent case brought to court; however, in general, discriminatory employment practices are difficult to prosecute effectively and remain pervasive in the United States.

In 2006 the federal government filed a lawsuit against a medical clinic in California because a manager used racial code words, including "reggin," which Barbara Feder Ostrov explains in "Discrimination at Work Growing Subtle" (*San Jose Mercury News*, August 12, 2006) is an "infamous racial slur spelled backward." An African-American file clerk was fired from her job after she complained about the racial slurs. The case underscored the changing nature of racial and ethnic discrimination in the workplace, as methods of intimidation become more subtle. This kind of subtle discrimination does not always lead to lawsuits. In fact, the Level Playing Field Institute reports in *The Cost of Employee Turnover Due Solely to Unfairness in the Workplace* (June 22, 2007, http://www.lpfi.org/sites/default/files/cl-executive-summary .pdf) that each year 2 million professionals and managers leave their jobs because they are "pushed out by cumulative small comments, whispered jokes and not-so-funny emails."

The U.S. Equal Employment Opportunity Commission (EEOC) won a settlement in a racial harassment lawsuit against Lockheed Martin in 2008. In the press release "Lockheed Martin to Pay $2.5 Million to Settle Racial Harassment Lawsuit" (January 2, 2008, http://www.eeoc .gov/eeoc/newsroom/release/1-2-08.cfm), the EEOC notes that Charles Daniels, an African-American electrician, was awarded $2.5 million after being harassed at job sites nationwide, including being threatened with lynching and other physical harm. Coworkers and a supervisor reportedly told Daniels that "we should do to blacks what Hitler did to the Jews" and "if the South had won then this would be a better country." The company failed to discipline the harassers when it was made aware of the situation.

In another high-profile case, in January 2012 Pepsi Beverages agreed to pay $3.1 million and to provide jobs and training to African-American applicants for positions at the company. The EEOC explains in the press release "Pepsi to Pay $3.13 Million and Made Major Policy Changes to Resolve EEOC Finding of Nationwide Hiring Discrimination against African Americans" (January 11, 2012, http:// www.eeoc.gov/eeoc/newsroom/release/1-11-12a.cfm) that Pepsi's use of the criminal background check policy discriminated against African-Americans. The company used arrest records to bar applicants from jobs, even if they had never been convicted, a policy that disproportionally affected African-Americans. Julie Schmid, the acting director of the EEOC's Minneapolis Area Office, stated, "When employers contemplate instituting a background check policy, the EEOC recommends that they take into consideration the nature and gravity of the offense, the time that has passed since the conviction and/or completion of the sentence, and the nature of the job sought in order to be sure that the exclusion is important for the particular position. Such exclusions can create an adverse impact based on race in violation of Title VII."

## U.S. Equal Employment Opportunity Commission

In May 2000 the EEOC issued new guidelines to facilitate the settlement of federal-sector discrimination complaints, including claims brought under Title VII. Under the administration of Chairperson Ida L. Castro (1953–), the EEOC sought to reform its complaint process for federal employees. The new directive authorizes federal agencies to enter into settlement of bias claims, including monetary payment.

In fiscal year (FY) 2010 the EEOC received 35,890 charges under Title VII alleging race-based discrimination. (See Table 4.5.) That same year the EEOC resolved 37,559 charges (some of these cases were carried over from the previous fiscal year). Of those, 3,325 (8.9%) were settled, with payments totaling $84.4 million to the charging parties. The percentage of settled cases was up substantially from FY 1997, when only 3.3% (1,206) were settled. In FY 2010 another 1,330 (3.5%) of the claims were found to have reasonable cause; 377 (1%) of these were charges with reasonable cause that closed after successful conciliation and 953 (2.5%) of them were charges with reasonable cause that closed after unsuccessful conciliation. Another 1,567 (4.2%) cases were withdrawn by the charging party on receipt of desired benefits ("withdrawals with benefits"). In other words, 6,222 cases of racial discrimination were found to have reasonable cause or were settled or withdrawn after the employer admitted culpability and submitted to a monetary settlement. Countless other incidents of racial discrimination in the workplace are never brought to the attention of the EEOC. Instead, victims suffer silently or leave their places of employment, as found by the Level Playing Field Institute Survey.

# TABLE 4.5

## Race-based charges filed and resolved under Title VII of the Civil Rights Act of 1964, fiscal years 1997–2010

| | Fiscal year | | | | | | | | | | | | | |
|---|---|---|---|---|---|---|---|---|---|---|---|---|---|---|
| | 1997 | 1998 | 1999 | 2000 | 2001 | 2002 | 2003 | 2004 | 2005 | 2006 | 2007 | 2008 | 2009 | 2010 |
| Receipts | 29,199 | 28,820 | 28,819 | 28,945 | 28,912 | 29,910 | 28,526 | 27,696 | 26,740 | 27,238 | 30,510 | 33,937 | 33,579 | 35,890 |
| Resolutions | 36,419 | 35,716 | 35,094 | 33,188 | 32,077 | 33,199 | 30,702 | 29,631 | 27,411 | 25,992 | 25,882 | 28,321 | 31,129 | 37,559 |
| **Resolutions by type** | | | | | | | | | | | | | | |
| Settlements | 1,206 | 1,460 | 2,138 | 2,802 | 2,549 | 3,059 | 2,890 | 2,927 | 2,801 | 3,039 | 2,945 | 3,065 | 3,065 | 3,325 |
| | 3.3% | 4.1% | 6.1% | 8.4% | 7.9% | 9.2% | 9.4% | 9.9% | 10.2% | 11.7% | 11.4% | 10.8% | 9.8% | 8.9% |
| Withdrawals with benefits | 912 | 823 | 1,036 | 1,150 | 1,203 | 1,200 | 1,125 | 1,088 | 1,167 | 1,177 | 1,235 | 1,435 | 1,530 | 1,567 |
| | 2.5% | 2.3% | 3.0% | 3.5% | 3.8% | 3.6% | 3.7% | 3.7% | 4.3% | 4.5% | 4.8% | 5.1% | 4.9% | 4.2% |
| Administrative closures | 8,395 | 7,871 | 7,213 | 5,727 | 5,626 | 5,043 | 4,759 | 4,261 | 3,674 | 3,436 | 3,931 | 3,964 | 4,803 | 5,018 |
| | 23.1% | 22.0% | 20.6% | 17.3% | 17.5% | 15.2% | 15.5% | 14.4% | 13.4% | 13.2% | 15.2% | 14.0% | 15.4% | 13.4% |
| No reasonable cause | 24,988 | 24,515 | 23,148 | 21,319 | 20,302 | 21,853 | 20,506 | 20,166 | 18,608 | 17,324 | 16,773 | 18,792 | 20,530 | 26,319 |
| | 68.6% | 68.6% | 66.0% | 64.2% | 63.3% | 65.8% | 66.8% | 68.1% | 67.9% | 66.7%, | 64.8% | 66.4% | 66.0% | 70.1% |
| Reasonable cause | 918 | 1,047 | 1,559 | 2,190 | 2,397 | 2,044 | 1,422 | 1,189 | 1,161 | 1,016 | 998 | 1,061 | 1,201 | 1,330 |
| | 2.5% | 2.9% | 4.4% | 6.6% | 7.5% | 6.2% | 4.6% | 4.0% | 4.2% | 3.9% | 3.9% | 3.7% | 3.9% | 3.5% |
| Successful conciliations | 248 | 287 | 382 | 529 | 691 | 580 | 392 | 330 | 377 | 292 | 285 | 355 | 392 | 377 |
| | 0.7% | 0.8% | 1.1% | 1.6% | 2.2% | 1.7% | 1.3% | 1.1% | 1.4% | 1.1% | 1.1% | 1.3% | 1.3% | 1.0% |
| Unsuccessful conciliations | 670 | 760 | 1,177 | 1,661 | 1,706 | 1,464 | 1,030 | 859 | 784 | 724 | 713 | 706 | 809 | 953 |
| | 1.8% | 2.1% | 3.4% | 5.0% | 5.3% | 4.4% | 3.4% | 2.9% | 2.9% | 2.8% | 2.8% | 2.5% | 2.6% | 2.5% |
| Merit resolutions | 3,036 | 3,330 | 4,733 | 6,142 | 6,149 | 6,303 | 5,437 | 5,204 | 5,129 | 5,232 | 5,178 | 5,565 | 5,796 | 6,222 |
| | 8.3% | 9.3% | 13.5% | 18.5% | 19.2% | 19.0% | 17.7% | 17.6% | 18.7% | 20.1% | 20.0% | 19.6% | 18.6% | 16.6% |
| Monetary benefits (millions)* | $41.8 | $32.2 | $53.2 | $61.7 | $86.5 | $81.1 | $69.6 | $61.1 | $76.5 | $61.4 | $67.7 | $79.3 | $82.4 | $84.4 |

*Does not include monetary benefits obtained through litigation.

SOURCE: "Race-Based Charges, FY 1997–FY 2010," in *Enforcement and Litigation Statistics*, U.S. Equal Employment Opportunity Commission, Office of Research, Information, and Planning, 2011, http://www.eeoc.gov/eeoc/statistics/enforcement/race.cfm (accessed January 15, 2012)

## Views of Economic Opportunities

Whites are much more likely than African-Americans to believe that members of minority groups have equal job opportunities in the United States. According to Frank Newport of the Gallup Organization, in *Little "Obama Effect" on Views about Race Relations* (October 29, 2009, http://www .gallup.com/poll/123944/little-obama-effect-views-race-relations.aspx), in 2008, 82% of whites, including Hispanics, said African-Americans have as good a chance as whites to get a job that they are qualified for, whereas only 49% of African-Americans thought so. An earlier Gallup poll surveyed Hispanics as well. In *Whites, Minorities Differ in Views of Economic Opportunities in U.S.* (July 10, 2006, http:// www.gallup.com/poll/23617/Whites-Minorities-Differ-Views-Economic-Opportunities-US.aspx), Joseph Carroll of the Gallup Organization reports on a June 2006 poll that asked the question: "Do you feel that racial minorities in this country have equal job opportunities as whites, or not?" There were stark differences in the responses of non-Hispanic whites and members of minority groups. Over half (53%) of non-Hispanic whites surveyed believed members of minority groups have equal job opportunities. By contrast, only a third (34%) of Hispanics surveyed believed this was true, down significantly from 46% in June 2001. Only 17% of African-Americans surveyed believed the job opportunities for minorities are equal to those of whites, down from 23% the previous year but basically unchanged from June 2001.

## WORKFORCE PROJECTIONS FOR 2018

In 2008 the percentage of the workforce that was Hispanic (14.3%) was higher than the percentage of the workforce that was African-American (11.5%). (See Table 4.6.) In addition, more Hispanics than African-Americans or non-Hispanic whites will enter the workforce through 2018, causing the group to make up an increasingly larger part of the workforce. The proportion of African-Americans in the labor force is expected to increase slightly to 12.1% in 2018, whereas the proportion of non-Hispanic whites is expected to actually decrease from 68.2% in 2008 to 64% in 2018. As recently as 1988, non-Hispanic whites made up nearly four-fifths (79%) of the workforce. The proportion of Hispanics in the workforce is expected to increase from 14.3% in 2008 to 17.6% in 2018. The growth of Hispanics in the workforce can be attributed to higher birthrates among that group and to increased immigration.

Asian-Americans are another fast-growing group in the labor force. The proportion of Asian-Americans in the workforce is expected to increase from 4.7% in 2008 to 5.6% in 2018. (See Table 4.6.) As with most other minority groups, increases reflect continued high immigration and higher fertility rates among some minority populations. By contrast, the non-Hispanic white population is decreasing its share of the labor force due to lower birthrates among

the majority group, relatively low immigration of non-Hispanic whites to the United States, and declining labor force participation by non-Hispanic white men, which is a reflection of the aging of the white male labor force.

## OCCUPATIONS
### African-Americans and Jobs

African-Americans are much less likely than whites or Asian-Americans to hold the jobs that require the most education and pay the highest salaries—those in management, professional, and related occupations. In 2010, 15 million African-Americans accounted for 10.8% of the civilian labor force aged 16 years and older. (See Table 4.7.) Only 29.1% of employed African-Americans held management, professional, or related occupations, compared with 37.9% of white workers. Women of both races were more likely to hold these positions, but only 33.8% of African-American women were managers or professionals, compared with 41.5% of white women. The proportion of African-Americans who held these positions had risen slightly from the previous year.

African-Americans are much more likely than whites to work in the poorly paid service occupations. In 2010, 25.1% of African-Americans worked in service occupations. (See Table 4.7.) By contrast, 16.6% of white Americans worked in service occupations in 2010.

Any growth in professional employment for African-Americans has generally occurred in fields at the lower end of the earnings scale. The BLS notes in *Employment and Earnings* (January 2012, http://www.bls.gov/cps/cpsa2011 .pdf) that 23.7% of all licensed practical and vocational nurses were African-American in 2011, but only 10.4% of registered nurses, 7.3% of nurse practitioners, 5.3% of physicians and surgeons, and 1% of dentists were African-American. The same pattern holds true for management positions. Even though 13.3% of education administrators and 11.3% of social and community service managers were African-American in 2011, only 6.6% of general and operations managers, 3% of construction managers, and 2.7% of chief executives were African-American.

In 2010 most African-Americans were concentrated in the management, professional, and related occupations (29.1%), sales and office occupations (25.1%), and service occupations (25.1%). (See Table 4.7.) However, African-Americans were underrepresented in management, professional, and related occupations (29.1%, compared with 37.2% of workers overall), and overrepresented in service occupations (25.1%, compared with 17.7% of workers overall).

### Hispanics and Jobs

Overall, Hispanics are less likely than African-Americans to hold professional and technical positions. In 2010 only 18.9% of employed Hispanics held management,

# TABLE 4.6

## Civilian labor force, by age, sex, race, and ethnicity, 1988, 1998, 2008, and projected 2018

[Numbers in thousands]

| Group | Level | | | | Change | | | Percent change | | | Percent distribution | | | | Annual growth rate (percent) | | |
|---|---|---|---|---|---|---|---|---|---|---|---|---|---|---|---|---|---|
| | 1988 | 1998 | 2008 | 2018 | 1988–98 | 1998–2008 | 2008–18 | 1988–98 | 1998–2008 | 2008–18 | 1988 | 1998 | 2008 | 2018 | 1988–98 | 1998–2008 | 2008–18 |
| Total, 16 years and older | 121,669 | 137,673 | 154,287 | 166,911 | 16,004 | 16,614 | 12,624 | 13.2 | 12.1 | 8.2 | 100.0 | 100.0 | 100.0 | 100.0 | 1.2 | 1.1 | 0.8 |
| **Age, years** | | | | | | | | | | | | | | | | | |
| 16 to 24 | 22,536 | 21,894 | 22,032 | 21,131 | −642 | 138 | −901 | −2.8 | 0.6 | −4.1 | 18.5 | 15.9 | 14.3 | 12.7 | −0.3 | 0.1 | −0.4 |
| 25 to 54 | 84,041 | 98,718 | 104,395 | 105,944 | 14,677 | 5,678 | 1,548 | 17.5 | 5.8 | 1.5 | 69.1 | 71.7 | 67.7 | 63.5 | 1.6 | 0.6 | 0.1 |
| 55 and older | 15,092 | 17,061 | 27,857 | 39,836 | 1,969 | 10,796 | 11,979 | 13.0 | 63.3 | 43.0 | 12.4 | 12.4 | 18.1 | 23.9 | 1.2 | 5.0 | 3.6 |
| **Sex:** | | | | | | | | | | | | | | | | | |
| Men | 66,927 | 73,959 | 82,520 | 88,682 | 7,032 | 8,561 | 6,162 | 10.5 | 11.6 | 7.5 | 55.0 | 53.7 | 53.5 | 53.1 | 1.0 | 1.1 | 0.7 |
| Women | 54,742 | 63,714 | 71,767 | 78,229 | 8,972 | 8,053 | 6,462 | 16.4 | 12.6 | 9.0 | 45.0 | 46.3 | 46.5 | 46.9 | 1.5 | 1.2 | 0.9 |
| **Race:** | | | | | | | | | | | | | | | | | |
| White | 104,756 | 115,415 | 125,635 | 132,490 | 10,659 | 10,220 | 6,855 | 10.2 | 8.9 | 5.5 | 86.1 | 83.8 | 81.4 | 79.4 | 1.0 | 0.9 | 0.5 |
| Black | 13,205 | 15,982 | 17,740 | 20,244 | 2,777 | 1,758 | 2,504 | 21.0 | 11.0 | 14.1 | 10.9 | 11.6 | 11.5 | 12.1 | 1.9 | 1.0 | 1.3 |
| Asian | 3,718 | 6,278 | 7,202 | 9,345 | 2,560 | 924 | 2,143 | 68.9 | 14.7 | 29.8 | 3.1 | 4.6 | 4.7 | 5.6 | 5.4 | 1.4 | 2.6 |
| All other groups* | — | — | 3,710 | 4,832 | — | — | 1,122 | — | — | 30.2 | — | — | 2.4 | 2.9 | — | — | 2.7 |
| **Ethnicity:** | | | | | | | | | | | | | | | | | |
| Hispanic origin | 8,982 | 14,317 | 22,024 | 29,304 | 5,335 | 7,707 | 7,280 | 59.4 | 53.8 | 33.1 | 7.4 | 10.4 | 14.3 | 17.6 | 4.8 | 4.4 | 2.9 |
| Other than Hispanic origin | 112,687 | 123,356 | 132,263 | 137,607 | 10,669 | 8,907 | 5,344 | 9.5 | 7.2 | 4.0 | 92.6 | 89.6 | 85.7 | 82.4 | 0.9 | 0.7 | 0.4 |
| White non-Hispanic | 96,141 | 101,767 | 105,210 | 106,834 | 5,626 | 3,443 | 1,624 | 5.9 | 3.4 | 1.5 | 79.0 | 73.9 | 68.2 | 64.0 | 0.6 | 0.3 | 0.2 |
| Age of baby boomers | 24 to 42 | 34 to 52 | 44 to 62 | 54 to 72 | — | — | — | — | — | — | — | — | — | — | — | — | — |

*The "all other groups" category includes (1) those classified as being of multiple racial origin and (2) the race categories of (2a) American Indian and Alaska Native and (2b) Native Hawaiian and other Pacific Islanders.
Notes: Dash indicates no data collected for category. Details may not sum to totals because of rounding.

SOURCE: Mitra Toossi, "Table 1. Civilian Labor Force, by Age, Sex, Race, and Ethnicity, 1988, 1998, 2008, and Projected 2018," in "Labor Force Projections to 2018: Older Workers Staying More Active," *Monthly Labor Review*, vol. 132, no. 11, November 2009, http://www.bls.gov/opub/mlr/2009/11/art3full.pdf (accessed January 15, 2012)

**TABLE 4.7**

### Employed persons by occupation, race, Hispanic origin, and sex, 2009–10

[Percent distribution]

| Occupation, race, and Hispanic or Latino ethnicity | Total | | Men | | Women | |
|---|---|---|---|---|---|---|
| | 2009 | 2010 | 2009 | 2010 | 2009 | 2010 |
| **Total** | | | | | | |
| Total, 16 years and over (thousands) | 139,877 | 139,064 | 73,670 | 73,359 | 66,208 | 65,705 |
| Percent | 100.0 | 100.0 | 100.0 | 100.0 | 100.0 | 100.0 |
| Management, professional, and related occupations | 37.3 | 37.2 | 34.5 | 34.2 | 40.5 | 40.6 |
| Management, business, and financial operations occupations | 15.4 | 15.1 | 16.7 | 16.3 | 13.9 | 13.7 |
| Professional and related occupations | 21.9 | 22.2 | 17.7 | 17.9 | 26.6 | 26.9 |
| Service occupations | 17.6 | 17.7 | 14.3 | 14.5 | 21.3 | 21.3 |
| Sales and office occupations | 24.2 | 24.0 | 17.0 | 16.9 | 32.2 | 32.0 |
| Sales and related occupations | 11.2 | 11.1 | 10.7 | 10.5 | 11.7 | 11.7 |
| Office and administrative support occupations | 13.0 | 13.0 | 6.3 | 6.4 | 20.4 | 20.3 |
| Natural resources, construction, and maintenance occupations | 9.5 | 9.4 | 17.3 | 17.0 | 0.9 | 0.9 |
| Farming, fishing, and forestry occupations | 0.7 | 0.7 | 1.0 | 1.0 | 0.3 | 0.4 |
| Construction and extraction occupations | 5.3 | 5.2 | 9.8 | 9.5 | 0.3 | 0.3 |
| Installation, maintenance, and repair occupations | 3.5 | 3.5 | 6.4 | 6.4 | 0.3 | 0.3 |
| Production, transportation, and material moving occupations | 11.4 | 11.6 | 17.0 | 17.4 | 5.2 | 5.2 |
| Production occupations | 5.5 | 5.8 | 7.5 | 7.9 | 3.3 | 3.4 |
| Transportation and material moving occupations | 5.9 | 5.9 | 9.5 | 9.5 | 1.9 | 1.9 |
| **White** | | | | | | |
| Total, 16 years and over (thousands) | 114,996 | 114,168 | 61,630 | 61,252 | 53,366 | 52,916 |
| Percent | 100.0 | 100.0 | 100.0 | 100.0 | 100.0 | 100.0 |
| Management, professional, and related occupations | 38.0 | 37.9 | 35.0 | 34.8 | 41.4 | 41.5 |
| Management, business, and financial operations occupations | 16.2 | 15.8 | 17.7 | 17.2 | 14.4 | 14.2 |
| Professional and related occupations | 21.8 | 22.1 | 17.3 | 17.6 | 27.0 | 27.3 |
| Service occupations | 16.5 | 16.6 | 13.4 | 13.6 | 20.1 | 20.1 |
| Sales and office occupations | 24.2 | 24.1 | 16.8 | 16.7 | 32.7 | 32.6 |
| Sales and related occupations | 11.4 | 11.2 | 10.9 | 10.7 | 11.8 | 11.7 |
| Office and administrative support occupations | 12.8 | 12.9 | 5.8 | 6.0 | 20.9 | 20.8 |
| Natural resources, construction, and maintenance occupations | 10.3 | 10.2 | 18.4 | 18.1 | 0.9 | 1.0 |
| Farming, fishing, and forestry occupations | 0.7 | 0.8 | 1.1 | 1.1 | 0.3 | 0.4 |
| Construction and extraction occupations | 5.8 | 5.6 | 10.6 | 10.3 | 0.3 | 0.3 |
| Installation, maintenance, and repair occupations | 3.7 | 3.7 | 6.7 | 6.7 | 0.3 | 0.3 |
| Production, transportation, and material moving occupations | 11.1 | 11.3 | 16.5 | 16.8 | 4.9 | 4.9 |
| Production occupations | 5.4 | 5.7 | 7.4 | 7.8 | 3.1 | 3.2 |
| Transportation and material moving occupations | 5.7 | 5.6 | 9.1 | 8.9 | 1.9 | 1.8 |
| **Black or African American** | | | | | | |
| Total, 16 years and over (thousands) | 15,025 | 15,010 | 6,817 | 6,865 | 8,208 | 8,145 |
| Percent | 100.0 | 100.0 | 100.0 | 100.0 | 100.0 | 100.0 |
| Management, professional, and related occupations | 29.2 | 29.1 | 23.8 | 23.5 | 33.7 | 33.8 |
| Management, business, and financial operations occupations | 10.1 | 10.2 | 9.6 | 9.8 | 10.5 | 10.7 |
| Professional and related occupations | 19.1 | 18.8 | 14.2 | 13.7 | 23.2 | 23.1 |
| Service occupations | 25.2 | 25.1 | 21.2 | 21.2 | 28.5 | 28.3 |
| Sales and office occupations | 25.2 | 25.1 | 18.5 | 18.3 | 30.8 | 30.7 |
| Sales and related occupations | 10.0 | 10.0 | 8.6 | 8.4 | 11.1 | 11.4 |
| Office and administrative support occupations | 15.3 | 15.1 | 10.0 | 9.9 | 19.7 | 19.4 |
| Natural resources, construction, and maintenance occupations | 6.1 | 5.8 | 12.4 | 11.9 | 0.8 | 0.7 |
| Farming, fishing, and forestry occupations | 0.3 | 0.3 | 0.5 | 0.5 | 0.1 | 0.2 |
| Construction and extraction occupations | 3.0 | 2.9 | 6.3 | 6.1 | 0.2 | 0.2 |
| Installation, maintenance, and repair occupations | 2.8 | 2.6 | 5.6 | 5.2 | 0.4 | 0.3 |
| Production, transportation, and material moving occupations | 14.3 | 15.0 | 24.0 | 25.1 | 6.2 | 6.5 |
| Production occupations | 5.9 | 6.1 | 8.6 | 8.8 | 3.6 | 3.8 |
| Transportation and material moving occupations | 8.5 | 8.9 | 15.5 | 16.3 | 2.6 | 2.7 |

professional, and related occupations, compared with 29.1% of African-Americans. (See Table 4.7.) The largest percentage of Hispanics worked in service occupations (26.4%), where they are seriously overrepresented, compared with 17.7% of workers overall in these low-paying occupations. More than one out of five (21.2%) Hispanic workers worked in sales and office occupations. Like African-Americans, Hispanics, except for Cuban-Americans who came to this country in 1959 following the Cuban revolution, are concentrated primarily in low-paying, low-skilled jobs.

In 2010, 19.9 million Hispanics worked, making up 14.3% of the workforce. (See Table 4.7.) According to the BLS, in *Employment and Earnings*, Hispanics were concentrated in low-paying jobs. In 2011 they made up 30.4% of janitors and building cleaners, 39.9% of maids and housekeepers, and 45.2% of grounds maintenance workers. They also made up 21.8% of the food preparation and serving occupations—31.5% of dining room and cafeteria attendants and bartender helpers, 30.4% of cooks, and 34.4% of dishwashers. However, they made

| Occupation, race, and Hispanic or Latino ethnicity | Total | | Men | | Women | |
|---|---|---|---|---|---|---|
| | 2009 | 2010 | 2009 | 2010 | 2009 | 2010 |
| **Asian** | | | | | | |
| Total, 16 years and over (thousands) | 6,635 | 6,705 | 3,551 | 3,588 | 3,084 | 3,117 |
| Percent | 100.0 | 100.0 | 100.0 | 100.0 | 100.0 | 100.0 |
| Management, professional, and related occupations | 48.8 | 47.0 | 50.1 | 47.7 | 47.4 | 46.1 |
|   Management, business, and financial operations occupations | 15.9 | 14.9 | 16.4 | 15.3 | 15.2 | 14.4 |
|   Professional and related occupations | 33.0 | 32.1 | 33.7 | 32.4 | 32.2 | 31.7 |
| Service occupations | 17.0 | 18.0 | 13.7 | 15.1 | 20.7 | 21.3 |
| Sales and office occupations | 21.2 | 21.1 | 18.0 | 17.6 | 25.0 | 25.2 |
|   Sales and related occupations | 11.3 | 11.4 | 11.6 | 11.2 | 11.1 | 11.7 |
|   Office and administrative support occupations | 9.9 | 9.7 | 6.4 | 6.3 | 13.9 | 13.6 |
| Natural resources, construction, and maintenance occupations | 4.0 | 3.9 | 7.1 | 6.7 | 0.4 | 0.6 |
|   Farming, fishing, and forestry occupations | 0.2 | 0.3 | 0.3 | 0.3 | 0.1 | 0.2 |
|   Construction and extraction occupations | 1.5 | 1.5 | 2.7 | 2.7 | 0.1 | 0.1 |
|   Installation, maintenance, and repair occupations | 2.3 | 2.1 | 4.1 | 3.7 | 0.2 | 0.3 |
| Production, transportation, and material moving occupations | 8.9 | 10.0 | 11.1 | 12.9 | 6.4 | 6.7 |
|   Production occupations | 5.6 | 6.6 | 5.8 | 7.4 | 5.5 | 5.7 |
|   Transportation and material moving occupations | 3.3 | 3.5 | 5.3 | 5.5 | 1.0 | 1.1 |
| **Hispanic or Latino ethnicity** | | | | | | |
| Total, 16 years and over (thousands) | 19,647 | 19,906 | 11,640 | 11,800 | 8,007 | 8,106 |
| Percent | 100.0 | 100.0 | 100.0 | 100.0 | 100.0 | 100.0 |
| Management, professional, and related occupations | 19.4 | 18.9 | 15.9 | 15.3 | 24.6 | 24.1 |
|   Management, business, and financial operations occupations | 8.4 | 7.8 | 7.9 | 7.3 | 9.1 | 8.7 |
|   Professional and related occupations | 11.1 | 11.0 | 8.0 | 8.0 | 15.5 | 15.4 |
| Service occupations | 25.8 | 26.4 | 21.2 | 21.8 | 32.4 | 33.2 |
| Sales and office occupations | 21.3 | 21.2 | 14.2 | 14.1 | 31.6 | 31.7 |
|   Sales and related occupations | 9.5 | 9.1 | 7.7 | 7.3 | 12.1 | 11.8 |
|   Office and administrative support occupations | 11.8 | 12.1 | 6.5 | 6.8 | 19.5 | 19.9 |
| Natural resources, construction, and maintenance occupations | 16.4 | 16.4 | 26.6 | 26.5 | 1.6 | 1.7 |
|   Farming, fishing, and forestry occupations | 1.9 | 2.1 | 2.6 | 2.7 | 1.0 | 1.2 |
|   Construction and extraction occupations | 10.8 | 10.5 | 18.0 | 17.5 | 0.3 | 0.3 |
|   Installation, maintenance, and repair occupations | 3.7 | 3.9 | 6.0 | 6.3 | 0.3 | 0.2 |
| Production, transportation, and material moving occupations | 17.1 | 17.1 | 22.2 | 22.4 | 9.8 | 9.3 |
|   Production occupations | 8.5 | 8.8 | 9.9 | 10.6 | 6.5 | 6.2 |
|   Transportation and material moving occupations | 8.6 | 8.2 | 12.3 | 11.8 | 3.3 | 3.1 |

Notes: Estimates for the above race groups (white, black or African American, and Asian) do not sum to totals because data are not presented for all races. Persons whose ethnicity is identified as Hispanic or Latino may be of any race. Updated population controls are introduced annually with the release of January data.

SOURCE: "10. Employed Persons by Occupation, Race, Hispanic or Latino Ethnicity, and Sex," in *Employment and Earnings*, U.S. Department of Labor, Bureau of Labor Statistics, 2011, http://www.bls.gov/cps/cpsaat10.pdf (accessed January 15, 2012)

up only 15.1% of first-line supervisors of food preparation and serving workers and 10.1% of bartenders.

Significant occupational differences exist among Hispanic subgroups. When it comes to job outlook, Cuban-Americans have traditionally done better in securing higher-paying jobs because they are often well educated. In 2010, 263,000 out of 850,000 (30.9%) Cuban-Americans in the workforce held management, professional, and related occupations. (See Table 4.8.) In contrast, 461,000 out of 1.6 million (28.6%) Puerto Ricans in the workforce and 2 million out of 12.6 million (16.1%) Mexican-Americans in the workforce held management, professional, and related occupations. Mexican-Americans were more likely to work in service occupations (3.4 million, or 26.7%) than in other occupations, especially in food preparation and serving occupations and building and grounds cleaning and maintenance occupations.

Puerto Ricans were more likely to work in sales and office occupations (449,000, or 27.9%) than in other occupations.

## Asian-Americans and Jobs

The higher educational attainment of many Asian-Americans has resulted in a greater proportion of them working in higher-paying jobs than do other racial and ethnic groups. In 2010 almost half (47%) of all Asian-Americans worked in management, professional, and related occupations—14.9% in management, business, and financial operations occupations and 32.1% in professional and related occupations. (See Table 4.7.) In comparison, only 37.9% of whites worked in these occupations, although the gap narrowed somewhat between 2009 and 2010. Asian-Americans were the next most likely to work in sales and office occupations (21.1%)

**TABLE 4.8**

## Employed Hispanic workers by sex, occupation, class of workers, full- or part-time status, and detailed ethnic group, 2009–10

[In thousands]

| | Hispanic or Latino ethnicity | | | | | | | |
| | Total[a] | | Mexican | | Puerto Rican | | Cuban | |
| Category | 2009 | 2010 | 2009 | 2010 | 2009 | 2010 | 2009 | 2010 |
|---|---|---|---|---|---|---|---|---|
| **Sex** | | | | | | | | |
| Total, 16 years and over | **19,647** | **19,906** | **12,478** | **12,622** | **1,594** | **1,612** | **795** | **850** |
| Men | 11,640 | 11,800 | 7,704 | 7,800 | 825 | 835 | 461 | 470 |
| Women | 8,007 | 8,106 | 4,774 | 4,822 | 769 | 777 | 334 | 379 |
| **Occupation** | | | | | | | | |
| Management, professional, and related occupations | 3,817 | 3,755 | 2,054 | 2,033 | 453 | 461 | 273 | 263 |
|   Management, business, and financial operations occupations | 1,642 | 1,562 | 884 | 859 | 182 | 178 | 129 | 113 |
|     Management occupations | 1,154 | 1,142 | 631 | 639 | 123 | 128 | 100 | 85 |
|     Business and financial operations occupations | 489 | 420 | 254 | 220 | 58 | 51 | 29 | 27 |
|   Professional and related occupations | 2,175 | 2,194 | 1,170 | 1,174 | 272 | 283 | 144 | 150 |
|     Computer and mathematical occupations | 189 | 194 | 100 | 103 | 26 | 32 | 13 | 10 |
|     Architecture and engineering occupations | 196 | 177 | 107 | 96 | 18 | 22 | 18 | 11 |
|     Life, physical, and social science occupations | 79 | 85 | 41 | 46 | 6 | 6 | 2 | 4 |
|     Community and social services occupations | 227 | 229 | 130 | 111 | 29 | 35 | 9 | 12 |
|     Legal occupations | 85 | 94 | 41 | 42 | 11 | 12 | 8 | 11 |
|     Education, training, and library occupations | 671 | 686 | 384 | 394 | 83 | 85 | 37 | 42 |
|     Arts, design, entertainment, sports, and media occupations | 239 | 244 | 126 | 124 | 28 | 26 | 14 | 18 |
|     Healthcare practitioner and technical occupations | 488 | 484 | 241 | 258 | 71 | 65 | 43 | 43 |
| Service occupations | 5,062 | 5,257 | 3,300 | 3,376 | 335 | 375 | 142 | 173 |
|   Healthcare support occupations | 456 | 506 | 268 | 284 | 47 | 66 | 20 | 22 |
|   Protective service occupations | 389 | 437 | 225 | 249 | 67 | 74 | 23 | 27 |
|   Food preparation and serving related occupations | 1,672 | 1,703 | 1,222 | 1,206 | 71 | 82 | 33 | 42 |
|   Building and grounds cleaning and maintenance occupations | 1,823 | 1,877 | 1,181 | 1,239 | 83 | 87 | 47 | 48 |
|   Personal care and service occupations | 721 | 734 | 403 | 399 | 67 | 67 | 20 | 34 |
| Sales and office occupations | 4,177 | 4,228 | 2,506 | 2,521 | 468 | 449 | 192 | 215 |
|   Sales and related occupations | 1,864 | 1,814 | 1,111 | 1,077 | 164 | 154 | 102 | 106 |
|   Office and administrative support occupations | 2,313 | 2,413 | 1,394 | 1,444 | 304 | 295 | 91 | 109 |
| Natural resources, construction, and maintenance occupations | 3,226 | 3,272 | 2,346 | 2,399 | 129 | 104 | 75 | 85 |
|   Farming, fishing, and forestry occupations | 377 | 412 | 350 | 378 | 2 | 2 | 1 | — |
|   Construction and extraction occupations | 2,123 | 2,090 | 1,545 | 1,511 | 58 | 50 | 43 | 54 |
|   Installation, maintenance, and repair occupations | 726 | 769 | 452 | 510 | 69 | 52 | 30 | 30 |
| Production, transportation, and material moving occupations | 3,364 | 3,395 | 2,272 | 2,294 | 209 | 222 | 112 | 114 |
|   Production occupations | 1,675 | 1,755 | 1,179 | 1,228 | 87 | 111 | 41 | 44 |
|   Transportation and material moving occupations | 1,689 | 1,640 | 1,093 | 1,066 | 122 | 112 | 71 | 69 |
| **Class of worker** | | | | | | | | |
| Agriculture: | | | | | | | | |
|   Wage and salary workers | 413 | 468 | 385 | 426 | 1 | 3 | 2 | 5 |
|   Self-employed workers | 13 | 11 | 12 | 8 | — | — | — | 1 |
|   Unpaid family workers | — | — | — | — | — | — | — | — |
| Nonagricultural industries: | | | | | | | | |
|   Wage and salary workers | 18,016 | 18,170 | 11,286 | 11,400 | 1,548 | 1,558 | 739 | 790 |
|     Government | 2,112 | 2,193 | 1,276 | 1,330 | 299 | 298 | 98 | 100 |
|     Private industries | 15,904 | 15,977 | 10,010 | 10,070 | 1,249 | 1,260 | 641 | 689 |
|       Private households | 296 | 264 | 158 | 148 | 8 | 2 | 7 | 7 |
|       Other industries | 15,608 | 15,713 | 9,853 | 9,922 | 1,241 | 1,258 | 634 | 682 |
|   Self-employed workers | 1,192 | 1,244 | 784 | 782 | 44 | 50 | 52 | 54 |
|   Unpaid family workers | 13 | 11 | 10 | 7 | — | — | 1 | — |
| **Full- or part-time status[b]** | | | | | | | | |
| Full-time workers | 15,971 | 16,106 | 10,118 | 10,171 | 1,308 | 1,321 | 662 | 696 |
| Part-time workers | 3,675 | 3,800 | 2,359 | 2,451 | 286 | 292 | 133 | 154 |

[a]Includes persons of Central or South American origin and of other Hispanic or Latino ethnicity, not shown separately.
[b]Employed persons are classified as full- or part-time workers based on their usual weekly hours at all jobs regardless of the number of hours they are at work during the reference week. Persons absent from work also are classified according to their usual status.
Notes: Persons whose ethnicity is identified as Hispanic or Latino may be of any race. Updated population controls are introduced annually with the release of January data. Dash indicates no data or data that do not meet publication criteria.

SOURCE: "13. Employed Hispanic or Latino Workers by Sex, Occupation, Class of Worker, Full- or Part-Time Status, and Detailed Ethnic Group," in *Employment and Earnings*, U.S. Department of Labor, Bureau of Labor Statistics, 2011, http://www.bls.gov/cps/cpsaat13.pdf (accessed January 15, 2012)

and service occupations (18%). In *Employment and Earnings*, the BLS indicates that even though only 4.9% of the workforce was of Asian origin, 6.1% of managers and professionals were Asian-American, and they were especially overrepresented among software developers, applications, and systems software (27.1%), medical scientists (25.1%), and physical scientists (19.9%)—three highly paid occupations.

However, the BLS reports that in 2011 Asian-Americans were underrepresented in natural resources, construction, and maintenance occupations (2%) and in installation, maintenance, and repair occupations (2.9%). Even though only 4.9% of service workers were Asian-American, 55.1% of miscellaneous personal appearance workers were Asian-American—reflecting the large number of Asian-Americans, particularly women, who work in nail salons and other personal care establishments.

### Native Americans and Alaskan Natives and Jobs

As stated previously, detailed data on Native American and Alaskan Native workers are difficult to obtain. However, the EEOC keeps some basic data on job patterns for minorities in private industry that includes Native Americans and Alaskan Natives as a separate category. In 2010 Native Americans made up only 0.5% of the total workforce. (See Table 4.9.) They made up only 0.3% of all executives and senior-level managers, 0.4% of all first- and midlevel officials and managers, and only 0.4% of professionals. However, Native Americans and Alaskan Natives were overrepresented among operatives (0.7%), laborers (0.6%), sales workers (0.6%), service workers (0.6%), and craft workers (0.8%).

## MINORITIES AND THE FEDERAL GOVERNMENT

Traditionally, white men have held most of the higher-level positions in the federal government. Along with cabinet members, who are selected by the president, these high-level officials wield the power in the federal government. This holds true for many agencies, including the Federal Bureau of Investigation, the U.S. Immigration and Customs Enforcement, and the U.S. Customs and Border Protection.

In *Federal Equal Opportunity Recruitment Program, FY 2010* (June 2011, http://main.opm.gov/About_OPM/Reports/FEORP/2010/feorp2010.pdf), the U.S. Office of Personnel Management finds that in FY 2010 minorities were overrepresented in the federal workforce with one exception: Hispanics were significantly underrepresented in federal jobs. African-Americans represented 17.7% of the federal workforce in FY 2010, but only 10% of the total civilian labor force. Asians and Pacific Islanders represented 5.6% of the federal workforce, but only 4.3% of the total civilian workforce. Native Americans represented 1.8% of the federal workforce, but only 0.6% of the total civilian labor force. Hispanics represented 8%

**TABLE 4.9**

Occupational employment in private industry, by race, ethnicity, sex, and industry, 2010

| Racial/ethnic group and sex | Total employment | Participation rate | | | | | | | | | |
|---|---|---|---|---|---|---|---|---|---|---|---|
| | | Executive/senior level officials & managers | First/mid level officials & managers | Professionals | Technicians | Sales workers | Office & clerical workers | Craft workers | Operatives | Laborers | Service workers |
| **All employees** | 100.00 | 100.00 | 100.00 | 100.00 | 100.00 | 100.00 | 100.00 | 100.00 | 100.00 | 100.00 | 100.00 |
| Men | 51.77 | 71.85 | 61.80 | 46.14 | 50.11 | 45.63 | 24.01 | 91.83 | 75.08 | 67.83 | 41.02 |
| Women | 48.23 | 28.15 | 38.20 | 53.86 | 49.89 | 54.37 | 75.99 | 8.17 | 24.92 | 32.17 | 58.98 |
| **White** | 65.72 | 88.13 | 79.93 | 75.21 | 69.62 | 68.43 | 65.59 | 71.48 | 60.35 | 46.24 | 50.21 |
| Men | 34.51 | 64.13 | 50.13 | 35.06 | 35.76 | 32.65 | 15.02 | 66.44 | 46.97 | 32.17 | 19.44 |
| Women | 31.21 | 24.00 | 29.80 | 40.15 | 33.86 | 35.78 | 50.57 | 5.04 | 13.37 | 14.07 | 30.77 |
| **Minority** | 34.28 | 11.87 | 20.07 | 24.79 | 30.38 | 31.57 | 34.41 | 28.52 | 39.65 | 53.76 | 49.79 |
| Men | 17.26 | 7.72 | 11.66 | 11.07 | 14.35 | 12.98 | 8.99 | 25.39 | 28.11 | 35.66 | 21.58 |
| Women | 17.02 | 4.15 | 8.41 | 13.71 | 16.03 | 18.60 | 25.42 | 3.13 | 11.54 | 18.10 | 28.21 |
| **Black** | 13.66 | 3.06 | 6.95 | 7.46 | 13.12 | 13.11 | 16.43 | 8.79 | 16.69 | 17.51 | 22.85 |
| Men | 6.09 | 1.58 | 3.53 | 2.44 | 4.84 | 5.06 | 3.83 | 7.61 | 11.80 | 11.67 | 8.85 |
| Women | 7.56 | 1.48 | 3.42 | 5.02 | 8.29 | 8.06 | 12.60 | 1.18 | 4.89 | 5.84 | 14.01 |
| **Hispanic** | 13.26 | 3.73 | 6.79 | 5.09 | 8.94 | 12.27 | 11.86 | 15.34 | 17.36 | 30.66 | 20.11 |
| Men | 7.40 | 2.48 | 4.27 | 2.33 | 4.98 | 5.29 | 3.31 | 14.05 | 12.65 | 20.56 | 9.77 |
| Women | 5.86 | 1.25 | 2.53 | 2.77 | 3.96 | 6.98 | 8.55 | 1.29 | 4.70 | 10.10 | 10.34 |
| **Asian American** | 5.52 | 4.16 | 5.14 | 10.79 | 6.59 | 3.80 | 4.06 | 2.80 | 4.09 | 3.57 | 4.33 |
| Men | 2.86 | 3.07 | 3.19 | 5.67 | 3.66 | 1.63 | 1.27 | 2.30 | 2.55 | 2.06 | 1.91 |
| Women | 2.66 | 1.09 | 1.95 | 5.12 | 2.93 | 2.16 | 2.80 | 0.49 | 1.54 | 1.50 | 2.43 |
| **American Indian** | 0.54 | 0.29 | 0.38 | 0.37 | 0.56 | 0.62 | 0.56 | 0.82 | 0.65 | 0.61 | 0.60 |
| Men | 0.28 | 0.19 | 0.24 | 0.16 | 0.27 | 0.24 | 0.14 | 0.73 | 0.48 | 0.42 | 0.24 |
| Women | 0.26 | 0.10 | 0.15 | 0.21 | 0.28 | 0.38 | 0.41 | 0.09 | 0.17 | 0.19 | 0.36 |
| **Hawaiian** | 0.39 | 0.17 | 0.23 | 0.33 | 0.38 | 0.39 | 0.40 | 0.28 | 0.35 | 0.53 | 0.56 |
| Men | 0.19 | 0.11 | 0.13 | 0.14 | 0.20 | 0.17 | 0.11 | 0.25 | 0.25 | 0.36 | 0.24 |
| Women | 0.20 | 0.06 | 0.11 | 0.19 | 0.18 | 0.22 | 0.29 | 0.03 | 0.10 | 0.17 | 0.32 |
| **Two or more races** | 0.91 | 0.46 | 0.57 | 0.75 | 0.78 | 1.39 | 1.10 | 0.49 | 0.51 | 0.88 | 1.34 |
| Men | 0.43 | 0.29 | 0.31 | 0.34 | 0.40 | 0.59 | 0.33 | 0.43 | 0.37 | 0.58 | 0.58 |
| Women | 0.48 | 0.17 | 0.26 | 0.41 | 0.38 | 0.80 | 0.78 | 0.05 | 0.14 | 0.29 | 0.76 |

SOURCE: Adapted from "2010 EEO-1 National Aggregate Report," in *2010 Job Patterns for Minorities and Women in Private Industry*, U.S. Equal Employment Opportunity Commission, 2011, http://www1.eeoc.gov/eeoc/statistics/employment/jobpat-eeo1/2010/index.cfm#select_label (accessed January 15, 2012)

of the federal workforce, but 13.6% of the total civilian workforce in FY 2010.

Even though minorities are generally overrepresented in the federal workforce, they are underrepresented at the senior pay grades. For example, African-Americans made up 17.7% of the federal workforce in FY 2010 but were overrepresented at the lowest pay grades. In FY 2010, 24.7% of employees in the lowest positions—General Schedule and Related (GSR) grades one to four—were African-American. Another 25.5% of GSR five to eight, 17% of GSR nine to 12, 12.8% of GSR 13 to 15, and just 6.7% of the senior pay levels were African-American. Asians and Pacific Islanders were also underrepresented at the senior pay levels, but less so than African-Americans, representing 6.3% of the GSR one-to-four pay levels and 6.4% of the senior pay levels. Hispanics represented 9.2% of the GSR one-to-four pay levels and only 4.1% of the senior pay levels. Native Americans represented 4.7% of the GSR one-to-four pay levels and only 0.9% of the senior pay levels.

A major contributor to this situation is time. It takes about 20 years to rise to the top of any organization. During the early 1990s few people of color held any management positions in the federal government. Another possible factor is partiality or discrimination. Some lower-level government employees believe they have been deprived of promotions because of their gender or race and have filed bias complaints.

## MINORITIES IN BUSINESS

The Census Bureau indicates in *2007 Survey of Business Owners* (June 7, 2011, http://www.census.gov/econ/sbo/get07sof.html?19) that in 2007, 83.4% of business owners in the United States were white. All minority groups except Asian-Americans were underrepresented among business owners when compared with their presence in the U.S. residential population aged 25 years and older. Only 8.3% of business owners were of Hispanic origin, even though in that year the adult U.S. population was 13.3% Hispanic. African-Americans represented only 7.1% of business owners, even though 12% of the adult U.S. population was African-American in that year. About 0.9% of business owners were Native American and Alaskan Native, which was essentially proportional to their representation in the adult U.S. population in 2007. Asian-Americans, who represented 5.7% of business owners, were overrepresented in comparison with their presence in the adult U.S. population, at 4.5%.

### Minority Women-Owned Businesses

According to the Census Bureau, in *2007 Survey of Business Owners*, only 28.8% of business owners in 2007 were women. The Center for Women's Business Research reports in "Key Facts about Women-Owned Businesses" (2012, http://www.womensbusinessresearchcenter.org/research/keyfacts/) that in 2008, 18.8% of women-owned businesses were owned by women of color. In that year there were 1.9 million firms majority owned by minority women in the United States. These businesses generated $165 billion in sales in 2008.

## Minority Set-Aside Programs under Increasing Attack

Many levels of government, including the federal government, have set-aside programs that award a certain percentage of contracts to minority- and women-owned businesses. These programs were developed to remedy the effects of past discrimination and to address the difficulties these firms faced in competing with larger, more established firms for government contracts. Minority businesses are often newer and smaller and have difficulty competing with older, larger businesses that know the process and can afford to make lower bids. Acquiring government contracts can be involved and confusing for businesses that are unfamiliar with the process. Governments, especially the federal government, are often slow to pay their bills, so businesses frequently have to borrow money to bridge the gap between the delivery of goods and services that must be paid for and the time it takes the government to pay them.

Even though the U.S. Supreme Court has not yet declared the use of racial classifications unconstitutional, it has ruled them suspect and subject to strict judicial scrutiny. As a result, set-aside programs came under increasing attack during the 1990s and at the turn of the 21st century.

In *Richmond v. J. A. Croson Co.* (488 U.S. 469 [1989]), the Supreme Court struck down a Richmond, Virginia, city ordinance that reserved 30% of city-financed construction contracts for minority-owned businesses. The court ruled that the ordinance violated equal protection because there was no "specific" and "identified" evidence of past discrimination, "public or private," against the Richmond Minority Business Enterprise in city contracting. The majority opinion, written by Justice Sandra Day O'Connor (1930–), also noted that the city had failed to "narrowly tailor" the remedy to accomplish any objective "except perhaps outright racial balancing." The opinion further stated that it was a "completely unrealistic" assumption that a 30% assignment to minority business enterprises in a particular trade would be a fair representation of the community.

In a similar case, Adarand Constructors, a white-owned company, sued the federal government, claiming the company failed to receive a government contract because racial preferences had violated the owner's right to equal protection under the Fifth Amendment. In 1989 the U.S. Department of Transportation awarded a contract for a federal highway project to a construction firm, that in turn subcontracted the job to a Disadvantaged Business Enterprise in compliance with the Subcontractor Compensation Clause. In *Adarand Constructors Inc.*

*v. Peña* (515 U.S. 200 [1995]), the Supreme Court expressed doubt in the validity of the affirmative action programs, which were based on the Surface Transportation and Uniform Relocation Assistance Act of 1987 that channeled $10 billion per year in construction contracts to women- and minority-owned businesses. The court, citing the need for stricter and narrower standards in determining racial preferences when awarding contracts, returned the case to the district court for review.

In June 2000 a federal court decided in *Associated General Contractors of Ohio v. Sandra A. Drabik* (No. 98-4393) that the Ohio state program of setting aside 5% of state construction projects for minority-owned businesses was unconstitutional. Even though that court had upheld the state's program in 1983, subsequent U.S. Supreme Court decisions required the federal court to apply a more stringent standard of judicial review and no longer allowed legislatures to use "implicit fact-finding of discrimination" to justify racial preferences and affirmative action programs such as set-aside programs.

In the meantime, the federal government created a new set-aside program in 1993 called the Small and Disadvantaged Business Set-Aside Program. This program supplemented other set-aside programs by allowing agencies to set aside some competitions solely for small and disadvantaged businesses with awards made through the agencies rather than through the government.

## TRIBAL CASINOS: A MATTER OF SELF-RULE

The Indian Gaming Regulatory Act of 1988 gives tribes "the exclusive right to regulate gaming on Indian lands if the gaming activity is not specifically prohibited by federal law and is conducted within a State which does not, as a matter of criminal law and public policy, prohibit such gaming activity." The law requires that only tribes, not individuals, run gaming operations. The tribes do not need state approval for class-two casinos, which are supposedly bingo halls but which in many cases have slot machine parlors that skirt the law. Class-three casinos offer slots, roulette, craps, and poker, and they require state approval. Thus, governors make deals with tribes, granting class-three approval in exchange for a share of the profits going to the state treasury. With many states facing severe budget problems, tribal gaming has become an attractive source of revenue. As a result, tribal gaming has gained considerable political influence. The National Indian Gaming Association reports in *Gaming Tribal Report* (July 6, 2011, http://www.nigc.gov/LinkClick.aspx?fileticket=0J7Yk1QNgX0%3d&tabid=943) that 240 out of 566 federally recognized Native American tribes were engaged in gaming in 2011. How much has tribal gaming helped the Native American population as a whole?

In "Wheel of Misfortune" (*Time*, December 16, 2002), Donald L. Barlett and James B. Steele provide a scathing and controversial review of tribal gaming.

According to Barlett and Steele, when tribal gaming emerged during the late 1980s "in a frenzy of cost cutting and privatization, Washington perceived gaming on reservations as a cheap way to wean tribes from government handouts, encourage economic development and promote tribal self-sufficiency." However, the 1988 Indian Gaming Regulatory Act "was so riddled with loopholes, so poorly written, so discriminatory and subject to such conflicting interpretations that 14 years later, armies of high-priced lawyers are still debating the definition of a slot machine." Barlett and Steele maintain that only a handful of tribal gaming establishments, those operating close to major population centers, are successful, whereas the overwhelming majority are either too small or too remote in location: "Casinos in California, Connecticut and Florida—states with only 3% of the Indian population—haul in 44% of all revenue, an average of $100,000 per Indian." Barlett and Steele state that in 2002 "290 Indian casinos in 28 states pulled in at least $12.7 billion in revenue. Of that sum, . . . the casinos kept more than $5 billion as profit. That would place overall Indian gaming among *Fortune* magazine's 20 most profitable U.S. corporations." However, "just 39 casinos generated $8.4 billion. In short, 13% of the casinos accounted for 66% of the take."

Also controversial was the authenticity of the tribes that were involved in gaming. According to Barlett and Steele, leaders of tribes involved in gaming "are free to set their own whimsical rules for admission, without regard to Indian heritage. They may exclude rivals, potential whistle-blowers and other legitimate claimants. The fewer tribe members, the larger the cut for the rest. Some tribes are booting out members, while others are limiting membership." Moreover, many "long-defunct tribes and extended families" have attempted to gain congressional certification to become involved in tribal gaming. In New York State some tribes that are not even recognized as New York tribes, including tribes from Oklahoma and Wisconsin, have teamed with area developers to buy land in the Catskills and elsewhere in the state in hopes of building casinos. They are opposed, however, by local communities—as well as by Donald Trump (1946–)—who fear further competition to casinos operating in Atlantic City, New Jersey.

By contrast, many proponents point out the positive effects of tribal gaming, arguing that it spurs economic development and helps tribes solidify tribal sovereignty. The immediate effect of tribal gaming seems to have done just that. For example, Thaddieus W. Conner and William A. Taggart studied tribal gaming in New Mexico and published their findings in "The Impact of Gaming on the Indian Nations in New Mexico" (*Social Science Quarterly*, vol. 90, no. 1, March 2009). The researchers find that gaming tribes have higher incomes, lower poverty, and improvement in some social areas when compared with nongaming tribes.

Stephen Cornell of the University of Arizona points out in "The Political Economy of American Indian Gaming" (*Annual Review of Law and Social Science*, vol. 4, December 2008) that tribal gaming has had positive economic, political, and social effects on both gaming and nongaming Native American reservations. In "Indian Gaming and Tribal Revenue Allocation Plans: A Case of 'Play to Pay'" (*Gaming Law Review and Economics*, vol. 15, no. 6, June 2011), Taggart and Conner point out that evidence suggests that tribal gaming has allowed tribes to provide for their members' general welfare, to fund tribal government operations, and to spur economic development.

Proponents of tribal gaming also point to a number of success stories. Marks and Spilde Contreras find that in 2007 tribal gaming reduced poverty and improved employment and income in the communities near the California casinos. The Oneidas of Wisconsin took advantage of a bingo hall to lower the tribe's unemployment rate during the early 1990s and used proceeds to build an elementary school and subsidize a Head Start program. The Suquamish in Washington State used gambling profits to buy back former reservation land. Only a handful of tribal casinos generate large revenues, but even those operations that break even create jobs that benefit many Native Americans. Furthermore, tribes not able to take advantage of gambling can benefit from revenue-sharing programs, such as the one that was set up in California.

## Tribal Casinos and the Global Economic Recession

Interestingly, tribal casinos were much less affected by the global economic recession than were nontribal casinos.

According to Howard Stutz, in "Gaming Revenue Tight in 2008" (*Las Vegas Review-Journal*, December 10, 2009), tribal casinos collected $26.8 billion in gaming revenue in 2008, a 1.5% increase over the previous year. Hugo Martín reports in "Recession Is in Play at California's Tribal Casinos" (*Los Angeles Times*, November 20, 2009) that the recession did not decrease the number of visitors to California's tribal casinos—although Atlantic City and Las Vegas did see drops in visitors—but it did affect how much money those visitors spent. The article "Tribal Casinos No Longer Sure Bet in Washington" (Associated Press, February 3, 2010) notes that even though a few Washington State tribal casinos closed and most casinos saw revenues drop in 2009, a few saw revenues increase. Furthermore, tribal casinos overall were performing more strongly than nontribal casinos. In the years following the end of the recession, tribal gaming rebounded. In "Indian Gaming Revenues Rise by 1.3 Percent" (*Las Vegas Review-Journal*, March 6, 2012), Stutz notes that revenues grew 1.3% between 2009 and 2010, and reached $26.7 billion in 2010, the largest single-year figure ever for tribal casinos. Nevertheless, that 1.3% increase was far below the double-digit increases that had been reported for Indian gaming between 1989 and 2006.

Regardless, wary that the future might see the curtailment in revenues, some tribes began to diversify by expanding their facilities into full-fledged resorts, whereas others started investing proceeds into nongaming businesses, thereby establishing an economic base independent of gambling.

## CHAPTER 5
# MONEY, INCOME, AND POVERTY STATUS

Income greatly influences where people live, what they eat, how they dress, what cars they drive or transportation they take, and what schools their children can attend. How much money and income people have is usually determined by their occupation, which is often directly related to their level of education. Racial and ethnic backgrounds can play a big role in all these factors as well.

## INCOME DIFFERENCES
### All Households

A household consists of a person or people who occupy the same housing unit and may have just one person (the householder who owns or rents the house). It may also consist of related family members (family household) or unrelated people (nonfamily household).

The median income (half of all households earned more and half earned less) of U.S. households in 2010, including money income before taxes but excluding the value of noncash benefits such as food stamps, Medicare (the federally administered system of health insurance for people aged 65 years and older and people with disabilities), Medicaid (the federally funded health care program for low-income people), public housing, and employer-provided benefits, was $49,445, down from $52,163 in 2007, before the global economic recession, which lasted from late 2007 to mid-2009. (See Table 5.1.) The decrease in median income in 2010 can be attributed to the recession, which resulted in soaring unemployment and underemployment rates. The median income varied substantially between races and ethnic groups. The median income of non-Hispanic white households was $54,620, which was considerably higher than that of Hispanic households ($37,759) and African-American households ($32,068). However, non-Hispanic white income was significantly less than the median household income of Asian-Americans ($64,308). Some of the reasons for these income disparities are discussed in this chapter.

### Married-Couple Households

In 2010 there were 58 million married-couple households in the United States, representing 48.9% of all households and 73.8% of all family households. (See Table 5.1.) Married couples tend to have a higher household income than do single householders, because often both the husband and wife work outside of the home. In 2010 married-couple households had a median income of $72,751. The median income for female-headed households with no husband present was substantially lower, at $32,031—only 44% of the median income of married-couple households. The median income for male-headed households with no wife present was also lower than the married-couple median but substantially higher than the median income for female-headed households, at $49,718.

### Minority Incomes

HISPANIC INCOME. Even though Table 5.1 shows that Hispanic households earned an average median income of $37,759 in 2010, down from $38,667 in 2009, the financial situation among Hispanic subgroups tends to vary. The U.S. Census Bureau notes in *The Hispanic Population in the United States: 2010* (June 2011, http://www.census.gov/population/www/socdemo/hispanic/cps2010.html) that in 2009 more than three out of 10 (31.8%) Hispanic households had money income under $25,000 per year, compared with just 21.7% of non-Hispanic white households. Among family households, more than a quarter (27.5%) of Hispanic families earned under $25,000 per year, compared with just 12.2% of non-Hispanic white families.

Among the Hispanic subgroups, however, the Census Bureau indicates that the yearly earnings outlook was best for Hispanic families of South American origin. (See Table 5.2.) Approximately 22.4% of South American family households earned under $25,000 per year in 2009, compared with 31% of Central American family

TABLE 5.1

## Median household and per capita income by selected characteristics, 2009 and 2010

| Characteristic | 2009 | | 2010 | | Percentage change in real median income (2010 less 2009) |
| | Number (thousands) | Median income (dollars) Estimate | Number (thousands) | Median income (dollars) Estimate | Estimate |
|---|---|---|---|---|---|
| **Households** | | | | | |
| All households | 117,538 | 50,599 | 118,682 | 49,445 | −2.3 |
| **Type of household** | | | | | |
| Family households | 78,833 | 62,276 | 78,613 | 61,544 | −1.2 |
| Married-couple | 58,410 | 73,016 | 58,036 | 72,751 | −0.4 |
| Female householder, no husband present | 14,843 | 33,135 | 15,019 | 32,031 | −3.3 |
| Male householder, no wife present | 5,580 | 48,878 | 5,559 | 49,718 | 1.7 |
| Nonfamily households | 38,705 | 30,947 | 40,069 | 29,730 | −3.9 |
| Female householder | 20,442 | 25,686 | 21,234 | 25,456 | −0.9 |
| Male householder | 18,263 | 37,215 | 18,835 | 35,627 | −4.3 |
| **Race* and Hispanic origin of householder** | | | | | |
| White | 95,489 | 52,717 | 96,144 | 51,846 | −1.7 |
| White, not Hispanic | 83,158 | 55,360 | 83,471 | 54,620 | −1.3 |
| Black | 14,730 | 33,122 | 15,065 | 32,068 | −3.2 |
| Asian | 4,687 | 66,550 | 4,747 | 64,308 | −3.4 |
| Hispanic (any race) | 13,298 | 38,667 | 13,665 | 37,759 | −2.3 |
| **Nativity of householder** | | | | | |
| Native born | 102,039 | 51,337 | 102,647 | 50,288 | −2.0 |
| Foreign born | 15,499 | 44,648 | 16,036 | 43,750 | −2.0 |
| Naturalized citizen | 7,834 | 52,833 | 8,277 | 52,642 | −0.4 |
| Not a citizen | 7,666 | 36,685 | 7,758 | 36,401 | −0.8 |
| **Residence** | | | | | |
| Inside principal cities | 38,850 | 45,592 | 39,472 | 44,049 | −3.4 |
| Outside principal cities | 59,529 | 57,516 | 59,793 | 56,140 | −2.4 |
| **Earnings of full-time, year-round workers** | | | | | |
| Men with earnings | 56,053 | 47,905 | 56,412 | 47,715 | −0.4 |
| Women with earnings | 43,217 | 36,877 | 42,834 | 36,931 | 0.1 |

*Federal surveys now give respondents the option of reporting more than one race. Therefore, two basic ways of defining a race group are possible. A group such as Asian may be defined as those who reported Asian and no other race (the race-alone or single-race concept) or as those who reported Asian regardless of whether they also reported another race (the race-alone-or-in-combination concept). This table shows data using the first approach (race alone). The use of the single-race population does not imply that it is the preferred method of presenting or analyzing data. The Census Bureau uses a variety of approaches. Information on people who reported more than one race, such as white **and** American Indian and Alaska Native or Asian **and** black or African American, is available from Census 2010 through American FactFinder. About 2.9 percent of people reported more than one race in Census 2010. Data for American Indians and Alaska Natives, Native Hawaiians and other Pacific Islanders, and those reporting two or more races are not shown separately in this table. Note: Income in 2010 dollars.

SOURCE: Adapted from Carmen DeNavas-Walt, Bernadette D. Proctor, and Jessica C. Smith, "Table 1. Income and Earnings Summary Measures by Selected Characteristics: 2009 and 2010," in *Income, Poverty, and Health Insurance Coverage in the United States: 2010*, U.S. Census Bureau, September 2011, http://www.census.gov/prod/2011pubs/p60–239.pdf (accessed December 11, 2011)

households, 31.5% of Cuban family households, 32.4% of Mexican family households, and 33.4% of Puerto Rican family households. Even though only 20.8% of Hispanic family households earned $75,000 or more per year, 30.8% of South American and 25.6% of Cuban family households did. In contrast, only 22.1% of Puerto Rican families, 19.3% of Mexican families, and 19.2% of Central American families earned $75,000 or more per year in 2009.

Hispanic incomes are relatively low for a variety of reasons, including language barriers and discrimination in the workplace. However, the lack of educational attainment is a major reason for low Hispanic incomes. In *Hispanic Population in the United States*, the Census Bureau indicates that in 2010, 21.2% of all Hispanics aged 25 years and older had less than a ninth-grade education, another 15.9% did not have a high school diploma, and only 13.9% had a bachelor's degree or higher.

**AFRICAN-AMERICAN INCOME.** African-American households had the lowest median income in 2010, at $32,068. (See Table 5.1.) As shown earlier, households that are headed by an unmarried adult have a substantially lower income than do married-couple households. This puts African-Americans at a disadvantage. Among those over the age of 15 years, African-Americans are far more likely than whites, Hispanics, or Asian-Americans to have never married. According to the Census Bureau, in *America's Families and Living Arrangements: 2010* (November 2010, http://www.census.gov/population/www/socdemo/hh-fam/cps2010.html), 46.8% of African-Americans aged 15 years and older had never been married in 2010, compared with 38.7% of Hispanics, 28.3% of Asian-Americans, and 26.1% of non-Hispanic whites.

However, the differences in marriage rates do not explain the entire discrepancy between household incomes

TABLE 5.2

**Total money income of households by type and Hispanic origin type of householder, 2009**

[Numbers in thousands. Civilian noninstitutionalized population.[a]]

| Household type and money income[d] | Total Hispanic | | Hispanic origin type[b] | | | | | | | | | | | |
| | | | Mexican | | Puerto Rican | | Cuban | | Central American | | South American | | Other Hispanic[c] | |
| | Number | Percent | Number | Percent | Number | Percent | Number | Percent | Number | Percent | Number | Percent | Number | Percent |
|---|---|---|---|---|---|---|---|---|---|---|---|---|---|---|
| **Total households** | 13,298 | 100.0 | 8,070 | 100.0 | 1,430 | 100.0 | 702 | 100.0 | 1,017 | 100.0 | 846 | 100.0 | 1,234 | 100.0 |
| Under $5,000 | 516 | 3.9 | 327 | 4.0 | 63 | 4.4 | 29 | 4.1 | 26 | 2.6 | 19 | 2.2 | 52 | 4.2 |
| $5,000 to $9,999 | 733 | 5.5 | 411 | 5.1 | 117 | 8.2 | 64 | 9.1 | 28 | 2.7 | 27 | 3.2 | 87 | 7.1 |
| $10,000 to $14,999 | 951 | 7.2 | 581 | 7.2 | 116 | 8.1 | 42 | 6.0 | 76 | 7.4 | 50 | 5.9 | 86 | 7.0 |
| $15,000 to $19,999 | 989 | 7.4 | 613 | 7.6 | 110 | 7.7 | 50 | 7.1 | 81 | 8.0 | 42 | 5.0 | 92 | 7.5 |
| $20,000 to $24,999 | 1,032 | 7.8 | 689 | 8.5 | 72 | 5.0 | 37 | 5.2 | 104 | 10.3 | 52 | 6.1 | 79 | 6.4 |
| $25,000 to $34,999 | 1,908 | 14.3 | 1,187 | 14.7 | 189 | 13.2 | 98 | 14.0 | 165 | 16.2 | 97 | 11.4 | 173 | 14.0 |
| $35,000 to $49,999 | 2,052 | 15.4 | 1,308 | 16.2 | 188 | 13.2 | 87 | 12.4 | 165 | 16.2 | 115 | 13.6 | 188 | 15.2 |
| $50,000 to $74,999 | 2,341 | 17.6 | 1,396 | 17.3 | 258 | 18.0 | 114 | 16.3 | 177 | 17.5 | 183 | 21.7 | 212 | 17.2 |
| $75,000 to $99,999 | 1,215 | 9.1 | 730 | 9.0 | 129 | 9.0 | 64 | 9.1 | 89 | 8.8 | 99 | 11.7 | 103 | 8.4 |
| $100,000 and over | 1,561 | 11.7 | 828 | 10.3 | 188 | 13.1 | 116 | 16.5 | 106 | 10.4 | 162 | 19.1 | 161 | 13.1 |
| **Family households[e]** | 10,412 | 100.0 | 6,564 | 100.0 | 1,009 | 100.0 | 473 | 100.0 | 831 | 100.0 | 627 | 100.0 | 909 | 100.0 |
| Under $5,000 | 341 | 3.3 | 228 | 3.5 | 40 | 3.9 | 9 | 1.9 | 19 | 2.3 | 9 | 1.5 | 36 | 4.0 |
| $5,000 to $9,999 | 393 | 3.8 | 254 | 3.9 | 52 | 5.2 | 20 | 4.2 | 21 | 2.6 | 11 | 1.8 | 34 | 3.8 |
| $10,000 to $14,999 | 613 | 5.9 | 418 | 6.4 | 54 | 5.3 | 20 | 4.3 | 47 | 5.7 | 22 | 3.5 | 51 | 5.6 |
| $15,000 to $19,999 | 739 | 7.1 | 484 | 7.4 | 76 | 7.5 | 29 | 6.0 | 54 | 6.5 | 32 | 5.1 | 65 | 7.2 |
| $20,000 to $24,999 | 771 | 7.4 | 543 | 8.3 | 41 | 4.0 | 23 | 4.9 | 78 | 9.4 | 30 | 4.8 | 57 | 6.2 |
| $25,000 to $34,999 | 1,507 | 14.5 | 976 | 14.9 | 135 | 13.3 | 76 | 16.1 | 130 | 15.6 | 67 | 10.7 | 123 | 13.6 |
| $35,000 to $49,999 | 1,667 | 16.0 | 1,092 | 16.6 | 140 | 13.9 | 58 | 12.3 | 142 | 17.1 | 86 | 13.8 | 149 | 16.4 |
| $50,000 to $74,999 | 1,958 | 18.8 | 1,192 | 18.2 | 197 | 19.6 | 85 | 17.9 | 161 | 19.4 | 149 | 23.8 | 174 | 19.1 |
| $75,000 to $99,999 | 1,067 | 10.2 | 651 | 9.9 | 104 | 10.4 | 56 | 11.8 | 82 | 9.8 | 88 | 14.0 | 86 | 9.5 |
| $100,000 and over | 1,356 | 13.0 | 727 | 11.1 | 170 | 16.9 | 97 | 20.6 | 96 | 11.6 | 133 | 21.1 | 133 | 14.6 |
| **Nonfamily households** | 2,885 | 100.0 | 1,507 | 100.0 | 421 | 100.0 | 229 | 100.0 | 186 | 100.0 | 219 | 100.0 | 325 | 100.0 |
| Under $5,000 | 175 | 6.1 | 99 | 6.6 | 23 | 5.5 | 20 | 8.7 | 7 | 3.9 | 10 | 4.4 | 16 | 5.0 |
| $5,000 to $9,999 | 340 | 11.8 | 156 | 10.4 | 64 | 15.3 | 44 | 19.2 | 6 | 3.5 | 16 | 7.3 | 53 | 16.3 |
| $10,000 to $14,999 | 338 | 11.7 | 164 | 10.9 | 62 | 14.8 | 22 | 9.5 | 28 | 15.3 | 28 | 12.6 | 35 | 10.7 |
| $15,000 to $19,999 | 250 | 8.7 | 130 | 8.6 | 34 | 8.2 | 22 | 9.4 | 27 | 14.5 | 10 | 4.8 | 27 | 8.2 |
| $20,000 to $24,999 | 261 | 9.0 | 146 | 9.7 | 31 | 7.4 | 14 | 6.0 | 26 | 14.0 | 21 | 9.8 | 22 | 6.8 |
| $25,000 to $34,999 | 401 | 13.9 | 211 | 14.0 | 54 | 12.9 | 22 | 9.8 | 35 | 18.8 | 29 | 13.4 | 49 | 15.2 |
| $35,000 to $49,999 | 385 | 13.3 | 216 | 14.4 | 48 | 11.4 | 29 | 12.7 | 23 | 12.4 | 29 | 13.3 | 39 | 12.1 |
| $50,000 to $74,999 | 383 | 13.3 | 204 | 13.5 | 61 | 14.4 | 30 | 13.0 | 17 | 9.0 | 34 | 15.7 | 38 | 11.7 |
| $75,000 to $99,999 | 148 | 5.1 | 79 | 5.2 | 25 | 5.9 | 8 | 3.7 | 7 | 3.8 | 12 | 5.4 | 17 | 5.3 |
| $100,000 and over | 205 | 7.1 | 102 | 6.8 | 17 | 4.1 | 19 | 8.2 | 9 | 5.0 | 29 | 13.3 | 28 | 8.7 |

[a]Plus armed forces living off post or with their families on post.
[b]Hispanic refers to people whose origin is Mexican, Puerto Rican, Cuban, Spanish-speaking Central or South American countries, or other Hispanic/Latino, regardless of race. Central American totals exclude Mexican. Household type is shown by the Hispanic origin type of the householder.
[c]This category includes Dominicans and people who responded "Hispanic," "Latino," or provided other general terms.
[d]Total money income is the sum of wages and salaries, net income from self-employment, and income other than earnings.
[e]Households in which at least one member is related to the person who owns or rents the occupied housing unit (householder).

SOURCE: "Table 24. Total Money Income of Households by Type and Hispanic Origin Type of Householder: 2009," in *The Hispanic Population in the United States: 2010*, U.S. Census Bureau, 2011, http://www.census.gov/population/www/socdemo/hispanic/cps2010.html (accessed December 11, 2011)

of non-Hispanic whites and African-Americans. Married-couple African-American households have lower incomes than married-couple non-Hispanic white households; also African-American female- and male-headed households have lower incomes than comparable non-Hispanic white households. The Census Bureau reports in the Current Population Survey (2011, http://www.bls.gov/cps/) that in 2010 African-American married-couple households had a median household income of $60,772, compared with a median household income of $77,416 among non-Hispanic white married-couple households. African-American families headed by a single mother had a median income of only $24,387, whereas non-Hispanic white single-mother families had a median income of $34,558. Lower educational attainment and discrimination in the workforce are two factors that may work together to lower the incomes of African-American households.

**ASIAN-AMERICAN INCOME.** Conversely, Asian-American households tend to have higher incomes than comparable non-Hispanic white households. The Census Bureau reports in the Current Population Survey that Asian-American married-couple households in 2010 had a median income of $84,665, which was higher than the median income of non-Hispanic white married-couple households. In addition, Asian-American single-mother families were decidedly better off than were their non-Hispanic white counterparts, with a median income of $42,014. This higher median income is probably almost entirely explained by the higher educational attainment of Asian-Americans.

**TABLE 5.4**

## People and families in poverty by selected characteristics, 2009 and 2010

[Numbers in thousands]

| Characteristic | 2009 Total | 2009 Below poverty Number | 2009 Below poverty Percent | 2010 Total | 2010 Below poverty Number | 2010 Below poverty Percent | Change in poverty (2010 less 2009)[a] Number | Change in poverty (2010 less 2009)[a] Percent |
|---|---|---|---|---|---|---|---|---|
| **People** | | | | | | | | |
| Total | 303,820 | 43,569 | 14.3 | 305,688 | 46,180 | 15.1 | 2,611 | 0.8 |
| **Family status** | | | | | | | | |
| In families | 249,384 | 31,197 | 12.5 | 249,855 | 33,007 | 13.2 | 1,809 | 0.7 |
| Householder | 78,867 | 8,792 | 11.1 | 78,633 | 9,221 | 11.7 | 429 | 0.6 |
| Related children under 18 | 73,410 | 14,774 | 20.1 | 73,227 | 15,730 | 21.5 | 956 | 1.4 |
| Related children under 6 | 25,104 | 5,983 | 23.8 | 25,096 | 6,343 | 25.3 | 360 | 1.4 |
| In unrelated subfamilies | 1,357 | 693 | 51.1 | 1,650 | 751 | 45.5 | 58 | −5.5 |
| Reference person | 521 | 253 | 48.7 | 641 | 274 | 42.6 | 20 | −6.0 |
| Children under 18 | 747 | 423 | 56.6 | 922 | 459 | 49.8 | 36 | −6.8 |
| Unrelated individuals | 53,079 | 11,678 | 22.0 | 54,183 | 12,422 | 22.9 | 743 | 0.9 |
| Male | 26,269 | 5,255 | 20.0 | 26,745 | 5,796 | 21.7 | 541 | 1.7 |
| Female | 26,811 | 6,424 | 24.0 | 27,438 | 6,626 | 24.1 | 202 | 0.2 |
| **Race[b] and Hispanic origin** | | | | | | | | |
| White | 242,047 | 29,830 | 12.3 | 243,013 | 31,650 | 13.0 | 1,819 | 0.7 |
| White, not Hispanic | 197,164 | 18,530 | 9.4 | 197,203 | 19,599 | 9.9 | 1,070 | 0.5 |
| Black | 38,556 | 9,944 | 25.8 | 38,965 | 10,675 | 27.4 | 732 | 1.6 |
| Asian | 14,005 | 1,746 | 12.5 | 14,324 | 1,729 | 12.1 | −17 | −0.4 |
| Hispanic (any race) | 48,811 | 12,350 | 25.3 | 49,869 | 13,243 | 26.6 | 893 | 1.3 |
| **Age** | | | | | | | | |
| Under 18 years | 74,579 | 15,451 | 20.7 | 74,494 | 16,401 | 22.0 | 950 | 1.3 |
| 18 to 64 years | 190,627 | 24,684 | 12.9 | 192,015 | 26,258 | 13.7 | 1,574 | 0.7 |
| 18 to 24 years | 29,313 | 6,071 | 20.7 | 29,651 | 6,507 | 21.9 | 436 | 1.2 |
| 25 to 34 years | 41,085 | 6,123 | 14.9 | 41,584 | 6,333 | 15.2 | 210 | 0.3 |
| 35 to 44 years | 40,447 | 4,756 | 11.8 | 39,842 | 5,028 | 12.6 | 272 | 0.9 |
| 45 to 54 years | 44,387 | 4,421 | 10.0 | 43,954 | 4,662 | 10.6 | 240 | 0.6 |
| 55 to 59 years | 19,172 | 1,792 | 9.3 | 19,554 | 1,972 | 10.1 | 180 | 0.7 |
| 60 to 64 years | 16,223 | 1,520 | 9.4 | 17,430 | 1,755 | 10.1 | 235 | 0.7 |
| 65 years and older | 38,613 | 3,433 | 8.9 | 39,179 | 3,520 | 9.0 | 87 | 0.1 |
| **Nativity** | | | | | | | | |
| Native born | 266,223 | 36,407 | 13.7 | 267,487 | 38,568 | 14.4 | 2,161 | 0.7 |
| Foreign born | 37,597 | 7,162 | 19.0 | 38,201 | 7,611 | 19.9 | 450 | 0.9 |
| Naturalized citizen | 16,024 | 1,736 | 10.8 | 16,797 | 1,906 | 11.3 | 169 | 0.5 |
| Not a citizen | 21,573 | 5,425 | 25.1 | 21,403 | 5,706 | 26.7 | 281 | 1.5 |
| **Region** | | | | | | | | |
| Northeast | 54,571 | 6,650 | 12.2 | 54,718 | 6,987 | 12.8 | 336 | 0.6 |
| Midwest | 65,980 | 8,768 | 13.3 | 66,006 | 9,148 | 13.9 | 380 | 0.6 |
| South | 112,165 | 17,609 | 15.7 | 113,137 | 19,072 | 16.9 | 1,463 | 1.2 |
| West | 71,103 | 10,542 | 14.8 | 71,827 | 10,973 | 15.3 | 431 | 0.5 |
| **Residence** | | | | | | | | |
| Inside metropolitan statistical areas | 256,028 | 35,655 | 13.9 | 258,025 | 38,325 | 14.9 | 2,670 | 0.9 |
| Inside principal cities | 97,725 | 18,261 | 18.7 | 98,655 | 19,465 | 19.7 | 1,204 | 1.0 |
| Outside principal cities | 158,302 | 17,394 | 11.0 | 159,370 | 18,860 | 11.8 | 1,466 | 0.8 |
| Outside metropolitan statistical areas[c] | 47,792 | 7,914 | 16.6 | 47,663 | 7,855 | 16.5 | −60 | −0.1 |
| **Work experience** | | | | | | | | |
| Total, 16 years and older | 238,095 | 29,625 | 12.4 | 239,917 | 31,382 | 13.1 | 1,758 | 0.6 |
| All workers | 154,772 | 10,680 | 6.9 | 153,141 | 10,666 | 7.0 | −15 | 0.1 |
| Worked full-time, year-round | 99,306 | 2,641 | 2.7 | 99,250 | 2,608 | 2.6 | −33 | — |
| Less than full-time, year-round | 55,466 | 8,039 | 14.5 | 53,891 | 8,057 | 15.0 | 18 | 0.5 |
| Did not work at least 1 week | 83,323 | 18,944 | 22.7 | 86,776 | 20,717 | 23.9 | 1,772 | 1.1 |
| **Disability status[d]** | | | | | | | | |
| Total, 18 to 64 years | 190,627 | 24,684 | 12.9 | 192,015 | 26,258 | 13.7 | 1,574 | 0.7 |
| With a disability | 14,644 | 3,655 | 25.0 | 14,935 | 4,165 | 27.9 | 510 | 2.9 |
| With no disability | 175,048 | 20,966 | 12.0 | 176,161 | 22,017 | 12.5 | 1,051 | 0.5 |

out of four African-American children (25.4%) and Hispanic children (26.9%) living in female-householder families lived below 50% of the poverty threshold, compared with 16.2% of non-Hispanic white children living in female-householder families.

The National School Lunch Program provides free or reduced-price meals to children from low-income families. Sometimes eligibility for the program is used as a rough guide to determine family income. Susan Aud, Mary Ann Fox, and Angelina KewalRamani note in *Status and Trends*

**TABLE 5.4**

**People and families in poverty by selected characteristics, 2009 and 2010** [CONTINUED]

[Numbers in thousands]

| Characteristic | 2009 | | | 2010 | | | Change in poverty (2010 less 2009)[a] | |
| --- | --- | --- | --- | --- | --- | --- | --- | --- |
| | Total | Below poverty | | Total | Below poverty | | Number | Percent |
| | | Number | Percent | | Number | Percent | | |
| **Families** | | | | | | | | |
| Total | 78,867 | 8,792 | 11.1 | 78,633 | 9,221 | 11.7 | 429 | 0.6 |
| **Type of family** | | | | | | | | |
| Married-couple | 58,428 | 3,409 | 5.8 | 58,047 | 3,596 | 6.2 | 188 | 0.4 |
| Female householder, no husband present | 14,857 | 4,441 | 29.9 | 15,026 | 4,745 | 31.6 | 304 | 1.7 |
| Male householder, no wife present | 5,582 | 942 | 16.9 | 5,560 | 880 | 15.8 | −62 | −1.1 |

—Represents or rounds to zero.

[a]Details may not sum to totals because of rounding.

[b]Federal surveys now give respondents the option of reporting more than one race. Therefore, two basic ways of defining a race group are possible. A group such as Asian may be defined as those who reported Asian and no other race (the race-alone or single-race concept) or as those who reported Asian regardless of whether they also reported another race (the race-alone-or-in-combination concept). This table shows data using the first approach (race alone). The use of the single-race population does not imply that it is the preferred method of presenting or analyzing data. The Census Bureau uses a variety of approaches. Information on people who reported more than one race, such as white and American Indian and Alaska Native or Asian and black or African American, is available from the Census 2010 through American FactFinder. About 2.9 percent of people reported more than one race in Census 2010. Data for American Indians and Alaska Natives, Native Hawaiians and other Pacific Islanders, and those reporting two or more races are not shown separately.

[c]The "outside metropolitan statistical areas" category includes both micropolitan statistical areas and territory outside of metropolitan and micropolitan statistical areas.

[d]The sum of those with and without a disability does not equal the total because disability status is not defined for individuals in the armed forces.

SOURCE: Carmen DeNavas-Walt, Bernadette D. Proctor, and Jessica C. Smith, "Table 4. People and Families in Poverty by Selected Characteristics: 2009 and 2010," in *Income, Poverty, and Health Insurance Coverage in the United States: 2010*, U.S. Census Bureau, September 2011, http://www.census.gov/prod/2011pubs/p60-239.pdf (accessed December 11, 2011).

---

*in the Education of Racial and Ethnic Groups* (July 2010, http://nces.ed.gov/pubs2010/2010015.pdf) that nationwide 48% of all fourth graders were eligible for free or reduced-price lunches in 2009. The percentages of African-American (74%) and Hispanic (77%) fourth graders who were eligible for these lunches were two and a half times the percentage of white (29%) fourth graders who were eligible. Also, a high proportion (68%) of Native American and Alaskan Native students were eligible. A third (34%) of Asian and Pacific Islander fourth graders were eligible for the reduced-price lunches.

The percentage of students who were eligible for the National School Lunch Program also varied by where they lived. African-American and Hispanic fourth graders who lived in a central city (80% and 82%, respectively), a town (83% and 84%, respectively), or a rural area (72% in both cases) were more likely than fourth graders who lived in the suburbs (65% and 70%, respectively) to be eligible for a free or reduced-price lunch—although all rates were significantly higher than average. (See Figure 5.2.) Asian and Pacific Islander fourth graders were the most likely to be eligible if they lived in a central city or a town, where 45% and 41% were eligible, respectively, rather than in the suburbs or a rural area, where only 25% and 23% were eligible, respectively. Native American and Alaskan Native fourth graders who lived in rural areas, including reservations, were the most likely to be eligible for the program. Almost three-quarters (72%) of Native American and Alaskan Native fourth graders in rural areas, compared with a little over half (52%) of Native American and Alaskan Native fourth graders in the suburbs, were eligible for a free or reduced-price lunch.

**The Haves and Have-Nots**

Lydia Saad of the Gallup Organization notes in *More Americans Say U.S. a Nation of Haves and Have-Nots* (July 11, 2008, http://www.gallup.com/poll/108769/More-Americans-Say-US-Nation-Haves-HaveNots.aspx) that in 2008 African-Americans were much more likely than non-Hispanic whites to believe that American society is divided into two groups: the haves and have-nots. Two-thirds (72%) of African-Americans answered that society is divided, whereas only 45% of non-Hispanic whites did. What is surprising, considering Hispanics' experience of lower income and higher poverty rates than non-Hispanic whites in the United States, Hispanics were only slightly more likely than non-Hispanic whites to answer that society is divided into the haves and have-nots. Only 49% of Hispanics said they believe society is divided; this was sharply up from a 2006 poll, however, perhaps reflecting the Hispanic experience of the recession that began in late 2007.

Part of the explanation for Hispanics' relative optimism might lie in their recent immigration experience. In "The Optimistic Immigrant: Among Latinos, the Recently Arrived Have the Most Hope for the Future" (May 30, 2006, http://pewresearch.org/pubs/28/the-optimistic-immigrant), Gabriel Escobar of the Pew Research Center points out what has been a historic truism in American society: that first-generation immigrants to the United States expect their children to have better opportunities than they have at present. Escobar notes that "Hispanics in general, and Hispanic immigrants in particular, are more inclined than blacks or whites to take an upbeat view about one of the most enduring tenets of the American dream—the idea that each

TABLE 5.5

**People with income below specified ratios of their poverty thresholds, by selected characteristics, 2010**

[Numbers in thousands]

| Characteristic | Total | Income-to-poverty ratio | | | | | | | |
| | | Under 0.50 | | Under 1.25 | | Under 1.50 | | Under 2.00 | |
| | | Number | Percent | Number | Percent | Number | Percent | Number | Percent |
| **All people** | 305,688 | 20,466 | 6.7 | 60,443 | 19.8 | 75,291 | 24.6 | 103,645 | 33.9 |
| **Age** | | | | | | | | | |
| Under 18 years | 74,494 | 7,369 | 9.9 | 20,741 | 27.8 | 24,853 | 33.4 | 32,467 | 43.6 |
| 18 to 24 years | 29,651 | 3,404 | 11.5 | 8,101 | 27.3 | 9,685 | 32.7 | 12,501 | 42.2 |
| 25 to 34 years | 41,584 | 2,993 | 7.2 | 8,203 | 19.7 | 10,220 | 24.6 | 14,141 | 34.0 |
| 35 to 44 years | 39,842 | 2,206 | 5.5 | 6,549 | 16.4 | 8,196 | 20.6 | 11,561 | 29.0 |
| 45 to 54 years | 43,954 | 2,001 | 4.6 | 6,147 | 14.0 | 7,702 | 17.5 | 10,813 | 24.6 |
| 55 to 59 years | 19,554 | 795 | 4.1 | 2,513 | 12.9 | 3,110 | 15.9 | 4,315 | 22.1 |
| 60 to 64 years | 17,430 | 708 | 4.1 | 2,415 | 13.9 | 3,052 | 17.5 | 4,297 | 24.7 |
| 65 years and older | 39,179 | 991 | 2.5 | 5,774 | 14.7 | 8,472 | 21.6 | 13,549 | 34.6 |
| **Race* and Hispanic origin** | | | | | | | | | |
| White | 243,013 | 13,315 | 5.5 | 42,298 | 17.4 | 53,446 | 22.0 | 75,297 | 31.0 |
| White, not Hispanic | 197,203 | 8,420 | 4.3 | 26,490 | 13.4 | 34,403 | 17.4 | 50,304 | 25.5 |
| Black | 38,965 | 5,254 | 13.5 | 13,237 | 34.0 | 15,715 | 40.3 | 20,005 | 51.3 |
| Asian | 14,324 | 834 | 5.8 | 2,219 | 15.5 | 2,820 | 19.7 | 4,056 | 28.3 |
| Hispanic (any race) | 49,869 | 5,460 | 10.9 | 17,299 | 34.7 | 20,816 | 41.7 | 27,243 | 54.6 |
| **Family status** | | | | | | | | | |
| In families | 249,855 | 13,749 | 5.5 | 43,705 | 17.5 | 54,587 | 21.8 | 76,733 | 30.7 |
| Householder | 78,633 | 3,964 | 5.0 | 12,217 | 15.5 | 15,443 | 19.6 | 22,091 | 28.1 |
| Related children under 18 | 73,227 | 6,927 | 9.5 | 19,990 | 27.3 | 24,002 | 32.8 | 31,497 | 43.0 |
| Related children under 6 | 25,096 | 2,911 | 11.6 | 7,858 | 31.3 | 9,207 | 36.7 | 11,796 | 47.0 |
| In unrelated subfamilies | 1,650 | 460 | 27.9 | 875 | 53.0 | 1,031 | 62.5 | 1,206 | 73.1 |
| Unrelated individuals | 54,183 | 6,257 | 11.5 | 15,863 | 29.3 | 19,673 | 36.3 | 25,705 | 47.4 |
| Male | 26,745 | 3,086 | 11.5 | 7,296 | 27.3 | 8,908 | 33.3 | 11,666 | 43.6 |
| Female | 27,438 | 3,170 | 11.6 | 8,568 | 31.2 | 10,766 | 39.2 | 14,039 | 51.2 |

*Federal surveys now give respondents the option of reporting more than one race. Therefore, two basic ways of defining a race group are possible. A group such as Asian may be defined as those who reported Asian and no other race (the race-alone or single-race concept) or as those who reported Asian regardless of whether they also reported another race (the race-alone-or-in-combination concept). This table shows data using the first approach (race alone). The use of the single-race population does not imply that it is the preferred method of presenting or analyzing data. The Census Bureau uses a variety of approaches. Information on people who reported more than one race, such as white and American Indian and Alaska Native or Asian and black or African American, is available from Census 2010 through American FactFinder. About 2.9 percent of people reported more than one race in Census 2010. Data for American Indians and Alaska Natives, Native Hawaiians and other Pacific Islanders, and those reporting two or more races are not shown separately.

Note: Details may not sum to totals because of rounding.

SOURCE: Carmen DeNavas-Walt, Bernadette D. Proctor, and Jessica C. Smith, "Table 6. People with Income below Specified Ratios of Their Poverty Thresholds by Selected Characteristics: 2010," in *Income, Poverty, and Health Insurance Coverage in the United States: 2010*, U.S. Census Bureau, September 2011, http://www.census.gov/prod/2011pubs/p60-239.pdf (accessed December 11, 2011)

generation will do better in life than the one that preceded it." Part of the explanation for this positive view lies in the general optimism of immigrants. Immigrants take on the challenge to move to an entirely new country because they strongly believe in their hope for the future.

## GOVERNMENT PROGRAMS

Because minorities are disproportionately poor, they have long accounted for a major portion of the welfare rolls across the United States. The U.S. government offers various forms of assistance to people living with economic hardship. Some of these programs are federally run, and others are run at the state level. In many cases states run federally mandated government programs, which can make tracking them complicated.

In 1996 Congress enacted the Personal Responsibility and Work Opportunity Reconciliation Act to reform the welfare system. The primary goal of the legislation was to get as many people as possible into the paid labor force and off the welfare rolls. The law set limits on how long people could receive welfare benefits. Aid to Families with Dependent Children, a guaranteed assistance program for low-income families, was eliminated and replaced in 1996 with the Temporary Assistance for Needy Families (TANF) program. The U.S. House of Representatives Committee on Ways and Means reports in *The Green Book* (2011, http://greenbook.waysandmeans.house.gov/2011/chapters) that the number of families receiving welfare had dropped from over 5 million in 1994 to 1.8 million in 2009, a decrease of 64.4%.

Gil Crouse, Susan Hauan, and Annette Waters Rogers of the U.S. Department of Health and Human Services (HHS) note in *Indicators of Welfare Dependence, Annual Report to Congress, 2008* (2008, http://aspe.hhs.gov/hsp/indicators08/) that in 2005, 32.9% of all non-Hispanic African-Americans received some portion of their total annual family income from means-tested assistance programs, which include TANF,

TABLE 5.6

**Percentage of related children under age 18 living below selected poverty levels, by age, family structure, race, and Hispanic origin, selected years 1980–2009**

| Characteristic | 1980 | 1985 | 1990 | 1995 | 2000 | 2005 | 2006 | 2007 | 2008 | 2009 |
|---|---|---|---|---|---|---|---|---|---|---|
| **Below 100% poverty** | | | | | | | | | | |
| **Related children\*** | | | | | | | | | | |
| Children in all families, total | 17.9 | 20.1 | 19.9 | 20.2 | 15.6 | 17.1 | 16.9 | 17.6 | 18.5 | 20.1 |
| Related children ages 0–5 | 20.3 | 22.6 | 23.0 | 23.7 | 17.8 | 20.0 | 20.0 | 20.8 | 21.3 | 23.8 |
| Related children ages 6–17 | 16.8 | 18.8 | 18.2 | 18.3 | 14.5 | 15.7 | 15.4 | 16.0 | 17.1 | 18.2 |
| White, non-Hispanic | 11.3 | 12.3 | 11.6 | 10.6 | 8.5 | — | — | — | — | — |
| White-alone, non-Hispanic | — | — | — | — | — | 9.5 | 9.5 | 9.7 | 10.0 | 11.2 |
| Black | 42.1 | 43.1 | 44.2 | 41.5 | 30.9 | — | — | — | — | — |
| Black-alone | — | — | — | — | — | 34.2 | 33.0 | 34.3 | 34.4 | 35.3 |
| Hispanic | 33.0 | 39.6 | 37.7 | 39.3 | 27.6 | 27.7 | 26.6 | 28.3 | 30.3 | 32.5 |
| Children in married-couple families, total | — | — | 10.2 | 10.0 | 8.0 | 8.5 | 8.1 | 8.5 | 9.9 | 11.0 |
| Related children ages 0–5 | — | — | 11.6 | 11.1 | 8.7 | 9.9 | 9.4 | 9.5 | 11.0 | 13.4 |
| Related children ages 6–17 | — | — | 9.5 | 9.4 | 7.6 | 7.7 | 7.5 | 8.0 | 9.2 | 9.8 |
| White, non-Hispanic | — | — | 6.8 | 5.9 | 4.7 | — | — | — | — | — |
| White-alone, non-Hispanic | — | — | — | — | — | 4.5 | 4.3 | 4.7 | 5.3 | 6.0 |
| Black | — | — | 18.1 | 12.8 | 8.8 | — | — | — | — | — |
| Black-alone | — | — | — | — | — | 12.5 | 12.0 | 11.0 | 11.0 | 15.2 |
| Hispanic | — | — | 26.5 | 28.4 | 20.7 | 20.1 | 18.5 | 19.2 | 22.1 | 23.9 |
| Children in female-householder families, no husband present, total | 50.8 | 53.6 | 53.4 | 50.3 | 40.1 | 42.8 | 42.1 | 43.0 | 43.5 | 44.4 |
| Related children ages 0–5 | 65.2 | 65.8 | 65.5 | 61.8 | 50.3 | 52.9 | 52.7 | 54.0 | 53.3 | 54.3 |
| Related children ages 6–17 | 45.5 | 48.3 | 47.3 | 44.6 | 35.7 | 38.3 | 37.4 | 37.8 | 38.7 | 39.6 |
| White, non-Hispanic | — | — | 39.6 | 33.5 | 28.0 | — | — | — | — | — |
| White-alone, non-Hispanic | — | — | — | — | — | 33.1 | 32.9 | 32.4 | 31.7 | 33.5 |
| Black | 64.8 | 66.9 | 64.7 | 61.6 | 49.3 | — | — | — | — | — |
| Black-alone | — | — | — | — | — | 50.2 | 49.7 | 50.4 | 51.9 | 50.6 |
| Hispanic | 65.0 | 72.4 | 68.4 | 65.7 | 49.8 | 50.2 | 47.2 | 51.6 | 51.9 | 52.2 |
| **Below 50% poverty** | | | | | | | | | | |
| **Related children\*** | | | | | | | | | | |
| Children in all families, total | — | — | 8.3 | 7.9 | 6.3 | 7.2 | 7.1 | 7.4 | 8.1 | 8.7 |
| Related children ages 0–5 | — | — | 10.3 | 10.4 | 7.9 | 8.9 | 9.2 | 9.6 | 10.1 | 11.0 |
| Related children ages 6–17 | — | — | 7.2 | 6.6 | 5.5 | 6.4 | 6.0 | 6.3 | 7.0 | 7.6 |
| White, non-Hispanic | — | — | 4.4 | 3.4 | 3.3 | — | — | — | — | — |
| White-alone, non-Hispanic | — | — | — | — | — | 3.6 | 3.9 | 3.9 | 4.1 | 4.5 |
| Black | — | — | 22.3 | 20.1 | 14.8 | — | — | — | — | — |
| Black-alone | — | — | — | — | — | 16.9 | 15.7 | 17.1 | 17.1 | 17.3 |
| Hispanic | — | — | 13.5 | 15.6 | 9.4 | 10.8 | 10.0 | 10.5 | 12.3 | 13.4 |
| Children in married-couple families, total | — | — | 2.7 | 2.6 | 2.2 | 2.4 | 2.2 | 2.6 | 3.2 | 3.6 |
| Related children ages 0–5 | — | — | 3.1 | 2.9 | 2.2 | 2.8 | 2.8 | 2.8 | 3.7 | 4.4 |
| Related children ages 6–17 | — | — | 2.4 | 2.5 | 2.2 | 2.1 | 1.9 | 2.5 | 2.9 | 3.2 |
| White, non-Hispanic | — | — | 1.9 | 1.4 | 1.5 | — | — | — | — | — |
| White-alone, non-Hispanic | — | — | — | — | — | 1.2 | 1.2 | 1.4 | 1.8 | 1.8 |
| Black | — | — | 3.9 | 2.9 | 3.1 | — | — | — | — | — |
| Black-alone | — | — | — | — | — | 4.5 | 2.9 | 4.4 | 4.4 | 6.0 |
| Hispanic | — | — | 6.7 | 8.6 | 4.4 | 5.2 | 4.7 | 5.4 | 6.3 | 7.3 |
| Children in female-householder families, no husband present, total | — | — | 27.7 | 23.8 | 18.9 | 21.8 | 21.1 | 21.2 | 22.3 | 22.2 |
| Related children ages 0–5 | — | — | 37.0 | 33.7 | 27.9 | 29.1 | 29.5 | 30.2 | 30.7 | 29.6 |
| Related children ages 6–17 | — | — | 23.0 | 18.9 | 15.2 | 18.5 | 17.4 | 17.0 | 18.3 | 18.7 |
| White, non-Hispanic | — | — | 19.1 | 13.1 | 12.0 | — | — | — | — | — |
| White-alone, non-Hispanic | — | — | — | — | — | 15.2 | 16.1 | 15.9 | 14.6 | 16.2 |
| Black | — | — | 36.8 | 32.2 | 24.2 | — | — | — | — | — |
| Black-alone | — | — | — | — | — | 26.1 | 26.0 | 25.9 | 26.8 | 25.4 |
| Hispanic | — | — | 31.9 | 32.5 | 24.8 | 27.7 | 22.9 | 24.4 | 28.5 | 26.9 |

—Not available.

\*Related children are persons ages 0–17 who are related to the householder by birth, marriage, or adoption, but are not themselves householders, spouses, or reference persons.

Notes: The 2004 data have been revised to reflect a correction to the weights in the 2005 Annual Social and Economic Supplement (ASEC). Data for 1999, 2000, and 2001 use Census 2000 population controls. Data for 2000 onward are from the expanded Current Population Survey (CPS) sample. The poverty level is based on money income and does not include noncash benefits, such as food stamps. Poverty thresholds reflect family size and composition and are adjusted each year using the annual average consumer price index level. In 2009, the poverty threshold for a two-parent, two-child family was $21,756. The levels shown here are derived from the ratio of the family's income to the family's poverty threshold.

SOURCE:: Adapted from "Table ECON1.A. Child Poverty: Percentage of All Children and Related Children Ages 0–17 Living below Selected Poverty Levels by Selected Characteristics, Selected Years 1980–2009," in *America's Children: Key National Indicators of Well-Being, 2011*, Federal Interagency Forum on Child and Family Statistics, July 2011, http://www.childstats.gov/pdf/ac2011/ac_11.pdf (accessed December 11, 2011)

Supplementary Security Income, and food stamps. (See Table 5.7.) One out of four (24%) Hispanics received means-tested assistance. Only 10.1% of non-Hispanic whites received such assistance. Moreover, 10.2% of non-Hispanic African-Americans received more than half of their total annual family income from means-tested assistance programs, compared with only 5.7% of Hispanics and only 2.2% of non-Hispanic whites.

**FIGURE 5.2**

**Percentage of public school 4th-graders eligible for free or reduced-price lunch, by school location and race and Hispanic origin, 2009**

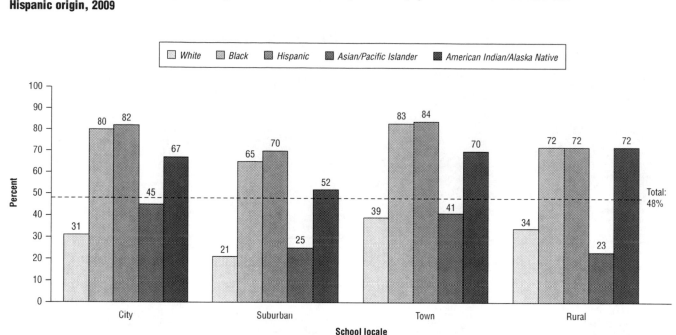

Notes: To be eligible for the national school lunch program, a student must be from a household with an income at or below 185 percent of the poverty level for reduced-price lunch or at or below 130 percent of the poverty level for free lunch. Race categories exclude persons of Hispanic ethnicity.

SOURCE: Susan Aud, Mary Ann Fox, and Angelina KewalRamani, "Figure 7.5a. Percentage of Public School 4th-Graders Eligible for Free or Reduced-Price Lunch, by School Locale and Race/Ethnicity: 2009," in *Status and Trends in the Education of Racial and Ethnic Groups*, U.S. Department of Education, National Center for Education Statistics, Institute of Education Sciences, 2010, http://nces.ed.gov/pubs2010/2010015.pdf (accessed November 30, 2011)

---

**TABLE 5.7**

**Percentage of total family income from means-tested assistance programs, by race, Hispanic origin, and age, 2005**

| | 0% | > 0% and ≤ 25% | > 25% and ≤ 50% | > 50% and ≤ 75% | > 75% and ≤ 100% | Total > 50% |
|---|---|---|---|---|---|---|
| **All persons** | 84.7 | 8.9 | 2.6 | 1.1 | 2.7 | 3.8 |
| **Racial/ethnic categories** | | | | | | |
| Non-Hispanic white | 89.9 | 6.4 | 1.4 | 0.6 | 1.6 | 2.2 |
| Non-Hispanic black | 67.1 | 15.9 | 6.8 | 3.2 | 7.0 | 10.2 |
| Hispanic | 76.0 | 14.1 | 4.2 | 1.7 | 3.9 | 5.7 |
| **Age categories** | | | | | | |
| Children ages 0–5 | 74.4 | 13.0 | 5.2 | 2.4 | 5.0 | 7.4 |
| Children ages 6–10 | 77.4 | 11.9 | 4.6 | 1.9 | 4.2 | 6.1 |
| Children ages 11–15 | 79.1 | 11.4 | 4.0 | 1.9 | 3.7 | 5.5 |
| Women ages 16–64 | 84.6 | 8.9 | 2.5 | 1.1 | 2.9 | 4.0 |
| Men ages 16–64 | 88.3 | 7.7 | 1.6 | 0.6 | 1.8 | 2.4 |
| Adults ages 65 and over | 89.7 | 6.3 | 1.8 | 0.7 | 1.5 | 2.2 |
| **Family categories** | | | | | | |
| Persons in married-couple families | 91.2 | 6.4 | 1.2 | 0.4 | 0.7 | 1.1 |
| Persons in female-headed families | 55.5 | 20.8 | 9.6 | 4.6 | 9.5 | 14.0 |
| Persons in male-headed families | 77.9 | 13.9 | 3.9 | 1.5 | 2.8 | 4.3 |
| Unrelated persons | 87.8 | 6.4 | 1.2 | 0.6 | 4.1 | 4.7 |

Notes: Means-tested assistance includes Temporary Assistance for Needy Families (TANF), Supplemental Security Income (SSI), and food stamps. Total >50% includes all persons with more than 50 percent of their total annual family income from these means-tested programs. Income includes cash income and the value of food stamps. Spouses are not present in the female-headed and male-headed family categories. Persons of Hispanic ethnicity may be of any race. Beginning in 2002, estimates for whites and blacks are for persons reporting a single race only. Persons who reported more than one race are included in the total of all persons but are not shown under any race category. Due to small sample size, American Indians/Alaska Natives, Asians and Native Hawaiians/other Pacific Islanders are included in the total for all persons but are not shown.

SOURCE: Gil Crouse, Susan Hauan, and Annette Waters Rogers, "Table IND 1a. Percentage of Total Income from Means-Tested Assistance Programs by Selected Characteristics: 2005," in *Indicators of Welfare Dependence, Annual Report to Congress, 2008*, U.S. Department of Health and Human Services, 2007, http://aspe.hhs.gov/hsp/indicators08/ch2.pdf (accessed December 11, 2011)

Therefore, Crouse, Hauan, and Waters Rogers indicate that non-Hispanic African-Americans are the most likely to receive means-tested assistance, especially food stamps—15.1% of non-Hispanic African-Americans received food stamps in 2005, compared with 8.5% of Hispanics and 4.1% of non-Hispanic whites. (See Table 5.8.) In addition, non-Hispanic African-Americans are more likely than Hispanics or non-Hispanic whites to receive assistance from multiple programs. Whereas a quarter (24.9%) of non-Hispanic African-Americans received means-tested assistance in 2005, 4.4% of them received both TANF and food stamps, compared with 2.7% of Hispanics and 0.7% of non-Hispanic whites.

The high number of female-headed families in the non-Hispanic African-American community may be part of the explanation for the high rate of means-tested assistance receipt. According to Crouse, Hauan, and Waters Rogers, more than four out of 10 (44.5%) individuals in female-headed families received means-tested assistance in 2005, compared with only 8.8% of individuals in married-couple families. In addition, individuals in female-headed families were the most likely to receive more than half of the annual family income from these programs—14% did so, compared with only 1.1% of individuals living in married-couple families. These percentages suggest that it is particularly difficult for single women with children to make ends meet without turning to government programs for assistance.

In spite of the work requirements of the welfare law, earnings contributed substantially less to the total family income of non-Hispanic African-American families than they did to non-Hispanic white or Hispanic families in 2005. Among families in poverty, earnings contributed only 35.3% of the total family income of non-Hispanic African-American families, but 41.9% of the total family income of non-Hispanic white families and 62.4% of the total family income of Hispanic families. (See Table 5.9.) Among families in extreme poverty, earnings contributed only 18.9% of the total family income of non-Hispanic African-American families, but 25.5% of the total family income of non-Hispanic white families and 32.7% of the total family income of Hispanic families.

The TANF program has been criticized since its inception in 1996. Critics maintain that the drop in the number of recipients cannot measure success. Caseloads initially decreased simply because the eligibility requirements were stiffened. As a result, many immigrants, especially Hispanics who were working poor, were denied aid, adversely affecting their children, who were U.S. citizens. Moreover, the type of work available to individuals on welfare was

**TABLE 5.8**

Percentage of population receiving assistance from Temporary Assistance for Needy Families (TANF), Food Stamps (FS), and/or Supplemental Security Income (SSI), by race, Hispanic origin, and age, 2005

| | | One program only | | | Two programs | |
| --- | --- | --- | --- | --- | --- | --- |
| | Any receipt | TANF | FS | SSI | TANF & FS | FS & SSI |
| **All persons** | 10.2 | 0.2 | 6.2 | 1.3 | 1.5 | 1.2 |
| **Racial/ethnic categories** | | | | | | |
| Non-Hispanic white | 6.7 | 0.1 | 4.1 | 0.9 | 0.7 | 0.8 |
| Non-Hispanic black | 24.9 | 0.5 | 15.1 | 2.0 | 4.4 | 2.9 |
| Hispanic | 14.6 | 0.4 | 8.5 | 1.7 | 2.7 | 1.3 |
| **Age categories** | | | | | | |
| Children ages 0–5 | 20.7 | 0.6 | 13.4 | 0.7 | 5.3 | 0.7 |
| Children ages 6–10 | 17.6 | 0.5 | 11.6 | 0.7 | 4.2 | 0.6 |
| Children ages 11–15 | 15.9 | 0.7 | 10.2 | 0.9 | 3.3 | 0.8 |
| Women ages 16–64 | 9.6 | 0.1 | 6.1 | 0.9 | 1.2 | 1.3 |
| Men ages 16–64 | 6.3 | 0.1 | 3.8 | 1.2 | 0.4 | 0.9 |
| Adults ages 65 and over | 8.0 | 0.0 | 2.4 | 3.1 | 0.0 | 2.4 |
| **Family categories** | | | | | | |
| Persons in married-couple families | 4.8 | 0.1 | 3.0 | 0.7 | 0.5 | 0.4 |
| Persons in female-headed families | 33.4 | 0.7 | 20.1 | 2.5 | 7.4 | 2.7 |
| Persons in male-headed families | 13.9 | 0.3 | 8.2 | 2.2 | 1.9 | 1.3 |
| Unrelated persons | 9.4 | 0.0 | 4.9 | 1.8 | 0.0 | 2.7 |

Notes: Categories are mutually exclusive. SSI receipt is based on individual receipt; AFDC/TANF and food stamp receipt are based on the full recipient unit. In practice, individuals do not tend to receive both AFDC/TANF and SSI; hence, no individual receives benefits from all three programs. The percentage of individuals receiving assistance from any one program in an average month (shown here) is lower than the percentage residing in families receiving assistance at some point over the course of a year. Spouses are not present in the female-headed and male-headed family categories.

Persons of Hispanic ethnicity may be of any race. Beginning in 2002, estimates for whites and blacks are for persons reporting a single race only. Persons who reported more than one race are included in the total for all persons but are not shown under any race category. Due to small sample size, American Indians/Alaska Natives, Asians and Native Hawaiians/other Pacific Islanders are included in the total for all persons but are not shown separately.

SOURCE: Gil Crouse, Susan Hauan, and Annette Waters Rogers, "Table IND 5a. Percentage of Population Receiving Assistance from Multiple Means-Tested Assistance Programs by Selected Characteristics: 2005," in *Indicators of Welfare Dependence, Annual Report to Congress, 2008*, U.S. Department of Health and Human Services, 2007, http://aspe.hhs.gov/hsp/indicators08/ch2.pdf (accessed December 11, 2011)

**TABLE 5.9**

Percentage of total family income from various sources, by poverty status, race and Hispanic origin, 2005

| | <50% poverty | <100% of poverty | <200% of poverty | 200%+ of poverty | All persons |
|---|---|---|---|---|---|
| **All persons** | | | | | |
| TANF, SSI and food stamps | 58.5 | 32.5 | 10.4 | 0.2 | 1.1 |
| Earnings | 25.3 | 46.6 | 68.2 | 86.6 | 84.9 |
| Other income | 16.2 | 20.8 | 21.4 | 13.2 | 13.9 |
| **Racial/ethnic categories** | | | | | |
| Non-Hispanic white | | | | | |
| TANF, SSI and food stamps | 53.1 | 29.9 | 8.0 | 0.1 | 0.6 |
| Earnings | 25.5 | 41.9 | 62.7 | 85.6 | 84.3 |
| Other income | 21.4 | 28.3 | 29.4 | 14.3 | 15.1 |
| Non-Hispanic black | | | | | |
| TANF, SSI and food stamps | 66.3 | 43.5 | 17.9 | 0.5 | 4.0 |
| Earnings | 18.9 | 35.3 | 60.6 | 88.1 | 82.5 |
| Other income | 14.7 | 21.2 | 21.6 | 11.5 | 13.5 |
| Hispanic | | | | | |
| TANF, SSI and food stamps | 55.6 | 26.5 | 9.4 | 0.5 | 2.7 |
| Earnings | 32.7 | 62.4 | 81.5 | 91.6 | 89.1 |
| Other income | 11.7 | 11.1 | 9.0 | 7.9 | 8.2 |
| **Age categories** | | | | | |
| Children ages 0–5 | | | | | |
| TANF, SSI and food stamps | 65.5 | 37.2 | 13.5 | 0.2 | 2.3 |
| Earnings | 22.8 | 52.0 | 78.0 | 94.6 | 92.1 |
| Other income | 11.6 | 10.7 | 8.5 | 5.2 | 5.7 |
| Children ages 6–10 | | | | | |
| TANF, SSI and food stamps | 65.1 | 35.5 | 12.0 | 0.2 | 1.9 |
| Earnings | 20.7 | 50.2 | 77.4 | 93.7 | 91.3 |
| Other income | 14.2 | 14.3 | 10.6 | 6.2 | 6.8 |
| Children ages 11–15 | | | | | |
| TANF, SSI and food stamps | 61.8 | 36.1 | 12.5 | 0.1 | 1.7 |
| Earnings | 22.6 | 47.3 | 74.3 | 92.0 | 89.8 |
| Other income | 15.6 | 16.6 | 13.2 | 7.9 | 8.5 |
| Women ages 16–64 | | | | | |
| TANF, SSI and food stamps | 55.6 | 33.3 | 11.2 | 0.2 | 1.1 |
| Earnings | 26.6 | 46.3 | 71.4 | 89.1 | 87.7 |
| Other income | 17.8 | 20.5 | 17.5 | 10.7 | 11.2 |
| Men ages 16–64 | | | | | |
| TANF, SSI and food stamps | 48.0 | 27.4 | 8.0 | 0.2 | 0.7 |
| Earnings | 34.4 | 53.1 | 76.4 | 90.2 | 89.3 |
| Other income | 17.6 | 19.5 | 15.5 | 9.6 | 10.0 |
| Adults ages 65 and over | | | | | |
| TANF, SSI and food stamps | 37.2 | 21.4 | 6.5 | 0.3 | 1.0 |
| Earnings | 9.2 | 6.5 | 9.9 | 40.2 | 36.6 |
| Other income | 53.6 | 72.2 | 83.5 | 59.5 | 62.4 |
| **Family categories** | | | | | |
| Persons in married-couple families | | | | | |
| TANF, SSI and food stamps | 49.7 | 22.4 | 5.9 | 0.1 | 0.5 |
| Earnings | 35.0 | 62.0 | 77.0 | 87.6 | 86.9 |
| Other income | 15.3 | 15.6 | 17.1 | 12.3 | 12.6 |
| Persons in female-headed families | | | | | |
| TANF, SSI and food stamps | 66.9 | 45.2 | 21.7 | 1.0 | 6.9 |
| Earnings | 17.8 | 36.4 | 58.6 | 81.9 | 75.3 |
| Other income | 15.2 | 18.4 | 19.7 | 17.1 | 17.8 |
| Persons in male-headed families | | | | | |
| TANF, SSI and food stamps | 65.8 | 31.2 | 11.0 | 0.5 | 2.0 |
| Earnings | 21.0 | 50.7 | 72.1 | 87.3 | 85.2 |
| Other income | 13.2 | 18.0 | 16.9 | 12.2 | 12.8 |

Notes: Total income is total annual family income, including the value of food stamps. Other income is non-means-tested, non-earnings income such as child support, alimony, pensions, Social Security benefits, interest and dividends. Poverty status categories are not mutually exclusive. Spouses are not present in the female-headed and male-headed family categories. Persons of Hispanic ethnicity may be of any race. Beginning in 2002, estimates for whites and blacks are for persons reporting a single race only. Persons who reported more than one race are included in the total for all persons but are not shown under any race category. Due to small sample size, American Indians/Alaska Natives, Asians and Native Hawaiians/other Pacific Islanders are included in the total for all persons but are not shown separately.
TANF = Temporary Assistance for Needy Families
SSI = Supplemental Security Income

SOURCE: Gil Crouse, Susan Hauan, and Annette Waters Rogers, "Table IND 1c. Percentage of Total Income from Various Sources by Poverty Status and Selected Characteristics: 2005," in *Indicators of Welfare Dependence, Annual Report to Congress, 2008*, U.S. Department of Health and Human Services, 2007, http://aspe.hhs.gov/hsp/indicators08/ch2.pdf (accessed December 11, 2011)

generally low paying, offered no health insurance or other benefits, and did little to lift welfare-to-work participants above the poverty level. So, despite falling numbers of TANF recipients, rising poverty levels perhaps provide a more telling portrayal of the program's progress. (See Figure 5.1 and Table 5.4.)

The American Recovery and Reinvestment Act, which was signed into law by President Barack Obama (1961–) in February 2009, contained a provision for a TANF emergency fund of $5 billion for fiscal years 2009 and 2010. The HHS explains in "Questions and Answers on the American Recovery and Reinvestment Act of 2009 (Recovery Act)" (2012, http://www.hhs.gov/recovery/programs/tanf/tanf-faq.html) that states could apply for monies from the emergency fund to help meet increased need for TANF funding among their residents. The act also provided some relief for the TANF work requirements. In "Walking away from a Win-Win-Win: Subsidized Jobs Slated to End Soon Are Helping Families, Businesses, and Communities Weather the Recession" (September 2, 2010, http://www.cbpp.org/cms/index.cfm?fa=view&id=3274), Liz Schott and LaDonna Pavetti of the Center on Budget and Policy Priorities report that the emergency fund subsidized jobs in 37 states for nearly 250,000 otherwise unemployed individuals. Regardless, the TANF emergency fund was allowed to expire in September 2010. The U.S. Senate reauthorized the TANF program in November 2010 without reviving the emergency fund, despite continuing high unemployment levels.

# CHAPTER 6
# HEALTH

The demographic profiles of African-Americans, Hispanics, Asian-Americans, Pacific Islanders, Native Americans, and Alaskan Natives differ considerably from those of the majority population in the United States. Because a high percentage of minorities live in urban areas, they are exposed to a greater number of environmental hazards, including pollution, traffic hazards, substandard and/or overcrowded housing, and crime. Occupational risks are also greater for minorities because a greater percentage of them are employed in potentially dangerous jobs. Poverty, which is experienced disproportionately by African-Americans, Hispanics, and Native Americans and Alaskan Natives, leads to poor nutrition, poor housing conditions, and poor access to health care. In addition, the amount of stress that is involved in facing daily discrimination and changing cultural environments as well as the lack of resources for solving stressful situations can play a critical role in the mental and physical health of minority groups.

As a whole, Hispanics enjoy better health on a variety of measures than do non-Hispanic whites, despite Hispanics' disadvantaged position, higher poverty rates, lower educational attainment, and the obstacles to health care that they encounter. This is most likely due in part to the fact that Hispanics in the United States are younger than the non-Hispanic white population. According to the U.S. Census Bureau, in *The Hispanic Population in the United States: 2010* (2011, http://www.census.gov/population/www/socdemo/hispanic/cps2010.html), 34.9% of the Hispanic population was under the age of 18 years in 2010, compared with 20.9% of the non-Hispanic white population. (See Table 6.1.) Conversely, only 5.8% of Hispanics were aged 65 years and older, compared with 15.6% of non-Hispanic whites.

This age differential is partly due to the higher fertility rate of Hispanics and partly to their recent immigration status—younger people tend to immigrate. According to

2010 census data that were analyzed by the Pew Hispanic Center in *Statistical Portrait of Hispanics in the United States, 2010* (February 21, 2012, http://www.pewhispanic .org/files/2012/02/Statistical-Portrait-of-Hispanics-in-the-United-States-2010_Apr-3.pdf), in 2010, 30.2% of Hispanics in the United States were foreign born, compared with 12.9% of the larger U.S. population. In addition, first-generation immigrants tend to have more children than do other Americans. In 2010, 8.1% of Hispanic women aged 15 to 44 years had given birth, compared with just 5.9% of non-Hispanic white women.

## HEALTH CARE
### Quality of Care

In *National Healthcare Disparities Report, 2010* (March 2011, http://www.ahrq.gov/qual/nhdr10/nhdr10 .pdf), the U.S. Department of Health and Human Services (HHS) defines quality health care in this way: "Health care seeks to prevent, diagnose, and treat disease and to improve the physical and mental well-being of all Americans.... Quality health care delivers these services in ways that are safe, timely, patient centered, efficient, and equitable." In other words, health care does not vary in quality because of personal characteristics such as race or ethnicity.

The HHS focuses on 42 core measures of quality and six core measures of access to care to compare the health care that is received across racial and ethnic groups. It finds that minorities consistently receive a poorer quality of care than do non-Hispanic whites. In 2010 African-Americans received poorer quality of care than whites for 21 out of 48 (43.8%) core quality measures, Native Americans and Alaskan Natives for nine out of 24 (37.5%) core quality measures, and Asian-Americans for four out of 19 (21.1%) core quality measures. (See Figure 6.1.) Hispanics received lower quality of care than non-Hispanic whites for 24 out of 43 (55.8%) core quality measures. Poor people received

## TABLE 6.1

**Population by sex, age, Hispanic origin, and race, 2010**

[Numbers in thousands. Civilian noninstitutionalized population.[a]]

| Sex and age | Total | | Hispanic | | Hispanic origin and race[b] | | | | | |
|---|---|---|---|---|---|---|---|---|---|---|
| | | | | | Non-Hispanic | | | | | |
| | | | | | Total | | White alone | | All other races | |
| | Number | Percent | Number | Percent | Number | Percent | Number | Percent | Number | Percent |
| **Both sexes** | **304,280** | **100.0** | **48,901** | **100.0** | **255,379** | **100.0** | **197,436** | **100.0** | **57,942** | **100.0** |
| Under 15 years | 62,112 | 20.4 | 14,613 | 29.9 | 47,499 | 18.6 | 33,624 | 17.0 | 13,875 | 23.9 |
| 15 years and over | 242,168 | 79.6 | 34,289 | 70.1 | 207,879 | 81.4 | 163,812 | 83.0 | 44,067 | 76.1 |
| Under 16 years | 66,185 | 21.8 | 15,416 | 31.5 | 50,769 | 19.9 | 36,012 | 18.2 | 14,757 | 25.5 |
| 16 years and over | 238,095 | 78.2 | 33,486 | 68.5 | 204,610 | 80.1 | 161,424 | 81.8 | 43,185 | 74.5 |
| Under 18 years | 75,040 | 24.7 | 17,056 | 34.9 | 57,984 | 22.7 | 41,190 | 20.9 | 16,794 | 29.0 |
| 18 years and over | 229,240 | 75.3 | 31,845 | 65.1 | 197,395 | 77.3 | 156,247 | 79.1 | 41,148 | 71.0 |
| Under 21 years | 87,581 | 28.8 | 19,464 | 39.8 | 68,117 | 26.7 | 48,727 | 24.7 | 19,390 | 33.5 |
| 21 years and over | 216,699 | 71.2 | 29,437 | 60.2 | 187,261 | 73.3 | 148,709 | 75.3 | 38,553 | 66.5 |
| Under 65 years | 265,667 | 87.3 | 46,087 | 94.2 | 219,580 | 86.0 | 166,701 | 84.4 | 52,879 | 91.3 |
| 65 years and over | 38,613 | 12.7 | 2,815 | 5.8 | 35,799 | 14.0 | 30,736 | 15.6 | 5,063 | 8.7 |
| **Male** | **149,485** | **100.0** | **25,147** | **100.0** | **124,338** | **100.0** | **97,005** | **100.0** | **27,333** | **100.0** |
| Under 15 years | 31,757 | 21.2 | 7,468 | 29.7 | 24,290 | 19.5 | 17,242 | 17.8 | 7,047 | 25.8 |
| 15 years and over | 117,728 | 78.8 | 17,679 | 70.3 | 100,049 | 80.5 | 79,763 | 82.2 | 20,286 | 74.2 |
| Under 16 years | 33,833 | 22.6 | 7,881 | 31.3 | 25,951 | 20.9 | 18,468 | 19.0 | 7,483 | 27.4 |
| 16 years and over | 115,653 | 77.4 | 17,265 | 68.7 | 98,387 | 79.1 | 78,537 | 81.0 | 19,850 | 72.6 |
| Under 18 years | 38,324 | 25.6 | 8,709 | 34.6 | 29,615 | 23.8 | 21,128 | 21.8 | 8,487 | 31.0 |
| 18 years and over | 111,162 | 74.4 | 16,438 | 65.4 | 94,723 | 76.2 | 75,877 | 78.2 | 18,846 | 69.0 |
| Under 21 years | 44,688 | 29.9 | 9,972 | 39.7 | 34,716 | 27.9 | 24,919 | 25.7 | 9,797 | 35.8 |
| 21 years and over | 104,797 | 70.1 | 15,175 | 60.3 | 89,622 | 72.1 | 72,086 | 74.3 | 17,536 | 64.2 |
| Under 65 years | 132,692 | 88.8 | 23,935 | 95.2 | 108,758 | 87.5 | 83,456 | 86.0 | 25,301 | 92.6 |
| 65 years and over | 16,793 | 11.2 | 1,212 | 4.8 | 15,581 | 12.5 | 13,549 | 14.0 | 2,032 | 7.4 |
| **Female** | **154,795** | **100.0** | **23,755** | **100.0** | **131,040** | **100.0** | **100,431** | **100.0** | **30,609** | **100.0** |
| Under 15 years | 30,355 | 19.6 | 7,145 | 30.1 | 23,210 | 17.7 | 16,382 | 16.3 | 6,828 | 22.3 |
| 15 years and over | 124,440 | 80.4 | 16,609 | 69.9 | 107,831 | 82.3 | 84,049 | 83.7 | 23,781 | 77.7 |
| Under 16 years | 32,352 | 20.9 | 7,534 | 31.7 | 24,818 | 18.9 | 17,544 | 17.5 | 7,274 | 23.8 |
| 16 years and over | 122,442 | 79.1 | 16,220 | 68.3 | 106,222 | 81.1 | 82,887 | 82.5 | 23,335 | 76.2 |
| Under 18 years | 36,716 | 23.7 | 8,347 | 35.1 | 28,369 | 21.6 | 20,061 | 20.0 | 8,307 | 27.1 |
| 18 years and over | 118,079 | 76.3 | 15,407 | 64.9 | 102,672 | 78.4 | 80,369 | 80.0 | 22,302 | 72.9 |
| Under 21 years | 42,893 | 27.7 | 9,492 | 40.0 | 33,401 | 25.5 | 23,808 | 23.7 | 9,593 | 31.3 |
| 21 years and over | 111,902 | 72.3 | 14,263 | 60.0 | 97,639 | 74.5 | 76,622 | 76.3 | 21,016 | 68.7 |
| Under 65 years | 132,974 | 85.9 | 22,152 | 93.3 | 110,822 | 84.6 | 83,244 | 82.9 | 27,578 | 90.1 |
| 65 years and over | 21,820 | 14.1 | 1,602 | 6.7 | 20,218 | 15.4 | 17,186 | 17.1 | 3,032 | 9.9 |

[a]Plus armed forces living off post or with their families on post.

[b]Hispanic refers to people whose origin is Mexican, Puerto Rican, Cuban, Spanish-speaking Central or South American countries, or other Hispanic/Latino, regardless of race.

SOURCE: Adapted from "Table 1. Population by Sex, Age, Hispanic Origin, and Race: 2010," in *The Hispanic Population in the United States: 2010*, U.S. Census Bureau, 2011, http://www.census.gov/population/www/socdemo/hispanic/cps2010.html (accessed December 16, 2011)

lower quality of care than high-income people (family incomes above 400% of the poverty level) in 19 out of 23 (82.6%) core quality measures. (It should be noted that people from minority groups are disproportionally poor.)

### Access to Care

In *National Healthcare Disparities Report, 2010*, the HHS measures access to health care, finding that minorities, particularly those of low socioeconomic status, face barriers to accessing health care that make receiving basic health services a struggle. Access is measured in several ways, including ability to get into the health care system, to get care within the health care system, and to find providers to meet their needs.

The HHS finds that in 2010 Hispanics had worse access to care than non-Hispanic whites for five out of six (83.3%) core access measures. (See Figure 6.2.) African-

Americans had worse access to care for two out of six (33.3%) core access measures, and Asian-Americans and Native Americans and Alaskan Natives had worse access to care for one out of six (16.7%) core access measures. Part of these differences in access to care for minority groups had to do with socioeconomics; people below the poverty level had worse access to care than did high-income people for every one of the access measures.

The HHS notes that disparities in health care are changing slowly or not at all. Across 179 measures of health care quality that were tracked between 2001 and 2008, approximately two-thirds showed modest improvement. Access, however, was actually worsening in 40.9% of the 22 measures of health care access and another 27.3% of the measures had not improved. Fewer than one out of five (20%) health care disparities faced by African-Americans, Native Americans and Alaskan Natives, and Hispanics had

**FIGURE 6.1**

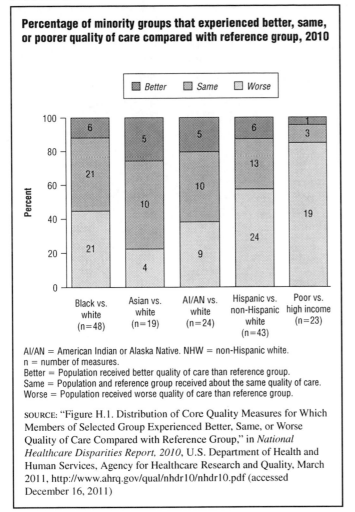

Percentage of minority groups that experienced better, same, or poorer quality of care compared with reference group, 2010

☒ Better  ☒ Same  ☐ Worse

AI/AN = American Indian or Alaska Native. NHW = non-Hispanic white.
n = number of measures.
Better = Population received better quality of care than reference group.
Same = Population and reference group received about the same quality of care.
Worse = Population received worse quality of care than reference group.

SOURCE: "Figure H.1. Distribution of Core Quality Measures for Which Members of Selected Group Experienced Better, Same, or Worse Quality of Care Compared with Reference Group," in *National Healthcare Disparities Report, 2010*, U.S. Department of Health and Human Services, Agency for Healthcare Research and Quality, March 2011, http://www.ahrq.gov/qual/nhdr10/nhdr10.pdf (accessed December 16, 2011)

**FIGURE 6.2**

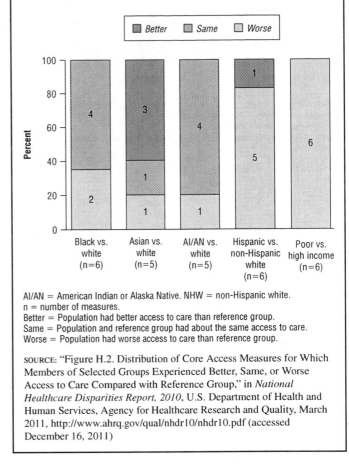

Percentage of minority groups that experienced better, same, or worse access to care compared with reference group, 2010

☒ Better  ☒ Same  ☐ Worse

AI/AN = American Indian or Alaska Native. NHW = non-Hispanic white.
n = number of measures.
Better = Population had better access to care than reference group.
Same = Population and reference group had about the same access to care.
Worse = Population had worse access to care than reference group.

SOURCE: "Figure H.2. Distribution of Core Access Measures for Which Members of Selected Groups Experienced Better, Same, or Worse Access to Care Compared with Reference Group," in *National Healthcare Disparities Report, 2010*, U.S. Department of Health and Human Services, Agency for Healthcare Research and Quality, March 2011, http://www.ahrq.gov/qual/nhdr10/nhdr10.pdf (accessed December 16, 2011)

narrowed between 2001 and 2008. The gap between Asian-Americans and non-Hispanic whites had narrowed for about 30% of the core measures during this period, but 70% showed no change.

**HEALTH INSURANCE.** Lack of health insurance is one formidable barrier to receiving health care. Carmen DeNavas-Walt, Bernadette D. Proctor, and Jessica C. Smith of the Census Bureau indicate in *Income, Poverty, and Health Insurance Coverage in the United States: 2010* (September 2011, http://www.census.gov/prod/2011pubs/p60-239.pdf) that 49.9 million people were uninsured in 2010. The lack of insurance coverage is a significant barrier to getting basic health care services. The HHS emphasizes in *National Healthcare Disparities Report, 2010* that uninsured people are more likely to have a poor health status and to die early because it is more difficult for the uninsured to get health care and therefore they are diagnosed at later disease stages and receive less therapeutic care.

In 2010 members of minority groups were much less likely to carry health insurance coverage than were their non-Hispanic white counterparts. On average, 30.7% of Hispanics, 20.8% of African-Americans, and 18.1% of

Asian-Americans lacked coverage. (See Table 6.2.) In comparison, 11.7% of non-Hispanic whites lacked health insurance coverage in 2010.

Those minorities who do have health insurance are more likely than non-Hispanic whites to be covered by government programs rather than by private health insurance. In 2009 members of all minority groups except for Asian-Americans were more likely to be covered by Medicaid (the federally funded health care program for low-income people) than were non-Hispanic whites. In that year Medicaid covered 10.4% of non-Hispanic whites and 9.9% of Asian-Americans. (See Table 6.3.) However, Medicaid covered 29.5% of African-Americans, 29.7% of Native Americans or Alaskan Natives, and 27.6% of Hispanics. Among Hispanics, Puerto Ricans were the most likely (32.1%) and Cubans were the least likely (16.7%) to be covered by Medicaid. The large proportion of minorities on Medicaid is in part explained by eligibility requirements; only poor and low-income people qualify, and members of these groups are disproportionately poor. However, Medicaid coverage does not necessarily translate into good or even adequate health care. Benjamin Le Cook of

**TABLE 6.2**

**People without health insurance coverage by selected characteristics, 2009–10**

[Numbers in thousands]

| Characteristic | 2009[a] | | | 2010 | | | Change in uninsured[b] | |
|---|---|---|---|---|---|---|---|---|
| | Total | Uninsured Number | Uninsured Percent | Total | Uninsured Number | Uninsured Percent | Number | Percent |
| **Total** | 304,280 | 48,985 | 16.1 | 306,110 | 49,904 | 16.3 | 919 | 0.2 |
| **Family status** | | | | | | | | |
| In families | 249,384 | 36,809 | 14.8 | 249,855 | 37,618 | 15.1 | 809 | 0.3 |
| Householder | 78,867 | 11,220 | 14.2 | 78,633 | 11,772 | 15.0 | 551 | 0.7 |
| Related children under 18 | 73,410 | 7,018 | 9.6 | 73,227 | 6,986 | 9.5 | −32 | — |
| Related children under 6 | 25,104 | 2,213 | 8.8 | 25,096 | 2,236 | 8.9 | 22 | 0.1 |
| In unrelated subfamilies | 1,357 | 344 | 25.3 | 1,650 | 428 | 25.9 | 84 | 0.6 |
| Unrelated individuals | 53,539 | 11,832 | 22.1 | 54,605 | 11,858 | 21.7 | 26 | −0.4 |
| **Race[c] and Hispanic origin** | | | | | | | | |
| White | 242,403 | 37,124 | 15.3 | 243,323 | 37,385 | 15.4 | 261 | — |
| White, not Hispanic | 197,436 | 22,715 | 11.5 | 197,423 | 23,093 | 11.7 | 378 | 0.2 |
| Black | 38,624 | 7,838 | 20.3 | 39,031 | 8,132 | 20.8 | 294 | 0.5 |
| Asian | 14,011 | 2,317 | 16.5 | 14,332 | 2,600 | 18.1 | 284 | 1.6 |
| Hispanic (any race) | 48,901 | 15,450 | 31.6 | 49,972 | 15,340 | 30.7 | −110 | −0.9 |
| **Age** | | | | | | | | |
| Under 65 years | 265,667 | 48,342 | 18.2 | 266,931 | 49,112 | 18.4 | 770 | 0.2 |
| Under 18 years | 75,040 | 7,313 | 9.7 | 74,916 | 7,307 | 9.8 | −6 | — |
| Under 19 years[d] | 79,317 | 8,058 | 10.2 | 79,288 | 7,952 | 10.0 | −107 | −0.1 |
| 19 to 25 years[d] | 29,389 | 9,221 | 31.4 | 29,692 | 8,828 | 29.7 | −393 | −1.6 |
| 18 to 24 years | 29,313 | 8,581 | 29.3 | 29,651 | 8,078 | 27.2 | −502 | −2.0 |
| 25 to 34 years | 41,085 | 11,530 | 28.1 | 41,584 | 11,804 | 28.4 | 274 | 0.3 |
| 35 to 44 years | 40,447 | 8,498 | 21.0 | 39,842 | 8,692 | 21.8 | 194 | 0.8 |
| 45 to 64 years | 79,782 | 12,421 | 15.6 | 80,939 | 13,231 | 16.3 | 810 | 0.8 |
| 65 years and older | 38,613 | 643 | 1.7 | 39,179 | 792 | 2.0 | 149 | 0.4 |
| **Nativity** | | | | | | | | |
| Native born | 266,674 | 36,305 | 13.6 | 267,884 | 36,881 | 13.8 | 576 | 0.2 |
| Foreign born | 37,606 | 12,680 | 33.7 | 38,226 | 13,023 | 34.1 | 343 | 0.4 |
| Naturalized citizen | 16,024 | 2,951 | 18.4 | 16,801 | 3,356 | 20.0 | 405 | 1.6 |
| Not a citizen | 21,581 | 9,729 | 45.1 | 21,424 | 9,667 | 45.1 | −62 | — |
| **Region** | | | | | | | | |
| Northeast | 54,654 | 6,434 | 11.8 | 54,782 | 6,779 | 12.4 | 345 | 0.6 |
| Midwest | 66,096 | 8,368 | 12.7 | 66,104 | 8,605 | 13.0 | 237 | 0.4 |
| South | 112,312 | 21,576 | 19.2 | 113,275 | 21,665 | 19.1 | 88 | −0.1 |
| West | 71,218 | 12,606 | 17.7 | 71,949 | 12,855 | 17.9 | 249 | 0.2 |
| **Residence** | | | | | | | | |
| Inside metropolitan statistical areas | 256,383 | 41,550 | 16.2 | 258,350 | 42,153 | 16.3 | 603 | 0.1 |
| Inside principal cities | 97,856 | 18,704 | 19.1 | 98,774 | 19,152 | 19.4 | 448 | 0.3 |
| Outside principal cities | 158,527 | 22,846 | 14.4 | 159,576 | 23,001 | 14.4 | 155 | — |
| Outside metropolitan statistical areas[e] | 47,897 | 7,435 | 15.5 | 47,760 | 7,752 | 16.2 | 316 | 0.7 |
| **Household income** | | | | | | | | |
| Less than $25,000 | 58,159 | 15,320 | 26.3 | 60,140 | 16,166 | 26.9 | 846 | 0.5 |
| $25,000 to $49,999 | 71,340 | 14,999 | 21.0 | 70,680 | 15,435 | 21.8 | 436 | 0.8 |
| $50,000 to $74,999 | 58,381 | 8,997 | 15.4 | 57,359 | 8,831 | 15.4 | −167 | — |
| $75,000 or more | 116,400 | 9,669 | 8.3 | 117,931 | 9,473 | 8.0 | −196 | −0.3 |
| **Work experience** | | | | | | | | |
| Total, 18 to 64 years old | 190,627 | 41,030 | 21.5 | 192,015 | 41,805 | 21.8 | 776 | 0.2 |
| All workers | 145,184 | 28,241 | 19.5 | 143,581 | 28,000 | 19.5 | −242 | — |
| Worked full-time, year-round | 95,808 | 14,095 | 14.7 | 95,549 | 14,311 | 15.0 | 216 | 0.3 |
| Less than full-time, year-round | 49,376 | 14,146 | 28.6 | 48,032 | 13,689 | 28.5 | −458 | −0.2 |
| Did not work at least 1 week | 45,443 | 12,788 | 28.1 | 48,434 | 13,806 | 28.5 | 1,017 | 0.4 |

Mathematica Policy Research Inc. in Cambridge, Massachusetts, notes in "Effect of Medicaid Managed Care on Racial Disparities in Health Care Access" (*Health Services Research*, vol. 42, no. 1, February 2007) that because Medicaid reimburses physicians at lower rates than do private insurance plans, fewer doctors accept it, thereby erecting more barriers for those covered by Medicaid to receiving adequate health care.

Nearly all people aged 65 years and older are covered by health insurance largely due to Medicare (the federally administered system of health insurance for people aged 65 years and older and people with disabilities). However, Medicaid additionally covers a much higher proportion of minorities of this age, whereas non-Hispanic whites tend to be covered by private insurance. For example, in 2008 only 5.4% of non-Hispanic whites aged

## TABLE 6.2

**People without health insurance coverage by selected characteristics, 2009–10** [CONTINUED]

[Numbers in thousands]

| Characteristic | 2009[a] Total | Uninsured Number | Percent | 2010 Total | Uninsured Number | Percent | Change in uninsured[b] Number | Percent |
|---|---|---|---|---|---|---|---|---|
| **Disability status[f]** | | | | | | | | |
| Total, 18 to 64 years old | 190,627 | 41,030 | 21.5 | 192,015 | 41,805 | 21.8 | 776 | 0.2 |
| With a disability | 14,644 | 2,348 | 16.0 | 14,935 | 2,577 | 17.3 | 230 | 1.2 |
| With no disability | 175,048 | 38,682 | 22.1 | 176,161 | 39,228 | 22.3 | 546 | 0.2 |

—Represents zero or rounds to zero.

[a]The data for 2009 were revised to reflect the results of enhancements to the editing process.

[b]Details may not sum to totals because of rounding.

[c]Federal surveys now give respondents the option of reporting more than one race. Therefore, two basic ways of defining a race group are possible. A group such as Asian may be defined as those who reported Asian and no other race (the race-alone or single-race concept) or as those who reported Asian regardless of whether they also reported another race (the race-alone-or-in-combination concept). This table shows data using the first approach (race alone). The use of the single-race population does not imply that it is the preferred method of presenting or analyzing data. The Census Bureau uses a variety of approaches. Information on people who reported more than one race, such as white **and** American Indian and Alaska Native or Asian **and** black or African American, is available from Census 2010 through American FactFinder. About 2.9 percent of people reported more than one race in Census 2010. Data for American Indians and Alaska Natives, Native Hawaiians and other Pacific Islanders, and those reporting two or more races are not shown separately.

[d]These age groups are of special interest because of the Affordable Care Act of 2010. Children under the age of 19 are eligible for Medicaid/CHIP (Children's Health Insurance Program) and individuals aged 19 to 25 may be a dependent on a parent's health plan.

[e]The "outside metropolitan statistical areas" category includes both micropolitan statistical areas and territory outside of metropolitan and micropolitan statistical areas.

[f]The sum of those with and without a disability does not equal the total because disability status is not defined for individuals in the armed forces.

SOURCE: Carmen DeNavas-Walt, Bernadette D. Proctor, and Jessica C. Smith, "Table 8. People without Health Insurance Coverage by Selected Characteristics: 2009 and 2010," in *Income, Poverty, and Health Insurance Coverage in the United States: 2010*, U.S. Census Bureau, September 2011, http://www.census.gov/prod/2011pubs/p60-239.pdf (accessed December 11, 2011)

---

65 years and older were covered by Medicaid, compared with 20% of non-Hispanic African-Americans and 21.1% of Hispanics. (See Table 6.4.) In 2008 non-Hispanic whites aged 65 years and older were more likely to be covered either by an employer-sponsored plan (35.4%) or by a Medigap plan (24.9%), both of which are forms of private health insurance, although in both cases the percentages covered by private plans had been dropping steadily since 1992. Nevertheless, lower proportions of minority groups were covered by private plans. In 2008, 23.2% of non-Hispanic African-Americans and 19.7% of Hispanics were covered by an employer-sponsored plan and 6.5% and 7.8%, respectively, were covered by a Medigap plan.

**DOCTOR VISITS.** Another measure of a group's access to care is the number of doctor visits that are made annually. Since the 1980s, as more outpatient clinics and other outreach health facilities have opened, Americans have had increased opportunities to seek medical help. However, in 2009 members of most minority groups were more likely than non-Hispanic whites to have not visited a doctor's office or emergency department in the previous 12 months. In that year, 23.8% of Hispanics, 21.7% of Native Americans or Alaskan Natives, 20.8% of Asian-Americans, and 14.4% of non-Hispanic African-Americans had not visited a health care provider. (See Table 6.5.) Only 12.9% of non-Hispanic whites had not visited a health care provider in that year.

This disparity can be explained in part by the disproportionate number of minorities who are poor or low income; these groups were more likely than non-low income people to make no visits to a doctor's office or emergency department in 2009. Nevertheless, only 15.8% of non-Hispanic whites and 15% of non-Hispanic African-Americans with incomes below the poverty level had not seen a doctor in 2009, compared with 26.7% of poor Hispanics. (See Table 6.5.) Disparities in health care persist, especially for Hispanics, even when controlling for poverty.

**INDIAN HEALTH SERVICE.** Federal funding for Native American health care is provided through the Indian Health Service (IHS; 2012, http://www.ihs.gov/index.cfm?module=ihsIntro), whose mission is "to raise the physical, mental, social, and spiritual health of American Indians and Alaska Natives to the highest level." The delivery of health care to Native Americans is complicated by the lack of services and the long distances that sometimes must be traveled to receive care. Alaskan Natives are often able to get preventive medical care only by flying to a medical facility, and even though transportation costs are covered for emergency care, they are not provided for routine care.

Many Native American tribes have invested some of the money earned from casinos to improve health services. For example, Herman Williams Jr. explains in "Gambling Expansion Advocates Ignore the Facts about Tribal Gaming" (*Tulalip–Quil Ceda Messenger*, March 2003) that the Tulalip Tribes in Washington State were able to build a new state-of-the-art health center as well as improve other social services and reduce unemployment with proceeds from tribal gaming. According to Kate Spilde, in "The

**TABLE 6.3**

**Medicaid coverage among persons under 65 years of age, by race and Hispanic origin, selected years 1984–2009**

| Characteristic | 1984[a] | 1989[a] | 1995[a] | 1997 | 2000[b] | 2004(1)[c] | 2004(2)[c] | 2007[c] | 2008[c] | 2009[a] |
|---|---|---|---|---|---|---|---|---|---|---|
| | | | | | Number in millions | | | | | |
| Total[d] | 14.0 | 15.4 | 26.6 | 22.9 | 23.2 | 31.1 | 31.6 | 36.2 | 38.4 | 42.4 |
| | | | | | Percent of population | | | | | |
| Total[d] | 6.8 | 7.2 | 11.5 | 9.7 | 9.5 | 12.3 | 12.5 | 13.9 | 14.7 | 16.1 |
| **Race[e]** | | | | | | | | | | |
| White only | 4.6 | 5.1 | 8.9 | 7.4 | 7.1 | 10.2 | 10.4 | 11.4 | 12.1 | 13.7 |
| Black or African American only | 20.5 | 19.0 | 28.5 | 22.4 | 21.2 | 24.5 | 24.9 | 27.7 | 28.3 | 29.5 |
| American Indian or Alaska Native only | 28.2* | 29.7 | 19.0 | 19.6 | 15.1 | 18.0 | 18.4 | 21.2 | 37.0 | 29.7 |
| Asian only | 8.7* | 8.8* | 10.5 | 9.6 | 7.5 | 9.6 | 9.8 | 8.7 | 9.2 | 9.9 |
| Native Hawaiian or other Pacific Islander only | — | — | — | — | * | * | * | * | * | * |
| 2 or more races | — | — | — | — | 19.1 | 19.0 | 19.3 | 27.9 | 24.7 | 30.1 |
| **Hispanic origin and race[e]** | | | | | | | | | | |
| Hispanic or Latino | 13.3 | 13.5 | 21.9 | 17.6 | 15.5 | 21.9 | 22.5 | 24.7 | 24.9 | 27.6 |
| Mexican | 12.2 | 12.4 | 21.6 | 17.2 | 14.0 | 21.9 | 22.4 | 25.9 | 25.4 | 28.4 |
| Puerto Rican | 31.5 | 27.3 | 33.4 | 31.0 | 29.4 | 28.5 | 29.1 | 28.0 | 31.0 | 32.1 |
| Cuban | 4.8* | 7.7* | 13.4 | 7.3 | 9.2 | 17.9 | 17.9 | 13.3 | 13.0 | 16.7 |
| Other Hispanic or Latino | 7.9 | 11.1 | 18.2 | 15.3 | 14.5 | 19.9 | 20.8 | 21.4 | 22.3 | 24.6 |
| Not Hispanic or Latino | 6.2 | 6.5 | 10.2 | 8.7 | 8.5 | 10.5 | 10.7 | 11.7 | 12.6 | 13.7 |
| White only | 3.7 | 4.1 | 7.1 | 6.1 | 6.1 | 7.8 | 7.9 | 8.5 | 9.2 | 10.4 |
| Black or African American only | 20.7 | 19.0 | 28.1 | 22.1 | 21.0 | 24.1 | 24.6 | 27.3 | 27.9 | 29.1 |

—Data not available.

*Estimates are considered unreliable.

[a]Data prior to 1997 are not strictly comparable with data for later years due to the 1997 questionnaire redesign.

[b]Estimates for 2000–2002 were calculated using 2000-based sample weights and may differ from estimates in other reports that used 1990-based sample weights for 2000–2002 estimates.

[c]Beginning in quarter 3 of the 2004 National Health Insurance Survey (NHIS), persons under 65 years with no reported coverage were asked explicitly about Medicaid coverage. Estimates were calculated without and with the additional information from this question in the columns labeled 2004(1) and 2004(2), respectively, and estimates were calculated with the additional information starting with 2005 data.

[d]Includes all other races not shown separately, those with unknown marital status, unknown disability status, and, in 1984 and 1989, persons with unknown poverty level.

[e]The race groups, white, black, American Indian or Alaska Native, Asian, Native Hawaiian or other Pacific Islander, and 2 or more races, include persons of Hispanic and non-Hispanic origin. Persons of Hispanic origin may be of any race. Starting with 1999 data, race-specific estimates are tabulated according to the 1997 Revisions to the Standards for the Classification of Federal Data on Race and Ethnicity and are not strictly comparable with estimates for earlier years. The five single-race categories plus multiple-race categories shown in the table conform to the 1997 Standards. Starting with 1999 data, race-specific estimates are for persons who reported only one racial group; the category 2 or more races includes persons who reported more than one racial group. Prior to 1999, data were tabulated according to the 1977 Standards with four racial groups and the Asian only category included Native Hawaiian or other Pacific Islander. Estimates for single-race categories prior to 1999 included persons who reported one race or, if they reported more than one race, identified one race as best representing their race. Starting with 2003 data, race responses of other race and unspecified multiple race were treated as missing, and then race was imputed if these were the only race responses. Almost all persons with a race response of other race were of Hispanic origin.

Notes: The category Medicaid coverage includes persons who had any of the following at the time of interview: Medicaid, other public assistance through 1996, state-sponsored health plan starting in 1997, or Children's Health Insurance Program (CHIP) starting in 1999; it includes those who also had another type of coverage in addition to one of these. In 2007, 11.2% of persons under 65 years of age reported being covered by Medicaid, 1.2% by state-sponsored health plans, and 1.5% by CHIP. The number of persons with Medicaid coverage was calculated by multiplying the percentage with Medicaid coverage by the number of persons under age 65 in the civilian non-institutionalized U.S. population. Percentages were calculated with unknown values excluded from denominators.

SOURCE: Adapted from "Table 137. Medicaid Coverage among Persons under 65 Years of Age, by Selected Characteristics: United States, Selected Years 1984–2009," in *Health, United States, 2010: With Special Feature on Death and Dying*, U.S. Department of Health and Human Services, Centers for Disease Control and Prevention, National Center for Health Statistics, 2011, http://www.cdc.gov/nchs/data/hus/hus10.pdf (accessed December 16, 2011).

Rumsey Band of the Wintun Indians: A Return to Self-Sufficiency" (February 2001, http://www.indiangaming.org/library/articles/rumsey-band.shtml), the Rumsey Band of the Wintun Indians in California operate the Rumsey Chapa-De Indian Health Clinic with profits from their casino, which also funds schools and contributes to the cultural life of the area. In "Tribes Hit the Jackpot" (*New Mexico Resources*, Fall 2003), Kevin Robinson-Avila reports that the Sandia Pueblo in New Mexico built a wellness center that provides free medical care to all tribe members as well as child care, education, and training. Barbara Wolfe et al. report in "The Income and Health Effects of Tribal Casino Gaming on American Indians" (*La Follette Policy Report*, vol. 19, no. 2, Spring 2010) that when one or more gaming tribes is present in a county, Native Americans residing in the area are more likely to carry health insurance and less likely to forgo health care when needed. In addition, several indicators of health status among Native Americans in casino gaming areas improve, including hypertension, obesity, diabetes, asthma, and disability.

## PREGNANCY AND BIRTH

### Prenatal Care

The importance of early prenatal care cannot be over-emphasized, as doctors are now better able to detect, and often correct, potential problems early in pregnancy. Every pregnant woman should receive prenatal care, and the National Center for Health Statistics (NCHS) believes the United States is capable of guaranteeing that more than 90% of pregnant women receive prenatal care during their first trimester of pregnancy.

**TABLE 6.4**

**Health insurance coverage of Medicare beneficiaries 65 years of age and over, by type of coverage and race and Hispanic origin, selected years 1992–2008**

[Data are based on household interviews of a sample of noninstitutionalized Medicare beneficiaries]

| Characteristic | Medicare Health Maintenance Organization[a] | | | | | Medicaid[b] | | | | |
|---|---|---|---|---|---|---|---|---|---|---|
| | 1992 | 1995 | 2000 | 2007 | 2008 | 1992 | 1995 | 2000 | 2007 | 2008 |
| **Age** | | | | | Number in millions | | | | | |
| 65 years and over | 1.1 | 2.6 | 5.9 | 7.3 | 8.1 | 2.7 | 2.8 | 2.7 | 3.3 | 3.2 |
| | | | | | Percent of population | | | | | |
| 65 years and over | 3.9 | 8.9 | 19.3 | 20.4 | 22.1 | 9.4 | 9.6 | 9.0 | 9.2 | 8.8 |
| 65–74 years | 4.2 | 9.5 | 20.6 | 21.0 | 22.9 | 7.9 | 8.8 | 8.5 | 8.8 | 8.2 |
| 75–84 years | 3.7 | 8.3 | 18.5 | 20.8 | 23.0 | 10.6 | 9.6 | 8.9 | 9.3 | 9.1 |
| 85 years and over | * | 7.3 | 16.3 | 17.0 | 16.5 | 16.6 | 13.6 | 11.2 | 11.4 | 10.3 |
| **Race and Hispanic origin** | | | | | | | | | | |
| White, not Hispanic or Latino | 3.6 | 8.4 | 18.4 | 18.5 | 20.2 | 5.6 | 5.4 | 5.1 | 5.7 | 5.4 |
| Black, not Hispanic or Latino | * | 7.9 | 20.7 | 27.9 | 28.5 | 28.5 | 30.3 | 23.6 | 18.8 | 20.0 |
| Hispanic | * | 15.5 | 27.5 | 36.7 | 37.5 | 39.0 | 40.5 | 28.7 | 24.4 | 21.1 |

| Characteristic | Employer-sponsored plan[c] | | | | | Medigap[d] | | | | |
|---|---|---|---|---|---|---|---|---|---|---|
| | 1992 | 1995 | 2000 | 2007 | 2008 | 1992 | 1995 | 2000 | 2007 | 2008 |
| **Age** | | | | | Number in millions | | | | | |
| 65 years and over | 12.5 | 11.3 | 10.7 | 12.1 | 12.0 | 9.9 | 9.5 | 7.6 | 7.9 | 7.9 |
| | | | | | Percent of population | | | | | |
| 65 years and over | 42.8 | 38.6 | 35.2 | 33.8 | 32.7 | 33.9 | 32.5 | 25.0 | 22.0 | 21.5 |
| 65–74 years | 46.9 | 41.1 | 36.6 | 35.1 | 34.0 | 31.4 | 29.9 | 21.7 | 20.4 | 19.6 |
| 75–84 years | 38.2 | 37.1 | 35.0 | 33.1 | 31.2 | 37.5 | 35.2 | 27.8 | 22.9 | 22.7 |
| 85 years and over | 31.6 | 30.2 | 29.4 | 30.2 | 31.1 | 38.3 | 37.6 | 31.1 | 26.2 | 26.3 |
| **Race and Hispanic origin** | | | | | | | | | | |
| White, not Hispanic or Latino | 45.9 | 41.3 | 38.6 | 36.8 | 35.4 | 37.2 | 36.2 | 28.3 | 25.3 | 24.9 |
| Black, not Hispanic or Latino | 25.9 | 26.7 | 22.0 | 25.8 | 23.2 | 13.6 | 10.2 | 7.5 | 7.3 | 6.5 |
| Hispanic | 20.7 | 16.9 | 15.8 | 16.2 | 19.7 | 15.8 | 10.1 | 11.3 | 7.7 | 7.8 |

| Characteristic | Medicare fee-for-service only or other[e] | | | | |
|---|---|---|---|---|---|
| | 1992 | 1995 | 2000 | 2007 | 2008 |
| **Age** | | | Number in millions | | |
| 65 years and over | 2.9 | 3.1 | 3.5 | 5.2 | 5.5 |
| | | | Percent of population | | |
| 65 years and over | 9.9 | 10.5 | 11.5 | 14.6 | 14.9 |
| 65–74 years | 9.7 | 10.7 | 12.6 | 14.8 | 15.2 |
| 75–84 years | 10.1 | 9.9 | 9.9 | 14.0 | 14.0 |
| 85 years and over | 10.8 | 11.3 | 12.1 | 15.2 | 15.8 |
| **Race and Hispanic origin** | | | | | |
| White, not Hispanic or Latino | 7.7 | 8.7 | 9.6 | 13.7 | 14.1 |
| Black, not Hispanic or Latino | 26.7 | 25.0 | 26.1 | 20.2 | 21.7 |
| Hispanic | 18.3 | 17.1 | 16.7 | 15.0 | 13.9 |

*Estimates are considered unreliable if the sample cell size is 50 or fewer.
—Data not available.
[a]Enrollee has Medicare Health Maintenance Organization (HMO) regardless of other insurance.
[b]Enrolled in Medicaid and not enrolled in a Medicare risk HMO.
[c]Private insurance plans purchased through employers (own, current, or former employer, family business, union, or former employer or union of spouse) and not enrolled in a Medicare risk HMO or Medicaid.
[d]Supplemental insurance purchased privately or through organizations such as AARP or professional organizations, and not enrolled in a Medicare risk HMO, Medicaid, or employer-sponsored plan.
[e]Medicare fee-for-service only or other public plans (except Medicaid).
Notes: Data for noninstitutionalized Medicare beneficiaries. Insurance categories are mutually exclusive. Persons with more than one type of coverage are categorized according to the order in which the health insurance categories appear. Data for additional years are available.

SOURCE: Adapted from "Table 139. Health Insurance Coverage of Medicare Beneficiaries 65 Years of Age and over, by Type of Coverage and Selected Characteristics: United States, Selected Years 1992–2008," in *Health, United States, 2010: With Special Feature on Death and Dying*, U.S. Department of Health and Human Services, Centers for Disease Control and Prevention, National Center for Health Statistics, 2011, http://www.cdc.gov/nchs/data/hus/hus10 .pdf (accessed December 16, 2011)

In 2007 an estimated 82% of women in the United States received prenatal care during their first trimester of pregnancy, but that percentage was significantly lower among some minority groups. (See Table 6.6.) Almost nine out of 10 (87.7%) non-Hispanic white women and four out of five (82.6%) Asian or Pacific Islander women received

**TABLE 6.5**

**Health care visits to doctor offices, emergency departments, and home visits within the past 12 months, by race and Hispanic origin and poverty level, 1997, 2008, and 2009**

[Data are based on household interviews of a sample of the civilian noninstitutionalized population]

| | Number of health care visits[a] | | | | | | | | | | | |
|---|---|---|---|---|---|---|---|---|---|---|---|---|
| | None | | | 1–3 visits | | | 4–9 visits | | | 10 or more visits | | |
| Characteristic | 1997 | 2008 | 2009 | 1997 | 2008 | 2009 | 1997 | 2008 | 2009 | 1997 | 2008 | 2009 |
| **Race[b, c]** | | | | | | Percent distribution | | | | | | |
| White only | 16.0 | 15.4 | 15.1 | 46.1 | 46.2 | 46.5 | 23.9 | 25.1 | 25.0 | 14.0 | 13.3 | 13.5 |
| Black or African American only | 16.8 | 15.4 | 14.6 | 46.1 | 48.3 | 46.8 | 23.2 | 24.2 | 24.8 | 13.9 | 12.2 | 13.8 |
| American Indian or Alaska Native only | 17.1 | 15.4 | 21.7 | 38.0 | 42.8 | 50.1 | 24.2 | 29.1 | 18.4 | 20.7 | 12.7 | 9.9 |
| Asian only | 22.8 | 18.2 | 20.8 | 49.1 | 53.7 | 50.6 | 19.7 | 20.9 | 20.7 | 8.3 | 7.2 | 8.0 |
| Native Hawaiian or other Pacific Islander only | — | * | * | — | * | * | — | * | * | — | * | * |
| 2 or more races | — | 11.9 | 16.2 | — | 44.9 | 41.4 | — | 25.2 | 28.9 | — | 18.0 | 13.4 |
| **Hispanic origin and race[b, c]** | | | | | | | | | | | | |
| Hispanic or Latino | 24.9 | 24.3 | 23.8 | 42.3 | 44.0 | 44.3 | 20.3 | 20.6 | 21.2 | 12.5 | 11.1 | 10.8 |
| Mexican | 28.9 | 26.6 | 25.9 | 40.8 | 43.4 | 44.5 | 18.5 | 19.1 | 20.1 | 11.8 | 11.0 | 9.5 |
| Not Hispanic or Latino | 15.4 | 13.7 | 13.7 | 46.7 | 47.3 | 47.2 | 24.0 | 25.6 | 25.5 | 13.9 | 13.4 | 13.7 |
| White only | 14.7 | 13.1 | 12.9 | 46.6 | 46.7 | 47.0 | 24.4 | 26.2 | 25.9 | 14.3 | 14.0 | 14.2 |
| Black or African American only | 16.9 | 15.2 | 14.4 | 46.1 | 48.7 | 46.6 | 23.1 | 23.9 | 25.2 | 13.8 | 12.1 | 13.8 |
| **Percent of poverty level[b, d]** | | | | | | | | | | | | |
| Below 100% | 20.6 | 19.1 | 19.4 | 37.8 | 39.3 | 39.2 | 22.7 | 23.9 | 23.5 | 18.9 | 17.6 | 17.9 |
| 100%–199% | 20.1 | 22.2 | 19.6 | 43.3 | 41.4 | 43.4 | 21.7 | 22.0 | 23.0 | 14.9 | 14.4 | 14.0 |
| 200%–399% | 16.4 | 16.0 | 16.3 | 47.2 | 47.3 | 47.0 | 23.6 | 24.6 | 24.1 | 12.8 | 12.1 | 12.5 |
| 400% or more | 12.8 | 10.3 | 10.9 | 49.8 | 51.4 | 50.3 | 24.9 | 26.5 | 26.7 | 12.5 | 11.8 | 12.1 |
| **Hispanic origin and race and percent of poverty level[b, c, d]** | | | | | | | | | | | | |
| Hispanic or Latino: | | | | | | | | | | | | |
| Below 100% | 30.2 | 26.8 | 26.7 | 34.8 | 39.8 | 38.6 | 19.9 | 19.2 | 20.3 | 15.0 | 14.3 | 14.4 |
| 100%–199% | 28.7 | 29.7 | 28.8 | 39.7 | 39.1 | 42.0 | 20.4 | 19.8 | 18.8 | 11.2 | 11.5 | 10.4 |
| 200%–399% | 20.7 | 23.8 | 21.4 | 47.4 | 46.4 | 47.2 | 19.8 | 20.4 | 22.3 | 12.1 | 9.4 | 9.1 |
| 400% or more | 15.2 | 14.8 | 14.7 | 50.4 | 52.2 | 51.8 | 22.6 | 22.9 | 24.1 | 11.8 | 10.2 | 9.5 |
| Not Hispanic or Latino: | | | | | | | | | | | | |
| White only: | | | | | | | | | | | | |
| Below 100% | 17.0 | 16.2 | 15.8 | 38.3 | 37.4 | 40.4 | 23.9 | 26.2 | 24.4 | 20.9 | 20.3 | 19.4 |
| 100%–199% | 17.3 | 19.2 | 15.9 | 44.1 | 40.5 | 42.7 | 22.2 | 23.2 | 25.1 | 16.3 | 17.0 | 16.3 |
| 200%–399% | 15.4 | 14.5 | 14.9 | 46.9 | 46.1 | 46.4 | 24.3 | 26.1 | 24.7 | 13.4 | 13.2 | 14.1 |
| 400% or more | 12.5 | 9.5 | 10.1 | 49.1 | 50.9 | 49.7 | 25.5 | 27.2 | 27.4 | 13.0 | 12.5 | 12.8 |
| Black or African American only: | | | | | | | | | | | | |
| Below 100% | 17.4 | 16.6 | 15.0 | 38.5 | 43.0 | 38.1 | 23.4 | 22.6 | 26.3 | 20.7 | 17.8 | 20.7 |
| 100%–199% | 18.8 | 18.9 | 16.7 | 43.7 | 46.3 | 45.4 | 22.9 | 22.7 | 25.2 | 14.5 | 12.2 | 12.7 |
| 200%–399% | 16.6 | 14.4 | 16.1 | 49.7 | 52.0 | 48.5 | 22.9 | 23.1 | 24.2 | 10.8 | 10.5 | 11.3 |
| 400% or more | 14.0 | 11.5 | 10.1 | 54.3 | 52.9 | 53.6 | 22.7 | 25.7 | 25.7 | 9.0 | 9.9 | 10.6 |

*Estimates are considered unreliable.
—Data not available.
[a]This table presents a summary measure of health care visits to doctor offices, emergency departments, and home visits during a 12-month period.
[b]Estimates are age-adjusted to the year 2000 standard population using six age groups: Under 18 years, 18–44 years, 45–54 years, 55–64 years, 65–74 years, and 75 years and over. The disability measure is age-adjusted using the five adult age groups.
[c]The race groups white, black, American Indian or Alaska Native, Asian, Native Hawaiian or other Pacific Islander, and 2 or more races include persons of Hispanic and non-Hispanic origin. Persons of Hispanic origin may be of any race. Starting with 1999 data, race-specific estimates are tabulated according to the 1997 Revisions to the Standards for the Classification of Federal Data on Race and Ethnicity and are not strictly comparable with estimates for earlier years. The five single-race categories plus multiple-race categories shown in the table conform to the 1997 Standards. Starting with 1999 data, race-specific estimates are for persons who reported only one racial group; the category 2 or more races includes persons who reported more than one racial group. Prior to 1999, data were tabulated according to the 1977 Standards with four racial groups and the Asian only category included Native Hawaiian or other Pacific Islander. Estimates for single-race categories prior to 1999 included persons who reported one race or, if they reported more than one race, identified one race as best representing their race. Starting with 2003 data, race responses of other race and unspecified multiple race were treated as missing, and then race was imputed if these were the only race responses. Almost all persons with a race response of other race were of Hispanic origin.
[d]Percent of poverty level is based on family income and family size and composition using U.S. Census Bureau poverty thresholds. Missing family income data were imputed for 1997 and beyond.
Notes: In 1997, the National Health Interview Survey questionnaire was redesigned. Data for additional years are available.

SOURCE: Adapted from "Table 79. Health Care Visits to Doctor Offices, Emergency Departments, and Home Visits within the Past 12 Months, by Selected Characteristics: United States, Selected Years 1997–2009," in *Health, United States, 2010: With Special Feature on Death and Dying*, U.S. Department of Health and Human Services, Centers for Disease Control and Prevention, National Center for Health Statistics, 2011, http://www.cdc.gov/nchs/data/hus/hus10.pdf (accessed December 16, 2011)

prenatal care during their first trimester. By contrast, only 72.4% of Hispanic women, 75% of non-Hispanic African-American women, and 68.3% of Native American or Alaskan Native women did so. It is worthy of note, however, that despite the low rates of first-trimester prenatal care among Hispanic women in general, Cuban women had among the highest rates of prenatal care of all racial and ethnic groups, at 83.6%.

TABLE 6.6

**Prenatal care for live births, according to detailed race and Hispanic origin of mother, selected years 1970–2000, and selected states 2006–07**

[Data are based on birth certificates]

| Prenatal care, race, and Hispanic origin of mother | 1970 | 1980 | 1990 | 2000 | 28 reporting areas (1989 revision) 2006[a] | 2007[a] | 18 reporting areas (2003 revision) 2006[b] | 2007[b] |
|---|---|---|---|---|---|---|---|---|
| **Prenatal care began during 1st trimester** | | | | Percent of live births[c] | | | | |
| All races | 68.0 | 76.3 | 75.8 | 83.2 | 82.4 | 82.0 | 69.0 | 67.5 |
| White | 72.3 | 79.2 | 79.2 | 85.0 | 84.4 | 84.0 | 70.9 | 69.5 |
| Black or African American | 44.2 | 62.4 | 60.6 | 74.3 | 75.6 | 75.0 | 58.3 | 57.0 |
| American Indian or Alaska Native | 38.2 | 55.8 | 57.9 | 69.3 | 68.9 | 68.3 | 54.3 | 53.2 |
| Asian or Pacific Islander[d] | — | 73.7 | 75.1 | 84.0 | 82.0 | 82.6 | 71.4 | 69.8 |
| Hispanic or Latina[e] | — | 60.2 | 60.2 | 74.4 | 72.3 | 72.4 | 57.7 | 56.1 |
| Mexican | — | 59.6 | 57.8 | 72.9 | 70.5 | 70.7 | 53.4 | 51.5 |
| Puerto Rican | — | 55.1 | 63.5 | 78.5 | 78.7 | 78.3 | 68.1 | 66.1 |
| Cuban | — | 82.7 | 84.8 | 91.7 | 83.3 | 83.6 | 80.4 | 78.9 |
| Central and South American | — | 58.8 | 61.5 | 77.6 | 71.8 | 71.7 | 61.0 | 59.0 |
| Other and unknown Hispanic or Latina | — | 66.4 | 66.4 | 75.8 | 78.3 | 79.0 | 63.5 | 63.7 |
| Not Hispanic or Latin[e] | | | | | | | | |
| White | — | 81.2 | 83.3 | 88.5 | 88.0 | 87.7 | 76.2 | 74.9 |
| Black or African American | — | 60.8 | 60.7 | 74.3 | 75.7 | 75.0 | 58.4 | 57.1 |
| **Prenatal care began during 3rd trimester or no prenatal care** | | | | | | | | |
| All races | 7.9 | 5.1 | 6.1 | 3.9 | 3.9 | 3.9 | 7.9 | 8.4 |
| White | 6.3 | 4.3 | 4.9 | 3.3 | 3.3 | 3.2 | 7.2 | 7.6 |
| Black or African American | 16.6 | 8.9 | 11.3 | 6.7 | 5.8 | 6.0 | 11.8 | 12.6 |
| American Indian or Alaska Native | 28.9 | 15.2 | 12.9 | 8.6 | 8.2 | 8.5 | 13.2 | 14.0 |
| Asian or Pacific Islander[d] | — | 6.5 | 5.8 | 3.3 | 3.9 | 3.6 | 7.1 | 7.7 |
| Hispanic or Latina[e] | — | 12.0 | 12.0 | 6.3 | 6.4 | 6.2 | 12.2 | 12.9 |
| Mexican | — | 11.8 | 13.2 | 6.9 | 6.8 | 6.5 | 14.2 | 15.1 |
| Puerto Rican | — | 16.2 | 10.6 | 4.5 | 4.1 | 3.9 | 6.7 | 7.8 |
| Cuban | — | 3.9 | 2.8 | 1.4 | 3.7 | 3.2 | 3.1 | 3.4 |
| Central and South American | — | 13.1 | 10.9 | 5.4 | 6.9 | 6.7 | 10.1 | 11.0 |
| Other and unknown Hispanic or Latina | — | 9.2 | 8.5 | 5.9 | 4.9 | 5.0 | 9.5 | 9.4 |
| Not Hispanic or Latina[e] | | | | | | | | |
| White | — | 3.5 | 3.4 | 2.3 | 2.3 | 2.3 | 5.2 | 5.5 |
| Black or African American | — | 9.7 | 11.2 | 6.7 | 5.8 | 6.0 | 11.8 | 12.6 |

—Data not available.

[a]Data are for the 28 reporting areas that used the 1989 Revision of the U.S. Standard Certificate of Live Birth for data on prenatal care in 2006 and 2007. Reporting areas that have implemented the 2003 Revision of the U.S. Standard Certificate of Live Birth are excluded because prenatal care data based on the 2003 revision are not comparable with data based on the 1989 and earlier revisions of the U.S. Standard Certificate of Live Birth.

[b]Data are for the 18 reporting areas that used the 2003 Revision of the U.S. Standard Certificate of Live Birth for data on prenatal care in 2006 and 2007. Reporting areas that used the 1989 Revision of the U.S. Standard Certificate of Live Birth are excluded because prenatal care data based on the 2003 revision are not comparable with data based on the 1989 or earlier revisions.

[c]Excludes live births where trimester when prenatal care began is unknown.

[d]Starting with 2003 data, estimates are not available for Asian or Pacific Islander subgroups during the transition from single-race to multiple-race reporting.

[e]Prior to 1993, data from states lacking an Hispanic-origin item on the birth certificate were excluded. Data for non-Hispanic white and non-Hispanic black women for years prior to 1989 are not nationally representative and are provided for comparison with Hispanic data.

Notes: Prior to 2003, all data are based on the 1989 and earlier revisions of the U.S. Standard Certificate of Live Birth. Data for 1970 and 1975 exclude births that occurred in states not reporting prenatal care. Starting in 2003 some states have implemented the 2003 Revision of the U.S. Standard Certificate of Live Birth on a voluntary basis. Data are not shown for 2006 and 2007 for the six states that implemented the 2003 revision mid-year 2006 or during 2007. California implemented a partial revision of the 2003 Revision of the U.S. Standard Certificate of Live Birth in 2006 but continued to use the 1989 revision format for data on prenatal care. The race groups white, black, American Indian or Alaska Native, and Asian or Pacific Islander include persons of Hispanic and non-Hispanic origin. Persons of Hispanic origin may be of any race. Starting with 2003 data, some states reported multiple-race data. The multiple-race data for these states were bridged to the single-race categories of the 1977 Office of Management and Budget standards for comparability with other states. Interpretation of trend data should take into consideration changes in reporting areas and immigration. Data for additional years are available.

SOURCE: "Table 5. Prenatal Care for Live Births, by Detailed Race and Hispanic Origin of Mother, United States, Selected Years 1970–2000, and Selected States 2006–2007," in *Health, United States, 2010: With Special Feature on Death and Dying*, U.S. Department of Health and Human Services, Centers for Disease Control and Prevention, National Center for Health Statistics, 2011, http://www.cdc.gov/nchs/data/hus/hus10.pdf (accessed December 16, 2011)

## Births and Fertility

Of the 4 million births in 2010, nearly 2.2 million were to non-Hispanic white mothers, 946,000 were to Hispanic mothers, 589,139 were to non-Hispanic African-American mothers, 246,915 were to Asian or Pacific Islander mothers, and 46,760 were to Native American or Alaskan Native mothers. (See Table 6.7.) The birthrate (live births per 1,000 population in a specified group) was highest among Hispanics (18.7), followed by non-Hispanic African-Americans (15.1) and Asians or Pacific Islanders (14.5). Native Americans or Alaskan Natives (11) and non-Hispanic whites (10.9) had the lowest birthrates.

The fertility rate refers to the number of live births per 1,000 women aged 15 to 44 years in a specified group. In

TABLE 6.7

**Total births and percentage of births with selected demographic characteristics, by race and Hispanic origin of mother, 2009–10**

| Race and Hispanic origin of mother | Number | | Birth rate | | Fertility rate | | Total fertility rate | | Percent of births to unmarried women | |
|---|---|---|---|---|---|---|---|---|---|---|
| | 2010 | 2009 | 2010 | 2009 | 2010 | 2009 | 2010 | 2009 | 2010 | 2009 |
| All races and origins[a] | 4,000,279 | 4,130,665 | 13.0 | 13.5 | 64.1 | 66.2 | 1,932.0 | 2,002.0 | 40.8 | 41.0 |
| Non-Hispanic white[b] | 2,161,669 | 2,212,552 | 10.9 | 11.2 | 58.7 | 59.6 | 1,791.0 | 1,830.0 | 29.0 | 29.0 |
| Non-Hispanic black[b] | 589,139 | 609,584 | 15.1 | 15.7 | 66.6 | 68.9 | 1,971.5 | 2,045.5 | 72.5 | 72.8 |
| American Indian or Alaska Native total[b, c] | 46,760 | 48,665 | 11.0 | 11.8 | 48.6 | 51.7 | 1,404.0 | 1,498.5 | 65.6 | 65.4 |
| Asian or Pacific Islander total[b, c] | 246,915 | 251,089 | 14.5 | 15.1 | 59.2 | 61.3 | 1,689.5 | 1,743.0 | 17.0 | 17.2 |
| Hispanic[d] | 946,000 | 999,548 | 18.7 | 20.3 | 80.3 | 86.5 | 2,352.5 | 2,531.5 | 53.3 | 53.2 |

[a]Includes births to white Hispanic and black Hispanic women and births with origin not stated, not shown separately.

[b]Race and Hispanic origin are reported separately on birth certificates. Persons of Hispanic origin may be of any race. Race categories are consistent with the 1977 Office of Management and Budget (OMB) standards. In 2010, thirty-eight states and the District of Columbia reported multiple-race data. The multiple-race data for these states were bridged to the single-race categories of the 1977 OMB standards for comparability with other states. Multiple-race reporting areas vary for 2009–2010.

[c]Includes persons of Hispanic origin according to the mother's reported race.

[d]Includes all persons of Hispanic origin of any race.

Notes: Data for 2010 are based on a continuous file of records received from the states. Figures for 2010 are based on weighted data rounded to the nearest individual. Birth rates are the total number of births per 1,000 population in specified group. Fertility rates are the total number of births (regardless of the age of the mother) per 1,000 women aged 15–44 years in specified group. Total fertility rates are sums of birth rates for 5-year age groups in specified group multiplied by 5. Population enumerated as of April 1 for 2010 and estimated as of July 1 for 2009. Rates for 2009 have been revised using (intercensal) population estimates based on the 2000 and 2010 census and may differ from rates previously published.

SOURCE: Brady E. Hamilton, Joyce A. Martin, and Stephanie J. Ventura, "Table 1. Selected Demographic Characteristics, by Race and Hispanic Origin of Mother: United States, Final 2009 and Preliminary 2010," in "Births: Preliminary Data for 2010," *National Vital Statistics Reports*, vol. 60, no. 2, November 2011, http://www.cdc.gov/nchs/data/nvsr/nvsr60/nvsr60_02.pdf (accessed November 14, 2011)

2010 Hispanic women had the highest fertility rate (80.3), followed by non-Hispanic African-American women (66.6) and Asian or Pacific Islander women (59.2). (See Table 6.7.) Non-Hispanic white women (58.7) and Native American or Alaskan Native women (48.6) had the lowest fertility rates. Even though Hispanic women had the highest fertility rate, it varied among Hispanics from different countries of origin. According to Joyce A. Martin et al. of the Centers for Disease Control and Prevention (CDC), in "Births: Final Data for 2009" (*National Vital Statistics Reports*, vol. 60, no. 1, November 3, 2011), in 2009 women of Central and South American origin had the highest fertility rate (115.7) among Hispanics, followed by women of Mexican origin (91.4), women of Puerto Rican origin (68.7), and women of Cuban origin (49.5).

## Low Birth Weight and Infant Mortality

The percentage of babies that were born with low birth weights increased between 1985 and 2006, before decreasing slightly in 2007. (See Table 6.8.) Low birth weight is defined as weighing between 3 pounds, 4 ounces and 5 pounds, 8 ounces (1,500 and 2,500 g). Very low birth weight is less than 3 pounds, 4 ounces. Low-birth-weight babies, as well as premature babies (born before 37 weeks of gestation), often suffer serious health problems and encounter developmental problems later in life. According to the CDC, 6.8% of babies born in 1985 weighed less than 5 pounds, 8 ounces, compared with 8.2% of babies born in 2007. (See Table 6.8.) In 2007 non-Hispanic African-Americans were twice as likely as Hispanics to have low-birth-weight babies. In that year, 13.9% of non-Hispanic African-American babies were born with low birth weights,

whereas 8.1% of Asian or Pacific Islander babies, 7.5% of Native American or Alaskan Native babies, 7.3% of non-Hispanic white babies, and 6.9% of Hispanic babies were born with low birth weights. The percentage of very low-birth-weight live births also increased during this period, from 1.2% in 1985 to 1.5% in 2007. Again, non-Hispanic African-American mothers (3.2%) faced more than twice the risk of having a very low-birth-weight baby than did all mothers (1.5%).

Marian F. MacDorman and T. J. Mathews of the CDC report in "Recent Trends in Infant Mortality in the United States" (October 2008, http://www.cdc.gov/nchs/data/data briefs/db09.pdf) that the infant mortality rate (the rate of deaths before one year of age) increased from 6.9 infant deaths per 1,000 live births in 2000 to 7 infant deaths per 1,000 live births in 2002. This increase was due primarily to an increase in the number of births of very low-birth-weight and preterm babies. The rate then decreased to 6.8 infant deaths per 1,000 live births in both 2003 and 2004, before increasing again to 6.9 infant deaths per 1,000 live births in 2005. Even though the infant mortality rate remained stagnant between 2000 and 2005, MacDorman and Mathews report that preliminary data suggest that the infant mortality rate declined to 6.7 infant deaths per 1,000 live births in 2006.

The infant mortality rate is much higher for some groups than for others. As Table 6.9 shows, in 2006 non-Hispanic African-Americans suffered the highest rate of infant mortality, with 13.4 infant deaths per 1,000 live births. This rate was more than double the rate of 5.6 infant deaths per 1,000 live births for non-Hispanic whites. Native Americans or

TABLE 6.8

**Low-birthweight live births, by detailed race, Hispanic origin, and smoking status of mother, selected years 1970–2007**

[Data are based on birth certificates]

| Birthweight, race and Hispanic origin of mother, and smoking status of mother | 1970 | 1975 | 1980 | 1985 | 1990 | 1995 | 2000 | 2005 | 2006 | 2007 |
|---|---|---|---|---|---|---|---|---|---|---|
| Low birthweight (less than 2,500 grams) | | | | | Percent of live births[a] | | | | | |
| **All races** | **7.93** | **7.38** | **6.84** | **6.75** | **6.97** | **7.32** | **7.57** | **8.19** | **8.26** | **8.22** |
| White | 6.85 | 6.27 | 5.72 | 5.65 | 5.70 | 6.22 | 6.55 | 7.16 | 7.21 | 7.16 |
| Black or African American | 13.90 | 13.19 | 12.69 | 12.65 | 13.25 | 13.13 | 12.99 | 13.59 | 13.59 | 13.55 |
| American Indian or Alaska Native | 7.97 | 6.41 | 6.44 | 5.86 | 6.11 | 6.61 | 6.76 | 7.36 | 7.52 | 7.46 |
| Asian or Pacific Islander[b] | — | — | 6.68 | 6.16 | 6.45 | 6.90 | 7.31 | 7.98 | 8.12 | 8.10 |
| Hispanic or Latina[c] | — | — | 6.12 | 6.16 | 6.06 | 6.29 | 6.41 | 6.88 | 6.99 | 6.93 |
| Mexican | — | — | 5.62 | 5.77 | 5.55 | 5.81 | 6.01 | 6.49 | 6.58 | 6.50 |
| Puerto Rican | — | — | 8.95 | 8.69 | 8.99 | 9.41 | 9.30 | 9.92 | 10.14 | 9.83 |
| Cuban | — | — | 5.62 | 6.02 | 5.67 | 6.50 | 6.49 | 7.64 | 7.14 | 7.66 |
| Central and South American | — | — | 5.76 | 5.68 | 5.84 | 6.20 | 6.34 | 6.78 | 6.81 | 6.71 |
| Other and unknown Hispanic or Latina | — | — | 6.96 | 6.83 | 6.87 | 7.55 | 7.84 | 8.27 | 8.54 | 8.61 |
| Not Hispanic or Latina:[c] | | | | | | | | | | |
| White | — | — | 5.69 | 5.61 | 5.61 | 6.20 | 6.60 | 7.29 | 7.32 | 7.28 |
| Black or African American | — | — | 12.71 | 12.62 | 13.32 | 13.21 | 13.13 | 14.02 | 13.97 | 13.90 |
| | | | | | | | | | 17 reporting areas | |
| Cigarette smoker[d] | — | — | — | — | * | * | * | * | 12.02 | 12.08 |
| Nonsmoker[d] | — | — | — | — | * | * | * | * | 7.69 | 7.61 |
| Very low birthweight (less than 1,500 grams) | | | | | | | | | | |
| **All races** | **1.17** | **1.16** | **1.15** | **1.21** | **1.27** | **1.35** | **1.43** | **1.49** | **1.49** | **1.49** |
| White | 0.95 | 0.92 | 0.90 | 0.94 | 0.95 | 1.06 | 1.14 | 1.20 | 1.20 | 1.19 |
| Black or African American | 2.40 | 2.40 | 2.48 | 2.71 | 2.92 | 2.97 | 3.07 | 3.15 | 3.05 | 3.11 |
| American Indian or Alaska Native | 0.98 | 0.95 | 0.92 | 1.01 | 1.01 | 1.10 | 1.16 | 1.17 | 1.28 | 1.27 |
| Asian or Pacific Islander[b] | — | — | 0.92 | 0.85 | 0.87 | 0.91 | 1.05 | 1.14 | 1.12 | 1.14 |
| Hispanic or Latina[c] | — | — | 0.98 | 1.01 | 1.03 | 1.11 | 1.14 | 1.20 | 1.19 | 1.21 |
| Mexican | — | — | 0.92 | 0.97 | 0.92 | 1.01 | 1.03 | 1.12 | 1.12 | 1.13 |
| Puerto Rican | — | — | 1.29 | 1.30 | 1.62 | 1.79 | 1.93 | 1.87 | 1.91 | 1.89 |
| Cuban | — | — | 1.02 | 1.18 | 1.20 | 1.19 | 1.21 | 1.50 | 1.28 | 1.27 |
| Central and South American | — | — | 0.99 | 1.01 | 1.05 | 1.13 | 1.20 | 1.19 | 1.13 | 1.15 |
| Other and unknown Hispanic or Latina | — | — | 1.01 | 0.96 | 1.09 | 1.28 | 1.42 | 1.36 | 1.36 | 1.44 |
| Not Hispanic or Latina:[c] | | | | | | | | | | |
| White | — | — | 0.87 | 0.91 | 0.93 | 1.04 | 1.14 | 1.21 | 1.20 | 1.19 |
| Black or African American | — | — | 2.47 | 2.67 | 2.93 | 2.98 | 3.10 | 3.27 | 3.15 | 3.20 |
| | | | | | | | | | 17 reporting areas | |
| Cigarette smoker[d] | — | — | — | — | * | * | * | * | 1.73 | 1.82 |
| Nonsmoker[d] | — | — | — | — | * | * | * | * | 1.41 | 1.40 |

— Data not available.

*Data not shown. Due to a change in reporting, data are not comparable to other years. See footnote d.

[a]Excludes live births with unknown birthweight. Percent based on live births with known birthweight.

[b]Starting with 2003 data, estimates are not available for Asian or Pacific Islander subgroups during the transition from single-race to multiple-race reporting.

[c]Prior to 1993, data from states lacking an Hispanic-origin item on the birth certificate were excluded. Data for non-Hispanic white and non-Hispanic black women for years prior to 1989 are not nationally representative and are provided for comparison with Hispanic data.

[d]Percent based on live births with known smoking status of mother and known birthweight. Only reporting areas that have implemented the 2003 Revision of the U.S. Standard Certificate of Live Birth are shown because maternal tobacco use data based on the 2003 revision are not comparable with data based on the 1989 or earlier revisions to the U.S. Standard Certificate of Live Birth. In addition, California did not require reporting of tobacco use during pregnancy. Data are for the 17 reporting areas that used the 2003 Revision of the U.S. Standard Certificate of Live Birth for data on smoking in 2006 and 2007.

Notes: The race groups, white, black, American Indian or Alaska Native, and Asian or Pacific Islander, include persons of Hispanic and non-Hispanic origin. Persons of Hispanic origin may be of any race. Starting with 2003 data, some states reported multiple-race data. The multiple-race data for these states were bridged to the single-race categories of the 1977 Office of Management and Budget standards for comparability with other states. Interpretation of trend data should take into consideration expansion of reporting areas and immigration. Data for additional years are available.

SOURCE: "Table 9. Low Birthweight Live Births, by Detailed Race, Hispanic Origin, and Smoking Status of Mother: United States, Selected Years 1970–2007," in *Health, United States, 2010: With Special Feature on Death and Dying*, U.S. Department of Health and Human Services, Centers for Disease Control and Prevention, National Center for Health Statistics, 2011, http://www.cdc.gov/nchs/data/hus/hus10.pdf (accessed December 16, 2011)

Alaskan Natives also had a relatively high rate of infant deaths, at 8.3 per 1,000 live births. Hispanic women (5.4 deaths per 1,000 live births) and Asian or Pacific Islander women (4.5 deaths per 1,000 live births) had the lowest infant mortality rates. However, Hispanic subgroups varied considerably. Puerto Rican infant mortality rates were quite high compared with other Hispanic subgroups, at 8 per 1,000 live births, whereas Central and South American infant mortality rates were quite low, at 4.5 per 1,000 live births. MacDorman and Mathews note that the relatively low infant mortality rates among most Hispanic subgroups remain unexplained.

According to the Pew Hispanic Center, in the fact sheet "Hispanic Health: Divergent and Changing" (January 2002, http://pewhispanic.org/files/factsheets/1.pdf), the connection

TABLE 6.9

**Infant, neonatal, and postneonatal mortality rates, by detailed race and Hispanic origin of mother, selected years 1983–2006**

[Data are based on linked birth and death certificates for infants]

| Race and Hispanic origin of mother | 1983[a] | 1985[a] | 1990[a] | 1995[b] | 2000[b] | 2004[b] | 2005[b] | 2006[b] |
|---|---|---|---|---|---|---|---|---|
| | Infant[c] deaths per 1,000 live births | | | | | | | |
| **All mothers** | **10.9** | **10.4** | **8.9** | **7.6** | **6.9** | **6.8** | **6.9** | **6.7** |
| White | 9.3 | 8.9 | 7.3 | 6.3 | 5.7 | 5.7 | 5.7 | 5.6 |
| Black or African American | 19.2 | 18.6 | 16.9 | 14.6 | 13.5 | 13.2 | 13.3 | 12.9 |
| American Indian or Alaska Native | 15.2 | 13.1 | 13.1 | 9.0 | 8.3 | 8.4 | 8.1 | 8.3 |
| Asian or Pacific Islander[d] | 8.3 | 7.8 | 6.6 | 5.3 | 4.9 | 4.7 | 4.9 | 4.5 |
| Hispanic or Latina[e, f] | 9.5 | 8.8 | 7.5 | 6.3 | 5.6 | 5.5 | 5.6 | 5.4 |
| Mexican | 9.1 | 8.5 | 7.2 | 6.0 | 5.4 | 5.5 | 5.5 | 5.3 |
| Puerto Rican | 12.9 | 11.2 | 9.9 | 8.9 | 8.2 | 7.8 | 8.3 | 8.0 |
| Cuban | 7.5 | 8.5 | 7.2 | 5.3 | 4.6 | 4.6 | 4.4 | 5.1 |
| Central and South American | 8.5 | 8.0 | 6.8 | 5.5 | 4.6 | 4.6 | 4.7 | 4.5 |
| Other and unknown Hispanic or Latina | 10.6 | 9.5 | 8.0 | 7.4 | 6.9 | 6.7 | 6.4 | 5.8 |
| Not Hispanic or Latina: | | | | | | | | |
| White[f] | 9.2 | 8.6 | 7.2 | 6.3 | 5.7 | 5.7 | 5.8 | 5.6 |
| Black or African American[f] | 19.1 | 18.3 | 16.9 | 14.7 | 13.6 | 13.6 | 13.6 | 13.4 |
| | Neonatal[c] deaths per 1,000 live births | | | | | | | |
| **All mothers** | **7.1** | **6.8** | **5.7** | **4.9** | **4.6** | **4.5** | **4.5** | **4.5** |
| White | 6.1 | 5.8 | 4.6 | 4.1 | 3.8 | 3.8 | 3.8 | 3.7 |
| Black or African American | 12.5 | 12.3 | 11.1 | 9.6 | 9.1 | 8.9 | 8.9 | 8.7 |
| American Indian or Alaska Native | 7.5 | 6.1 | 6.1 | 4.0 | 4.4 | 4.3 | 4.0 | 4.3 |
| Asian or Pacific Islander[d] | 5.2 | 4.8 | 3.9 | 3.4 | 3.4 | 3.2 | 3.4 | 3.2 |
| Hispanic or Latina[e, f] | 6.2 | 5.7 | 4.8 | 4.1 | 3.8 | 3.8 | 3.9 | 3.7 |
| Mexican | 5.9 | 5.4 | 4.5 | 3.9 | 3.6 | 3.7 | 3.8 | 3.7 |
| Puerto Rican | 8.7 | 7.6 | 6.9 | 6.1 | 5.8 | 5.3 | 5.9 | 5.4 |
| Cuban | *5.0 | 6.2 | 5.3 | *3.6 | *3.2 | *2.8 | *3.1 | 3.6 |
| Central and South American | 5.8 | 5.6 | 4.4 | 3.7 | 3.3 | 3.4 | 3.2 | 3.1 |
| Other and unknown Hispanic or Latina | 6.4 | 5.6 | 5.0 | 4.8 | 4.6 | 4.7 | 4.3 | 3.7 |
| Not Hispanic or Latina: | | | | | | | | |
| White[f] | 5.9 | 5.6 | 4.5 | 4.0 | 3.8 | 3.7 | 3.7 | 3.6 |
| Black or African American[f] | 12.0 | 11.9 | 11.0 | 9.6 | 9.2 | 9.1 | 9.1 | 9.0 |
| | Postneonatal[c] deaths per 1,000 live births | | | | | | | |
| **All mothers** | **3.8** | **3.6** | **3.2** | **2.6** | **2.3** | **2.3** | **2.3** | **2.2** |
| White | 3.2 | 3.1 | 2.7 | 2.2 | 1.9 | 1.9 | 2.0 | 1.9 |
| Black or African American | 6.7 | 6.3 | 5.9 | 5.0 | 4.3 | 4.3 | 4.3 | 4.2 |
| American Indian or Alaska Native | 7.7 | 7.0 | 7.0 | 5.1 | 3.9 | 4.2 | 4.0 | 4.0 |
| Asian or Pacific Islander[d] | 3.1 | 2.9 | 2.7 | 1.9 | 1.4 | 1.5 | 1.5 | 1.4 |
| Hispanic or Latina[e, f] | 3.3 | 3.2 | 2.7 | 2.1 | 1.8 | 1.7 | 1.8 | 1.7 |
| Mexican | 3.2 | 3.2 | 2.7 | 2.1 | 1.8 | 1.7 | 1.7 | 1.6 |
| Puerto Rican | 4.2 | 3.5 | 3.0 | 2.8 | 2.4 | 2.5 | 2.4 | 2.6 |
| Cuban | *2.5 | *2.3 | *1.9 | *1.7 | * | *1.7 | *1.4 | *1.4 |
| Central and South American | 2.6 | 2.4 | 2.4 | 1.9 | 1.4 | 1.2 | 1.5 | 1.4 |
| Other and unknown Hispanic or Latina | 4.2 | 3.9 | 3.0 | 2.6 | 2.3 | 2.0 | 2.1 | 2.1 |
| Not Hispanic or Latina: | | | | | | | | |
| White[f] | 3.2 | 3.0 | 2.7 | 2.2 | 1.9 | 2.0 | 2.1 | 1.9 |
| Black or African American[f] | 7.0 | 6.4 | 5.9 | 5.0 | 4.4 | 4.5 | 4.5 | 4.4 |

*Estimates are considered unreliable. Rates preceded by an asterisk are based on fewer than 50 deaths in the numerator. Rates not shown are based on fewer than 20 deaths in the numerator.
[a]Rates based on unweighted birth cohort data.
[b]Rates based on a period file using weighted data.
[c]Infant (under 1 year of age), neonatal (under 28 days), and postneonatal (28 days–11 months).
[d]Starting with 2003 data, estimates are not available for Asian or Pacific Islander subgroups during the transition from single-race to multiple-race reporting.
[e]Persons of Hispanic origin may be of any race.
[f]Prior to 1995, data are shown only for states with an Hispanic-origin item on their birth certificates.
Notes: The race groups white, black, American Indian or Alaska Native, and Asian or Pacific Islander include persons of Hispanic and non-Hispanic origin. Starting with 2003 data, some states reported multiple-race data. The multiple-race data for these states were bridged to the single-race categories of the 1977 Office of Management and Budget standards for comparability with other states. Data for additional years are available.

SOURCE: "Table 15. Infant, Neonatal, and Postneonatal Mortality Rates, by Detailed Race and Hispanic Origin of Mother: United States, Selected Years 1983–2006," in *Health, United States, 2010: With Special Feature on Death and Dying,* U.S. Department of Health and Human Services, Centers for Disease Control and Prevention, National Center for Health Statistics, 2011, http://www.cdc.gov/nchs/data/hus/hus10.pdf (accessed December 16, 2011)

between low income and low educational attainment and high infant mortality seems to be more complicated than previously thought. Even though Hispanics have a higher rate of poverty and lower educational attainment than do non-Hispanic whites, they have a consistently lower infant mortality rate. Researchers speculate that greater social support, less high-risk behavior, and dietary factors may explain the differences. However, as Hispanic immigrants begin to adopt the lifestyle of the American mainstream, experts worry that the health of this population will decline and the infant mortality rates will rise.

Furthermore, the view of low birth weight as a result of low income and low educational attainment is complicated by other research that shows even professional, middle-class, and educated African-American women have a higher risk than their white counterparts of having low-birth-weight babies. Ziba Kashef indicates in "Persistent Peril: Why African American Babies Have the Highest Infant Mortality Rate in the Developed World" (*RaceWire*, February 2003) that "researchers have found that even when they control for such varied factors as poverty, housing, employment, medical risk, abuse, social support and so on, 90 percent of the differences in birth weight between black and white moms remains unaccounted for." Marian F. MacDorman of the CDC notes in "Race and Ethnic Disparities in Fetal Mortality, Preterm Birth, and Infant Mortality in the United States: An Overview" (*Seminars in Perinatology*, vol. 35, no. 4, August 2011) that risk factors for poor birth outcomes, including teen childbearing, advanced maternal age, low socioeconomic status, low educational achievement, maternal smoking, and lack of maternal care, do not explain all the disparities in birth outcomes. As a result, some experts, such as Paula Braveman of the University of California, San Francisco, in "Racial Disparities at Birth: The Puzzle Persists" (*Issues in Science and Technology*, vol. 24, no. 2, Winter 2008), have begun to look at factors such as chronic emotional stress resulting from living in a racially biased society to explain the poorer birth outcomes of African-American mothers.

## DISEASES AND MINORITY POPULATIONS
### Cancer

Cancer is the uncontrolled spread of abnormal cells and can lead to death if left unchecked. Cancer incidence varies according to racial and ethnic background. Risk factors such as occupation, use of tobacco and alcohol, sexual and reproductive behaviors, and nutritional and dietary habits influence the development of cancer. Cancer screening, treatment, and mortality rates also vary by race and ethnicity.

African-Americans have both the highest cancer incidence and the highest cancer mortality rates of all racial and ethnic groups, whereas the cancer incidence and mortality rates of other minority groups are relatively low. The Surveillance, Epidemiology, and End Results (SEER) Program of the National Cancer Institute (NCI) is the most authoritative source of information on cancer incidence, mortality, and survival in the United States. Nadia Howlader et al. of the NCI report in *SEER Cancer Statistics Review, 1975–2009* (April 2012, http://seer.cancer.gov/csr/1975_2009_pops09/)

that the incidence rates of all cancers between 2005 and 2009 were:

- 627.1 per 100,000 African-American men and 398.3 per 100,000 African-American women
- 542.7 per 100,000 white men and 423.1 per 100,000 white women
- 402 per 100,000 Hispanic men and 324.1 per 100,000 Hispanic women
- 352.7 per 100,000 Native American and Alaskan Native men and 313.8 per 100,000 Native American and Alaskan Native women
- 342.6 per 100,000 Asian and Pacific Islander men and 299.4 per 100,000 Asian and Pacific Islander women

The mortality rates of all cancers between 2005 and 2009 were:

- 288.3 per 100,000 African-American men and 174.6 per 100,000 African-American women
- 216.7 per 100,000 white men and 150.8 per 100,000 white women
- 146.3 per 100,000 Hispanic men and 100.5 per 100,000 Hispanic women
- 184.9 per 100,000 Native American and Alaskan Native men and 135.9 per 100,000 Native American and Alaskan Native women
- 132.6 per 100,000 Asian and Pacific Islander men and 93.2 per 100,000 Asian and Pacific Islander women

The incidence rates of cancer declined for all racial and ethnic groups between 1999 and 2008. (See Table 6.10.) This decline was highest among African-Americans, whose annual percent change during this period was −1%. The annual percent change for Hispanics was −0.8%; for whites, −0.7%; for Native Americans and Alaskan Natives, −0.6%; and for Asians and Pacific Islanders, −0.4%. The death rates also declined for all groups. Again, the most pronounced annual percent change was among African-Americans (−2%), followed by Hispanics (−1.7%), whites and Asians and Pacific Islanders (−1.4%), and Native Americans and Alaskan Natives (−0.4%). (See Table 6.11.)

Howlader et al. note that more non-Hispanic whites survived five years after the diagnosis of invasive cancer than did African-Americans in the 20-year period between 1988 and 2008. About two-thirds (65%) of non-Hispanic whites survived five years, compared with only 55.1% of African-Americans. Much of this difference in survival can be attributed to later diagnosis of cancer in African-Americans because of lower screening rates and less access to health care. Among the most diagnosed cancers for all groups in the United States are breast cancer, prostate cancer, lung and bronchus cancer, and colon

**TABLE 6.10**

**Cancer incidence rates and trends for the top 15 cancer sites[a], by race and Hispanic origin, 2004–08**

[Both sexes]

| All races | Rate[b] 2004–2008 | APC[c] 1999–2008 |
|---|---|---|
| All sites | 464.4 | −0.7* |
| Prostate[f] | 69.7 | −1.6* |
| Breast | 67.0 | −1.4* |
| Lung and bronchus | 62.0 | −1.3* |
| Colon and rectum | 47.2 | −2.4* |
| Urinary bladder | 21.1 | −0.4* |
| Melanoma of the skin | 20.8 | 1.9* |
| Non-Hodgkin lymphoma | 19.8 | 0.2 |
| Kidney and renal pelvis | 14.6 | 3.0* |
| Corpus and uterus, NOS[f] | 12.8 | −0.1 |
| Leukemia | 12.5 | −0.4 |
| Pancreas | 12.0 | 1.1* |
| Thyroid | 11.0 | 6.2* |
| Oral cavity and pharynx | 10.6 | −0.4 |
| Stomach | 7.7 | −1.6* |
| Liver & IBD[g] | 7.3 | 3.0* |

| White | Rate[b] 2004–2008 | APC[c] 1999–2008 |
|---|---|---|
| All sites | 471.8 | −0.7* |
| Breast | 68.2 | −1.8* |
| Prostate[f] | 67.4 | −1.7* |
| Lung and bronchus | 63.3 | −1.2* |
| Colon and rectum | 46.5 | −2.6* |
| Melanoma of the skin | 24.3 | 2.3* |
| Urinary bladder | 22.9 | −0.4 |
| Non-Hodgkin lymphoma | 20.7 | 0.2 |
| Kidney and renal pelvis | 15.1 | 2.8* |
| Corpus and uterus, NOS[f] | 13.2 | −0.4 |
| Leukemia | 13.1 | −0.4 |
| Pancreas | 11.9 | 1.1* |
| Thyroid | 11.5 | 6.4* |
| Oral cavity and pharynx | 10.8 | −0.1 |
| Ovary[f, h] | 7.2 | −1.8* |
| Brain and ONS[g] | 7.1 | −0.5 |

| Black | Rate[b] 2004–2008 | APC[c] 1999–2008 |
|---|---|---|
| All sites | 491.2 | −1.0* |
| Prostate[f] | 97.4 | −2.5* |
| Lung and bronchus | 72.7 | −1.8* |
| Breast | 68.8 | 0.1 |
| Colon and rectum | 57.8 | −1.8* |
| Kidney and renal pelvis | 16.5 | 2.9* |
| Pancreas | 15.9 | 0.9 |
| Non-Hodgkin lymphoma | 14.8 | 0.6 |
| Urinary bladder | 13.1 | −0.3 |
| Corpus and uterus, NOS[f] | 12.0 | 2.2* |
| Stomach | 11.9 | −1.6* |
| Myeloma | 11.9 | 0.4 |
| Oral cavity and pharynx | 9.9 | −2.8* |
| Leukemia | 9.8 | −1.1 |
| Liver & IBD[g] | 9.2 | 3.6* |
| Thyroid | 6.5 | 6.1* |

| Asian/Pacific Islander | Rate[b] 2004–2008 | APC[c] 1999–2008 |
|---|---|---|
| All sites | 315.9 | −0.4* |
| Breast | 51.2 | 0.5 |
| Colon and rectum | 39.4 | −1.9* |
| Lung and bronchus | 39.0 | −0.9* |
| Prostate[f] | 38.4 | −2.0* |
| Liver & IBD[g] | 14.6 | 0.5 |
| Non-Hodgkin lymphoma | 13.3 | −0.5 |
| Stomach | 13.0 | −3.1* |
| Thyroid | 10.9 | 5.0* |
| Corpus and uterus, NOS[f] | 9.9 | 1.8* |
| Pancreas | 9.5 | 1.2* |
| Urinary bladder | 9.3 | 0.4 |
| Oral cavity and pharynx | 7.9 | −0.5 |
| Kidney and renal pelvis | 7.7 | 4.9* |
| Leukemia | 7.3 | −0.6 |
| Ovary[f, h] | 5.4 | −0.3 |

| American Indian/Alaska Native[d] | Rate[b] 2004–2008 | APC[c] 1999–2008 |
|---|---|---|
| All sites | 319.9 | −0.6 |
| Lung and bronchus | 44.5 | 0.4 |
| Breast | 42.3 | 0.1 |
| Colon and rectum | 41.4 | −2.3 |
| Prostate[f] | 33.0 | −1.9 |
| Kidney and renal pelvis | 17.6 | 3.3* |
| Liver & IBD[g] | 12.2 | 3.4 |
| Non-Hodgkin lymphoma | 11.5 | −1.4 |
| Pancreas | 10.6 | 1.6 |
| Stomach | 10.6 | −5.0 |
| Corpus and uterus, NOS[f] | 9.0 | 0.8 |
| Urinary bladder | 8.3 | — |
| Leukemia | 7.6 | 1.5 |
| Oral cavity and pharynx | 7.0 | −4.0 |
| Thyroid | 6.3 | 0.8 |
| Ovary[f, h] | 5.8 | −4.0 |

| Hispanic[e] | Rate[b] 2004–2008 | APC[c] 1999–2008 |
|---|---|---|
| All sites | 356.1 | −0.8* |
| Prostate[f] | 56.8 | −2.2* |
| Breast | 49.0 | −0.7* |
| Colon and rectum | 38.3 | −1.0* |
| Lung and bronchus | 32.5 | −1.5* |
| Non-Hodgkin lymphoma | 17.2 | 0.3 |
| Kidney and renal pelvis | 14.5 | 2.9* |
| Urinary bladder | 11.6 | −1.0 |
| Stomach | 11.5 | −1.8* |
| Liver & IBD[g] | 11.1 | 2.0* |
| Pancreas | 10.9 | 0.7 |
| Corpus and uterus, NOS[f] | 10.0 | 1.4* |
| Leukemia | 9.8 | 0.4 |
| Thyroid | 9.4 | 5.0* |
| Ovary[f, h] | 6.3 | −0.9 |
| Oral cavity and pharynx | 6.2 | −0.7 |

and rectum cancer. These cancers are examined in more detail in the following sections.

**BREAST CANCER.** Even though a smaller proportion of African-American women (119.9 per 100,000 females between 2004 and 2008) were diagnosed with breast cancer than were non-Hispanic white women (133.2 per 100,000), a higher proportion of African-American women (32 per 100,000 females between 2004 and 2008) died of the disease than did white women (23.4 per 100,000). (See Figure 6.3.) For years, experts assumed that the difference in mortality rates was due to poor health care and late

**TABLE 6.10**

**Cancer incidence rates and trends for the top 15 cancer sites[a], by race and Hispanic origin, 2004–08** [CONTINUED]

[Both sexes]

[a]Top 15 cancer sites selected based on 2004–2008 age-adjusted rates for the race/ethnic group.
[b]Incidence data used in calculating the rates are from the 17 Surveillance, Epidemiology, and End Results (SEER) areas (San Francisco, Connecticut, Detroit, Hawaii, Iowa, New Mexico, Seattle, Utah, Atlanta, San Jose-Monterey, Los Angeles, Alaska Native registry, rural Georgia, California excluding San Francisco, San Jose-Monterey, Los Angeles, Kentucky, Louisiana and New Jersey). Rates are age-adjusted to the 2000 U.S. standard population (19 age groups—Census P25–1130).
[c]The APC is the Annual Percent Change over the time interval. Incidence data used in calculating the trends are from the 13 SEER areas (San Francisco, Connecticut, Detroit, Hawaii, Iowa, New Mexico, Seattle, Utah, Atlanta, San Jose-Monterey, Los Angeles, Alaska Native registry and rural Georgia). Trends are based on rates age-adjusted to the 2000 U.S. standard population (19 age groups—Census P25–1130).
[d]Rates for American Indian/Alaska Native are based on the CHSDA (Contract Health Service Delivery Area) counties.
[e]Hispanic is not mutually exclusive from whites, blacks, Asian/Pacific Islanders, and American Indians/Alaska Natives. Incidence data for Hispanics are based on National Health Insurance Awards (NHIA) and exclude cases from the Alaska Native registry.
[f]NOS = Not Otherwise Specified. The rates for sex-specific cancer sites are calculated using the population for both sexes combined.
[g]IBD = Intrahepatic bile duct. ONS = Other nervous system.
[h]Ovary excludes borderline cases or histologies 8,442, 8,451, 8,462, 8,472, and 8,473.
*The APC is significantly different from zero (p < 0.05).
—Statistic not shown. Rate based on less than 16 cases for the time interval. Trend based on less than 10 cases for at least one year within the time interval.

SOURCE: N. Howlader et al., eds., "Table 1.23. Age-Adjusted SEER Incidence Rates and Trends for the Top 15 Cancer Sites by Race/Ethnicity," in *SEER Cancer Statistics Review, 1975–2008*, National Cancer Institute, 2011, http://seer.cancer.gov/csr/1975_2008/results_merged/topic_topfifteen.pdf (accessed December 16, 2011)

treatment for African-American women. However, Rob Stein reports in "Blacks Getting Equal Health Care Are Still More Likely to Die from Some Cancers" (*Washington Post*, July 8, 2009) that a large study involving 20,000 cancer patients finds that despite equal care, African-American women with breast or ovarian cancer were more likely than white women with these cancers to die of the disease. The researcher Kathy S. Albain of Loyola University stated, "This is almost certainly related to a mix of factors across races pertaining to tumor biology and inherited factors."

In "African American Women and Breast Cancer" (June 29, 2006, http://www.susanlovemd.com/pdfs/african_american_bc.pdf), Sue Rochman of the Dr. Susan Love Research Foundation explains that African-American women may be more susceptible to a more deadly form of the cancer. Tumors from African-American women have been found to contain more actively dividing cells than tumors from white women. The tumor cells in African-American women also lack hormone receptors, which is another indicator of a poor prognosis. After peaking during the early 1990s, the death rate from breast cancer for African-American women showed some improvement by 2008. (See Figure 6.3.)

Hispanics, Asians and Pacific Islanders, and Native Americans and Alaskan Natives are less likely to be diagnosed with breast cancer or to die from breast cancer than either whites or African-Americans. The incidence rates of breast cancer between 2004 and 2008 were 77.9 per 100,000 female Native Americans and Alaskan Natives, 92.1 per 100,000 female Hispanics, and 93.7 per 100,000 female Asians and Pacific Islanders. Between 2004 and 2008 the mortality rates of breast cancer were lowest for Asians and Pacific Islanders, at 12.2 per 100,000, despite their higher incidence rate. The mortality rate for Hispanics was highest of the three groups, at 15.1 per 100,000. Figure 6.3 shows the

mortality rates of these three groups compared with those of African-American and white women.

**PROSTATE CANCER.** African-American men have a particularly high incidence of and mortality rate for prostate cancer. Between 2004 and 2008 the prostate cancer incidence rate among African-American men was 233.8 cases per 100,000 population, compared with a rate of only 153.1 cases per 100,000 population among non-Hispanic whites. (See Figure 6.4.) During this period African-American men had a mortality rate of 54.9 per 100,000 males from prostate cancer, compared with 22.6 deaths per 100,000 non-Hispanic white men. Even though the incidence and mortality rates for prostate cancer decreased for both groups between the early 1990s and 2008, the incidence and mortality rates for African-American men remained substantially higher than for all other races and ethnic groups.

Hispanics, Asians and Pacific Islanders, and Native Americans and Alaskan Natives have lower rates of prostate cancer incidence and lower rates of prostate cancer mortality than do African-Americans or non-Hispanic whites. (See Figure 6.4.) The incidence rates of prostate cancer between 2004 and 2008 were 129 per 100,000 Hispanic men, 88.3 per 100,000 Asian and Pacific Islander men, and 75.3 per 100,000 Native American and Alaskan Native men. The mortality rate of prostate cancer was lowest for Asian and Pacific Islander males, at 10.5 per 100,000 males, despite their higher incidence rate. The mortality rates for Hispanic and Native American and Alaskan Native males were much higher at 18.5 per 100,000 males and 16.9 per 100,000 males, respectively.

**LUNG AND BRONCHUS CANCER.** According to Howlader et al., in *SEER Cancer Statistics Review*, lung cancer is the deadliest cancer in the United States; the five-year survival rate for all races was only 16.3% of those diagnosed

## TABLE 6.11

**Cancer mortality rates and trends for the top 15 cancer sites[a], by race and Hispanic origin, 2004–08**

[Both sexes]

### All Races

| | Rate[b] 2004–2008 | APC[c] 1999–2008 |
|---|---|---|
| All sites | 181.3 | −1.5* |
| Lung and bronchus | 51.6 | −1.3* |
| Colon and rectum | 17.1 | −2.9* |
| Breast | 13.2 | −2.2* |
| Pancreas | 10.8 | 0.4* |
| Prostate[f] | 9.3 | −3.0* |
| Leukemia | 7.1 | −1.1* |
| Non-Hodgkin lymphoma | 6.7 | −3.1* |
| Liver & IBD[g] | 5.3 | 2.3* |
| Ovary[f] | 4.7 | −1.3* |
| Urinary bladder | 4.4 | 0.1 |
| Esophagus | 4.3 | −0.3 |
| Brain and ONS[g] | 4.3 | −1.0* |
| Kidney and renal pelvis | 4.0 | −0.6* |
| Stomach | 3.7 | −3.1* |
| Myeloma | 3.5 | −1.6* |

### White

| | Rate[b] 2004–2008 | APC[c] 1999–2008 |
|---|---|---|
| All sites | 180.0 | −1.4* |
| Lung and bronchus | 52.1 | −1.2* |
| Colon and rectum | 16.6 | −3.0* |
| Breast | 12.8 | −2.3* |
| Pancreas | 10.6 | 0.5* |
| Prostate[f] | 8.6 | −2.8* |
| Leukemia | 7.4 | −1.0* |
| Non-Hodgkin lymphoma | 7.0 | −3.1* |
| Liver & IBD[g] | 4.9 | 2.4* |
| Ovary[f] | 4.9 | −1.2* |
| Brain and ONS[g] | 4.6 | −0.9* |
| Urinary bladder | 4.6 | 0.3* |
| Esophagus | 4.4 | 0.4 |
| Kidney and renal pelvis | 4.1 | −0.6* |
| Stomach | 3.2 | −3.2* |
| Myeloma | 3.2 | −1.5* |

### Black

| | Rate[b] 2004–2008 | APC[c] 1999–2008 |
|---|---|---|
| All sites | 220.8 | −2.0* |
| Lung and bronchus | 57.0 | −2.0* |
| Colon and rectum | 24.3 | −2.4* |
| Breast | 19.0 | −1.4* |
| Prostate[f] | 19.0 | −3.7* |
| Pancreas | 13.9 | −0.1 |
| Stomach | 7.2 | −3.4* |
| Liver & IBD[g] | 7.1 | 2.5* |
| Myeloma | 6.6 | −1.8* |
| Leukemia | 6.3 | −1.0* |
| Esophagus | 4.9 | −4.4* |
| Non-Hodgkin lymphoma | 4.7 | −2.6* |
| Corpus and uterus, NOS[f] | 4.3 | 0.3 |
| Ovary[f] | 4.2 | −1.3* |
| Kidney and renal pelvis | 4.0 | −0.6* |
| Urinary bladder | 3.7 | −0.8 |

### Asian/Pacific Islander

| | Rate[b] 2004–2008 | APC[c] 1999–2008 |
|---|---|---|
| All sites | 110.9 | −1.4* |
| Lung and bronchus | 26.2 | −1.0* |
| Colon and rectum | 11.4 | −1.6* |
| Liver & IBD[g] | 10.0 | −1.0 |
| Pancreas | 7.6 | 0.3 |
| Stomach | 7.0 | −3.9* |
| Breast | 6.8 | −0.9 |
| Non-Hodgkin lymphoma | 4.3 | −2.7* |
| Prostate[f] | 4.2 | −3.5* |
| Leukemia | 3.8 | −1.5* |
| Ovary[f] | 2.8 | 0.5 |
| Oral cavity and pharynx | 2.0 | −2.5* |
| Brain and ONS[g] | 1.9 | −0.4 |
| Esophagus | 1.9 | −0.7 |
| Kidney and renal pelvis | 1.9 | 0.9 |
| Myeloma | 1.7 | −0.9 |

### American Indian/Alaska Native[d]

| | Rate[b] 2004–2008 | APC[c] 1999–2008 |
|---|---|---|
| All sites | 159.6 | −0.4 |
| Lung and bronchus | 41.0 | 0.3 |
| Colon and rectum | 16.5 | −0.5 |
| Breast | 9.7 | 0.4 |
| Pancreas | 9.2 | 2.3 |
| Liver & IBD[g] | 9.1 | 1.7 |
| Prostate[f] | 8.2 | −0.6 |
| Kidney and renal pelvis | 6.2 | −0.7 |
| Stomach | 5.8 | −4.5* |
| Leukemia | 4.8 | 1.0 |
| Non-Hodgkin lymphoma | 4.7 | −3.8 |
| Ovary[f] | 3.8 | −0.7 |
| Esophagus | 3.8 | −0.5 |
| Myeloma | 3.0 | −5.0* |
| Oral cavity and pharynx | 2.4 | −1.2 |
| Brain and ONS[g] | 2.4 | 4.9 |

### Hispanic[e]

| | Rate[b] 2004–2008 | APC[c] 1999–2008 |
|---|---|---|
| All sites | 121.0 | −1.7* |
| Lung and bronchus | 21.8 | −2.1* |
| Colon and rectum | 12.6 | −2.0* |
| Pancreas | 8.3 | 0.0 |
| Breast | 8.3 | −1.9* |
| Liver & IBD[g] | 8.1 | 1.4* |
| Prostate[f] | 7.4 | −2.8* |
| Stomach | 5.9 | −3.2* |
| Non-Hodgkin lymphoma | 5.2 | −2.6* |
| Leukemia | 4.8 | −1.5* |
| Kidney and renal pelvis | 3.6 | −0.4 |
| Ovary[f] | 3.3 | −0.8 |
| Myeloma | 2.8 | −2.4* |
| Brain and ONS[g] | 2.8 | −0.7 |
| Esophagus | 2.3 | −1.4* |
| Urinary bladder | 2.3 | −1.0 |

between 2001 and 2007. African-Americans have a particularly high incidence of lung cancer and mortality rate compared with other groups. Between 2004 and 2008 the lung cancer incidence rate among African-Americans was 72.7 cases per 100,000 population, compared with a rate of 67.8 cases per 100,000 non-Hispanic whites, 44.5 cases per 100,000 Native Americans and Alaskan Natives, 39 cases per 100,000 Asians and Pacific Islanders, and 32.5 per 100,000 Hispanics. (See Figure 6.5.) Both the incidence and mortality rates for lung cancer decreased between the 1990s and 2008, especially for Hispanics and African-Americans; however, the incidence and mortality rates for

## TABLE 6.11

**Cancer mortality rates and trends for the top 15 cancer sites[a], by race and Hispanic origin, 2004–08** [CONTINUED]

[Both sexes]

[a]Top 15 cancer sites selected based on 2004–2008 age-adjusted rates for the race/ethnic group.
[b]Mortality data used in calculating the rates are analyzed from US mortality files provided by the National Center for Health Statistics, the Centers for Disease Control (CDC). Rates are age-adjusted to the 2000 U.S. standard population (19 age groups—Census P25–1130).
[c]The APC is the Annual Percent Change over the time interval. Mortality data used in calculating the trends are analyzed from US mortality files provided by the National Center for Health Statistics, CDC. Trends are based on rates age-adjusted to the 2000 U.S. standard population (19 age groups—Census P25–1130).
[d]Rates for American Indian/Alaska Native are based on the CHSDA (Contract Health Service Delivery Area) counties.
[e]Hispanic is not mutually exclusive from whites, blacks, Asian/Pacific Islanders, and American Indians/Alaska Natives.
The 2004–2008 Hispanic death rates do not include deaths from the District of Columbia and North Dakota.
The 1999–2008 Hispanic mortality trends do not include deaths from the District of Columbia, Minnesota, New Hampshire and North Dakota.
[f]NOS = Not Otherwise Specified. The rates for sex-specific cancer sites are calculated using the population for both sexes combined.
[g]IBD = Intrahepatic Bile Duct. ONS = Other Nervous System.
*The APC is significantly different from zero (p < 0.05).
—Statistic not shown. Rate based on less than 16 cases for the time interval. Trend based on less than 10 cases for at least one year within the time interval.

SOURCE: N. Howlader et al., eds., "Table 1.26. Age-Adjusted U.S. Death Rates and Trends for the Top 15 Cancer Sites by Race/Ethnicity," in *SEER Cancer Statistics Review, 1975–2008*, National Cancer Institute, 2011, http://seer.cancer.gov/csr/1975_2008/results_merged/topic_topfifteen.pdf (accessed December 16, 2011)

African-Americans remained substantially higher than for all other races and ethnic groups.

**COLON AND RECTUM CANCER.** Colon and rectum cancer is the fourth-most frequently diagnosed cancer in the United States after prostate cancer, breast cancer, and lung and bronchus cancer; it is also the second-most deadly. African-Americans are diagnosed more frequently than other groups. Between 2004 and 2008 African-Americans had an incidence of 57.8 cases per 100,000 population, compared with a rate of 47.6 per 100,000 non-Hispanic whites, 41.4 per 100,000 Native Americans and Alaskan Natives, 39.4 per 100,000 Asians and Pacific Islanders, and 38.3 per 100,000 Hispanics. (See Figure 6.6.) African-Americans also had the highest mortality rate from colon and rectum cancer, at 24.3 deaths per 100,000 population, compared with 16.9 deaths per 100,000 non-Hispanic whites, 12.6 deaths per 100,000 Hispanics, 12.5 deaths per 100,000 Native Americans and Alaskan Natives, and 11.4 deaths per 100,000 Asians and Pacific Islanders. Both the incidence and mortality rates of colon and rectum cancer steadily decreased for non-Hispanic whites between the mid-1980s and 2008, whereas the incidence and mortality rates for African-Americans remained relatively constant until 2002, when they began to drop.

### Heart Disease and Stroke

Heart disease includes coronary and hypertensive heart diseases and heart failure. According to the HHS, in *National Healthcare Disparities Report, 2010*, each year approximately 17.6 million Americans suffer from coronary heart disease. About 8.5 million heart attacks occur each year, and 5.8 million Americans have heart failure.

The rates of heart disease vary considerably by race, with higher rates for African-Americans. Along with age, sex, and race, heredity is one of the risk factors for heart disease that cannot be changed. However, because of their higher rates of incidence of heart disease and stroke, African-Americans are encouraged to control other risk factors, including the use of tobacco and alcohol, blood pressure and cholesterol levels, physical activity, weight, and stress.

**HIGH BLOOD PRESSURE.** Véronique L. Roger et al. explain in *Heart Disease and Stroke Statistics—2012 Update* (*Circulation*, vol. 125, no. 1, December 15, 2011) that the prevalence of high blood pressure (hypertension) in both non-Hispanic African-American men and women is significantly higher than in non-Hispanic white men and women and that the prevalence of high blood pressure among Hispanics and Asian-Americans is lower than in the non-Hispanic white community. Among adults aged 20 years and older, 33.9% of non-Hispanic white males and 31.3% of non-Hispanic white females had high blood pressure in 2008; 43% of non-Hispanic African-American males and 45.7% of non-Hispanic African-American females had high blood pressure in that year. However, the rates of high blood pressure among Hispanics (24.7%) and Asian-Americans (20.5%) were much lower, while the rate for Native Americans and Alaskan Natives (30%) was comparable to that of non-Hispanic whites. Roger et al. note that the prevalence of high blood pressure among non-Hispanic African-Americans in the United States is among the highest in the world. Compared with non-Hispanic whites, non-Hispanic African-Americans develop high blood pressure earlier in life and their average blood pressure is much higher. As a result, non-Hispanic African-Americans had nearly twice the risk of a nonfatal stroke than did non-Hispanic whites, a 1.8 times greater rate of fatal stroke than did non-Hispanic whites, and a 1.5 times greater rate of death from heart disease than did non-Hispanic whites in 2008.

FIGURE 6.3

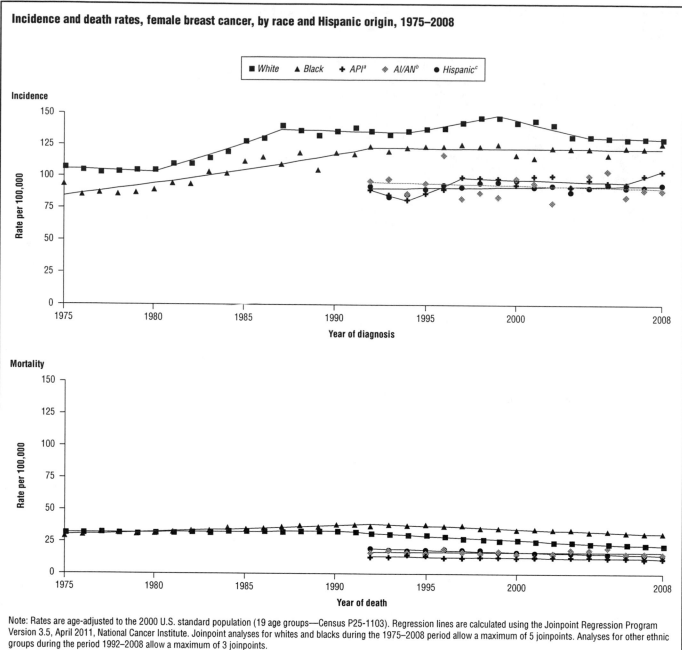

**Incidence and death rates, female breast cancer, by race and Hispanic origin, 1975–2008**

Note: Rates are age-adjusted to the 2000 U.S. standard population (19 age groups—Census P25-1103). Regression lines are calculated using the Joinpoint Regression Program Version 3.5, April 2011, National Cancer Institute. Joinpoint analyses for whites and blacks during the 1975–2008 period allow a maximum of 5 joinpoints. Analyses for other ethnic groups during the period 1992–2008 allow a maximum of 3 joinpoints.

[a]API = Asian/Pacific Islander.

[b]AI/AN = American Indian/Alaska Native. Rates for American Indian/Alaska Native are based on the CHSDA (Contract Health Service Delivery Area) counties.

[c]Hispanic is not mutually exclusive from whites, blacks, Asian/Pacific Islanders, and American Indians/Alaska Natives. Incidence data for Hispanics are based on the National Health Insurance Awards (NHIA) and exclude cases from the Alaska Native Registry. Mortality data for Hispanics exclude cases from Connecticut, the District of Columbia, Maryland, Minnesota, New Hampshire, New York, North Dakota, Oklahoma, and Vermont.

SOURCE: N. Howlader et al., eds., "SEER Incidence and U.S. Death Rates: Cancer of the Female Breast," in *SEER Cancer Statistics Review, 1975–2008*, National Cancer Institute, 2011, http://seer.cancer.gov/csr/1975_2008/results_merged/sect_04_breast.pdf (accessed December 16, 2011)

**DEATHS FROM HEART DISEASE.** The NCHS indicates in *Health, United States, 2010* (2011, http://www.cdc.gov/nchs/data/hus/hus10.pdf) that the death rate from heart disease was higher for males (when compared with females) among all racial and ethnic groups (at 237.7 per 100,000 and 154 per 100,000, respectively), but that the rate declined between 1990 and 2007 for all groups. African-American males had the highest death rate from heart disease in 2007, at 305.9 deaths per 100,000 population,

down from 485.4 deaths per 100,000 population in 1990. Hispanic males (165), Native American and Alaskan Native males (159.8), and Asian and Pacific Islander males (126) all had lower death rates from heart disease than did non-Hispanic white males (239.8).

The NCHS reports that females die of heart disease at high rates as well, although not at the rate that males do. In 2007 African-American females had the highest death rate

## FIGURE 6.4

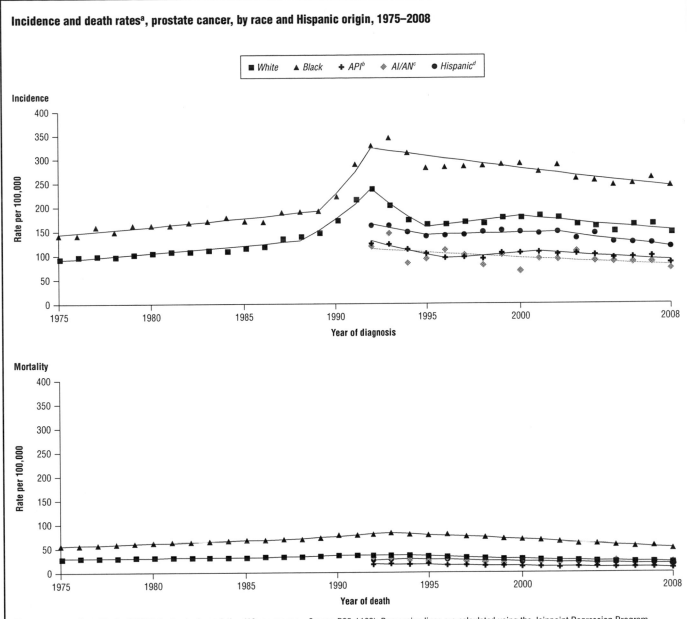

**Incidence and death rates[a], prostate cancer, by race and Hispanic origin, 1975–2008**

■ White ▲ Black + API[b] ◈ AI/AN[c] ● Hispanic[d]

[a]Rates are age-adjusted to the 2000 U.S. standard population (19 age groups—Census P25-1103). Regression lines are calculated using the Joinpoint Regression Program Version 3.5, April 2011, National Cancer Institute. Joinpoint analyses for whites and blacks during the 1975–2008 period allow a maximum of 5 joinpoints. Analyses for other ethnic groups during the period 1992–2008 allow a maximum of 3 joinpoints.
[b]API = Asian/Pacific Islander.
[c]AI/AN = American Indian/Alaska Native. Rates for American Indian/Alaska Native are based on the CHSDA (Contract Health Service Delivery Area) counties.
[d]Hispanic is not mutually exclusive from whites, blacks, Asian/Pacific Islanders, and American Indians/Alaska Natives. Incidence data for Hispanics are based on National Health Insurance Awards (NHIA) and exclude cases from the Alaska Native Registry. Mortality data for Hispanics exclude cases from Connecticut, the District of Columbia, Maine, Maryland, Minnesota, New Hampshire, New York, North Dakota, Oklahoma, and Vermont.

SOURCE: N. Howlader et al., eds., "SEER Incidence and U.S. Death Rates: Cancer of the Prostate," in *SEER Cancer Statistics Review, 1975–2008*, National Cancer Institute, 2011, http://seer.cancer.gov/csr/1975_2008/results_merged/sect_23_prostate.pdf (accessed December 16, 2011)

for heart disease of all racial and ethnic groups, at 204.5 deaths per 100,000 population, down significantly from the 1990 rate of 327.5 deaths per 100,000 population. Non-Hispanic white females had the next highest death rate from heart disease, at 153 deaths per 100,000 population. Hispanic females (111.8), Native American and Alaskan Native females (99.8), and Asian and Pacific Islander females (82)

all had lower death rates from heart disease than did African-American and non-Hispanic white women. The death rates for all females from heart disease had declined since 1990.

### Alzheimer's Disease

Alzheimer's disease is a progressive brain disorder that gradually destroys a person's memory and ability to

**FIGURE 6.5**

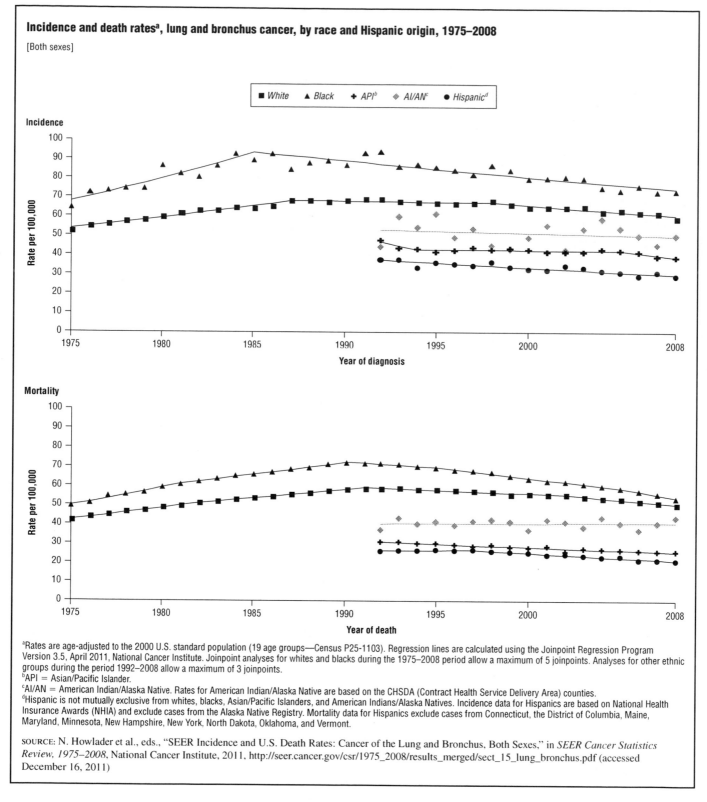

**Incidence and death rates[a], lung and bronchus cancer, by race and Hispanic origin, 1975–2008**

[Both sexes]

■ *White*    ▲ *Black*    + *API[b]*    ◈ *AI/AN[c]*    ● *Hispanic[d]*

**Incidence**

Rate per 100,000

Year of diagnosis

**Mortality**

Rate per 100,000

Year of death

[a]Rates are age-adjusted to the 2000 U.S. standard population (19 age groups—Census P25-1103). Regression lines are calculated using the Joinpoint Regression Program Version 3.5, April 2011, National Cancer Institute. Joinpoint analyses for whites and blacks during the 1975–2008 period allow a maximum of 5 joinpoints. Analyses for other ethnic groups during the period 1992–2008 allow a maximum of 3 joinpoints.
[b]API = Asian/Pacific Islander.
[c]AI/AN = American Indian/Alaska Native. Rates for American Indian/Alaska Native are based on the CHSDA (Contract Health Service Delivery Area) counties.
[d]Hispanic is not mutually exclusive from whites, blacks, Asian/Pacific Islanders, and American Indians/Alaska Natives. Incidence data for Hispanics are based on National Health Insurance Awards (NHIA) and exclude cases from the Alaska Native Registry. Mortality data for Hispanics exclude cases from Connecticut, the District of Columbia, Maine, Maryland, Minnesota, New Hampshire, New York, North Dakota, Oklahoma, and Vermont.

SOURCE: N. Howlader et al., eds., "SEER Incidence and U.S. Death Rates: Cancer of the Lung and Bronchus, Both Sexes," in *SEER Cancer Statistics Review, 1975–2008*, National Cancer Institute, 2011, http://seer.cancer.gov/csr/1975_2008/results_merged/sect_15_lung_bronchus.pdf (accessed December 16, 2011)

reason, communicate, and carry out daily activities. As it progresses, it also tends to affect personality and behavior and may result in anxiety, paranoia, and delusions or hallucinations. The disease can last from three to 20 years, and eventually the loss of brain function will cause death. Even though the underlying causes of Alzheimer's disease remain unclear, some research indicates that

minorities, particularly African-Americans, are at a greater risk of developing the disease.

In 1992 scientists first discovered that people with the apolipoprotein E gene (*APOE-ε4*; approximately 25% of the total population) have a greater risk for developing the disease. Most early research into the connection between the

FIGURE 6.6

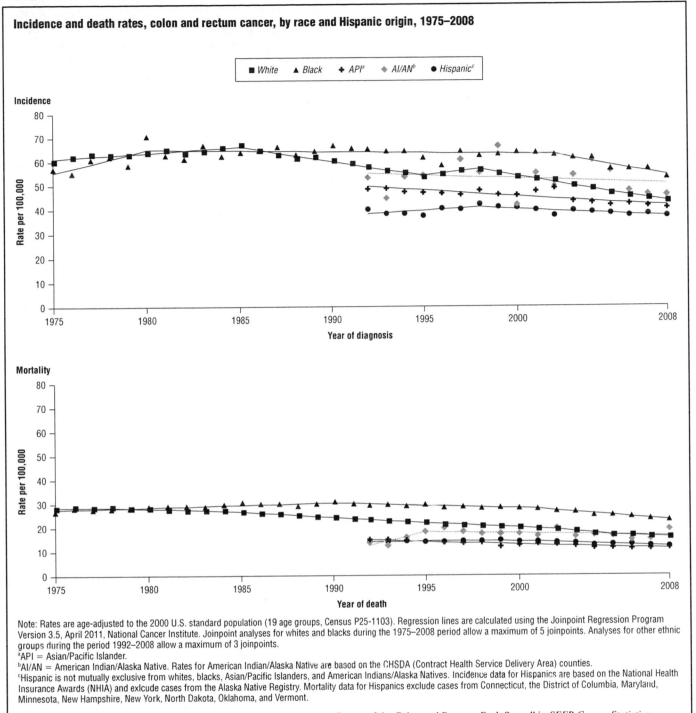

Incidence and death rates, colon and rectum cancer, by race and Hispanic origin, 1975–2008

Note: Rates are age-adjusted to the 2000 U.S. standard population (19 age groups, Census P25-1103). Regression lines are calculated using the Joinpoint Regression Program Version 3.5, April 2011, National Cancer Institute. Joinpoint analyses for whites and blacks during the 1975–2008 period allow a maximum of 5 joinpoints. Analyses for other ethnic groups during the period 1992–2008 allow a maximum of 3 joinpoints.
[a]API = Asian/Pacific Islander.
[b]AI/AN = American Indian/Alaska Native. Rates for American Indian/Alaska Native are based on the CHSDA (Contract Health Service Delivery Area) counties.
[c]Hispanic is not mutually exclusive from whites, blacks, Asian/Pacific Islanders, and American Indians/Alaska Natives. Incidence data for Hispanics are based on the National Health Insurance Awards (NHIA) and exlcude cases from the Alaska Native Registry. Mortality data for Hispanics exclude cases from Connecticut, the District of Columbia, Maryland, Minnesota, New Hampshire, New York, North Dakota, Oklahoma, and Vermont.

SOURCE: N. Howlader et al., eds., "SEER Incidence and U.S. Death Rates: Cancer of the Colon and Rectum, Both Sexes," in *SEER Cancer Statistics Review, 1975–2008*, National Cancer Institute, 2011, http://seer.cancer.gov/csr/1975_2008/results_merged/sect_06_colon_rectum.pdf (accessed December 16, 2011)

gene and the development of Alzheimer's disease concluded that the increased risk associated with the *APOE*-є4 gene applies only to whites. However, Kathryn Sawyer et al. point out in "Racial Differences in the Influence of the APOE Epsilon 4 Allele on Cognitive Decline in a Sample of Community-Dwelling Older Adults" (*Gerontology*, vol. 55, no. 1, January 2009) that earlier studies had methodo-

logical problems, including racial bias in the assessment of dementia among the elderly, that obscured the link between the gene and the risk factors in minority communities. Contrary to earlier studies, Sawyer et al. find that the allele predicted Alzheimer's disease in both African-Americans and whites and that those with the gene declined faster than those without the gene.

The Alzheimer's Association emphasizes in *2010 Alzheimer's Disease Facts and Figures* (2010, http://www.alz.org/documents_custom/report_alzfactsfigures2010.pdf) that African-Americans have about twice the risk as whites to develop Alzheimer's disease or another form of dementia, while Hispanics are about 1.5 times as likely to develop these diseases. For example, the Alzheimer's Association estimates that 32.5% of African-Americans aged 75 to 85 years have some cognitive impairment, while 23.7% of Hispanics and just 9.8% of whites have these impairments at this age. In a study of 2,162 individuals in New York City, about 9.1% of African-Americans, 7.5% of Hispanics, and 2.9% of whites aged 65 to 74 years were found to have Alzheimer's disease or another form of dementia; about 27.9% of Hispanics, 19.9% of African-Americans, and just 10.9% of whites aged 75 to 84 years were found to have these diseases. Since the turn of the 21st century, discoveries of risk factors for Alzheimer's disease—high blood pressure and high cholesterol—have begun to provide some explanation for this increased risk, as these risk factors are disproportionately present in the African-American and Hispanic communities. The Alzheimer's Association stresses the importance of getting effective medical therapies for vascular disease and its risk factors, as these drugs could potentially protect against Alzheimer's disease as well.

## Diabetes

Diabetes is a chronic disease in which the body does not produce or use insulin properly, leading to cells being starved for sugar and often resulting in damage to the heart, kidneys, and eyes. According to the NCHS, in *Health, United States, 2010*, diabetes was the seventh-deadliest disease in the United States in 2007. In fact, the death rate due to diabetes is on the rise at the same time that the death rates due to other diseases such as cancer and heart disease are declining. In "Age-Adjusted Percentage of Civilian, Noninstitutionalized Population with Diagnosed Diabetes, by Race and Sex, United States, 1980–2010" (December 27, 2011, http://www.cdc.gov/diabetes/statistics/prev/national/figraceethsex.htm), the CDC reports that in 2010, 9.7% of African-American males and 9.5% of African-American females had been diagnosed with diabetes, and 6.8% of white males and 5.4% of white females had diabetes. The rates for all groups had been markedly rising over the course of the previous two decades.

Diabetes is a dangerous disease because it can cause many different complications, including heart disease, kidney failure, and loss of circulation in the extremities. The lack of circulation in the lower limbs can lead to infection of small wounds and gangrene, which can eventually require leg amputation. Diabetes requires effective management of hemoglobin A1c and lipids, as well as regular examination of the eyes and feet and yearly influenza immunizations. However, the rates of receiving all three diabetic management services vary by race and ethnic group. The HHS explains in *National Healthcare Disparities Report, 2010* that non-Hispanic whites were more likely than either African-Americans or Hispanics to receive the recommended services between 2002 and 2007, although less than a majority of all groups had received the services in the past year. (See Figure 6.7.)

**FIGURE 6.7**

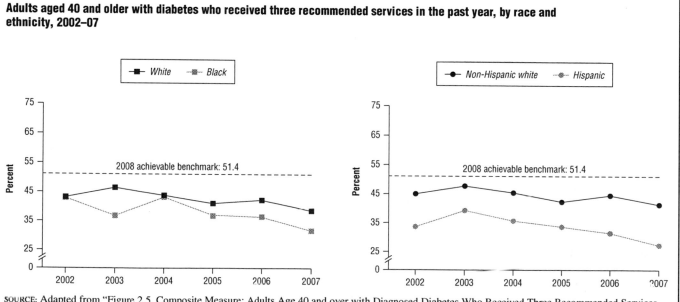

Adults aged 40 and older with diabetes who received three recommended services in the past year, by race and ethnicity, 2002–07

SOURCE: Adapted from "Figure 2.5. Composite Measure: Adults Age 40 and over with Diagnosed Diabetes Who Received Three Recommended Services for Diabetes in the Calendar Year (Hemoglobin A1c Test, Dilated Eye Examination, and Foot Examination), by Race, Ethnicity, Family Income, and Education, 2002–2007," in *National Healthcare Disparities Report, 2010*, U.S. Department of Health and Human Services, Agency for Healthcare Research and Quality, March 2011, http://www.ahrq.gov/qual/nhdr10/nhdr10.pdf (accessed December 16, 2011)

## AIDS

The acquired immunodeficiency syndrome (AIDS) is caused by a virus that affects the body's immune system, making it difficult to fight invasions from infection or other foreign substances. As a result, people who have AIDS are subject to a number of opportunistic infections, primarily *Pneumocystis carinii* pneumonia and Kaposi's sarcoma, a form of skin cancer. AIDS, which is caused by the human immunodeficiency virus (HIV), is not transmitted casually, but only through the transfer of bodily fluids, such as blood, semen, and vaginal secretions. There are only four methods of transmission: contaminated blood, sexual transmission, contaminated syringes from injection drug use, and perinatal (around the time of birth) transmission from a mother to her child or through breast milk.

Minorities have been especially hard hit by the AIDS epidemic. The CDC notes in *HIV Surveillance Report: Diagnoses of HIV Infection and AIDS in the United States and Dependent Areas, 2009* (February 2011, http://www.cdc.gov/hiv/surveillance/resources/reports/2009report/pdf/2009 SurveillanceReport.pdf) that of the estimated 682,668 people living with HIV in 40 states and five U.S. dependent areas in 2008, 315,838 (46.3%) were African-American, 215,806 (31.6%) were white, and 134,241 (19.7%) were Hispanic. (See Table 6.12.) Asian-Americans and Native Americans and Alaskan Natives were the least likely groups to be living with HIV, at less than 1% (4,290 and 2,387, respectively) each. An estimated 490,696 individuals were living with AIDS at year-end 2008 across the nation. Again, African-Americans were overrepresented; 209,175 (42.6%) were African-American. (See Table 6.13.)

In "Pregnancy and Childbirth" (October 10, 2007, http://www.cdc.gov/hiv/topics/perinatal/), the CDC explains that children primarily get HIV in utero from infected mothers. Far more AIDS cases have been diagnosed among African-American children than among children of other racial or ethnic backgrounds. Through 2009, 5,787 cases among African-American children, 1,862 cases among Hispanic children, and 1,602 cases among white children had been diagnosed. (See Table 6.14.) Only 48 cases had been diagnosed among Asian-American children, and only 31 cases had been diagnosed among Native American and Alaskan Native children. The use of antiretroviral drugs has greatly diminished the rate of infection of the children of HIV-positive mothers; the use of these drugs reduces the rate of transmission from 25% to about 2%. The rate of diagnosis among African-American children dropped from 30 cases in 2006 to eight in 2009—a decrease of 73.3%. Only three cases were diagnosed among Hispanic children and only one case among white children in 2009.

The methods of transmission of HIV among the adolescent and adult population differ considerably by race. In 2009 white men with HIV had overwhelmingly contracted the disease through homosexual (male-to-male sexual) con-tact; 8,608 of 10,093 (85.3%) contracted HIV in this way. (See Table 6.15.) Most Asian-American men who were diagnosed with HIV in 2009 (293 out of 363 cases, or 80.7%) had also contracted the disease through male-to-male sexual contact. Even though male-to-male sexual contact was the method of transmission for the plurality of African-American men (10,128 of 14,898, or 68%) and Hispanic men (4,418 of 5,972, or 74%), a significant proportion of African-American men (1,333 of 14,898, or 8.9%) and Hispanic men (592 of 5,972, or 9.9%) had contracted HIV through injection drug use. A sizable proportion of African-American men with HIV had contracted the disease through high-risk heterosexual (male-to-female sexual) contact (3,029 of 14,898, or 20.3%).

Most men who had contracted AIDS in 2009 had also done so through male-to-male sexual contact or injection drug use. Among men who were diagnosed with AIDS in that year, 79.5% (6,457 of 8,121) of white men had contracted the disease through homosexual contact, as did 74.5% (260 of 349) of Asian-American men, 68.1% (3,649 of 5,359) of Hispanic men, and 55.8% (6,185 of 11,093) of African-American men. (See Table 6.16.) Another 14.9% (1,652 of 11,093) of African-American men, 13% (695 of 5,359) of Hispanic men, 7.1% (574 of 8,121) of white men, and 6% (21 of 349) of Asian-American men contracted AIDS through injection drug use.

The transmission patterns of HIV and AIDS are quite different among women. In 2009 most cases of HIV had been transmitted to women through heterosexual contact with an infected partner. About 76.8% (1,304 of 1,699) of white women, 82.3% (1,113 of 1,352) of Hispanic women, 87.3% (5,787 of 6,627) of African-American women, and 93.2% (96 of 103 women) of Asian-American women contracted HIV in this way. (See Table 6.15.) These patterns were similar among women who were diagnosed with AIDS in 2009. (See Table 6.16.)

African-Americans are extremely overrepresented in new diagnoses of HIV/AIDS each year. However, the disparities in the care that they received earlier in the epidemic had lessened significantly by 2007. In *National Healthcare Disparities Report, 2010*, the HHS states that "without adequate treatment, as HIV disease progresses, CD4 cell counts fall and patients become increasingly susceptible to opportunistic infections." The HHS notes that the receipt of antiretroviral therapy (to prevent HIV-infected people from developing AIDS) and drug therapy to prevent *Pneumocystis carinii* pneumonia did not differ significantly by race or ethnicity in 2007.

### Sickle-Cell Anemia in African-Americans

In "Facts about Sickle Cell Disease" (September 16, 2011, http://www.cdc.gov/ncbddd/sicklecell/facts.html), the CDC explains that sickle-cell anemia, a hereditary disease that primarily strikes African-American people in

**TABLE 6.12**

**Persons living with a diagnosis of HIV infection, by race and Hispanic origin and selected characteristics, 2008**

| | American Indian/Alaska Native | | Asian[a] | | Black/African American | | Hispanic/Latino[b] | | Native Hawaiian/other Pacific Islander | | White | | Multiple races | | Total[c] | |
|---|---|---|---|---|---|---|---|---|---|---|---|---|---|---|---|---|
| | No. | Est. no.[d] | No. | Est. no.[d] | No. | Est. no.[d] | No. | Est. no.[d] | No. | Est. no.[d] | No. | Est. no.[d] | No. | Est. no.[d] | No. | Est. no.[d,e] |
| **Age at end of year** | | | | | | | | | | | | | | | | |
| <13 | 11 | 12 | 32 | 34 | 1,974 | 2,045 | 545 | 572 | 0 | 0 | 341 | 354 | 58 | 61 | 2,963 | 3,079 |
| 13–14 | 0 | 0 | 3 | 3 | 854 | 872 | 265 | 274 | 0 | 0 | 128 | 130 | 14 | 14 | 1,267 | 1,297 |
| 15–19 | 19 | 20 | 18 | 19 | 4,362 | 4,557 | 1,266 | 1,325 | 0 | 0 | 775 | 800 | 82 | 85 | 6,522 | 6,806 |
| 20–24 | 79 | 83 | 117 | 126 | 12,968 | 13,677 | 3,534 | 3,764 | 16 | 16 | 3,459 | 3,652 | 310 | 324 | 20,485 | 21,643 |
| 25–29 | 188 | 197 | 298 | 316 | 21,376 | 22,199 | 7,850 | 8,275 | 32 | 34 | 8,662 | 9,021 | 560 | 589 | 38,973 | 40,637 |
| 30–34 | 263 | 269 | 576 | 609 | 27,395 | 28,174 | 12,209 | 12,745 | 52 | 54 | 13,519 | 13,936 | 749 | 776 | 54,790 | 56,591 |
| 35–39 | 376 | 381 | 817 | 854 | 38,669 | 39,446 | 17,815 | 18,443 | 49 | 50 | 25,413 | 25,936 | 1,152 | 1,176 | 84,362 | 86,358 |
| 40–44 | 443 | 445 | 792 | 826 | 53,373 | 54,148 | 24,931 | 25,619 | 46 | 48 | 41,660 | 42,226 | 1,608 | 1,635 | 122,993 | 125,088 |
| 45–49 | 410 | 411 | 576 | 593 | 55,492 | 56,079 | 24,311 | 24,856 | 41 | 42 | 47,913 | 48,269 | 1,764 | 1,783 | 130,693 | 132,222 |
| 50–54 | 284 | 283 | 417 | 429 | 44,158 | 44,448 | 17,496 | 17,876 | 26 | 27 | 33,226 | 33,321 | 1,219 | 1,228 | 96,973 | 97,759 |
| 55–59 | 162 | 161 | 225 | 232 | 27,392 | 27,472 | 10,149 | 10,379 | 17 | 17 | 19,900 | 19,888 | 737 | 743 | 58,698 | 59,010 |
| 60–64 | 66 | 66 | 131 | 134 | 12,709 | 12,691 | 5,351 | 5,479 | 9 | 9 | 10,394 | 10,349 | 317 | 317 | 29,034 | 29,104 |
| ≥65 | 59 | 60 | 113 | 116 | 10,130 | 10,032 | 4,552 | 4,635 | 7 | 7 | 7,987 | 7,923 | 250 | 248 | 23,150 | 23,074 |
| **Transmission category** | | | | | | | | | | | | | | | | |
| **Male adult or adolescent** | | | | | | | | | | | | | | | | |
| Male-to-male sexual contact | 982 | 1,122 | 1,799 | 2,573 | 79,826 | 103,423 | 43,764 | 53,939 | 169 | 203 | 128,536 | 144,992 | 3,253 | 3,824 | 258,469 | 310,498 |
| Injection drug use | 177 | 199 | 114 | 209 | 30,789 | 41,512 | 21,020 | 26,039 | 7 | 10 | 12,345 | 13,763 | 906 | 1,078 | 65,384 | 82,901 |
| Male-to-male sexual contact and injection drug use | 212 | 243 | 81 | 113 | 10,994 | 13,944 | 5,270 | 6,223 | 6 | 9 | 13,153 | 14,311 | 503 | 570 | 30,225 | 35,472 |
| Heterosexual contact[f] | 119 | 139 | 322 | 424 | 28,243 | 39,673 | 9,895 | 12,049 | 16 | 19 | 6,542 | 7,587 | 588 | 702 | 45,739 | 60,631 |
| Other[g] | 201 | 8 | 896 | 35 | 46,413 | 773 | 15,859 | 330 | 36 | 1 | 19,475 | 1,483 | 845 | 32 | 84,152 | 2,673 |
| **Subtotal** | **1,691** | **1,712** | **3,212** | **3,354** | **196,265** | **199,324** | **95,808** | **98,579** | **234** | **242** | **180,051** | **182,136** | **6,095** | **6,206** | **483,969** | **492,174** |
| **Female adult or adolescent** | | | | | | | | | | | | | | | | |
| Injection drug use | 160 | 205 | 34 | 78 | 17,433 | 26,068 | 7,072 | 9,447 | 9 | 11 | 8,728 | 10,789 | 623 | 827 | 34,073 | 47,489 |
| Heterosexual contact[f] | 323 | 432 | 428 | 761 | 54,238 | 83,277 | 17,473 | 23,658 | 32 | 50 | 15,632 | 20,933 | 1,301 | 1,767 | 89,465 | 131,003 |
| Other[g] | 158 | 10 | 388 | 41 | 36,776 | 907 | 7,647 | 220 | 20 | 2 | 7,537 | 504 | 650 | 25 | 53,313 | 1,713 |
| **Subtotal** | **641** | **647** | **850** | **881** | **108,447** | **110,252** | **32,192** | **33,325** | **61** | **63** | **31,897** | **32,226** | **2,574** | **2,620** | **176,851** | **180,206** |
| **Child (<13 yrs at diagnosis)** | | | | | | | | | | | | | | | | |
| Perinatal | 22 | 23 | 38 | 40 | 5,574 | 5,679 | 2,016 | 2,069 | 0 | 0 | 1,082 | 1,097 | 124 | 127 | 8,859 | 9,038 |
| Other[h] | 6 | 6 | 15 | 15 | 564 | 581 | 258 | 267 | 0 | 0 | 347 | 346 | 26 | 27 | 1,220 | 1,246 |
| **Subtotal** | **28** | **29** | **53** | **55** | **6,138** | **6,260** | **2,274** | **2,336** | **0** | **0** | **1,429** | **1,444** | **150** | **154** | **10,079** | **10,284** |
| **Total[i]** | **2,360** | **2,387** | **4,115** | **4,290** | **310,852** | **315,838** | **130,274** | **134,241** | **295** | **305** | **213,377** | **215,806** | **8,820** | **8,981** | **670,903** | **682,668** |

Note: Data include persons with a diagnosis of HIV infection regardless of stage of disease at diagnosis.

aIncludes Asian/Pacific Islander legacy cases.

bHispanics/Latinos can be of any race.

cIncludes persons of unknown race/ethnicity.

dEstimated numbers resulted from statistical adjustment that accounted for reporting delays and missing risk-factor information, but not for incomplete reporting.

eBecause the estimated totals were calculated independently of the corresponding values for each subpopulation, the subpopulation values may not sum to the totals shown here.

fHeterosexual contact with a person known to have, or to be at high risk for, HIV infection.

gIncludes hemophilia, blood transfusion, perinatal exposure, and risk factor not reported or not identified.

hIncludes hemophilia, blood transfusion, and risk factor not reported or not identified.

iBecause column totals for estimated numbers were calculated independently of the values for the subpopulations, the values in each column may not sum to the column total.

SOURCE: "Table 17b. Persons Living with a Diagnosis of HIV Infection, by Race/Ethnicity and Selected Characteristics, Year-end 2008—40 States and 5 U.S. Dependent Areas with Confidential Name-Based HIV Infection Reporting," in HIV Surveillance Report, 2009, vol. 21, U.S. Department of Health and Human Services, Centers for Disease Control and Prevention, February 2011, http://www.cdc.gov/hiv/surveillance/resources/reports/2009report/pdf/table17b.pdf (accessed December 16, 2011)

# TABLE 6.13

## Persons living with an AIDS diagnosis, by race and Hispanic origin and selected characteristics, 2008

| | American Indian/Alaska Native | | Asian[a] | | Black/African American | | Hispanic/Latino[b] | | Native Hawaiian/other Pacific Islander | | White | | Multiple races | | Total[c] | |
|---|---|---|---|---|---|---|---|---|---|---|---|---|---|---|---|---|
| | No. | Est. no.[d] | No. | Est. no.[d] | No. | Est. no.[d] | No. | Est. no.[d] | No. | Est. no.[d] | No. | Est. no.[d] | No. | Est. no.[d] | No. | Est. no.[d,e] |
| **Age at end of year** | | | | | | | | | | | | | | | | |
| <13 | 2 | 2 | 6 | 6 | 469 | 481 | 131 | 134 | 2 | 2 | 79 | 82 | 12 | 13 | 701 | 720 |
| 13–14 | 1 | 1 | 3 | 3 | 406 | 413 | 123 | 125 | 1 | 1 | 68 | 70 | 9 | 9 | 612 | 624 |
| 15–19 | 7 | 7 | 9 | 9 | 1,843 | 1,899 | 567 | 587 | 2 | 2 | 315 | 322 | 40 | 42 | 2,783 | 2,868 |
| 20–24 | 20 | 21 | 42 | 45 | 3,829 | 4,037 | 1,448 | 1,533 | 5 | 5 | 856 | 903 | 104 | 110 | 6,304 | 6,654 |
| 25–29 | 73 | 78 | 181 | 196 | 8,111 | 8,490 | 3,932 | 4,164 | 26 | 27 | 2,796 | 2,946 | 224 | 236 | 15,343 | 16,138 |
| 30–34 | 132 | 136 | 406 | 431 | 13,568 | 14,044 | 7,645 | 7,978 | 42 | 44 | 6,055 | 6,288 | 429 | 451 | 28,278 | 29,371 |
| 35–39 | 263 | 266 | 821 | 862 | 23,500 | 24,087 | 13,435 | 13,866 | 64 | 66 | 15,536 | 15,936 | 758 | 779 | 54,388 | 55,873 |
| 40–44 | 353 | 352 | 949 | 979 | 37,399 | 38,046 | 20,929 | 21,354 | 87 | 89 | 30,926 | 31,338 | 1,118 | 1,141 | 91,787 | 93,325 |
| 45–49 | 371 | 370 | 826 | 845 | 42,023 | 42,498 | 21,412 | 21,680 | 94 | 95 | 39,823 | 39,988 | 1,381 | 1,403 | 105,957 | 106,907 |
| 50–54 | 256 | 253 | 644 | 654 | 34,971 | 35,147 | 15,407 | 15,501 | 59 | 60 | 29,486 | 29,368 | 955 | 963 | 81,821 | 81,989 |
| 55–59 | 137 | 135 | 429 | 433 | 21,898 | 21,873 | 9,033 | 9,067 | 34 | 34 | 18,829 | 18,646 | 610 | 621 | 50,993 | 50,832 |
| 60–64 | 65 | 64 | 237 | 240 | 10,278 | 10,234 | 4,757 | 4,777 | 12 | 12 | 10,074 | 9,923 | 268 | 269 | 25,702 | 25,530 |
| ≥65 | 49 | 48 | 177 | 179 | 8,046 | 7,926 | 4,067 | 4,025 | 11 | 11 | 7,674 | 7,476 | 187 | 186 | 20,225 | 19,865 |
| **Transmission category** | | | | | | | | | | | | | | | | |
| **Male adult or adolescent** | | | | | | | | | | | | | | | | |
| Male-to-male sexual contact | 723 | 786 | 2,515 | 3,152 | 54,121 | 65,600 | 39,026 | 45,962 | 264 | 300 | 102,341 | 110,279 | 2,208 | 2,555 | 201,271 | 228,727 |
| Injection drug use | 173 | 187 | 150 | 231 | 27,487 | 34,234 | 16,646 | 19,795 | 16 | 18 | 11,034 | 11,914 | 759 | 888 | 56,274 | 67,287 |
| Male-to-male sexual contact and injection drug use | 231 | 245 | 165 | 191 | 9,964 | 11,465 | 5,260 | 5,876 | 21 | 22 | 12,944 | 13,514 | 456 | 503 | 29,045 | 31,822 |
| Heterosexual contact[f] | 76 | 86 | 368 | 403 | 19,760 | 26,041 | 7,802 | 9,123 | 20 | 22 | 4,754 | 5,313 | 400 | 472 | 33,135 | 41,467 |
| Other[g] | 108 | 12 | 779 | 72 | 25,279 | 948 | 11,189 | 562 | 35 | 2 | 10,879 | 1,582 | 550 | 45 | 48,857 | 3,224 |
| **Subtotal** | 1,311 | 1,315 | 3,927 | 4,049 | 136,611 | 138,288 | 79,923 | 81,318 | 356 | 364 | 141,952 | 142,603 | 4,373 | 4,463 | 368,582 | 372,528 |
| **Female adult or adolescent** | | | | | | | | | | | | | | | | |
| Injection drug use | 133 | 158 | 50 | 80 | 14,918 | 20,313 | 5,453 | 6,925 | 11 | 14 | 6,701 | 7,851 | 481 | 630 | 27,754 | 35,981 |
| Heterosexual contact[f] | 192 | 237 | 475 | 658 | 33,991 | 46,851 | 12,188 | 15,210 | 46 | 60 | 9,762 | 11,753 | 785 | 1,046 | 57,451 | 75,831 |
| Other[g] | 82 | 12 | 260 | 78 | 18,278 | 1,172 | 4,444 | 458 | 21 | 6 | 3,569 | 550 | 408 | 35 | 27,070 | 2,311 |
| **Subtotal** | 407 | 407 | 785 | 816 | 67,187 | 68,336 | 22,085 | 22,593 | 78 | 79 | 20,032 | 20,154 | 1,674 | 1,711 | 112,275 | 114,123 |
| **Child (<13 yrs at diagnosis)** | | | | | | | | | | | | | | | | |
| Perinatal | 10 | 10 | 14 | 14 | 2,451 | 2,459 | 826 | 828 | 5 | 5 | 478 | 475 | 42 | 42 | 3,827 | 3,835 |
| Other[h] | 1 | 1 | 4 | 4 | 91 | 92 | 52 | 52 | 0 | 0 | 55 | 54 | 5 | 5 | 208 | 208 |
| **Subtotal** | 11 | 11 | 18 | 18 | 2,542 | 2,551 | 878 | 880 | 5 | 5 | 533 | 529 | 47 | 47 | 4,035 | 4,043 |

# TABLE 6.13

## Persons living with an AIDS diagnosis, by race and Hispanic origin and selected characteristics, 2008 [CONTINUED]

| Region of residence | American Indian/Alaska Native | | Asian[a] | | Black/African American | | Hispanic/Latino[b] | | Native Hawaiian/other Pacific Islander | | White | | Multiple races | | Total[c] | |
|---|---|---|---|---|---|---|---|---|---|---|---|---|---|---|---|---|
| | No. | Est. no.[d] | No. | Est. no.[d] | No. | Est. no.[d] | No. | Est. no.[d] | No. | Est. no.[d] | No. | Est. no.[d] | No. | Est. no.[d] | No. | Est. no.[d,e] |
| Northeast | 134 | 139 | 1,084 | 1,141 | 59,809 | 61,821 | 37,419 | 38,899 | 24 | 25 | 34,259 | 34,899 | 2,996 | 3,123 | 135,812 | 140,136 |
| Midwest | 204 | 202 | 345 | 357 | 23,213 | 23,341 | 5,075 | 5,192 | 15 | 16 | 22,159 | 22,126 | 654 | 666 | 51,668 | 51,902 |
| South | 445 | 452 | 655 | 677 | 107,291 | 107,814 | 23,709 | 23,871 | 64 | 66 | 57,981 | 58,081 | 1,852 | 1,842 | 192,021 | 192,827 |
| West | 944 | 938 | 2,625 | 2,687 | 15,835 | 16,007 | 25,756 | 26,284 | 329 | 334 | 48,071 | 48,133 | 584 | 583 | 94,182 | 95,003 |
| U.S. dependent areas | 2 | 2 | 21 | 21 | 193 | 192 | 10,927 | 10,544 | 7 | 8 | 47 | 48 | 9 | 8 | 11,211 | 10,828 |
| **Total[f]** | **1,729** | **1,733** | **4,730** | **4,883** | **206,341** | **209,175** | **102,886** | **104,791** | **439** | **449** | **162,517** | **163,286** | **6,095** | **6,222** | **484,894** | **490,696** |

[a]Includes Asian/Pacific Islander legacy cases.
[b]Hispanics/Latinos can be of any race.
[c]Includes persons of unknown race/ethnicity.
[d]Estimated numbers resulted from statistical adjustment that accounted for reporting delays and missing risk-factor information, but not for incomplete reporting.
[e]Because the estimated totals were calculated independently of the corresponding values for each subpopulation, the subpopulation values may not sum to the totals shown here.
[f]Heterosexual contact with a person known to have, or to be at high risk for, HIV infection.
[g]Includes hemophilia, blood transfusion, perinatal exposure, and risk factor not reported or not identified.
[h]Includes hemophilia, blood transfusion, and risk factor not reported or not identified.
[i]Because column totals for estimated numbers were calculated independently of the values for the subpopulations, the values in each column may not sum to the column total.

SOURCE: "Table 18b. Persons Living with an AIDS Diagnosis, by Race/Ethnicity and Selected Characteristics, Year-end 2008—United States and 5 U.S. Dependent Areas with Confidential Name-Based HIV Infection Reporting," in HIV Surveillance Report, 2009, vol. 21, U.S. Department of Health and Human Services, Centers for Disease Control and Prevention, February 2011, http://www.cdc.gov/hiv/surveillance/resources/reports/2009report/pdf/table18b.pdf (accessed December 16, 2011)

**TABLE 6.14**

**AIDS diagnoses among children less than 13 years of age, by race and Hispanic origin, 2006–09 and cumulative**

| Race/ethnicity | 2006 No. | 2006 Estimated[a] No. | 2006 Estimated[a] Rate | 2007 No. | 2007 Estimated[a] No. | 2007 Estimated[a] Rate | 2008 No. | 2008 Estimated[a] No. | 2008 Estimated[a] Rate | 2009 No. | 2009 Estimated[a] No. | 2009 Estimated[a] Rate | Cumulative[b] No. | Cumulative[b] Est. no.[a] |
|---|---|---|---|---|---|---|---|---|---|---|---|---|---|---|
| American Indian/Alaska Native | 0 | 0 | 0.0 | 0 | 0 | 0.0 | 0 | 0 | 0.0 | 0 | 0 | 0.0 | 31 | 31 |
| Asian[c] | 1 | 1 | 0.0 | 0 | 0 | 0.0 | 2 | 2 | 0.1 | 0 | 0 | 0.0 | 47 | 48 |
| Black/African American | 28 | 30 | 0.4 | 21 | 22 | 0.3 | 20 | 23 | 0.3 | 6 | 8 | 0.1 | 5,736 | 5,787 |
| Hispanic/Latino[d] | 4 | 4 | 0.0 | 4 | 4 | 0.0 | 3 | 3 | 0.0 | 3 | 3 | 0.0 | 1,847 | 1,862 |
| Native Hawaiian/other Pacific Islander | 0 | 0 | 0.0 | 0 | 0 | 0.0 | 0 | 0 | 0.0 | 0 | 0 | 0.0 | 7 | 7 |
| White | 3 | 3 | 0.0 | 4 | 4 | 0.0 | 6 | 7 | 0.0 | 1 | 1 | 0.0 | 1,592 | 1,602 |
| Multiple races | 1 | 1 | 0.1 | 0 | 0 | 0.0 | 4 | 4 | 0.3 | 0 | 0 | 0.0 | 108 | 109 |
| **Total[e]** | **37** | **39** | **0.1** | **29** | **31** | **0.1** | **35** | **40** | **0.1** | **10** | **13** | **0.0** | **9,369[f]** | **9,448** |

[a]Estimated numbers resulted from statistical adjustment that accounted for reporting delays, but not for incomplete reporting. Rates are per 100,000 population.
[b]From the beginning of the epidemic through 2009.
[c]Includes Asian/Pacific Islander legacy cases.
[d]Hispanics/Latinos can be of any race.
[e]Because column totals for estimated numbers were calculated independently of the values for the subpopulations, the values in each column may not sum to the column total.
[f]Includes children of unknown race/ethnicity.

SOURCE: "Table 6a. AIDS Diagnoses among Children <13 Years of Age, by Race/Ethnicity, 2006–2009 and Cumulative—United States," in *HIV Surveillance Report, 2009*, vol. 21, U.S. Department of Health and Human Services, Centers for Disease Control and Prevention, February 2011, http://www.cdc.gov/hiv/surveillance/resources/reports/2009report/pdf/table6ab.pdf (accessed December 16, 2011)

the United States, is a blood disorder in which defective hemoglobin causes red blood cells to become sickle shaped, rather than round. This can create blockages in small arteries and can result in many problems, including chronic anemia, episodes of intense pain, strokes, and death. Scientists believe the genetic trait arose randomly in Africa and survived as a defense against malaria. The disease can be inherited only when both parents have the sickle-cell trait and the child inherits the defective gene from both parents. The CDC notes in "Sickle Cell Disease (SCD)" (September 16, 2011, http://www.cdc.gov/NCBDDD/sicklecell/data.html) that an estimated one out of every 12 African-Americans is a carrier for sickle-cell anemia, and about one out of every 500 African-American infants is born with it. Of the more than 90,000 Americans who had sickle-cell anemia in 2011, most were of African descent.

## BEHAVIORS THAT THREATEN HEALTH

### Cigarette Smoking

Nicotine is the drug in tobacco that causes addiction; cigarette smoking is the most popular method of taking nicotine in the United States. The National Institutes of Health indicates in the press release "Most Behaviors Preceding Major Causes of Preventable Death Have Begun by Young Adulthood" (January 11, 2006, http://www.nih.gov/news/pr/jan2006/nichd-11.htm) that tobacco use is the leading cause of preventable death in the United States. According to the CDC, in "Trends in the Prevalence of Tobacco Use" (2010, http://www.cdc.gov/healthyyouth/yrbs/pdf/us_tobacco_trend_yrbs.pdf), the national Youth Risk Behavior Survey finds that on three key measures smoking among teens had decreased between 1999 and

2009: those who had ever tried cigarette smoking (decreased from 70.4% to 46.3%), those who smoked cigarettes on at least one day in the past 30 days (decreased from 34.8% to 19.5%), and those who smoked cigarettes on 20 or more days in the past 30 days (decreased from 16.8% to 7.3%). Nevertheless, a significant proportion of young people still smoke. Smoking during pregnancy causes an increased risk of stillborn, premature birth, low birth weight, and sudden infant death syndrome. The tar in cigarettes increases the user's risk of lung cancer and other bronchial diseases, and the carbon monoxide in the smoke increases the chance of cardiovascular diseases.

In 2010 Native Americans and Alaskan Natives were more likely to smoke than any other group: 35.8% reported smoking during the past month, 42.2% during the past year, and 74.4% had smoked at some point during their lifetime. (See Table 6.17.) Non-Hispanic whites were the next most likely to smoke: 29.5% had smoked during the past month, 34.9% during the past year, and 74.9% during their lifetime. Non-Hispanic African-Americans were slightly more likely to smoke than Hispanics: 27.3% had smoked during the past month, compared with 21.9% of Hispanics; 31.5% had smoked during the past year, compared with 28.3% of Hispanics; and 58.6% had smoked during their lifetime, compared with 55.7% of Hispanics. Asian-Americans were the least likely to smoke; only 12.5% reported smoking during the past month, 17.3% during the past year, and 43.3% during their lifetime.

The Substance Abuse and Mental Health Services Administration reports in *Results from the 2010 National Survey on Drug Use and Health: Detailed Tables* (September

**TABLE 6.15**

**Diagnoses of HIV infection, by race and Hispanic origin, age, and transmission category, 2009**

| | American Indian/Alaska Native | | | Asian | | | Black/African American | | | Hispanic/Latino[a] | | | Native Hawaiian/other Pacific Islander | | | White | | | Multiple races | | | Total | | |
|---|---|---|---|---|---|---|---|---|---|---|---|---|---|---|---|---|---|---|---|---|---|---|---|---|
| | No. | Estimated[b] No. | Rate | No. | Estimated[b] No. | Rate | No. | Estimated[b] No. | Rate | No. | Estimated[b] No. | Rate | No. | Estimated[b] No. | Rate | No. | Estimated[b] No. | Rate | No. | Estimated[b] No. | Rate | No. | Estimated[b,c] No. | Rate |
| **Age at diagnosis (yr)** | | | | | | | | | | | | | | | | | | | | | | | | |
| <13 | 0 | 0 | 0.0 | 3 | 4 | 0.3 | 107 | 127 | 2.0 | 20 | 23 | 0.3 | 0 | 0 | 0.0 | 10 | 11 | 0.0 | 1 | 1 | 0.1 | 141 | 166 | 0.4 |
| 13–14 | 0 | 0 | 0.0 | 1 | 1 | 0.6 | 13 | 14 | 1.4 | 3 | 3 | 0.3 | 0 | 0 | 0.0 | 2 | 2 | 0.1 | 0 | 0 | 0.0 | 19 | 21 | 0.3 |
| 15–19 | 4 | 4 | 2.6 | 8 | 10 | 2.3 | 1,274 | 1,482 | 51.9 | 224 | 264 | 10.3 | 1 | 1 | 11.3 | 219 | 248 | 2.4 | 22 | 26 | 8.5 | 1,752 | 2,036 | 12.0 |
| 20–24 | 19 | 23 | 13.5 | 44 | 52 | 10.5 | 3,313 | 3,895 | 144.7 | 830 | 970 | 38.3 | 4 | 5 | 35.3 | 1,047 | 1,208 | 11.2 | 70 | 85 | 34.3 | 5,327 | 6,237 | 36.9 |
| 25–29 | 27 | 31 | 19.9 | 64 | 76 | 12.7 | 2,525 | 2,987 | 117.0 | 1,053 | 1,225 | 44.5 | 5 | 5 | 21.9 | 1,334 | 1,546 | 14.6 | 72 | 84 | 40.0 | 5,078 | 5,951 | 35.2 |
| 30–34 | 29 | 33 | 25.7 | 76 | 87 | 13.1 | 2,009 | 2,370 | 107.1 | 977 | 1,145 | 42.3 | 3 | 3 | 41.7 | 1,150 | 1,323 | 13.8 | 48 | 56 | 34.8 | 4,294 | 5,020 | 32.5 |
| 35–39 | 20 | 23 | 18.8 | 82 | 97 | 13.9 | 1,959 | 2,335 | 105.1 | 923 | 1,059 | 42.2 | 5 | 4 | 28.4 | 1,397 | 1,638 | 15.9 | 64 | 75 | 52.8 | 4,448 | 5,232 | 32.6 |
| 40–44 | 25 | 28 | 22.9 | 49 | 61 | 10.2 | 2,124 | 2,524 | 114.3 | 855 | 984 | 44.9 | 3 | 5 | 49.5 | 1,605 | 1,868 | 16.7 | 41 | 47 | 38.1 | 4,704 | 5,519 | 33.6 |
| 45–49 | 20 | 24 | 17.4 | 30 | 35 | 6.6 | 1,936 | 2,293 | 98.9 | 635 | 740 | 38.4 | 3 | 4 | 36.3 | 1,463 | 1,704 | 13.2 | 54 | 65 | 50.0 | 4,141 | 4,865 | 27.1 |
| 50–54 | 7 | 8 | 6.6 | 18 | 22 | 4.8 | 1,482 | 1,753 | 82.5 | 361 | 421 | 27.8 | 3 | 4 | 41.3 | 934 | 1,083 | 8.4 | 29 | 33 | 27.8 | 2,834 | 3,323 | 19.3 |
| 55–59 | 10 | 12 | 11.8 | 9 | 11 | 2.8 | 863 | 1,023 | 58.9 | 206 | 242 | 20.8 | 3 | 0 | 0.0 | 574 | 683 | 5.9 | 29 | 34 | 34.0 | 1,691 | 2,004 | 13.4 |
| 60–64 | 0 | 0 | 0.0 | 3 | 4 | 1.2 | 387 | 455 | 35.7 | 117 | 140 | 15.9 | 1 | 1 | 20.5 | 263 | 299 | 3.0 | 9 | 1 | 1.3 | 772 | 900 | 7.2 |
| ≥65 | 2 | 3 | 1.7 | 8 | 10 | 1.7 | 328 | 393 | 13.9 | 114 | 131 | 6.8 | 1 | 1 | 11.7 | 162 | 188 | 0.7 | 9 | 10 | 6.0 | 624 | 736 | 2.3 |
| **Transmission category** | | | | | | | | | | | | | | | | | | | | | | | | |
| **Male adult or adolescent** | | | | | | | | | | | | | | | | | | | | | | | | |
| Male-to-male sexual contact | 60 | 91 | — | 171 | 293 | — | 6,212 | 10,128 | — | 2,894 | 4,418 | — | 14 | 22 | — | 5,928 | 8,608 | — | 209 | 287 | — | 15,488 | 23,846 | — |
| Injection drug use | 11 | 16 | — | 8 | 16 | — | 410 | 1,333 | — | 269 | 592 | — | 1 | 1 | — | 304 | 462 | — | 15 | 29 | — | 1,018 | 2,449 | — |
| Male-to-male sexual contact and injection drug use | 9 | 16 | — | 5 | 7 | — | 128 | 389 | — | 115 | 199 | — | 0 | 0 | — | 362 | 501 | — | 13 | 18 | — | 632 | 1,131 | — |
| Heterosexual contact[d] | 9 | 13 | — | 26 | 44 | — | 1,411 | 3,029 | — | 466 | 755 | — | 2 | 2 | — | 318 | 505 | — | 34 | 49 | — | 2,266 | 4,399 | — |
| Other[e] | 29 | 1 | — | 95 | 3 | — | 4,405 | 19 | — | 1,401 | 7 | — | 5 | 0 | — | 1,761 | 17 | — | 53 | 0 | — | 7,749 | 47 | — |
| Subtotal | 118 | 137 | 18.4 | 305 | 363 | 12.7 | 12,556 | 14,898 | 122.2 | 5,145 | 5,972 | 48.3 | 22 | 26 | 41.2 | 8,673 | 10,093 | 14.8 | 324 | 383 | 41.3 | 27,153 | 31,872 | 32.7 |
| **Female adult or adolescent** | | | | | | | | | | | | | | | | | | | | | | | | |
| Injection drug use | 4 | 9 | — | 2 | 6 | — | 248 | 826 | — | 108 | 234 | — | 0 | 0 | — | 219 | 387 | — | 10 | 22 | — | 591 | 1,483 | — |
| Heterosexual contact[d] | 16 | 43 | — | 45 | 96 | — | 2,231 | 5,787 | — | 514 | 1,113 | — | 6 | 8 | — | 587 | 1,304 | — | 54 | 111 | — | 3,453 | 8,461 | — |
| Other[e] | 25 | 0 | — | 40 | 1 | — | 3,168 | 14 | — | 531 | 6 | — | 1 | 0 | — | 671 | 8 | — | 51 | 0 | — | 4,487 | 29 | — |
| Subtotal | 45 | 51 | 6.6 | 87 | 103 | 3.4 | 5,647 | 6,627 | 47.8 | 1,153 | 1,352 | 11.9 | 7 | 8 | 13.3 | 1,477 | 1,699 | 2.4 | 115 | 132 | 13.4 | 8,531 | 9,973 | 9.8 |
| **Child (<13 yrs at diagnosis)** | | | | | | | | | | | | | | | | | | | | | | | | |
| Perinatal | 0 | 0 | — | 3 | 4 | — | 82 | 96 | — | 18 | 20 | — | 0 | 0 | — | 8 | 9 | — | 1 | 1 | — | 112 | 131 | — |
| Other[f] | 0 | 0 | — | 0 | 0 | — | 25 | 31 | — | 2 | 2 | — | 0 | 0 | — | 2 | 2 | — | 0 | 0 | — | 29 | 35 | — |
| Subtotal | 0 | 0 | 0.0 | 3 | 4 | 0.3 | 107 | 127 | 2.0 | 20 | 23 | 0.3 | 0 | 0 | 0.0 | 10 | 11 | 0.0 | 1 | 1 | 0.1 | 141 | 166 | 0.4 |
| **Total[g]** | 163 | 189 | 9.8 | 395 | 470 | 6.4 | 18,320 | 21,552 | 66.6 | 6,318 | 7,347 | 22.8 | 29 | 34 | 21.0 | 10,160 | 11,803 | 7.2 | 440 | 516 | 16.7 | 35,825 | 42,011 | 17.4 |

Note: Data include persons with a diagnosis of HIV infection regardless of stage of disease at diagnosis.

[a]Hispanics/Latinos can be of any race.

[b]Estimated numbers resulted from statistical adjustment that accounted for reporting delays and missing risk-factor information, but not for incomplete reporting. Rates are per 100,000 population. Rates are not calculated by transmission category because of the lack of denominator data.

[c]Because the estimated totals were calculated independently of the corresponding values for each subpopulation, the subpopulation values may not sum to the totals shown here.

[d]Heterosexual contact with a person known to have, or to be at high risk for, HIV infection.

[e]Includes hemophilia, blood transfusion, perinatal exposure, and risk factor not reported or not identified.

[f]Includes hemophilia, blood transfusion, and risk factor not reported or not identified.

[g]Because column totals for estimated numbers were calculated independently of the values for the subpopulations, the values in each column may not sum to the column total.

SOURCE: "Table 3a. Diagnoses of HIV Infection, by Race/Ethnicity and Selected Characteristics, 2009—40 States with Confidential Name-Based HIV Infection Reporting," in *HIV Surveillance Report, 2009*, vol. 21, U.S. Department of Health and Human Services, Centers for Disease Control and Prevention, February 2011, http://www.cdc.gov/hiv/surveillance/resources/reports/2009report/pdf/table3a.pdf (accessed December 16, 2011)

**TABLE 6.16**

**AIDS diagnoses, by race and Hispanic origin, age, and transmission category, 2009**

| | American Indian/Alaska Native | | | Asian[a] | | | Black/African American | | | Hispanic/Latino[b] | | | Native Hawaiian/other Pacific Islander | | | White | | | Multiple races | | | Total | | |
|---|---|---|---|---|---|---|---|---|---|---|---|---|---|---|---|---|---|---|---|---|---|---|---|---|
| | No. | Est. No. | Rate | No. | Est. No. | Rate | No. | Est. No. | Rate | No. | Est. No. | Rate | No. | Est. No. | Rate | No. | Est. No. | Rate | No. | Est. No. | Rate | No. | Est. No.[d] | Rate |
| **Age at diagnosis (yr)** | | | | | | | | | | | | | | | | | | | | | | | | |
| <13 | 0 | 0 | 0.0 | 0 | 0 | 0.0 | 6 | 8 | 0.1 | 3 | 3 | 0.0 | 0 | 0 | 0.0 | 1 | 1 | 0.0 | 0 | 0 | 0.0 | 10 | 13 | 0.0 |
| 13–14 | 0 | 0 | 0.0 | 0 | 0 | 0.0 | 24 | 38 | 3.2 | 15 | 20 | 1.2 | 0 | 0 | 0.0 | 0 | 0 | 0.0 | 0 | 0 | 0.0 | 39 | 58 | 0.7 |
| 15–19 | 2 | 2 | 1.1 | 4 | 5 | 0.7 | 257 | 334 | 10.2 | 72 | 90 | 2.2 | 0 | 0 | 0.0 | 32 | 39 | 0.3 | 9 | 13 | 2.9 | 376 | 484 | 2.2 |
| 20–24 | 8 | 9 | 4.2 | 14 | 17 | 1.9 | 1,026 | 1,298 | 41.8 | 328 | 415 | 10.7 | 2 | 3 | 7.4 | 262 | 319 | 2.4 | 27 | 34 | 8.9 | 1,667 | 2,095 | 9.7 |
| 25–29 | 17 | 20 | 10.7 | 40 | 55 | 5.0 | 1,367 | 1,722 | 58.4 | 675 | 871 | 21.0 | 6 | 8 | 19.9 | 601 | 740 | 5.7 | 47 | 61 | 18.6 | 2,753 | 3,476 | 16.0 |
| 30–34 | 18 | 21 | 13.3 | 57 | 72 | 6.0 | 1,504 | 1,878 | 73.1 | 836 | 1,058 | 26.2 | 4 | 5 | 12.7 | 761 | 948 | 8.1 | 47 | 61 | 24.8 | 3,227 | 4,043 | 20.3 |
| 35–39 | 18 | 23 | 15.0 | 78 | 96 | 7.7 | 1,753 | 2,219 | 85.8 | 840 | 1,059 | 28.2 | 6 | 7 | 21.0 | 1,100 | 1,364 | 10.9 | 93 | 125 | 57.1 | 3,888 | 4,893 | 23.8 |
| 40–44 | 22 | 27 | 17.7 | 55 | 72 | 6.6 | 2,047 | 2,603 | 100.4 | 890 | 1,130 | 34.2 | 4 | 5 | 15.0 | 1,392 | 1,731 | 12.7 | 92 | 121 | 62.3 | 4,502 | 5,689 | 27.1 |
| 45–49 | 19 | 24 | 14.1 | 39 | 54 | 5.3 | 2,027 | 2,581 | 94.6 | 692 | 882 | 30.5 | 8 | 10 | 31.9 | 1,433 | 1,809 | 11.5 | 85 | 106 | 52.8 | 4,303 | 5,466 | 23.9 |
| 50–54 | 14 | 19 | 12.1 | 13 | 17 | 1.9 | 1,589 | 2,027 | 81.5 | 443 | 567 | 25.0 | 6 | 8 | 30.9 | 1,003 | 1,255 | 8.0 | 70 | 90 | 48.4 | 3,138 | 3,983 | 18.3 |
| 55–59 | 7 | 8 | 6.3 | 11 | 14 | 1.7 | 860 | 1,095 | 54.0 | 249 | 318 | 18.5 | 1 | 1 | 5.1 | 558 | 706 | 5.0 | 37 | 49 | 32.4 | 1,723 | 2,191 | 11.5 |
| 60–64 | 1 | 1 | 1.4 | 10 | 12 | 2.0 | 405 | 517 | 34.6 | 121 | 155 | 12.2 | 2 | 2 | 14.3 | 258 | 314 | 2.6 | 8 | 10 | 8.0 | 805 | 1,010 | 6.4 |
| ≥65 | 1 | 1 | 0.6 | 8 | 14 | 1.1 | 331 | 420 | 12.7 | 121 | 151 | 5.5 | 1 | 1 | 4.0 | 194 | 242 | 0.8 | 13 | 17 | 6.6 | 669 | 846 | 2.1 |
| **Transmission category** | | | | | | | | | | | | | | | | | | | | | | | | |
| **Male adult or adolescent** | | | | | | | | | | | | | | | | | | | | | | | | |
| Male-to-male sexual contact | 64 | 90 | — | 145 | 260 | — | 3,651 | 6,185 | — | 2,263 | 3,649 | — | 26 | 37 | — | 4,403 | 6,457 | — | 221 | 328 | — | 10,773 | 17,005 | — |
| Injection drug use | 10 | 15 | — | 12 | 21 | — | 742 | 1,652 | — | 341 | 695 | — | 1 | 1 | — | 386 | 574 | — | 31 | 54 | — | 1,523 | 3,012 | — |
| Male-to-male sexual contact and injection drug use | 8 | 11 | — | 9 | 17 | — | 295 | 550 | — | 190 | 302 | — | 4 | 5 | — | 470 | 658 | — | 24 | 38 | — | 1,000 | 1,580 | — |
| Heterosexual contact[e] | 7 | 10 | — | 30 | 49 | — | 1,400 | 2,628 | — | 406 | 683 | — | 0 | 0 | — | 258 | 390 | — | 47 | 73 | — | 2,148 | 3,832 | — |
| Other[f] | 13 | 2 | — | 70 | 3 | — | 2,595 | 79 | — | 1,022 | 30 | — | 4 | 0 | — | 980 | 43 | — | 57 | 1 | — | 4,741 | 158 | — |
| Subtotal | 102 | 127 | 13.8 | 266 | 349 | 6.5 | 8,683 | 11,093 | 78.0 | 4,222 | 5,359 | 28.9 | 35 | 43 | 24.2 | 6,497 | 8,121 | 9.8 | 380 | 495 | 35.0 | 20,185 | 25,587 | 20.6 |
| **Female adult or adolescent** | | | | | | | | | | | | | | | | | | | | | | | | |
| Injection drug use | 4 | 8 | — | 2 | 6 | — | 474 | 1,135 | — | 143 | 314 | — | 0 | 0 | — | 245 | 409 | — | 32 | 57 | — | 900 | 1,930 | — |
| Heterosexual contact[e] | 13 | 20 | — | 28 | 68 | — | 2,108 | 4,411 | — | 511 | 1,010 | — | 4 | 7 | — | 502 | 915 | — | 75 | 130 | — | 3,241 | 6,561 | — |
| Other[f] | 8 | 0 | — | 33 | 5 | — | 1,925 | 93 | — | 406 | 33 | — | 1 | 0 | — | 350 | 20 | — | 41 | 4 | — | 2,764 | 155 | — |
| Subtotal | 25 | 28 | 2.9 | 63 | 80 | 1.3 | 4,507 | 5,639 | 35.1 | 1,060 | 1,357 | 7.9 | 5 | 7 | 4.0 | 1,097 | 1,344 | 1.5 | 148 | 192 | 12.7 | 6,905 | 8,647 | 6.7 |
| **Child (<13 yrs at diagnosis)** | | | | | | | | | | | | | | | | | | | | | | | | |
| Perinatal | 0 | 0 | — | 0 | 0 | — | 6 | 8 | — | 2 | 2 | — | 0 | 0 | — | 1 | 1 | — | 0 | 0 | — | 9 | 12 | — |
| Other[g] | 0 | 0 | — | 0 | 0 | — | 0 | 0 | — | 1 | 1 | — | 0 | 0 | — | 0 | 0 | — | 0 | 0 | — | 1 | 1 | — |
| Subtotal | 0 | 0 | 0.0 | 0 | 0 | 0.0 | 6 | 8 | 0.1 | 3 | 3 | 0.0 | 0 | 0 | 0.0 | 1 | 1 | 0.0 | 0 | 0 | 0.0 | 10 | 13 | 0.0 |

TABLE 6.16

**AIDS diagnoses, by race and Hispanic origin, age, and transmission category, 2009** [CONTINUED]

| Region of residence | American Indian/Alaska Native[a] | | | Asian[a] | | | Black/African American | | | Hispanic/Latino[b] | | | Native Hawaiian/other Pacific Islander | | | White | | | Multiple races | | | Total | | |
|---|---|---|---|---|---|---|---|---|---|---|---|---|---|---|---|---|---|---|---|---|---|---|---|---|
| | No. | Estimated[c] No. | Rate | No. | Estimated[c] No. | Rate | No. | Estimated[c] No. | Rate | No. | Estimated[c] No. | Rate | No. | Estimated[c] No. | Rate | No. | Estimated[c] No. | Rate | No. | Estimated[c] No. | Rate | No. | Estimated[d] No. | Rate |
| Northeast | 2 | 3 | 2.0 | 68 | 99 | 3.4 | 2,787 | 3,956 | 64.4 | 1,550 | 2,186 | 33.2 | 8 | 11 | 49.8 | 1,221 | 1,681 | 4.3 | 171 | 236 | 37.1 | 5,807 | 8,171 | 14.8 |
| Midwest | 16 | 26 | 6.3 | 30 | 37 | 2.3 | 1,702 | 2,178 | 32.0 | 344 | 449 | 10.2 | 1 | 1 | 4.2 | 1,264 | 1,602 | 3.0 | 78 | 101 | 11.9 | 3,435 | 4,394 | 6.6 |
| South | 30 | 34 | 4.5 | 76 | 95 | 3.3 | 7,862 | 9,525 | 44.5 | 1,881 | 2,171 | 12.6 | 8 | 10 | 15.0 | 3,108 | 3,693 | 5.3 | 223 | 278 | 19.4 | 13,188 | 15,806 | 13.9 |
| West | 79 | 94 | 8.7 | 155 | 197 | 3.2 | 845 | 1,082 | 32.6 | 1,510 | 1,913 | 9.5 | 23 | 28 | 8.4 | 2,002 | 2,490 | 6.4 | 56 | 71 | 4.3 | 4,670 | 5,875 | 8.2 |
| **Total[h]** | **127** | **155** | **6.6** | **329** | **429** | **3.1** | **13,196** | **16,741** | **44.4** | **5,285** | **6,719** | **13.9** | **40** | **50** | **11.2** | **7,595** | **9,467** | **4.7** | **528** | **686** | **15.1** | **27,100** | **34,247** | **11.2** |

[a]Includes Asian/Pacific Islander legacy cases.

[b]Hispanics/Latinos can be of any race.

[c]Estimated numbers resulted from statistical adjustment that accounted for reporting delays and missing risk-factor information, but not for incomplete reporting. Rates are per 100,000 population. Rates are not calculated by transmission category because of the lack of denominator data.

[d]Because the estimated totals were calculated independently of the corresponding values for each subpopulation, the subpopulation values may not sum to the totals shown here.

[e]Heterosexual contact with a person known to have, or to be at high risk for, HIV infection.

[f]Includes hemophilia, blood transfusion, perinatal exposure, and risk factor not reported or not identified.

[g]Includes hemophilia, blood transfusion, and risk factor not reported or not identified.

[h]Because column totals for estimated numbers were calculated independently of the values for the subpopulations, the values in each column may not sum to the column total.

SOURCE: "Table 4a. AIDS Diagnoses, by Race/Ethnicity and Selected Characteristics, 2009—United States," in *HIV Surveillance Report, 2009*, vol. 21, U.S. Department of Health and Human Services, Centers for Disease Control and Prevention, February 2011, http://www.cdc.gov/hiv/surveillance/resources/reports/2009report/pdf/table4a.pdf (accessed December 16, 2011)

TABLE 6.17

**Tobacco product use by age, gender, and race and Hispanic origin, 2009 and 2010**

[Percentages]

| Demographic characteristic | Lifetime (2009) | Lifetime (2010) | Past year (2009) | Past year (2010) | Past month (2009) | Past month (2010) |
|---|---|---|---|---|---|---|
| **Total** | **69.1** | **68.7** | **33.1** | **32.8** | **27.7** | **27.4** |
| **Age** | | | | | | |
| 12–17 | 26.9[b] | 24.9 | 19.3[a] | 18.0 | 11.6[a] | 10.7 |
| 18–25 | 69.6 | 68.6 | 52.3 | 51.1 | 41.6 | 40.8 |
| 26 or older | 74.4 | 74.2 | 31.5 | 31.4 | 27.3 | 27.2 |
| **Gender** | | | | | | |
| Male | 76.4 | 76.2 | 40.1 | 40.3 | 33.5 | 33.7 |
| Female | 62.3 | 61.5 | 26.5 | 25.7 | 22.2 | 21.5 |
| **Hispanic origin and race** | | | | | | |
| Not Hispanic or Latino | 71.3 | 70.9 | 33.7 | 33.6 | 28.4 | 28.4 |
| White | 75.8 | 74.9 | 35.3 | 34.9 | 29.6 | 29.5 |
| Black or African American | 58.0 | 58.6 | 30.4 | 31.5 | 26.5 | 27.3 |
| American Indian or Alaska Native | 81.7 | 74.4 | 45.7 | 42.2 | 41.8 | 35.8 |
| Native Hawaiian or other Pacific Islander | c | c | c | c | c | c |
| Asian | 38.4 | 43.3 | 15.1 | 17.3 | 11.9 | 12.5 |
| Two or more races | 71.1 | 70.3 | 42.5 | 38.7 | 36.6 | 32.0 |
| Hispanic or Latino | 56.0 | 55.7 | 29.3 | 28.3 | 23.2 | 21.9 |

Note: Tobacco products include cigarettes, smokeless tobacco (i.e., chewing tobacco or snuff), cigars, or pipe tobacco. Tobacco product use in the past year excludes past year pipe tobacco use, but includes past month pipe tobacco use.
[a]Difference between estimate and 2010 estimate is statistically significant at the 0.05 level.
[b]Difference between estimate and 2010 estimate is statistically significant at the 0.01 level.
[c]Low precision; no estimate reported.

SOURCE: "Table 2.17B. Tobacco Product Use in Lifetime, Past Year, and Past Month among Persons Aged 12 or Older, by Demographic Characteristics: Percentages, 2009 and 2010," in *Results from the 2010 National Survey on Drug Use and Health: Detailed Tables*, U.S. Department of Health and Human Services, Substance Abuse and Mental Health Services Administration, Office of Applied Studies, September 2011, http://www.samhsa.gov/data/NSDUH/2k10ResultsTables/Web/PDFW/Sect2peTabs17to21.pdf (accessed December 16, 2011)

2011, http://www.samhsa.gov/data/nsduh/2k10Results Tables/Web/HTML/TOC.htm) that cigarette smoking is most prevalent among those aged 18 to 25 years, regardless of race or ethnic group. Among people in this age group, whites are overwhelmingly more likely to smoke than their African-American or Hispanic counterparts. In 2010, 47% of 18- to 25-year-old whites had smoked during the past month, compared with 31.2% of Hispanics and 32.1% of African-Americans.

## Diet and Nutrition

The Healthy Eating Index is computed periodically by the U.S. Department of Agriculture's Center for Nutrition Policy and Promotion (CNPP). In "Diet Quality of Low-Income and Higher Income Americans in 2003–04 as Measured by the Healthy Eating Index—2005" (December 2008, http://www.cnpp.usda.gov/Publications/NutritionIn sights/Insight42.pdf), the CNPP finds that the diet of all Americans is deficient, with the average American scoring a failing grade of 57.5 out of 100. Americans do not eat enough dark green and orange vegetables, legumes, and whole grains, and eat too much sodium, solid fats, and added sugars.

In "Obesity: Halting the Epidemic by Making Health Easier" (2009, http://www.cdc.gov/nccdphp/publications/AAG/pdf/obesity.pdf), the CDC states that "increased food intake, nonhealthful foods, and physical inactivity" by Americans resulted in an "obesity epidemic." Obesity can put people at risk for a variety of obesity-related diseases, including type 2 diabetes, cardiovascular disease, high blood pressure, liver and gallbladder disease, sleep apnea, osteoarthritis, some forms of cancer, and gynecological problems. Even though rates of obesity are high among the entire U.S. population, obesity is more likely among some groups. The CDC reports in "Differences in Prevalence of Obesity among Black, White, and Hispanic Adults—United States, 2006–2008" (*Morbidity and Mortality Weekly Report*, vol. 58, no. 27, July 17, 2009) that between 2006 and 2008, 35.7% of non-Hispanic African-Americans were obese; non-Hispanic African-American women were particularly likely to be obese (39.2%). Hispanics also had elevated rates of obesity compared with non-Hispanic whites (28.7% and 23.7%, respectively); Hispanic women (29.4%) were more likely than Hispanic men (27.8%) to be obese. Among non-Hispanic whites, men (25.4%) were more likely to be obese than women (21.8%).

One reason that Asians and Pacific Islanders enjoy better health than other racial and ethnic groups is their diet. The typical Asian and Pacific Islander diet is low in fat and cholesterol. The staple food for many Asians and Pacific Islanders is rice. The consumption of vegetables is relatively high, and pork and fish are also commonly eaten. Dairy products are used less frequently in Asian cuisine. The traditional sources of calcium are soybean curd, sardines, and green, leafy vegetables, which are all healthy sources of nutrients. As a result, Patricia M. Barnes, Patricia F. Adams, and Eve Powell-Griner of the CDC note in *Health Characteristics of the Asian Adult Population: United States, 2004–2006* (January 22, 2008, http://www.cdc.gov/nchs/data/ad/ad394.pdf) that between 2004 and 2006, 59.3% of Asian-Americans had a healthy weight, compared with 39.7% of whites, 31.5% of Hispanics, 29.7% of African-Americans, and 28.6% of Native Americans and Alaskan Natives.

## Drug Abuse

ALCOHOL. Alcohol depresses the central nervous system. The consumption of small amounts of alcohol can actually have a beneficial effect on the body. However, when consumed in larger amounts, alcohol impairs judgment and increases reaction time, can interfere with prescription and nonprescription medications in adverse ways, and can cause serious damage to developing fetuses. Chronic health consequences of excessive drinking include increased risk of liver cirrhosis, pancreatitis, certain types of cancer, high blood pressure, and psychological disorders. Addiction to alcohol is a chronic disease that is often progressive and sometimes fatal.

In 2010 Asian-Americans, Native Americans and Alaskan Natives, Hispanics, and non-Hispanic African-Americans were all less likely to report having used alcohol in the past month than were non-Hispanic whites. (See Table 6.18.) The rate of binge alcohol use, which is defined as five or more drinks on one occasion in at least one day in the previous month, was lowest among Asian-Americans (12.4%) and non-Hispanic African-Americans (19.8%). Hispanics (25.1%) and Native Americans and Alaskan Natives (24.7%) had rates that were comparable to or higher than that of non-Hispanic whites (24%) in 2010. The rates of heavy alcohol use, which is defined as drinking five or more drinks on each of five or more days in the past 30 days, were highest among non-Hispanic whites (7.7%) and lowest among Asian-Americans (2.4%) in 2010. At the same time, non-Hispanic African-Americans (4.5%), Hispanics (5.1%), and Native Americans and Alaskan Natives (6.9%) were found to be heavy alcohol users.

ILLICIT DRUG USE. According to the CDC, illicit drugs include marijuana/hashish, cocaine (including crack), heroin, hallucinogens, inhalants, and any prescription-type psychotherapeutic drug that is used nonmedically. In 2010 the rates of illicit drug use during the past month were highest for non-Hispanic African-Americans (10.7%) and Native Americans and Alaskan Natives (12.1%), followed closely by non-Hispanic whites (9.1%). (See Table 6.19.) The rates of illicit

**TABLE 6.18**

Alcohol use, binge alcohol use, and heavy alcohol use in the past month among persons aged 12 or older, by age, gender, and race and Hispanic origin, 2009 and 2010

| Demographic characteristic | Alcohol use (2009) | Alcohol use (2010) | Binge alcohol use (2009) | Binge alcohol use (2010) | Heavy alcohol use (2009) | Heavy alcohol use (2010) |
|---|---|---|---|---|---|---|
| Total | 51.9 | 51.8 | 23.7 | 23.1 | 6.8 | 6.7 |
| **Age** | | | | | | |
| 12–17 | 14.7[a] | 13.6 | 8.8[b] | 7.8 | 2.1[a] | 1.7 |
| 18–25 | 61.8 | 61.5 | 41.7 | 40.6 | 13.7 | 13.6 |
| 26 or older | 54.9 | 54.9 | 22.4 | 21.9 | 6.2 | 6.1 |
| **Gender** | | | | | | |
| Male | 57.6 | 57.4 | 31.6 | 30.9 | 10.3 | 10.1 |
| Female | 46.5 | 46.5 | 16.1 | 15.7 | 3.5 | 3.4 |
| **Hispanic origin and race** | | | | | | |
| Not Hispanic or Latino | 53.6 | 53.5 | 23.4 | 22.7 | 7.1 | 6.9 |
| White | 56.7 | 56.7 | 24.8 | 24.0 | 7.9 | 7.7 |
| Black or African American | 42.8 | 42.8 | 19.8 | 19.8 | 4.5 | 4.5 |
| American Indian or Alaska Native | 37.1 | 36.6 | 22.2 | 24.7 | 8.3 | 6.9 |
| Native Hawaiian or other Pacific Islander | * | * | * | * | 3.6 | * |
| Asian | 37.6 | 38.4 | 11.1 | 12.4 | 1.5 | 2.4 |
| Two or more races | 47.6 | 45.2 | 24.1 | 21.5 | 6.4 | 5.8 |
| Hispanic or Latino | 41.7 | 41.8 | 25.0 | 25.1 | 5.2 | 5.1 |

*Low precision; no estimate reported.

Notes: Binge alcohol use is defined as drinking five or more drinks on the same occasion (i.e., at the same time or within a couple of hours of each other) on at least 1 day in the past 30 days. Heavy alcohol use is defined as drinking five or more drinks on the same occasion on each of 5 or more days in the past 30 days; all heavy alcohol users are also binge alcohol users.

[a]Difference between estimate and 2010 estimate is statistically significant at the 0.05 level.
[b]Difference between estimate and 2010 estimate is statistically significant at the 0.01 level.

SOURCE: "Table 2.42B. Alcohol Use, Binge Alcohol Use, and Heavy Alcohol Use in the Past Month among Persons Aged 12 or Older, by Demographic Characteristics: Percentages, 2009 and 2010," in *Results from the 2010 National Survey on Drug Use and Health: Detailed Tables*, U.S. Department of Health and Human Services, Substance Abuse and Mental Health Services Administration, Office of Applied Studies, September 2011, http://www.samhsa.gov/data/NSDUH/2k10ResultsTables/Web/PDFW/Sect2peTabs37to46.pdf (accessed December 16, 2011)

TABLE 6.19

**Illicit drug use by age, gender, and race and Hispanic origin, 2009 and 2010**

| Demographic characteristic | Lifetime (2009) | Lifetime (2010) | Past year (2009) | Past year (2010) | Past month (2009) | Past month (2010) |
|---|---|---|---|---|---|---|
| Total | 47.1 | 47.1 | 15.1 | 15.3 | 8.7 | 8.9 |
| **Age** | | | | | | |
| 12–17 | 26.8 | 25.7 | 19.5 | 19.4 | 10.0 | 10.1 |
| 18–25 | 58.1 | 57.0 | 36.0 | 35.0 | 21.2 | 21.5 |
| 26 or older | 47.8 | 48.1 | 10.9 | 11.3 | 6.3 | 6.6 |
| **Gender** | | | | | | |
| Male | 51.9 | 52.2 | 17.9 | 18.2 | 10.8 | 11.2 |
| Female | 42.6 | 42.3 | 12.4 | 12.5 | 6.6 | 6.8 |
| **Hispanic origin and race** | | | | | | |
| Not Hispanic or Latino | 48.7 | 48.8 | 15.1 | 15.3 | 8.8 | 9.1 |
| White | 51.2 | 50.9 | 15.3 | 15.3 | 8.8 | 9.1 |
| Black or African American | 43.5 | 45.1 | 15.9 | 16.8 | 9.6 | 10.7 |
| American Indian or Alaska Native | 64.8 | 58.4 | 27.1 | 22.6 | 18.3 | 12.1 |
| Native Hawaiian or other Pacific Islander | * | * | * | 10.4 | * | 5.4 |
| Asian | 20.1 | 25.2 | 6.2 | 8.7 | 3.7 | 3.5 |
| Two or more races | 55.8 | 57.4 | 23.4 | 22.4 | 14.3 | 12.5 |
| Hispanic or Latino | 37.6 | 37.2 | 14.9 | 15.3 | 7.9 | 8.1 |

*Low precision; no estimate reported.
Note: Illicit drugs include marijuana/hashish, cocaine (including crack), heroin, hallucinogens, inhalants, or prescription-type psychotherapeutics used nonmedically, including data from original methamphetamine questions but not including new methamphetamine items added in 2005 and 2006.

SOURCE: "Table 1.19B. Illicit Drug Use in Lifetime, Past Year, and Past Month among Persons Aged 12 or Older, by Demographic Characteristics: Percentages, 2009 and 2010," in *Results from the 2010 National Survey on Drug Use and Health: Detailed Tables*, U.S. Department of Health and Human Services, Substance Abuse and Mental Health Services Administration, Office of Applied Studies, September 2011, http://www.samhsa.gov/data/NSDUH/2k10ResultsTables/Web/PDFW/Sect1peTabs19to23.pdf (accessed December 16, 2011)

drug use during the past month were lowest for Asian-Americans (3.5%) and Hispanics (8.1%). Native Americans and Alaskan Natives (22.6%) had the highest rates of illicit drug use during the past year, followed by non-Hispanic African-Americans (16.8%), non-Hispanic whites (15.3%), Hispanics (15.3%), and Asian-Americans (8.7%). Lifetime illicit drug use was also highest among Native Americans and Alaskan Natives (58.4%), followed by non-Hispanic whites (50.9%), non-Hispanic African-Americans (45.1%), Hispanics (37.2%), and Asian-Americans (25.2%).

## LIFE EXPECTANCY AND DEATH

### Life Expectancy

Women tend to live longer than men, and whites are likely to live longer than African-Americans. When comparing the life expectancies of African-American and white babies, African-American males born in 2008 had the shortest life expectancy of 70.2 years, whereas white females had the longest life expectancy of 80.7 years. (See Figure 6.8.) African-American females had a life expectancy of 76.9 years, and white males had a life expectancy of 75.9 years. The life expectancy of all groups at birth had risen since 1970, especially for African-Americans. In 2008 African-Americans died at a higher rate than whites (1.2 African-Americans died for every 1 white death). (See Table 6.20.)

### Leading Causes of Death

In 2008 heart disease was the leading cause of death among Americans, with 186.5 deaths per 100,000 popula-

**FIGURE 6.8**

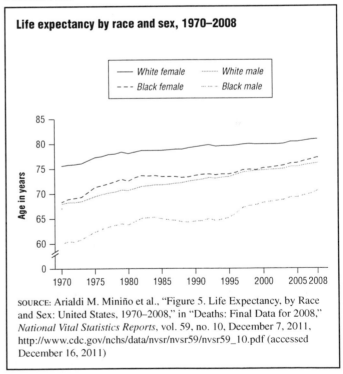

**Life expectancy by race and sex, 1970–2008**

White female · · · · · · White male
- - - Black female · · · · · · Black male

Age in years

SOURCE: Arialdi M. Miniño et al., "Figure 5. Life Expectancy, by Race and Sex: United States, 1970–2008," in "Deaths: Final Data for 2008," *National Vital Statistics Reports*, vol. 59, no. 10, December 7, 2011, http://www.cdc.gov/nchs/data/nvsr/nvsr59/nvsr59_10.pdf (accessed December 16, 2011)

tion. (See Table 6.20.) Cancers (malignant neoplasms) were the second-leading cause of death, with 175.3 deaths per 100,000 population, followed by chronic lower respiratory diseases, which caused 44 deaths per 100,000 population. Cerebrovascular diseases and accidents rounded

TABLE 6.20

## Deaths by causes of death, race, Hispanic origin, and sex, 2007–08

| Rank[a] | Cause of death (based on the ICD-10, 2004) | Number | Percent of total deaths | 2008 crude death rate | Age-adjusted death rate | | | |
|---|---|---|---|---|---|---|---|---|
| | | | | | 2008 | Percent change 2007 to 2008 | Ratio Male to female | Ratio Black[b] to white |
| — | All causes | 2,471,984 | 100.0 | 813.0 | 758.3 | −0.2 | 1.4 | 1.2 |
| 1 | Diseases of heart (I00-I09,I11,I13,I20-I51) | 616,828 | 25.0 | 202.9 | 186.5 | −2.3 | 1.5 | 1.3 |
| 2 | Malignant neoplasms (C00-C97) | 565,469 | 22.9 | 186.0 | 175.3 | −1.7 | 1.4 | 1.2 |
| 3 | Chronic lower respiratory diseases (J40-J47) | 141,090 | 5.7 | 46.4 | 44.0 | 7.8 | 1.3 | 0.7 |
| 4 | Cerebrovascular diseases (I60-I69) | 134,148 | 5.4 | 44.1 | 40.7 | −3.6 | 1.0 | 1.5 |
| 5 | Accidents (unintentional injuries) (V01-X59, Y85-Y86) | 121,902 | 4.9 | 40.1 | 38.8 | −3.0 | 2.1 | 0.8 |
| 6 | Alzheimer's disease (G30) | 82,435 | 3.3 | 27.1 | 24.4 | 7.5 | 0.8 | 0.8 |
| 7 | Diabetes mellitus (E10-E14) | 70,553 | 2.9 | 23.2 | 21.8 | −3.1 | 1.4 | 2.0 |
| 8 | Influenza and pneumonia (J09-J18)[c] | 56,284 | 2.3 | 18.5 | 16.9 | 4.3 | 1.3 | 1.1 |
| 9 | Nephritis, nephrotic syndrome and nephrosis (N00-N07, N17-N19, N25-N27) | 48,237 | 2.0 | 15.9 | 14.8 | 2.1 | 1.4 | 2.2 |
| 10 | Intentional self-harm (suicide) (U03[d], X60-X84, Y87.0) | 36,035 | 1.5 | 11.9 | 11.6 | 2.7 | 3.9 | 0.4 |
| 11 | Septicemia (A40-A41) | 35,927 | 1.5 | 11.8 | 11.1 | 0.9 | 1.2 | 2.1 |
| 12 | Chronic liver disease and cirrhosis (K70, K73-K74) | 29,963 | 1.2 | 9.9 | 9.2 | 1.1 | 2.1 | 0.7 |
| 13 | Essential hypertension and hypertensive renal disease (I10, I12, I15) | 25,742 | 1.0 | 8.5 | 7.7 | 4.1 | 1.0 | 2.5 |
| 14 | Parkinson's disease (G20-G21) | 20,483 | 0.8 | 6.7 | 6.4 | 0.0 | 2.3 | 0.4 |
| 15 | Assault (homicide) (U01-U02[d], X85-Y09, Y87.1) | 17,826 | 0.7 | 5.9 | 5.9 | −3.3 | 3.9 | 5.3 |
| — | All other causes (residual) | 469,062 | 19.0 | 154.3 | — | — | — | — |

—Category not applicable.

ICD-10 = *International Classification of Diseases, Tenth Revision.*

[a]Rank based on number of deaths.

[b]Multiple-race data were reported by 27 states and the District of Columbia in 2008. The multiple-race data for these reporting areas were bridged to the single-race categories of the 1977 OMB standards for comparability with other reporting areas.

[c]New ICD-10 code J09 (Influenza due to identified avian influenza virus) was added to the category in 2007.

[d]Not part of the *International Classification of Diseases, Tenth Revision*, Second Edition. Beginning with data for 2001, the National Center for Health Statistics introduced categories U01-U03 for classifying and coding deaths due to acts of terrorism.

Notes: Crude death rates on an annual basis per 100,000 population; age-adjusted rates per 100,000 U.S. standard population. Data for specified races other than white and black should be interpreted with caution because of inconsistencies between reporting race on death certificates and on censuses and surveys. Race categories are consistent with the 1977 Office of Management and Budget (OMB) standards. Cause-of-death coding changes in 2007 and 2008 may affect comparability of data between 2008 and previous years for various causes of death.

SOURCE: Arialdi M. Miniño et al., "Table B. Percentage of Total Deaths, Death Rates, Age-Adjusted Death Rates for 2008, Percentage Change in Age-Adjusted Death Rates from 2007 to 2008, and Ratio of Age-Adjusted Death Rates by Race and Sex for the 15 Leading Causes of Death for the Total Population in 2008: United States," in "Deaths: Final Data for 2008," *National Vital Statistics Reports*, vol. 59, no. 10, December 7, 2011, http://www.cdc.gov/nchs/data/nvsr/nvsr59/nvsr59_10.pdf (accessed December 16, 2011)

out the top-five leading causes of death that year, with 40.7 and 38.8 deaths per 100,000 population, respectively.

In *Health, United States, 2010*, the NCHS notes that in 2007 heart disease was the leading cause of death among every racial or ethnic group except Asians or Pacific Islanders, among whom it was the second-leading cause of death. That year 531,636 whites died of heart disease, accounting for 25.6% of deaths among whites that year; 71,209 African-Americans (24.6%), 29,021 Hispanics (21.4%), 10,574 Asians or Pacific Islanders (23.2%), and 2,648 Native Americans or Alaskan Natives (18.4%) died of heart disease in 2007. Cancer was the second-leading cause of death among most groups.

Suicide and homicide were responsible for more deaths among some groups than others. The NCHS reports that in 2007, suicide was particularly high among Native Americans or Alaskan Natives and Asians or Pacific Islanders; it was the eighth-leading cause of death among both groups. Homicide ranked as the sixth-leading cause of death among African-Americans and the eighth-leading cause of death among Hispanics.

**HOMICIDE.** The NCHS indicates in *Health, United States, 2010* that homicides are disproportionately high in the African-American population and that the high homicide rate among African-Americans is one of the reasons African-American men in their 20s and 30s have a higher death rate than men this age in other ethnic and racial groups. In 2007, 7,584 African-American males were murdered; overall, African-American males had a homicide death rate of 37.1 per 100,000 population. The highest rate of death by homicide was among African-American men aged 15 to 24 years (85.3 per 100,000 population), followed by African-American men aged 25 to 34 years (82.5 per 100,000 population) and African-American men aged 35 to 44 years (41.2 per 100,000 population). In comparison, there were 4.9 homicides per 100,000 non-Hispanic white men aged 15 to 24 years, 6.2 homicides per 100,000 non-Hispanic white men aged 25 to 34 years, and 5.1 homicides per 100,000 non-Hispanic white men aged 35 to 44 years.

According to the NCHS, in 2007 Hispanics, like African-Americans, had a higher homicide rate than most other groups, particularly among youth. The homicide rate for Hispanic men aged 15 to 24 years was 30 per 100,000 population and for Hispanic men aged 25 to 34 years it was 19.9 per 100,000 population. Even so, between 1990 and 2007 the homicide death rate among all Hispanic men dropped from 27.4 to 11.2 per 100,000 population.

**HIV AND AIDS.** The difference in the HIV/AIDS death rate among races and ethnic groups is staggering, with a much higher rate among African-Americans than any other group of Americans. In 2008, 8,176 African-Americans died from AIDS, compared with 4,766 whites, 2,524 Hispanics, 80 Asian-Americans, and 79 Native Americans and Alaskan Natives. (See Table 6.21.) African-Americans had the highest rate of AIDS deaths, at 21.9 per 100,000

population. In *Health, United States, 2010*, the NCHS reports that the HIV/AIDS death rate for African-American males in 2007 was 24.5 per 100,000 population, compared with 6.3 per 100,000 Hispanic males, 3.6 per 100,000 Native American or Alaskan Native males, 2.5 per 100,000 non-Hispanic white males, and 0.8 per 100,000 Asian or Pacific Islander males. The death rate for African-American females in 2007 was also extremely high in comparison with other groups, at 11.3 per 100,000 population, compared with 1.8 per 100,000 Hispanic females, 1.7 per 100,000 Native American or Alaskan Native females, and 0.5 per 100,000 non-Hispanic white females.

TABLE 6.21

**Deaths of persons with an AIDS diagnosis, by year of death, age, race and Hispanic origin, and transmission category, 2006–08 and cumulative**

| | 2006 | | | 2007 | | | 2008 | | | Cumulative[b] | |
|---|---|---|---|---|---|---|---|---|---|---|---|
| | | Estimated[a] | | | Estimated[a] | | | Estimated[a] | | | |
| | No. | No. | Rate | No. | No. | Rate | No. | No. | Rate | No. | Est. no.[a] |
| **Age at death (yr)** | | | | | | | | | | | |
| <13 | 12 | 13 | 0.0 | 5 | 6 | 0.0 | 3 | 4 | 0.0 | 4,915 | 4,949 |
| 13–14 | 3 | 3 | 0.0 | 9 | 11 | 0.1 | 0 | 0 | 0.0 | 283 | 289 |
| 15–19 | 43 | 46 | 0.2 | 34 | 39 | 0.2 | 33 | 40 | 0.2 | 1,175 | 1,205 |
| 20–24 | 166 | 179 | 0.8 | 140 | 161 | 0.8 | 133 | 165 | 0.8 | 9,027 | 9,188 |
| 25–29 | 443 | 478 | 2.3 | 415 | 476 | 2.3 | 375 | 486 | 2.3 | 44,716 | 45,358 |
| 30–34 | 864 | 935 | 4.8 | 753 | 861 | 4.4 | 627 | 799 | 4.1 | 97,541 | 98,967 |
| 35–39 | 1,864 | 2,016 | 9.6 | 1,627 | 1,862 | 8.9 | 1,234 | 1,578 | 7.6 | 120,966 | 123,266 |
| 40–44 | 3,048 | 3,294 | 14.8 | 2,628 | 2,992 | 13.7 | 2,107 | 2,674 | 12.5 | 110,488 | 113,308 |
| 45–49 | 3,278 | 3,546 | 15.6 | 2,910 | 3,310 | 14.5 | 2,490 | 3,153 | 13.8 | 79,542 | 82,168 |
| 50–54 | 2,612 | 2,811 | 13.8 | 2,487 | 2,822 | 13.5 | 2,232 | 2,792 | 13.0 | 49,759 | 51,708 |
| 55–59 | 1,651 | 1,781 | 9.8 | 1,541 | 1,745 | 9.6 | 1,657 | 2,064 | 11.1 | 28,709 | 29,913 |
| 60–64 | 847 | 913 | 6.8 | 854 | 969 | 6.7 | 922 | 1,154 | 7.7 | 16,314 | 16,981 |
| ≥65 | 931 | 1,004 | 2.7 | 860 | 973 | 2.6 | 941 | 1,178 | 3.0 | 16,496 | 17,197 |
| **Race/ethnicity** | | | | | | | | | | | |
| American Indian/Alaska Native | 73 | 80 | 3.5 | 65 | 76 | 3.3 | 63 | 79 | 3.4 | 1,745 | 1,813 |
| Asian[c] | 96 | 103 | 0.8 | 63 | 74 | 0.6 | 64 | 80 | 0.6 | 2,957 | 3,034 |
| Black/African American | 8,140 | 8,783 | 24.0 | 7,483 | 8,522 | 23.1 | 6,507 | 8,176 | 21.9 | 233,641 | 240,627 |
| Hispanic/Latino[d] | 2,454 | 2,608 | 5.9 | 2,167 | 2,393 | 5.3 | 2,061 | 2,524 | 5.4 | 87,475 | 89,297 |
| Native Hawaiian/other Pacific Islander | 5 | 6 | 1.3 | 8 | 9 | 2.1 | 10 | 12 | 2.7 | 338 | 347 |
| White | 4,597 | 5,017 | 2.5 | 4,089 | 4,721 | 2.4 | 3,684 | 4,766 | 2.4 | 248,009 | 253,397 |
| Multiple races | 395 | 419 | 10.1 | 388 | 431 | 10.0 | 363 | 448 | 10.1 | 5,615 | 5,827 |
| **Transmission category** | | | | | | | | | | | |
| Male adult or adolescent | | | | | | | | | | | |
| Male-to-male sexual contact | 4,794 | 6,107 | — | 4,436 | 6,020 | — | 3,810 | 5,884 | — | 263,652 | 286,164 |
| Injection drug use | 2,564 | 3,217 | — | 2,153 | 2,857 | — | 1,906 | 2,811 | — | 106,241 | 119,333 |
| Male-to-male sexual contact and injection drug use | 1,179 | 1,398 | — | 1,020 | 1,270 | — | 876 | 1,235 | — | 41,214 | 44,448 |
| Heterosexual contact[e] | 1,217 | 1,667 | — | 1,090 | 1,623 | — | 1,064 | 1,748 | — | 22,201 | 28,311 |
| Other[f] | 1,826 | 136 | — | 1,721 | 121 | — | 1,653 | 116 | — | 43,036 | 9,414 |
| **Subtotal** | **11,580** | **12,525** | **10.4** | **10,420** | **11,891** | **9.8** | **9,309** | **11,794** | **9.6** | **476,344** | **487,671** |
| Female adult or adolescent | | | | | | | | | | | |
| Injection drug use | 1,394 | 1,824 | — | 1,246 | 1,718 | — | 1,130 | 1,715 | — | 43,152 | 50,144 |
| Heterosexual contact[e] | 1,743 | 2,527 | — | 1,633 | 2,490 | — | 1,412 | 2,443 | — | 37,660 | 46,541 |
| Other[f] | 994 | 88 | — | 920 | 77 | — | 854 | 77 | — | 17,296 | 4,599 |
| **Subtotal** | **4,131** | **4,438** | **3.5** | **3,799** | **4,285** | **3.4** | **3,396** | **4,235** | **3.3** | **98,108** | **101,284** |

**TABLE 6.21**

**Deaths of persons with an AIDS diagnosis, by year of death, age, race and Hispanic origin, and transmission category, 2006–08 and cumulative** [CONTINUED]

| | 2006 | Estimated[a] | | 2007 | Estimated[a] | | 2008 | Estimated[a] | | Cumulative[b] | |
|---|---|---|---|---|---|---|---|---|---|---|---|
| | No. | No. | Rate | No. | No. | Rate | No. | No. | Rate | No. | Est. no.[a] |
| Child (<13 yrs at diagnosis) | | | | | | | | | | | |
| Perinatal | 44 | 47 | — | 38 | 44 | — | 45 | 54 | — | 4,882 | 4,938 |
| Other[c] | 7 | 8 | — | 6 | 7 | — | 4 | 5 | — | 597 | 603 |
| **Subtotal** | **51** | **55** | **0.1** | **44** | **51** | **0.1** | **49** | **59** | **0.1** | **5,479** | **5,541** |
| Region of residence | | | | | | | | | | | |
| Northeast | 4,438 | 4,692 | 8.6 | 3,887 | 4,197 | 7.6 | 3,472 | 4,004 | 7.3 | 189,360 | 192,050 |
| Midwest | 1,451 | 1,641 | 2.5 | 1,311 | 1,614 | 2.4 | 1,201 | 1,656 | 2.5 | 57,457 | 59,734 |
| South | 7,536 | 8,123 | 7.5 | 7,131 | 8,149 | 7.4 | 6,424 | 8,332 | 7.4 | 214,701 | 221,508 |
| West | 2,337 | 2,562 | 3.7 | 1,934 | 2,267 | 3.2 | 1,657 | 2,096 | 3.0 | 118,413 | 121,204 |
| **Total[h]** | **15,762** | **17,018** | **5.7** | **14,263** | **16,226** | **5.4** | **12,754** | **16,088** | **5.3** | **579,931** | **594,496** |

Notes: Deaths of persons with an AIDS diagnosis may be due to any cause.
[a]Estimated numbers resulted from statistical adjustment that accounted for reporting delays and missing risk-factor information, but not for incomplete reporting. Rates are per 100,000 population. Rates are not calculated by transmission category because of the lack of denominator data.
[b]From the beginning of the epidemic through 2008.
[c]Includes Asian/Pacific Islander legacy cases.
[d]Hispanics/Latinos can be of any race.
[e]Heterosexual contact with a person known to have, or to be at high risk for, HIV infection.
[f]Includes hemophilia, blood transfusion, perinatal exposure, and risk factor not reported or not identified.
[g]Includes hemophilia, blood transfusion, and risk factor not reported or not identified.
[h]Includes persons of unknown race/ethnicity. Because column totals for estimated numbers were calculated independently of the values for the subpopulations, the values in each column may not sum to the column total.

SOURCE: "Table 12a. Deaths of Persons with an AIDS Diagnosis, by Year of Death and Selected Characteristics, 2006–2008 and Cumulative—United States," in *HIV Surveillance Report, 2009, vol. 21,* U.S. Department of Health and Human Services, Centers for Disease Control and Prevention, February 2011, http://www.cdc.gov/hiv/surveillance/resources/reports/2009report/pdf/table12a.pdf (accessed December 16, 2011)

## CHAPTER 7
# CRIME

## VICTIMIZATION OF MINORITIES

Certain groups in U.S. society, including the poor, younger people, males, African-Americans, Hispanics, and residents of inner cities, are more likely to be victimized and are more vulnerable to violence than other groups. As discussed in other chapters of this book, African-Americans and Hispanics are more likely to be poor and to be unemployed than are whites. These factors put minorities at an especially high risk of being victimized.

### Violent Crimes

Non-Hispanic African-Americans are more likely than individuals of other races to be victims of violent crimes. In *Criminal Victimization, 2010* (September 2011, http://bjs .ojp.usdoj.gov/content/pub/pdf/cv10.pdf), Jennifer L. Truman of the Bureau of Justice Statistics (BJS) reports that in 2010, 20.8 per 1,000 non-Hispanic African-Americans were victims of a violent crime, compared with 15.6 per 1,000 Hispanics and 13.6 per 1,000 non-Hispanic whites. (See Table 7.1.) Native Americans or Alaskan Natives had an even higher rate of violent victimizations, at 42.2 per 1,000 people, whereas Asians or Pacific Islanders had a very low rate, at 6.3 per 1,000 people. People who reported that they were two or more races had twice the rate of violent victimizations as did non-Hispanic African-Americans, at 52.6 per 1,000 people.

Shannan M. Catalano of the BJS reports in *Criminal Victimization, 2005* (September 2006, http://bjs.ojp.usdoj .gov/content/pub/pdf/cv05.pdf) that even though minorities were particularly likely to be victimized, the rate of violent crimes in each racial and ethnic group declined significantly between 1993 and 2005. The rate of violent crimes committed against Hispanics had dropped 54.7%, the rate of violent crimes committed against African-Americans had dropped 59.9%, and the rate of violent crimes committed against people of other minority groups had dropped 65.1%. Truman reports that the overall rate of violent crime

dropped an additional 8.8% between 2005 and 2010, with an especially large decrease between 2009 and 2010, and this decrease held true for all racial and ethnic groups.

The rates of violent crimes by type of crime show that minorities are more likely than non-Hispanic whites to be victims of some types of violent crime and about equally likely to be victims of other types of violent crime. In 2010 non-Hispanic African-Americans were about twice as likely as non-Hispanic whites to be victims of aggravated assault (4.7 per 1,000 and 2.6 per 1,000, respectively) and of robbery (3.6 per 1,000 and 1.4 per 1,000, respectively). (See Table 7.1.) Hispanics had rates of aggravated assault and robbery (2.3 and 2.7, respectively) that were similar to the rates for non-Hispanic whites. People who reported that they were multiracial were much more likely than any other group to be victims of simple assault (34.9 per 1,000) or any assault (43.5 per 1,000).

**REPORTING VIOLENT CRIMES.** Truman finds that in general non-Hispanic African-Americans are less likely to report violent crimes to the police than are Hispanics or non-Hispanic whites. In 2010, 48% of non-Hispanic African-American male victims of violent crimes reported them to police, whereas 50% of non-Hispanic white male victims and 53.4% of Hispanic male victims did so. (See Table 7.2.) Non-Hispanic African-American females were more likely to report violent crimes than were non-Hispanic white females (55.4% and 52.4%, respectively), but less likely than Hispanic females (62.5%). In contrast, Hispanics were much less likely than either non-Hispanic African-Americans or non-Hispanic whites to report property crimes to the police.

**HOMICIDE.** African-Americans are also more likely than people of other races to be victims of homicides. African-American males aged 18 to 24 years had the highest homicide victimization rate in the last half of the 20th century and into the 21st century. According to James Alan Fox and Marianne W. Zawitz of the BJS, in *Homicide*

TABLE 7.1

### Rates of violent crime, by gender, race, Hispanic origin, and age of victim, 2010

| Demographic characteristic of victim | Population | Percent of total population | Violent victimizations per 1,000 persons age 12 or older | | | | | |
| | | | Total | Rape/sexual assault | Robbery | Total assault | Aggravated assault | Simple assault |
|---|---|---|---|---|---|---|---|---|
| **Total** | 255,961,940 | 100% | 14.9 | 0.7 | 1.9 | 12.3 | 2.8 | 9.5 |
| **Sex** | | | | | | | | |
| Male | 124,987,510 | 48.8% | 15.7 | 0.1[c] | 2.4 | 13.1 | 3.4 | 9.7 |
| Female | 130,974,430 | 51.2 | 14.2 | 1.3 | 1.4 | 11.5 | 2.3 | 9.2 |
| **Race/Hispanic origin** | | | | | | | | |
| White[a] | 173,740,280 | 67.9% | 13.6 | 0.7 | 1.4 | 11.6 | 2.6 | 9.0 |
| Black[a] | 30,371,120 | 11.9 | 20.8 | 1.1[c] | 3.6 | 16.1 | 4.7 | 11.4 |
| Hispanic | 35,836,220 | 14.0 | 15.6 | 0.8[c] | 2.7 | 12.0 | 2.3 | 9.8 |
| American Indian or Alaskan Native[a] | 1,373,440 | 0.5 | 42.2 | [b, c] | 4.3[c] | 37.9 | 19.5[c] | 18.3[c] |
| Asian or Pacific Islander[a] | 12,135,210 | 4.7 | 6.3 | 0.6[c] | 1.1[c] | 4.5 | 0.5[c] | 4.0 |
| Two or more races[a] | 2,505,670 | 1.0 | 52.6 | 1.2[c] | 8.0[c] | 43.5 | 8.5[c] | 34.9 |
| **Age** | | | | | | | | |
| 12–14 | 12,102,730 | 4.7% | 27.5 | 2.7[c] | 0.7[c] | 24.1 | 5.8 | 18.3 |
| 15–17 | 12,332,800 | 4.8 | 23.0 | 1.7[c] | 2.7[c] | 18.6 | 3.9 | 14.7 |
| 18–20 | 13,109,120 | 5.1 | 33.9 | 1.1[c] | 5.9 | 26.9 | 6.9 | 20.0 |
| 21–24 | 16,757,880 | 6.5 | 26.9 | 1.5[c] | 3.7 | 21.7 | 8.0 | 13.7 |
| 25–34 | 41,712,030 | 16.3 | 18.8 | 1.3 | 2.5 | 15.0 | 3.3 | 11.7 |
| 35–49 | 63,157,240 | 24.7 | 12.6 | 0.6 | 1.5 | 10.4 | 1.9 | 8.6 |
| 50–64 | 58,096,490 | 22.7 | 10.9 | [b, c] | 1.3 | 9.7 | 2.1 | 7.6 |
| 65 or older | 38,693,630 | 15.1 | 2.4 | 0.1[c] | 0.6[c] | 1.7 | 0.2[c] | 1.5 |

[a]Excludes persons of Hispanic origin.
[b]Less than 0.05.
[c]Interpret with caution; estimate based on 10 or fewer sample cases.

SOURCE: Jennifer L. Truman, "Table 9. Violent Victimizations, by Type of Crime, Sex, Race, Hispanic Origin, and Age of Victim, 2010," in *Criminal Victimization, 2010*, U.S. Department of Justice, Bureau of Justice Statistics, September 2011, http://www.bjs.gov/content/pub/pdf/cv10.pdf (accessed December 26, 2011)

TABLE 7.2

### Crime reported to the police, by gender, race, and Hispanic origin, 2010

| Demographic characteristic of victim | Violent victimization | Property victimization |
|---|---|---|
| **Total** | 51.0% | 39.3% |
| **Male** | 48.8% | 41.1% |
| White[a] | 50.0 | 41.1 |
| Black[a] | 48.0 | 42.5 |
| Hispanic | 53.4 | 36.1 |
| Other* | 19.1[b] | 46.7 |
|    American Indian or Alaskan Native[a] | 16.4[b] | 64.9 |
|    Asian or Pacific Islander[a] | 22.4[b] | 41.7 |
| Two or more races[a] | 37.5[b] | 50.3 |
| **Female** | 53.3% | 37.6% |
| White[a] | 52.4 | 38.4 |
| Black[a] | 55.4 | 39.6 |
| Hispanic | 62.5 | 33.1 |
| Other* | 74.4 | 32.0 |
|    American Indian or Alaskan Native[a] | 44.5[b] | 38.7[b] |
|    Asian or Pacific Islander[a] | 86.1 | 28.9 |
| Two or more races[a] | 17.5[b] | 34.1 |

Note: For violent victimizations, the characteristics apply to the victim. For property victimizations, the characteristics apply to the head of household.
[a]Excludes persons of Hispanic origin.
[b]Interpret with caution; estimate based on 10 or fewer sample cases.

SOURCE: Jennifer L. Truman, "Table 8. Victimizations Reported to the Police, by Sex, Race, and Hispanic Origin of Victim, 2010," in *Criminal Victimization, 2010*, U.S. Department of Justice, Bureau of Justice Statistics, September 2011, http://www.bjs.gov/content/pub/pdf/cv10.pdf (accessed December 26, 2011)

*Trends in the United States* (January 2010, http://bjs.ojp.usdoj.gov/content/pub/pdf/htius.pdf), this proportion rose from 89.8 homicide victims per 100,000 population in 1976 to a high of 183.5 homicides per 100,000 population in 1993. By 2005 the homicide rate for African-American males of this age group had dropped to 102 homicides per 100,000 population. The homicide victimization rate among white men aged 18 to 24 years had also risen, from 11.3 homicides per 100,000 population in 1976 to 12.2 homicides per 100,000 population in 2005. There was a spike in homicides among young white males during the early 1990s, with the victimization rate topping out at 18.2 in 1991. Among African-American and white women, the homicide victimization rate decreased in all age categories between 1976 and 2005. Nevertheless, African-Americans are overrepresented among homicide victims; in 2010, 49.8% of all homicide victims were African-American, and the majority of them were in their 20s. (See Table 7.3.)

The circumstances surrounding homicides vary from racial group to racial group. African-Americans are overrepresented as both victims and offenders in all types of homicide compared with their presence in the U.S. population as a whole, but they are also overrepresented compared with their already heightened representation among homicide victims in homicides involving drugs. According to Fox and Zawitz, even though 46.9% of all

## TABLE 7.3

**Homicide victims by age, sex, and race, 2010**

| Age | Total | Sex | | | Race | | | |
|---|---|---|---|---|---|---|---|---|
| | | Male | Female | Unknown | White | Black | Other | Unknown |
| **Total** | **12,996** | **10,058** | **2,918** | **20** | **6,043** | **6,470** | **331** | **152** |
| Percent distribution | 100.0 | 77.4 | 22.5 | 0.2 | 46.5 | 49.8 | 2.5 | 1.2 |
| Under 18* | 1,277 | 890 | 386 | 1 | 599 | 622 | 37 | 19 |
| Under 22* | 3,172 | 2,540 | 631 | 1 | 1,278 | 1,800 | 65 | 29 |
| 18 and over* | 11,566 | 9,069 | 2,493 | 4 | 5,385 | 5,797 | 291 | 93 |
| Infant (under 1) | 186 | 91 | 94 | 1 | 121 | 56 | 5 | 4 |
| 1 to 4 | 313 | 192 | 121 | 0 | 174 | 120 | 11 | 8 |
| 5 to 8 | 85 | 44 | 41 | 0 | 55 | 26 | 4 | 0 |
| 9 to 12 | 43 | 28 | 15 | 0 | 20 | 17 | 3 | 3 |
| 13 to 16 | 363 | 288 | 75 | 0 | 140 | 212 | 9 | 2 |
| 17 to 19 | 1,231 | 1,065 | 166 | 0 | 425 | 779 | 20 | 7 |
| 20 to 24 | 2,256 | 1,944 | 312 | 0 | 813 | 1,387 | 40 | 16 |
| 25 to 29 | 1,964 | 1,627 | 337 | 0 | 753 | 1,157 | 34 | 20 |
| 30 to 34 | 1,541 | 1,286 | 253 | 2 | 626 | 865 | 35 | 15 |
| 35 to 39 | 1,072 | 820 | 252 | 0 | 495 | 535 | 31 | 11 |
| 40 to 44 | 882 | 635 | 247 | 0 | 477 | 366 | 31 | 8 |
| 45 to 49 | 838 | 589 | 249 | 0 | 502 | 306 | 26 | 4 |
| 50 to 54 | 686 | 508 | 178 | 0 | 426 | 237 | 19 | 4 |
| 55 to 59 | 473 | 329 | 143 | 1 | 288 | 154 | 25 | 6 |
| 60 to 64 | 325 | 199 | 126 | 0 | 217 | 90 | 17 | 1 |
| 65 to 69 | 189 | 125 | 64 | 0 | 132 | 53 | 3 | 1 |
| 70 to 74 | 137 | 80 | 56 | 1 | 103 | 26 | 8 | 0 |
| 75 and over | 259 | 109 | 150 | 0 | 217 | 33 | 7 | 2 |
| Unknown | 153 | 99 | 39 | 15 | 59 | 51 | 3 | 40 |

*Does not include unknown ages.

SOURCE: "Expanded Homicide Data Table 2. Murder Victims by Age, Sex, and Race, 2010," in *Crime in the United States, 2010,* U.S. Department of Justice, Federal Bureau of Investigation, September 2011, http://www.fbi.gov/about-us/cjis/ucr/crime-in-the-u.s/2010/crime-in-the-u.s.-2010/tables/10shrtbl02.xls (accessed December 26, 2011)

## TABLE 7.4

**Race and sex of homicide victims by race and sex of offender, 2010**

[Single victim/single offender]

| Race of victim | Total | Race of offender | | | | Sex of offender | | |
|---|---|---|---|---|---|---|---|---|
| | | White | Black | Other | Unknown | Male | Female | Unknown |
| White | 3,327 | 2,777 | 447 | 40 | 63 | 2,975 | 289 | 63 |
| Black | 2,720 | 218 | 2,459 | 7 | 36 | 2,439 | 245 | 36 |
| Other race | 179 | 47 | 30 | 98 | 4 | 156 | 19 | 4 |
| Unknown race | 58 | 20 | 14 | 2 | 22 | 31 | 5 | 22 |
| **Sex of victim** | | | | | | | | |
| Male | 4,362 | 1,929 | 2,255 | 93 | 85 | 3,872 | 405 | 85 |
| Female | 1,864 | 1,113 | 681 | 52 | 18 | 1,698 | 148 | 18 |
| Unknown sex | 58 | 20 | 14 | 2 | 22 | 31 | 5 | 22 |

Note: This table is based on incidents where some information about the offender is known by law enforcement; therefore, when the offender age, sex, and race are all reported as unknown, these data are excluded from the table.

SOURCE: "Expanded Homicide Data Table 6. Murder: Race and Sex of Victim by Race and Sex of Offender, 2010," in *Crime in the United States, 2010,* U.S. Department of Justice, Federal Bureau of Investigation, September 2011, http://www.fbi.gov/about-us/cjis/ucr/crime-in-the-u.s/2010/crime-in-the-u.s.-2010/tables/10shrtbl06.xls (accessed December 26, 2011)

homicide victims between 1976 and 2005 were African-American, they represented 61.6% of all victims of drug-related homicides. Also, African-Americans were overrepresented as victims among gang-related homicides (39%), sex-related homicides (30.5%), and workplace killings (12.2%). Approximately 50.9% of all victims killed by guns were African-American, whereas only 16.9% of all victims were killed by poison.

Most murders are intraracial (of the same race). In 2010, 2,777 of 3,327 (83.5%) white murder victims were murdered by other whites. (See Table 7.4.) That same year, 2,459 of 2,720 (90.4%) African-American murder victims were murdered by other African-Americans. A low percentage of African-American perpetrators kill white victims, whereas an even smaller percentage of white perpetrators kill African-American victims.

## Property Crimes

According to Truman, people with lower incomes are more likely to be victims of property crime than are people with higher incomes. Because members of most minority groups are disproportionately poor, they are more likely to be victims of property crime. In 2010 the rate of victimization of property crime was 168.7 per 1,000 households with incomes less than $7,500; 170.4 per 1,000 households with incomes between $7,500 and $14,999; 144.9 per 1,000 households with incomes between $15,000 and $24,999; 133.9 per 1,000 households with incomes between $25,000 and $34,999; 120.5 per 1,000 households with incomes between $35,000 and $49,999; and 115.4 per 1,000 households with incomes between $50,000 and $74,999. Only in the highest income group, households earning $75,000 or more, does the property crime rate go up again, to 119.3 per 1,000 households. This rate was still substantially lower than among the lowest-income households. Those with the lowest incomes are often forced to live in the least safe areas and have the fewest resources with which to protect themselves from crime.

## Hate Crimes

The Hate Crime Statistics Act of 1990 required the U.S. attorney general to provide the "acquisition and publication of data about crimes that manifest prejudice based on race, religion, homosexuality or heterosexuality, or ethnicity." The Violent Crime and Law Enforcement Act of 1994 amended the Hate Crime Statistics Act to include crimes that are motivated by discrimination against people with physical and/or mental disabilities. For an offense to be considered a hate crime, the law enforcement investigation must reveal sufficient evidence to lead to the conclusion that the offender's actions were motivated by his or her bias against a certain group. Therefore, data on hate crimes must be considered underreported, as many incidents and offenses that are motivated by bias go uncounted without sufficient evidence concerning this motivation. Even though hate crimes can be perpetrated against members of majority groups, most hate crimes are directed at minorities: racial minorities, religious minorities, ethnic minorities, gay and lesbian people, or people with disabilities.

The hate crime data collection program counts one offense for each victim of crimes against people, but only one offense for each distinct crime against property, regardless of the number of victims; therefore, the number of victims is higher than the number of offenses. Of the 7,699 hate-bias offenses reported in 2010, 3,725 were racially motivated and 1,040 were motivated by ethnicity or national origin. (See Table 7.5.) Of the offenses that were racially motivated, 2,600 were committed against African-Americans and 679 were committed against whites. Another 190 were committed against Asians and Pacific Islanders and 45 were committed against Native Americans and Alaskan Natives. Of the offenses that were motivated by ethnicity or national origin, 681 were anti-Hispanic and 359 were directed against people of another ethnic minority. Of the offenses that were perpetrated against African-Americans in 2010, 933 were intimidation, 486 were simple assault, and 315 were aggravated assault. (See Table 7.6.) Of the offenses that were perpetrated against Hispanics, 227 were intimidation, 183 were simple assault, and 112 were aggravated assault.

The Intelligence Project (2012, http://www.splcenter.org/intel/map/hate.jsp) of the Southern Poverty Law Center in Montgomery, Alabama, a private organization that monitors hate groups and paramilitary organizations nationwide, reports that there were 1,018 active hate group chapters in 2011, up from 888 in 2007. These groups included racist groups such as chapters of the Ku Klux Klan, racist skinhead groups (a particularly violent element of the white supremacist movement), neo-Confederate groups (an alliance of southern heritage organizations that claims allegiance to the antebellum South), and others. The project also tracks black separatist groups that typically oppose integration and want separate institutions for African-Americans. Even though the project recognizes that this black racism is in part a response to centuries of white racism, it believes that a criterion for considering a group racist should be applied to all groups regardless of color. Mary Potok of the Southern Poverty Law Center states in "The 'Patriot' Movement Explodes" (*Intelligence Report*, no. 145, Spring 2012) that there were 1,274 "Patriot" groups (groups that see the federal government as their primary enemy) in 2011, a 755% growth since the end of 2008, after Barack Obama (1961–) was elected president. Potok also notes that 196 neo-Nazi groups, 184 nativist extremist groups, 152 Ku Klux Klan chapters, 131 black separatist groups, 130 racist skinhead groups, 111 white nationalist groups, 32 neo-Confederate groups, 30 Christian identity groups, and many other types of hate groups were operating nationwide in 2011.

## Crime at School

Even though students are less likely to be victimized at school than they are away from school, any crime at school, especially violent crimes, justifiably horrifies students and the community at large. In *Indicators of School Crime and Safety: 2010* (November 2010, http://nces.ed.gov/pubs2011/2011002.pdf), Simone Robers et al. state that "any instance of crime or violence at school not only affects the individuals involved but also may disrupt the educational process and affect bystanders, the school itself, and the surrounding community."

Racial and ethnic minorities are disproportionately affected by crimes at school. Rachel Dinkes, Emily Forrest Cataldi, and Wendy Lin-Kelly note in *Indicators of School Crime and Safety: 2007* (December 2007, http://nces.ed.gov/

**TABLE 7.5**

**Hate-bias incidents, 2010**

| Bias motivation | Incidents | Offenses | Victims[a] | Known offenders[b] |
|---|---|---|---|---|
| Total | 6,628 | 7,699 | 8,208 | 6,008 |
| Single-bias incidents | 6,624 | 7,690 | 8,199 | 6,001 |
| **Race:** | **3,135** | **3,725** | **3,949** | **2,934** |
| Anti-White | 575 | 679 | 697 | 649 |
| Anti-Black | 2,201 | 2,600 | 2,765 | 1,974 |
| Anti-American Indian/Alaskan Native | 44 | 45 | 47 | 43 |
| Anti-Asian/Pacific Islander | 150 | 190 | 203 | 156 |
| Anti-multiple races, group | 165 | 211 | 237 | 112 |
| **Religion:** | **1,322** | **1,409** | **1,552** | **606** |
| Anti-Jewish | 887 | 922 | 1,040 | 346 |
| Anti-Catholic | 58 | 61 | 65 | 22 |
| Anti-Protestant | 41 | 46 | 47 | 6 |
| Anti-Islamic | 160 | 186 | 197 | 125 |
| Anti-other religion | 123 | 134 | 141 | 72 |
| Anti-multiple religions, group | 48 | 53 | 55 | 30 |
| Anti-Atheism/Agnosticism/etc. | 5 | 7 | 7 | 5 |
| **Sexual orientation:** | **1,277** | **1,470** | **1,528** | **1,516** |
| Anti-male homosexual | 739 | 851 | 876 | 904 |
| Anti-female homosexual | 144 | 167 | 181 | 152 |
| Anti-homosexual | 347 | 403 | 420 | 412 |
| Anti-heterosexual | 21 | 21 | 22 | 21 |
| Anti-bisexual | 26 | 28 | 29 | 27 |
| **Ethnicity/national origin:** | **847** | **1,040** | **1,122** | **887** |
| Anti-Hispanic | 534 | 681 | 747 | 593 |
| Anti-other ethnicity/national origin | 313 | 359 | 375 | 294 |
| **Disability:** | **43** | **46** | **48** | **58** |
| Anti-physical | 19 | 22 | 24 | 28 |
| Anti-mental | 24 | 24 | 24 | 30 |
| **Multiple-bias incidents[c]** | **4** | **9** | **9** | **7** |

[a]The term *victim* may refer to a person, business, institution, or society as a whole.
[b]The term *known offender* does not imply that the identity of the suspect is known, but only that an attribute of the suspect has been identified, which distinguishes him/her from an unknown offender.
[c]In a *multiple-bias incident,* two conditions must be met: (a) more than one offense type must occur in the incident and (b) at least two offense types must be motivated by different biases.

SOURCE: "Table 1. Incidents, Offenses, Victims, and Known Offenders by Bias Motivation, 2010," in *Hate Crime Statistics, 2010*, U.S. Department of Justice, Federal Bureau of Investigation, November 2011, http://www.fbi.gov/about-us/cjis/ucr/hate-crime/2010/tables/table-1-incidents-offenses-victims-and-known-offenders-by-bias-motivation-2010.xls (accessed December 26, 2011)

pubs2008/2008021.pdf) that all types of crimes (theft, violent, and serious violent) are the most likely to occur in urban, rather than in suburban or rural, schools. In 2005, the most recent year that data on school location were available as of April 2012, the rate of school crime in urban schools was 64 per 1,000 students, whereas the rate in suburban schools was 55 per 1,000 students and the rate in rural schools was 50 per 1,000 students. The rate of violent crime was particularly high in urban schools, at 34 per 1,000 students, compared with 19 and 21 per 1,000 students in suburban and rural schools, respectively.

Robers et al. find that the rate of crimes per 1,000 students in 2008 was higher among African-Americans (68) and slightly higher among Hispanics (47) than among whites (44). (See Table 7.7.) However, African-American and Hispanic students were much more likely than other groups to report that gangs were present at school in 2007. (See Figure 7.1.) More than a third of African-Americans (38%) and Hispanics (36%) reported that gangs were present at school, whereas only 17% of Asian-American students and 16% of white students did.

Drugs are another serious problem at school. Dinkes, Kemp, and Baum note that "the availability of drugs on school property has a disruptive and corrupting influence on the school environment." In 2009, 23% of students reported that drugs had been made available to them on school property during the previous 12 months. However, this percentage varied by race and ethnicity. Native Americans and Alaskan Natives (34%) were the most likely to have had drugs made available to them on school property during the previous 12 months, followed by Hispanics (31%), Pacific Islanders and Native Hawaiians (28%), African-Americans (22%), whites (20%), and Asian-Americans (18%). (See Figure 7.2.)

Students are also the target of hate-related words and see hate-related graffiti at school all too often. In 2007 students were asked if someone at school had called them a derogatory word having to do with their race, ethnicity,

# TABLE 7.6

## Hate crimes by bias motivation, 2010

| Bias motivation | Total offenses | Crimes against persons | | | | | | Crimes against property | | | | | | | Crimes against society[a] |
|---|---|---|---|---|---|---|---|---|---|---|---|---|---|---|---|
| | | Murder and nonnegligent manslaughter | Forcible rape | Aggravated assault | Simple assault | Intimidation | Other[a] | Robbery | Burglary | Larceny-theft | Motor Vehicle theft | Arson | Destruction/ damage/ vandalism | Other[a] | |
| **Total** | 7,699 | 7 | 4 | 888 | 1,681 | 2,231 | 13 | 146 | 125 | 175 | 16 | 43 | 2,321 | 35 | 14 |
| **Single-bias incidents** | 7,690 | 7 | 4 | 886 | 1,679 | 2,231 | 13 | 146 | 125 | 173 | 16 | 43 | 2,318 | 35 | 14 |
| **Race:** | 3,725 | 1 | 2 | 444 | 755 | 1,227 | 5 | 53 | 61 | 84 | 7 | 12 | 1,045 | 18 | 11 |
| Anti-white | 679 | 0 | 2 | 92 | 192 | 157 | 3 | 32 | 22 | 49 | 6 | 0 | 111 | 10 | 3 |
| Anti-black | 2,600 | 1 | 0 | 315 | 486 | 933 | 2 | 19 | 25 | 16 | 1 | 11 | 781 | 5 | 5 |
| Anti-American Indian/Alaskan Native | 45 | 0 | 0 | 3 | 12 | 2 | 0 | 1 | 1 | 17 | 0 | 0 | 5 | 3 | 1 |
| Anti-Asian/Pacific Islander | 190 | 0 | 0 | 15 | 42 | 73 | 0 | 0 | 7 | 1 | 0 | 0 | 52 | 0 | 0 |
| Anti-multiple races, group | 211 | 0 | 0 | 19 | 23 | 62 | 0 | 1 | 6 | 1 | 0 | 1 | 96 | 0 | 2 |
| **Religion:** | 1,409 | 3 | 0 | 35 | 133 | 321 | 1 | 11 | 29 | 38 | 1 | 17 | 816 | 4 | 0 |
| Anti-Jewish | 922 | 0 | 0 | 12 | 65 | 201 | 0 | 9 | 6 | 8 | 0 | 2 | 619 | 0 | 0 |
| Anti-Catholic | 61 | 0 | 0 | 0 | 5 | 7 | 0 | 0 | 6 | 10 | 1 | 0 | 31 | 1 | 0 |
| Anti-Protestant | 46 | 0 | 0 | 0 | 1 | 3 | 0 | 0 | 5 | 3 | 0 | 1 | 33 | 0 | 0 |
| Anti-Islamic | 186 | 0 | 0 | 17 | 46 | 69 | 0 | 1 | 1 | 3 | 0 | 1 | 47 | 1 | 0 |
| Anti-other religion | 134 | 3 | 0 | 4 | 11 | 25 | 1 | 1 | 9 | 8 | 0 | 12 | 59 | 1 | 0 |
| Anti-multiple religions, group | 53 | 0 | 0 | 2 | 5 | 15 | 0 | 0 | 1 | 5 | 0 | 1 | 23 | 1 | 0 |
| Anti-Atheism/Agnosticism/etc. | 7 | 0 | 0 | 0 | 0 | 1 | 0 | 0 | 1 | 1 | 0 | 0 | 4 | 0 | 0 |
| **Sexual orientation:** | 1,470 | 2 | 1 | 247 | 495 | 331 | 6 | 56 | 19 | 24 | 4 | 7 | 273 | 5 | 0 |
| Anti-male homosexual | 851 | 1 | 0 | 158 | 301 | 190 | 3 | 39 | 6 | 12 | 1 | 5 | 134 | 1 | 0 |
| Anti-female homosexual | 167 | 0 | 1 | 23 | 40 | 52 | 3 | 2 | 4 | 2 | 1 | 0 | 39 | 0 | 0 |
| Anti-homosexual | 403 | 0 | 0 | 58 | 139 | 84 | 0 | 15 | 8 | 3 | 1 | 2 | 92 | 1 | 0 |
| Anti-heterosexual | 21 | 0 | 0 | 3 | 7 | 1 | 0 | 0 | 0 | 1 | 0 | 0 | 8 | 1 | 0 |
| Anti-bisexual | 28 | 1 | 0 | 5 | 8 | 4 | 0 | 0 | 1 | 6 | 1 | 0 | 0 | 2 | 0 |
| **Ethnicity/national origin:** | 1,040 | 1 | 1 | 154 | 276 | 347 | 0 | 23 | 15 | 20 | 4 | 7 | 183 | 7 | 2 |
| Anti-Hispanic | 681 | 1 | 1 | 112 | 183 | 227 | 0 | 16 | 9 | 11 | 3 | 5 | 105 | 7 | 1 |
| Anti-other ethnicity/national origin | 359 | 0 | 0 | 42 | 93 | 120 | 0 | 7 | 6 | 9 | 1 | 2 | 78 | 0 | 1 |
| **Disability:** | 46 | 0 | 0 | 6 | 20 | 5 | 1 | 3 | 1 | 7 | 0 | 0 | 1 | 1 | 1 |
| Anti-physical | 22 | 0 | 0 | 4 | 8 | 5 | 1 | 0 | 0 | 3 | 0 | 0 | 0 | 0 | 1 |
| Anti-mental | 24 | 0 | 0 | 2 | 12 | 0 | 0 | 3 | 1 | 4 | 0 | 0 | 1 | 1 | 0 |
| **Multiple-bias incidents[b]** | 9 | 0 | 0 | 2 | 2 | 0 | 0 | 0 | 0 | 2 | 0 | 0 | 3 | 0 | 0 |

[a]Includes additional offenses collected in the National Incident-Based Reporting System.

[b]In a *multiple-bias incident*, two conditions must be met: (a) more than one type must occur in the incident and (b) at least two offense types must be motivated by different biases.

SOURCE: Table 4. Offenses: Offense Type by Bias Motivation, 2010, in *Hate Crime Statistics, 2010*, U.S. Department of Justice, Federal Bureau of Investigation, November 2011, http://www.fbi.gov/about-us/cjis/ucr/hate-crime/2010/tables/table-4-offenses-offense-type-by-bias-motivation-2010.xls (accessed December 26, 2011)

TABLE 7.7

**Number of student-reported nonfatal crimes against students ages 12–18 and rate of crimes per 1,000 students at school, by type of crime and selected characteristics, 2008**

| Student characteristic | Number of crimes | | | | Rate of crimes per 1,000 students | | | |
|---|---|---|---|---|---|---|---|---|
| | Total | Theft | Violent | Serious violent[a] | Total | Theft | Violent | Serious violent[a] |
| **At school** | | | | | | | | |
| Total | 1,248,800 | 619,000 | 629,800 | 113,300 | 47 | 24 | 24 | 4 |
| **Sex** | | | | | | | | |
| Male | 736,900 | 350,800 | 386,100 | 75,400 | 55 | 26 | 29 | 6 |
| Female | 511,900 | 268,100 | 243,700 | 37,900[c] | 40 | 21 | 19 | 3[c] |
| **Age** | | | | | | | | |
| 12–14 | 589,800 | 267,300 | 322,600 | 58,000 | 49 | 22 | 27 | 5 |
| 15–18 | 658,900 | 351,700 | 307,200 | 55,300 | 46 | 25 | 21 | 4 |
| **Race/ethnicity[b]** | | | | | | | | |
| White | 696,500 | 327,200 | 369,300 | 35,400[c] | 44 | 21 | 23 | 2[c] |
| Black | 259,700 | 117,300 | 142,400 | 28,000[c] | 68 | 31 | 37 | 7[c] |
| Hispanic | 240,200 | 140,100 | 100,100 | 44,000[c] | 47 | 27 | 20 | 9[c] |
| Other | 52,300 | 34,400 | 17,900[c] | 5,800[c] | 32 | 21 | 11[c] | 4[c] |
| **Household income** | | | | | | | | |
| Less than $15,000 | 108,200 | 27,900 | 80,300 | 8,100[c] | 72 | 19 | 54 | 5[c] |
| $15,000–29,999 | 113,900 | 68,900 | 45,000 | 8,400[c] | 41 | 25 | 16 | 3[c] |
| $30,000–49,999 | 207,700 | 109,100 | 98,700 | 26,000[c] | 49 | 26 | 23 | 6[c] |
| $50,000–74,999 | 212,100 | 92,400 | 119,700 | 21,400[c] | 56 | 24 | 31 | 6[c] |
| $75,000 or more | 310,100 | 187,500 | 122,600 | 10,400[c] | 41 | 25 | 16 | 1[c] |

[a]Serious violent crimes are also included in violent crimes.
[b]Other includes Asians, Pacific Islanders, and American Indians (including Alaska Natives). Race categories exclude persons of Hispanic ethnicity.
[c]Interpret data with caution. Estimate based on 10 or fewer sample cases.
Note: Serious violent crimes include rape, sexual assault, robbery, and aggravated assault. Violent crimes include serious violent crimes and simple assault. Theft includes purse snatching, pick pocketing, all burglaries, attempted forcible entry, and all attempted and completed thefts except motor vehicle thefts. Theft does not include robbery in which threat or use of force is involved. Total crimes include violent crimes and theft. "At school" includes inside the school building, on school property, or on the way to or from school. Although *Indicators 2* and *3* present information on similar topics, the survey sources for these two indicators differ with respect to time coverage and administration. Population size is 26,314,000 students ages 12–18 in 2008. Detail may not sum to totals because of rounding and missing data on student characteristics. Estimates of number of crimes are rounded to the nearest 100.

SOURCE: Simone Robers et al., "Table 2.2. Number of Student-Reported Nonfatal Crimes against Students Ages 12–18 and Rate of Crimes per 1,000 Students at School, by Type of Crime and Selected Student Characteristics: 2008," in *Indicators of School Crime and Safety: 2010*, National Center for Education Statistics and Bureau of Justice Statistics, November 2010, http://nces.ed.gov/pubs2011/2011002.pdf (accessed December 26, 2011)

**FIGURE 7.1**

**Percentage of students ages 12–18 who reported that gangs were present at school during the school year, by school sector and race and Hispanic origin, 2007**

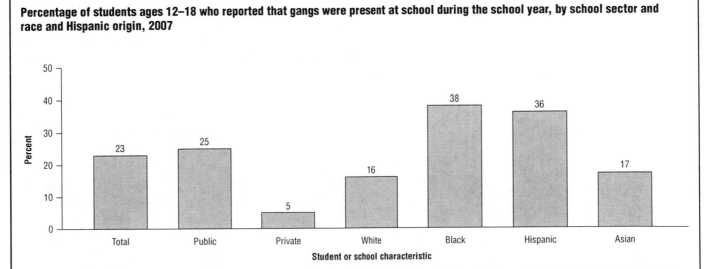

Notes: Race categories exclude persons of Hispanic ethnicity. All gangs, whether or not they are involved in violent or illegal activity, are included. "At school" includes the school building, on school property, on a school bus, or going to and from school.

SOURCE: Simone Robers et al., "Figure 8.1. Percentage of Students Ages 12–18 Who Reported That Gangs Were Present at School during the School Year, by School Sector and Race/Ethnicity: 2007," in *Indicators of School Crime and Safety: 2010*, National Center for Education Statistics and Bureau of Justice Statistics, November 2010, http://nces.ed.gov/pubs2011/2011002.pdf (accessed December 26, 2011)

FIGURE 7.2

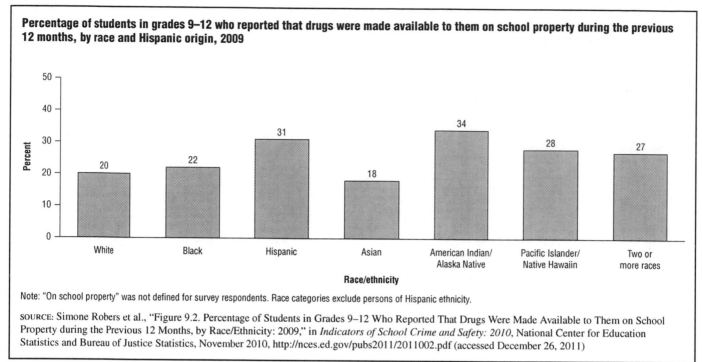

**Percentage of students in grades 9–12 who reported that drugs were made available to them on school property during the previous 12 months, by race and Hispanic origin, 2009**

Note: "On school property" was not defined for survey respondents. Race categories exclude persons of Hispanic ethnicity.

SOURCE: Simone Robers et al., "Figure 9.2. Percentage of Students in Grades 9–12 Who Reported That Drugs Were Made Available to Them on School Property during the Previous 12 Months, by Race/Ethnicity: 2009," in *Indicators of School Crime and Safety: 2010*, National Center for Education Statistics and Bureau of Justice Statistics, November 2010, http://nces.ed.gov/pubs2011/2011002.pdf (accessed December 26, 2011)

religion, gender, sexual orientation, or disability and if they had seen any hate-inspired graffiti in the past six months at school. Ten percent of all students had been the target of hate-related words in the past six months—11% each of African-American, Hispanic, and Asian-American students and 9% of white students. (See Figure 7.3.) More than a third (35%) of all students had seen hate-related graffiti at school; this varied little by race or ethnic group. Robers et al. indicate that of all African-American students surveyed, 7.1% reported being the target of hate-related words related to their race; among Hispanic students, 6.2% reported being the target of hate-related words related to their race and 6.7% reported being the target of hate-related words related to their ethnicity. Students were more likely to report being targeted for their race (4.6%) and ethnicity (2.9%) than for any other reason, including religion, disability, gender, or sexual orientation.

## MINORITIES AS OFFENDERS

African-Americans (particularly males) commit a higher number of offenses as a proportion of the population than do other groups. According to the Federal Bureau of Investigation, in *Crime in the United States, 2010* (September 2011, http://www.fbi.gov/about-us/cjis/ucr/crime-in-the-u.s/2010/crime-in-the-u.s.-2010/), 5,770 (53.4%) of 10,870 known murderers that year were African-American. (See Table 7.8.) Of those 5,770 known African-American murderers, 497 (8.6%) were under the age of 18 years and 2,035 (35.3%) were under the age of 22 years. African-Americans who committed murder were on average younger than their white counterparts.

According to Fox and Zawitz, the circumstances under which African-American and white homicide offenders commit their crimes vary by race. African-American offenders are the most likely to commit homicides related to illegal drug activity. Between 1976 and 2005, 65% of homicide offenders who had committed their crimes under drug-related circumstances were African-American. A high proportion of felony murders (deaths that occur during violent crimes such as burglary, sexual assault, or robbery) between these years were committed by African-Americans (59.3%) as well. By contrast, whites committed a disproportionate number of workplace murders (70.5%), sex-related murders (54.7%), and gang-related murders (54.3%). African-American offenders committed the majority of homicides using guns (56.4%), and whites committed the majority of murders using arson (55.7%) and poison (79.8%).

Fox and Zawitz find that whites are more likely than African-Americans to commit homicide in the context of an intimate victim-offender relationship or family relationship. Between 1976 and 2005 whites committed 54.4% of homicides of intimate partners, whereas African-Americans committed 43.4%. During this same period, whites committed 59.2% of homicides of family members, whereas African-Americans committed 38.5% of these murders. Most of the perpetrators who killed infants (55.4%) or elder family members (54.5%) were white.

## MINORITIES IN PRISONS AND JAILS

In December 2010 there were more non-Hispanic African-American males in state and federal prisons than there were non-Hispanic white or Hispanic males. Out of

FIGURE 7.3

Percentage of students ages 12–18 who reported being targets of hate-related words and seeing hate-related graffiti at school during the school year, by selected student and school characteristics, 2007

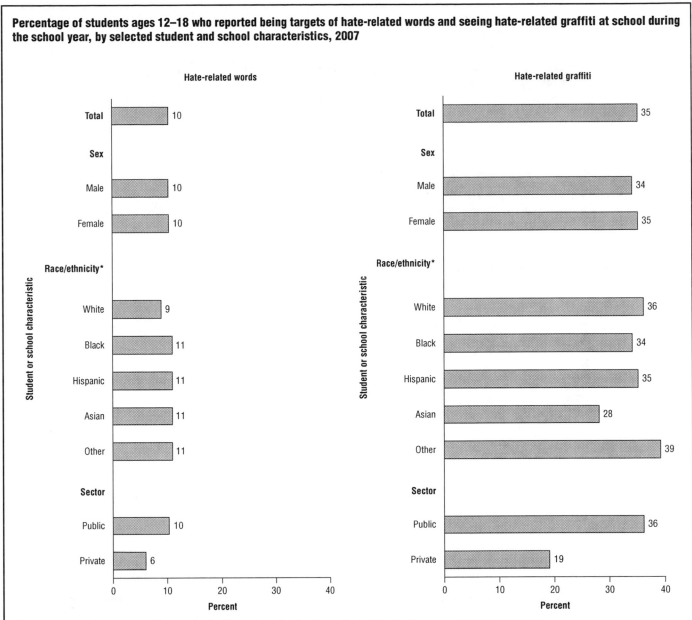

*Race categories exclude persons of Hispanic ethnicity. Other includes American Indian, Alaska Native, Pacific Islander, and more than one race.
Notes: "At school" includes the school building, on school property, on a school bus, and going to and from school. "Hate-related" refers to derogatory terms used by others in reference to students' personal characteristics.

SOURCE: Simone Robers et al., "Figure 10.1. Percentage of Students Ages 12–18 Who Reported Being Targets of Hate-Related Words and Seeing Hate-Related Graffiti at School during the School Year, by Selected Student and School Characteristics: 2007," in *Indicators of School Crime and Safety: 2010*, National Center for Education Statistics and Bureau of Justice Statistics, November 2010, http://nces.ed.gov/pubs2011/2011002.pdf (accessed December 26, 2011)

a total of 1.4 million incarcerated males, 558,700 were non-Hispanic African-American, 449,400 were non-Hispanic white, and 325,700 were Hispanic. (See Table 7.9.) Men between the ages of 25 and 34 made up the largest proportion of all males in the prison population.

The rate of incarceration for non-Hispanic African-American males greatly exceeds the rates for non-Hispanic white and Hispanic males. In December 2010 the rate for non-Hispanic African-American males was 3,059 inmates for every 100,000 U.S. residents. (See Table 7.10.) This

proportion was much higher than that among non-Hispanic whites, with 456 inmates for every 100,000 residents imprisoned during the same period. Among Hispanic men there were 1,252 inmates for every 100,000 residents, more than double the rate of imprisonment for non-Hispanic whites but much lower than the rate of imprisonment for non-Hispanic African-Americans.

Even though non-Hispanic white women (48,000) outnumbered non-Hispanic African-American women (26,600) in federal and state prisons in December 2010, non-Hispanic

## TABLE 7.8

**Murder offenders by age, sex, and race, 2010**

| Age | Total | Sex | | | Race | | | |
|---|---|---|---|---|---|---|---|---|
| | | Male | Female | Unknown | White | Black | Other | Unknown |
| **Total** | **15,094** | **9,972** | **1,075** | **4,047** | **4,849** | **5,770** | **251** | **4,224** |
| Percent distribution | 100.0 | 66.1 | 7.1 | 26.8 | 32.1 | 38.2 | 1.7 | 28.0 |
| Under 18* | 802 | 726 | 76 | 0 | 272 | 497 | 22 | 11 |
| Under 22* | 3,239 | 2,981 | 257 | 1 | 1,104 | 2,035 | 65 | 35 |
| 18 and over* | 9,445 | 8,442 | 990 | 13 | 4,477 | 4,643 | 225 | 100 |

*Does not include unknown ages.

SOURCE: Adapted from "Expanded Homicide Data Table 3. Murder Offenders by Age, Sex, and Race, 2010," in *Crime in the United States, 2010*, U.S. Department of Justice, Federal Bureau of Investigation, September 2011, http://www.fbi.gov/about-us/cjis/ucr/crime-in-the-u.s/2010/crime-in-the-u.s.-2010/tables/10shrtbl03.xls (accessed December 26, 2011)

## TABLE 7.9

**Estimated number of sentenced prisoners under state and federal jurisdiction, by sex, race, Hispanic origin, and age, December 31, 2010**

| Age | Male | | | | Female | | | |
|---|---|---|---|---|---|---|---|---|
| | Total[a] | White[b] | Black[b] | Hispanic | Total[a] | White[b] | Black[b] | Hispanic |
| **Total[c]** | **1,439,000** | **449,400** | **558,700** | **325,700** | **105,200** | **48,000** | **26,600** | **18,700** |
| 18–19 | 20,800 | 3,900 | 10,400 | 5,300 | 800 | 300 | 300 | 200 |
| 20–24 | 172,400 | 42,600 | 74,800 | 44,600 | 10,900 | 4,600 | 2,900 | 2,300 |
| 25–29 | 234,200 | 64,400 | 94,400 | 62,000 | 17,800 | 7,900 | 4,400 | 3,800 |
| 30–34 | 234,300 | 64,000 | 95,300 | 62,100 | 17,900 | 8,200 | 4,300 | 3,500 |
| 35–39 | 198,800 | 58,500 | 77,900 | 49,700 | 15,600 | 7,300 | 3,800 | 2,700 |
| 40–44 | 181,400 | 60,900 | 67,900 | 37,500 | 15,400 | 7,100 | 4,000 | 2,500 |
| 45–49 | 162,900 | 59,100 | 59,700 | 28,500 | 13,100 | 6,100 | 3,500 | 1,700 |
| 50–54 | 113,500 | 43,000 | 40,900 | 17,900 | 7,700 | 3,600 | 2,100 | 1,100 |
| 55–59 | 61,400 | 24,600 | 21,300 | 9,300 | 3,500 | 1,600 | 900 | 500 |
| 60–64 | 31,800 | 14,700 | 9,300 | 4,600 | 1,500 | 800 | 300 | 200 |
| 65 or older | 25,200 | 13,500 | 5,500 | 3,600 | 1,000 | 500 | 200 | 100 |

Note: Data source used to estimate race and Hispanic origin changed in 2010 and data source for age distributions was enhanced between 2009 and 2010. Use caution when comparing to prior years. Counts based on prisoners with a sentence of more than 1 year.
[a]Includes American Indians, Alaska Natives, Asians, Native Hawaiians, other Pacific Islanders, and persons identifying two or more races.
[b]Excludes persons of Hispanic or Latino origin.
[c]Includes persons under age 18.

SOURCE: Paul Guerino, Paige M. Harrison, and William J. Sabol, "Appendix Table 13. Estimated Number of Sentenced Prisoners under State or Federal Jurisdiction, by Sex, Race, Hispanic Origin, and Age, December 31, 2010," in *Prisoners in 2010*, U.S. Department of Justice, Bureau of Justice Statistics, December 2011, http://bjs.ojp.usdoj.gov/content/pub/pdf/p10.pdf (accessed December 26, 2011)

African-American women were incarcerated at nearly three times the rate of non-Hispanic white women (133 per 100,000 residents and 47 per 100,000 residents, respectively). (See Table 7.9 and Table 7.10.) In that year, there were 18,700 Hispanic women in state and federal prisons; they were incarcerated at one and a half times the rate of non-Hispanic white women (77 per 100,000 residents).

The National Criminal Justice Association (NCJA) discusses in "Minorities in the Criminal Justice System" (July 22, 2003, http://www.ncja.org/Content/Navigation Menu/PoliciesPractices/PolicyStatements/ArchivedPolicy Statements/default.htm) the overrepresentation of minorities among the ranks of offenders in the criminal justice system. It notes that social factors play a role in this overrepresentation, including the lack of employment and educational opportunities, poor economic conditions, the lack of minority role models, and the negative portrayal of minorities

in the media. Observing that an estimated 4.4% of white males will enter prison during their lifetime, compared with 16% of Hispanic males and 28% of African-American males, the NCJA indicates that state and local criminal justice policy makers must continually address minority-related criminal justice issues. Among these issues are the overrepresentation of minorities in both the juvenile and adult criminal justice populations and the underrepresentation of minorities in law enforcement, corrections, and legal professions; conscious and unconscious tensions between members of minority groups and law enforcement personnel; accurate reporting of hate crimes; racial profiling by law enforcement and its effects on community relations and prison crowding; racially biased effects of drug laws and enforcement strategies; minorities' equal access to the court system; racially biased sentencing patterns; and unequal socioeconomic conditions. However, Robert D. Crutchfield, April Fernandes, and Jorge

**TABLE 7.10**

Estimated rate of sentenced prisoners under state and federal jurisdiction, per 100,000 U.S. residents, by sex, race, Hispanic origin, and age, December 31, 2010

| Age | Male | | | | Female | | | |
|---|---|---|---|---|---|---|---|---|
| | Total[a] | White[b] | Black[b] | Hispanic | Total[a] | White[b] | Black[b] | Hispanic |
| Total[c] | 938 | 456 | 3,059 | 1,252 | 67 | 47 | 133 | 77 |
| 18–19 | 459 | 148 | 1,547 | 560 | 20 | 11 | 40 | 31 |
| 20–24 | 1,503 | 635 | 4,594 | 1,898 | 103 | 72 | 182 | 121 |
| 25–29 | 2,088 | 975 | 6,318 | 2,694 | 169 | 124 | 299 | 202 |
| 30–34 | 2,250 | 1,055 | 7,265 | 2,795 | 176 | 136 | 309 | 188 |
| 35–39 | 2,005 | 990 | 6,570 | 2,476 | 159 | 124 | 289 | 153 |
| 40–44 | 1,744 | 911 | 5,610 | 2,136 | 148 | 106 | 289 | 156 |
| 45–49 | 1,482 | 784 | 4,728 | 1,893 | 116 | 81 | 238 | 117 |
| 50–54 | 1,046 | 550 | 3,424 | 1,489 | 69 | 45 | 149 | 88 |
| 55–59 | 646 | 345 | 2,228 | 1,027 | 34 | 22 | 76 | 55 |
| 60–64 | 389 | 231 | 1,256 | 676 | 17 | 12 | 33 | 29 |
| 65 or older | 142 | 95 | 416 | 292 | 4 | 3 | 7 | 8 |

Note: Data source used to estimate race and Hispanic origin changed in 2010 and data source for age distributions was enhanced between 2009 and 2010. Use caution when comparing to prior years. Counts based on prisoners with a sentence of more than 1 year.
[a]Includes American Indians, Alaska Natives, Asians, Native Hawaiians, other Pacific Islanders, and persons identifying two or more races.
[b]Excludes persons of Hispanic or Latino origin.
[c]Includes persons under age 18.

SOURCE: Paul Guerino, Paige M. Harrison, and William J. Sabol, "Appendix Table 15. Estimated Number of Sentenced Prisoners under State or Federal Jurisdiction per 100,000 U.S. Residents, by Sex, Race, Hispanic Origin, and Age, December 31, 2010," in *Prisoners in 2010*, U.S. Department of Justice, Bureau of Justice Statistics, December 2011, http://bjs.ojp.usdoj.gov/content/pub/pdf/p10.pdf (accessed December 26, 2011)

Martinez analyze in "Racial and Ethnic Disparity and Criminal Justice: How Much Is Too Much?" (*Journal of Criminal Law and Criminology*, vol. 100, no. 3, Summer 2010) the statistics on arrests, pretrial processing procedures, trials, and sentencing and do not find any evidence of "obvious discrimination or racial or ethnic bias."

In "Schools and Prisons: Fifty Years after *Brown v. Board of Education*" (April 20, 2004, http://www.sentencingproject.org/Admin/Documents/publications/rd_brownvboard.pdf), Marc Mauer and Ryan Scott King of the Sentencing Project call attention to the dramatic rise in imprisonment in the African-American community after 1954. According to Mauer and King, this rise resulted from a punitive crime policy that disproportionately affects African-Americans. They note that the causes for the rising imprisonment rate of African-Americans include higher crime rates, the War on Drugs, disparities in crack-cocaine and powder-cocaine sentencing policies, school-zone drug laws, three-strikes policies, inadequate defense resources for poor people, and zero-tolerance policies in schools. They state that "at current rates of incarceration, one of every three black males born today can expect to be imprisoned at some point in his lifetime. Whether or not one believes that current crime control policies are 'working' to reduce crime, such an outcome should be shocking to all Americans. Imposing a crime policy with such profound racial dynamics calls into question the nation's commitment to a free and democratic society."

The Sentencing Project identifies in *Reducing Racial Disparity in the Criminal Justice System: A Manual for Practitioners and Policymakers* (August 2008, http://www.sentencingproject.org/doc/publications/rd_reducingracialdisparity.pdf) several causes for this racial disparity. It finds that there is little support for the belief that members of minority groups commit more crimes; instead, they are more likely to be involved in crimes that police observe themselves, are more likely to be arrested, and are more likely to receive longer sentences than whites. In addition, members of minority communities do not have the same access to health care, employment opportunities, and treatment programs. Some laws, such as the War on Drugs, have a disproportionate impact on minority communities. Finally, the Sentencing Project cites overt racial bias, stating, "So long as racism exists within society at large, it will be found within the criminal justice system."

In "Addressing Racial Disparities in Incarceration" (*Prison Journal*, vol. 91, no. 3, 2011), Marc Mauer notes that "1 of every 3 African American males born today can expect to go to prison in his lifetime, as can 1 of every 6 Latino males, compared to 1 in 17 White males." With this in mind, he makes several suggestions to address the racial disparity in the criminal justice system. First, he argues that the intersection of race and class in the criminal justice system is powerful and that a lack of access to resources is a major contributor to racial disparities. He suggests that courts should have options other than jail for offenders. He also suggests that the nation should invest in education and boost high school completion rates. In addition, state legislatures should consider adopting racial impact statement policies, which require that any proposed sentencing legislation be analyzed for undue racial effects before that legislation is passed. Finally, racial fairness policy goals and commissions should be adopted and implemented in all states to assess how interrelated decisions produce racial disparities in imprisonment, and policy and practice decisions should be routinely examined for undue racial impact.

## Racial Disparities in Sentencing

In 1984 the U.S. Sentencing Commission (USSC) set forth sentencing guidelines in the Sentencing Reform Act of 1984, which was designed to implement uniform sentencing practices that would eliminate disparities based on race. In November 2004 the USSC released *Fifteen Years of Guidelines Sentencing: An Assessment of How Well the Federal Criminal Justice System Is Achieving the Goals of Sentencing Reform* (http://www.ussc.gov/Research/Research _Projects/Miscellaneous/15_Year_Study/15_year_study_full .pdf), which evaluated the effectiveness of these practices. The USSC concludes that remaining disparity in sentencing is the result of sentencing rules and charging practices that have "institutionalized" disparity. In fact, variables such as mandatory minimums and plea bargaining have had "a greater adverse impact on Black offenders than did the factors taken into account by judges in the discretionary system...prior to [the] guidelines implementation."

Tushar Kansal of the Sentencing Project examines in *Racial Disparity in Sentencing: A Review of the Literature* (January 2005, http://www.sentencingproject.org/ doc/publications/rd_sentencing_review.pdf) the literature about the nature of this ongoing racial disparity. Kansal finds that in noncapital cases racially discriminatory sentencing outcomes do exist, but that they are not uniform or extensive. Kansal notes that the following groups suffer harsher sentencing: young African-American and Hispanic males, especially if unemployed; African-Americans convicted of harming white victims; and African-American and Hispanic defendants convicted of less serious (nonviolent) crimes. An examination of death-penalty cases finds that if the murder victim was white, the defendant was more likely to receive the death sentence, and in the federal system minority defendants, especially African-Americans, were more likely to receive a death sentence than were white defendants.

In "Criminal Sentencing Policies Disproportionately Hurt Black Americans, Mauer Says" (November 6, 2007, http:// www.law.virginia.edu/html/news/2007_fall/mauer.htm), Shea Connelly reports on a talk that Marc Mauer of the Sentencing Project gave at Virginia Law School in 2007. Mauer identified the War on Drugs as a prime causal agent in the disproportionate number of African-Americans who are incarcerated. He pointed out that communities with monetary resources do not deal with kids with drug problems through the criminal justice system, but through treatment programs. By contrast, poor communities often call on the police to deal with drug-abuse problems. Because minorities are disproportionately poor, the strict sentencing laws arising from the War on Drugs have fallen heavily on

them. Harsher penalties for the possession of crack cocaine, which is more common in low-income communities, as opposed to powder cocaine, which is more common in white and affluent communities, have also contributed heavily to the problem of racial disparities in the criminal justice system.

Ashley Nellis and Ryan S. King examine in *No Exit: The Expanding Use of Life Sentences in America* (July 2009, http://sentencingproject.org/doc/publications/publications/inc _noexitseptember2009.pdf) racial disparities in life sentences. The researchers note that this type of sentence has grown dramatically not in response to higher crime rates but in response to a policy of imposing harsher punishments. In 2008, 140,610 prisoners nationwide were serving life sentences, up from 34,000 in 1984. Of these, 41,095 were serving sentences with no possibility of parole, an increase of 22% since 2003. Nellis and King find that minority prisoners served a disproportionate share of life sentences. In 2008 two out of three (66.4%) prisoners serving life sentences were people of color—48.3% were African-American and 14.4% were Hispanic, whereas 33.4% were white. Among the 6,807 juveniles serving life sentences nationwide, 47.3% were African-American, 23.7% were Hispanic, and 22.7% were white.

## Native Americans in Jail

Todd D. Minton of the BJS notes in *Jails in Indian Country, 2010* (December 2011, http://bjs.ojp.usdoj.gov/ content/pub/pdf/jic10.pdf) that at midyear 2010, 75 Native American country jails, detention centers, and other correctional facilities confined 2,119 inmates. This represented a 2.6% decrease from the year before; however, overall the number of inmates held in Native American country jails increased by 21% between 2004 and 2010. These 2,119 inmates were only a small proportion of the total number of Native Americans that were being held in jails and prisons; 78,900 were being held nationwide. At midyear 2010 Native Americans had an incarceration rate of 950 per 100,000 residents. Between 2000 and 2010 the number of Native Americans in correctional facilities nationwide grew about 4.1% annually.

Minton reports that most inmates of Native American country jails were male; at midyear 2010, 23% of those being held were female and 77% were male. About 12% of those being held were juveniles. Among the 59% of inmates who were convicted of a crime (the other 41% were being held before trial), 13% had been convicted of domestic violence, 11% of assault, 10% of driving while intoxicated, 5% of drug offenses, 2% of rape or sexual assault, 5% of other violent crimes, and 54% of other crimes.

## Parole and Probation

Because African-Americans account for the largest proportion of prison and jail inmates, it is no surprise that

African-Americans also outnumber other racial and ethnic groups in the nation's parole system. The parole system grants inmates early release from prison with fewer rights than the general population and under monitored conditions.

In 2010 the race and ethnicity of parolees was equivalent to their proportion of the state and federal prison population. Of the 1.5 million prison inmates in December 2010, 585,300 (37.9%) were non-Hispanic African-American, and 39% of inmates paroled from prisons and jails at year-end 2010 were African-American. (See Table 7.9 and Table 7.11.) In the same year, 344,400 (22.3%) were Hispanic, and 18% of those on parole were Hispanic.

The proportion of non-Hispanic whites on probation, a system where people who are convicted of a crime are under supervision by a probation officer rather than incarcerated, is quite disproportionate to their representation in the criminal justice system. At year-end 2010, 55% of probationers were non-Hispanic white, compared with the 32.2% of non-Hispanic whites who were in prisons and jails. (See Table 7.12 and Table 7.9.) By comparison, only 30% of probationers were non-Hispanic African-American, whereas 37.9% of inmates were non-Hispanic African-American, and 13% of probationers were Hispanic, whereas 22.3% of inmates were Hispanic. These numbers show that non-Hispanic white offenders are more likely than minority offenders to receive the more lenient sentence of probation.

Hispanics also face harsher treatment in the federal court system. The Sentencing Project points out in "Hispanic Prisoners in the United States" (August 2003, http://www.sentencingproject.org/doc/publications/inc_hispanic

**TABLE 7.11**

**Characteristics of adults on parole, 2000, 2009, and 2010**

| Characteristics | 2000 | 2009 | 2010 |
|---|---|---|---|
| Total | 100% | 100% | 100% |
| **Sex** | | | |
| Male | 88% | 88% | 88% |
| Female | 12 | 12 | 12 |
| **Race and Hispanic origin** | | | |
| White[a] | 38% | 41% | 42% |
| Black[a] | 40 | 39 | 39 |
| Hispanic/Latino | 21 | 18 | 18 |
| American Indian/Alaska Native[a] | 1 | 1 | 1 |
| Asian/Native Hawaiian/other Pacific Islander[a] | — | 1 | 1 |
| Two or more races[a] | * | — | — |
| **Status of supervision** | | | |
| Active | 83% | 85% | 82% |
| Inactive | 4 | 4 | 7 |
| Absconder | 7 | 5 | 6 |
| Supervised out of state | 5 | 4 | 4 |
| Financial conditions remaining | * | — | — |
| Other | 1 | 2 | 2 |
| **Maximum sentence to incarceration** | | | |
| Less than 1 year | 3% | 5% | 5% |
| 1 year or more | 97 | 95 | 95 |
| **Most serious offense** | | | |
| Violent | * | 27% | 27% |
| Sex offense | * | 8 | 8 |
| Other violent | * | 19 | 19 |
| Property | * | 23 | 24 |
| Drug | * | 36 | 35 |
| Weapon | * | 3 | 3 |
| Other[b] | * | 10 | 12 |

Note: Each characteristic is based on parolees with a known status. Detail may not sum to total due to rounding.
—Less than 0.5%.
*Not available.
[a]Excludes persons of Hispanic/Latino origin.
[b]Includes public-order offenses.

source: Lauren E. Glaze and Thomas P. Bonczar, "Appendix Table 15. Characteristics of Adults on Parole, 2000, 2009, and 2010," in *Probation and Parole in the United States, 2010*, U.S. Department of Justice, Bureau of Justice Statistics, November 2011, http://bjs.ojp.usdoj.gov/content/pub/pdf/ppus10.pdf (accessed December 26, 2011)

**TABLE 7.12**

**Characteristics of adults on probation, 2000, 2009, and 2010**

| Characteristics | 2000 | 2009 | 2010 |
|---|---|---|---|
| Total | 100% | 100% | 100% |
| **Sex** | | | |
| Male | 78% | 76% | 76% |
| Female | 22 | 24 | 24 |
| **Race and Hispanic origin** | | | |
| White[a] | 54% | 55% | 55% |
| Black[a] | 31 | 30 | 30 |
| Hispanic/Latino | 13 | 13 | 13 |
| American Indian/Alaska Native[a] | 1 | 1 | 1 |
| Asian/Native Hawaiian/other Pacific Islander[a] | 1 | 1 | 1 |
| Two or more races[a] | * | — | — |
| **Status of supervision** | | | |
| Active | 76% | 72% | 73% |
| Residential/other treatment program | * | 1 | 1 |
| Financial conditions remaining | * | 1 | 1 |
| Inactive | 9 | 6 | 6 |
| Absconder | 9 | 8 | 9 |
| Supervised out of jurisdiction | 3 | 3 | 2 |
| Warrant status | * | 6 | 6 |
| Other | 3 | 2 | 2 |
| **Type of offense** | | | |
| Felony | 52% | 50% | 50% |
| Misdemeanor | 46 | 47 | 47 |
| Other infractions | 2 | 2 | 2 |
| **Most serious offense** | | | |
| Violent | * | 19% | 19% |
| Domestic violence | * | 4 | 3 |
| Sex offense | * | 3 | 3 |
| Other violent offense | * | 13 | 12 |
| Property | * | 26 | 28 |
| Drug | 24 | 26 | 26 |
| Public-order | 24 | 18 | 18 |
| DWI/DUI | 18 | 15 | 15 |
| Other traffic offense | 6 | 4 | 3 |
| Other[b] | 52 | 10 | 10 |

Note: Each characteristic is based on probationers with a known status. Detail may not sum to total due to rounding.
—Less than 0.5%.
*Not available.
[a]Excludes persons of Hispanic/Latino origin.
[b]Includes violent and property offenses in 2000 because those data were not collected separately.

source: Lauren E. Glaze and Thomas P. Bonczar, "Appendix Table 5. Characteristics of Adults on Probation, 2000, 2009, and 2010," in *Probation and Parole in the United States, 2010*, U.S. Department of Justice, Bureau of Justice Statistics, November 2011, http://bjs.ojp.usdoj.gov/content/pub/pdf/ppus10.pdf (accessed December 26, 2011)

prisoners.pdf) that Hispanic defendants are about one-third as likely as non-Hispanic defendants (22.7% versus 63.1%) to be released before their cases come to trial. In *Uneven Justice: State Rates of Incarceration by Race and Ethnicity* (July 2007, http://www.sentencingproject.org/doc/publications/rd_stateratesofincbyraceandethnicity.pdf), Mauer and King indicate that between 1990 and 2005 the proportion of prisoners who were Hispanic had risen 43%. By 2007 one out of every six Hispanic males born could expect to be incarcerated during their lifetime if current trends continued.

### Minorities on Death Row

Tracy L. Snell of the BJS reports in *Capital Punishment, 2010* (December 2011, http://bjs.ojp.usdoj.gov/content/pub/pdf/cp10st.pdf) that at year-end 2010, 3,158 state and federal prisoners were incarcerated under the sentence of death. (See Table 7.13.) Non-Hispanic whites made up 55.4% (1,750) and non-Hispanic African-Americans made up 41.7% (1,316) of all death-row prisoners. Only 2.9% were of other races. Of those whose ethnicity was known, 12.3% were Hispanic (Hispanics could be either African-American or white).

Of those sentenced to death row in 2010, 45 (43.3%) were non-Hispanic white and 42 (40.4%) were non-Hispanic African-American. (See Table 7.13.) Hispanics made up 21.2% of those sentenced to death row in that year.

Between 1977 and 2010, 7,879 prisoners had been under the sentence of death. (See Table 7.14.) Of those prisoners, 3,816 (48.4%) were non-Hispanic white, 3,225 (40.9%) were non-Hispanic African-American, and 715 (9.1%) were Hispanic. Non-Hispanic white prisoners under the sentence of death were slightly more likely than average (18.3% versus 15.7%) to actually be executed, whereas non-Hispanic African-Americans (13.1%) and Hispanics (13.4%) on death row were slightly less likely to be executed.

### GANGS

Testifying before the U.S. Senate's Committee on the Judiciary, Steven R. Wiley (April 23, 1997, http://www.hi-ho.ne.jp/taku77/refer/gang.htm) of the Federal Bureau of Investigation explained that law enforcement agencies define a street gang as a "group of people that form an allegiance based on various social needs and engage in acts injurious to public health and safety." Law enforcement officers surveyed for the National Youth Gang Survey Analysis (2011, http://www.nationalgangcenter.gov/Survey-Analysis) by the National Youth Gang Center emphasize that gang members generally use tattoos, colors, or other symbols to identify themselves as part of a gang and that important definitional characteristics of gangs include claiming "turf," committing crimes together, and having a leader. Even though gangs have been involved with the drug trade for many years, gang-related deadly violence is more likely to come from territorial conflicts.

Gangs are often (but not always) racially or ethnically based. As a rule, ethnic gangs require that all members belong to a particular race or ethnic group. Erika Harrell of the BJS indicates in "Violence by Gang Members, 1993–2003" (June 2005, http://bjs.ojp.usdoj.gov/content/pub/pdf/vgm03.pdf), the most recent BJS publication on this topic as of April 2012, that between 1998 and 2003, 6% of all violent crimes were perpetrated by gang members.

The most frightening crime committed by gangs is murder. Fox and Zawitz find that more than half of all gang-related homicides between 1976 and 2005 involved whites. Approximately 57.5% of gang-related homicide victims during this period were white, and 54.3% of offenders were also white. African-Americans were the victims of gang-related homicides 39% of the time, and 41.2% of offenders were African-American.

The National Youth Gang Center notes in the National Youth Gang Survey Analysis the following trends:

- Even though the gang problem declined between 1995 and the turn of the 21st century, it then experienced a resurgence; between 2006 and 2009 the prevalence rate of gang activities remained fairly constant

- In 2009, 34.5% of jurisdictions reported gang problems

- Gang problems are highly prevalent in larger cities; specifically, 86.3% of law enforcement agencies serving cities with populations of 50,000 or more reported gang problems in 2009, compared with 51.8% of suburban counties, 32.9% of smaller cities, and 17% of rural counties

- Between 2005 and 2009, 79.8% of cities larger than 50,000 people consistently reported gang activity, compared with 38.9% of suburban counties, 23.8% of smaller cities, and 11% of rural counties

Furthermore, violence by perceived gang members declined between 1993 and 2003. Harrell states that in 1994 violent victimizations by gang members peaked at about 1.1 million, then fell to 341,000 in 2003. During this 11-year period, Hispanic victims were more likely than white or African-American victims to perceive their attackers as gang members. The rate of violence by victim-perceived gang members was 5.7 per 1,000 Hispanics, 4.1 per 1,000 African-Americans, and 2.4 per 1,000 non-Hispanic whites during this period. However, homicides by gang members have not declined. In 1993, 5.6% of all homicides were gang related; in 2003, 6.5% of all homicides were gang related. The National Youth Gang Center reports that there was a steady increase in gang-related homicides among those agencies that reported gang-related homicide data in 2009. In fact, the increase was getting larger over time; between 2002 and 2009 the number of gang-related homicides increased 2.1%, between 2005 and 2009 it increased 7.2%, and between 2008 and 2009 it increased 10.7%.

**TABLE 7.13**

## Prisoners under sentence of death, by region, jurisdiction, and race, 2009 and 2010

| Region and jurisdiction | Prisoners under sentence of death, 12/31/09 | | | Received under sentence of death, 2010 | | | Removed from death row (excluding executions), 2010[a] | | | Executed, 2010 | | | Prisoners under sentence of death, 12/31/10 | | |
|---|---|---|---|---|---|---|---|---|---|---|---|---|---|---|---|
| | Total[b] | White[c] | Black[c] | Total[b] | White[c] | Black[c] | Total[b] | White[c] | Black[c] | Total[b] | White[c] | Black[c] | Total[b] | White[c] | Black[c] |
| U.S. total | 3,173 | 1,779 | 1,318 | 104 | 45 | 42 | 73 | 41 | 31 | 46 | 33 | 13 | 3,158 | 1,750 | 1,316 |
| Federal[d] | 56 | 26 | 29 | 3 | 3 | 0 | 1 | 0 | 1 | 0 | 0 | 0 | 58 | 29 | 28 |
| State | 3,117 | 1,753 | 1,289 | 101 | 42 | 42 | 72 | 41 | 30 | 46 | 33 | 13 | 3,100 | 1,721 | 1,288 |
| **Northeast** | 229 | 84 | 136 | 3 | 1 | 2 | 6 | 3 | 3 | 0 | 0 | 0 | 226 | 82 | 135 |
| Connecticut | 10 | 4 | 6 | 1 | 1 | 0 | 1 | 1 | 0 | 0 | 0 | 0 | 10 | 4 | 6 |
| New Hampshire | 1 | 0 | 1 | 0 | 0 | 0 | 0 | 0 | 0 | 0 | 0 | 0 | 1 | 0 | 1 |
| New York | 0 | 0 | 0 | 0 | 0 | 0 | 0 | 0 | 0 | 0 | 0 | 0 | 0 | 0 | 0 |
| Pennsylvania | 218 | 80 | 129 | 2 | 0 | 2 | 5 | 2 | 3 | 0 | 0 | 0 | 215 | 78 | 128 |
| **Midwest** | 265 | 142 | 120 | 9 | 3 | 5 | 10 | 3 | 7 | 8 | 3 | 5 | 256 | 139 | 113 |
| Illinois | 14 | 10 | 4 | 1 | 1 | 0 | 0 | 0 | 0 | 0 | 0 | 0 | 15 | 11 | 4 |
| Indiana | 13 | 10 | 3 | 0 | 0 | 0 | 0 | 0 | 0 | 0 | 0 | 0 | 13 | 10 | 3 |
| Kansas | 9 | 5 | 4 | 0 | 0 | 0 | 1 | 0 | 1 | 0 | 0 | 0 | 8 | 5 | 3 |
| Missouri | 51 | 29 | 22 | 0 | 0 | 0 | 2 | 1 | 1 | 0 | 0 | 0 | 49 | 28 | 21 |
| Nebraska | 11 | 8 | 2 | 1 | 0 | 0 | 0 | 0 | 0 | 0 | 0 | 0 | 12 | 8 | 2 |
| Ohio | 165 | 78 | 85 | 7 | 2 | 5 | 7 | 2 | 5 | 8 | 3 | 5 | 157 | 75 | 80 |
| South Dakota | 2 | 2 | 0 | 0 | 0 | 0 | 0 | 0 | 0 | 0 | 0 | 0 | 2 | 2 | 0 |
| **South** | 1,661 | 912 | 726 | 45 | 21 | 22 | 41 | 22 | 18 | 35 | 27 | 8 | 1,630 | 884 | 722 |
| Alabama | 202 | 103 | 98 | 7 | 4 | 3 | 3 | 1 | 2 | 5 | 4 | 1 | 201 | 102 | 98 |
| Arkansas | 42 | 18 | 24 | 1 | 0 | 0 | 1 | 1 | 0 | 0 | 0 | 0 | 42 | 17 | 24 |
| Delaware | 17 | 9 | 8 | 0 | 0 | 0 | 0 | 0 | 0 | 0 | 0 | 0 | 17 | 9 | 8 |
| Florida | 390 | 256 | 134 | 14 | 6 | 8 | 11 | 8 | 3 | 1 | 1 | 0 | 392 | 253 | 139 |
| Georgia | 104 | 54 | 49 | 0 | 0 | 0 | 2 | 0 | 1 | 2 | 2 | 0 | 100 | 52 | 48 |
| Kentucky | 35 | 29 | 6 | 2 | 1 | 1 | 3 | 1 | 2 | 0 | 0 | 0 | 34 | 29 | 5 |
| Louisiana | 83 | 29 | 53 | 2 | 1 | 1 | 0 | 0 | 0 | 1 | 1 | 0 | 84 | 29 | 54 |
| Maryland | 5 | 1 | 4 | 0 | 0 | 0 | 0 | 0 | 0 | 0 | 0 | 0 | 5 | 1 | 4 |
| Mississippi | 60 | 28 | 31 | 4 | 2 | 2 | 1 | 1 | 0 | 3 | 3 | 0 | 60 | 26 | 33 |
| North Carolina | 159 | 65 | 86 | 4 | 3 | 1 | 5 | 2 | 3 | 0 | 0 | 0 | 158 | 66 | 84 |
| Oklahoma | 77 | 42 | 31 | 0 | 0 | 0 | 3 | 3 | 0 | 3 | 2 | 1 | 71 | 37 | 30 |
| South Carolina | 55 | 25 | 30 | 2 | 0 | 2 | 1 | 1 | 0 | 0 | 0 | 0 | 56 | 24 | 32 |
| Tennessee | 89 | 49 | 38 | 1 | 1 | 0 | 4 | 1 | 3 | 0 | 0 | 0 | 86 | 49 | 35 |
| Texas | 330 | 198 | 127 | 8 | 3 | 4 | 6 | 3 | 3 | 17 | 12 | 5 | 315 | 186 | 123 |
| Virginia | 13 | 6 | 7 | 0 | 0 | 0 | 1 | 0 | 1 | 3 | 2 | 1 | 9 | 4 | 5 |
| **West** | 962 | 615 | 307 | 44 | 17 | 13 | 15 | 13 | 2 | 3 | 3 | 0 | 988 | 616 | 318 |
| Arizona | 130 | 108 | 17 | 9 | 2 | 3 | 5 | 5 | 0 | 1 | 1 | 0 | 133 | 104 | 20 |
| California | 683 | 401 | 250 | 24 | 8 | 7 | 8 | 6 | 2 | 0 | 0 | 0 | 699 | 403 | 255 |
| Colorado | 2 | 0 | 2 | 1 | 0 | 1 | 0 | 0 | 0 | 0 | 0 | 0 | 3 | 0 | 3 |
| Idaho | 15 | 15 | 0 | 2 | 2 | 0 | 1 | 1 | 0 | 0 | 0 | 0 | 16 | 16 | 0 |
| Montana | 2 | 2 | 0 | 0 | 0 | 0 | 0 | 0 | 0 | 0 | 0 | 0 | 2 | 2 | 0 |
| Nevada | 78 | 46 | 31 | 4 | 3 | 1 | 1 | 1 | 0 | 0 | 0 | 0 | 81 | 48 | 32 |
| New Mexico | 2 | 2 | 0 | 0 | 0 | 0 | 0 | 0 | 0 | 0 | 0 | 0 | 2 | 2 | 0 |
| Oregon | 31 | 27 | 3 | 3 | 1 | 1 | 0 | 0 | 0 | 0 | 0 | 0 | 34 | 28 | 4 |
| Utah | 10 | 8 | 1 | 0 | 0 | 0 | 0 | 0 | 0 | 1 | 1 | 0 | 9 | 7 | 1 |
| Washington | 8 | 5 | 3 | 1 | 1 | 0 | 0 | 0 | 0 | 1 | 1 | 0 | 8 | 5 | 3 |
| Wyoming | 1 | 1 | 0 | 0 | 0 | 0 | 0 | 0 | 0 | 0 | 0 | 0 | 1 | 1 | 0 |

Note: Some figures shown for year end 2009 are revised from those reported in *Capital Punishment, 2009–Statistical Tables*, BJS Web, NCJ 231676. The revised figures include 11 inmates who were either reported late to the National Prisoner Statistics program or were not in custody of state correctional authorities on December 31, 2009 (3 in Georgia, 2 in Arkansas, and 1 each in Alabama, Florida, Texas, Idaho, Nevada, and the Federal Bureau of Prisons) and exclude 11 inmates who were relieved of a death sentence before December 31, 2009 (3 in Nevada; 2 each in Illinois, Oklahoma, and Texas; and 1 each in Indiana, Florida, North Carolina, Arizona, and California). Data for December 31, 2009, also include 3 inmates who were erroneously reported as being removed from under sentence of death (1 each in Alabama, Florida, and North Carolina).

[a]Includes 15 deaths from natural causes (5 in Florida; 2 each in Pennsylvania, Texas, and California; and 1 each in Oklahoma, South Carolina, Tennessee, and Arizona), 4 deaths from suicide (1 each in Georgia, Texas, Arizona, and California), and 1 death from a drug overdose (California).
[b]Includes American Indians, Alaska Natives, Asians, Native Hawaiians, other Pacific Islanders, and Hispanic inmates for whom no other race was identified.
[c]Counts of white and black inmates include persons of Hispanic/Latino origin.
[d]Excludes persons held under armed forces jurisdiction with a military death sentence for murder.

SOURCE: Tracy L. Snell, "Table 4. Prisoners under Sentence of Death, by Region, Jurisdiction, and Race, 2009 and 2010," in *Capital Punishment, 2010—Statistical Tables*, U.S. Department of Justice, Bureau of Justice Statistics, December 2011, http://bjs.ojp.usdoj.gov/content/pub/pdf/cp10st.pdf (accessed December 26, 2011)

**TABLE 7.14**

**Executions and other dispositions of inmates sentenced to death, by race and Hispanic origin, 1977–2010**

| Race/Hispanic origin | Total under sentence of death 1977–2010[b] | Prisoners executed | | Prisoners who received other dispositions[a] | |
|---|---|---|---|---|---|
| | | Number | Percent of total | Number | Percent of total |
| Total | 7,879 | 1,234 | 15.7% | 3,487 | 44.3% |
| White[c] | 3,816 | 700 | 18.3% | 1,710 | 44.8% |
| Black[c] | 3,225 | 424 | 13.1 | 1,497 | 46.4 |
| Hispanic | 715 | 96 | 13.4 | 231 | 32.3 |
| All other races[c, d] | 123 | 14 | 11.4 | 49 | 39.8 |

Note: In 1972, the U.S. Supreme Court invalidated capital punishment statutes in several states (*Furman v. Georgia,* 408 U.S. 238 (1972)), effecting a moratorium on executions. Executions resumed in 1977 when the Supreme Court found that revisions to several state statutes had effectively addressed the issues previously held unconstitutional (*Gregg v. Georgia,* 428 U.S. 153 (1976) and its companion cases).

[a]Includes persons removed from a sentence of death because of statutes struck down on appeal, sentences or convictions vacated, commutations, or death by other than execution.
[b]Includes 5 persons sentenced to death prior to 1977 who were still under sentence of death on December 31, 2010; 374 persons sentenced to death prior to 1977 whose death sentence was removed between 1977 and December 31, 2010; and 7,500 persons sentenced to death between 1977 and 2010.
[c]Excludes persons of Hispanic/Latino origin.
[d]Includes American Indians, Alaska Natives, Asians, Native Hawaiians, and other Pacific Islanders.

SOURCE: Tracy L. Snell, "Table 13. Executions and Other Dispositions of Inmates Sentenced to Death, by Race and Hispanic Origin, 1977–2010," in *Capital Punishment, 2010—Statistical Tables*, U.S. Department of Justice, Bureau of Justice Statistics, December 2011, http://bjs.ojp.usdoj.gov/content/pub/pdf/cp10st.pdf (accessed December 26, 2011)

# CHAPTER 8
# POLITICAL PARTICIPATION

*A truly postethnic America would be one in which the ethno-racial component in identity would loom less large than it now does in politics.*

—David A. Hollinger, *Postethnic America: Beyond Multiculturalism* (1995)

David A. Hollinger's words point out the large divide between minority groups and the majority in the political life of the nation. Not only are there racial and ethnic divides in voter registration and voter turnout but also there are differences in voting by minorities when compared with the majority group. Specifically, minority groups largely cast their support behind Democratic candidates. In addition, only in the last 20 years of the 20th century did minority candidates running for office achieve much success. By November 2008, however, an African-American candidate had done the unthinkable: Barack Obama (1961–), a U.S. senator from Illinois, had been elected the 44th president of the United States.

Perry Bacon Jr. states in "Can Obama Count on the Black Vote?" (*Time*, January 23, 2007) that "much of Obama's overall appeal stems from his image as practically a post-racial politician. Not only does he have a mixed-race background, with a white mother from Kansas and a black father from Kenya, but his rhetoric, most notably his 2004 Democratic National Convention speech, emphasizes the importance of Americans moving beyond political, religious and racial differences." Obama did not rely on racial appeals in the same way that previous African-American candidates—notably Jesse Jackson (1941–) in his runs for the Democratic nomination—had done. According to Dan Balz and Jon Cohen, in "Blacks Shift to Obama, Poll Finds" (*Washington Post*, February 28, 2007), this emphasis allowed him to appeal to a large portion of the white electorate, and early in the primary season African-Americans shifted their support from Hillary Rodham Clinton (1947–), the front-runner, to Obama. Minority voters turned out in record numbers to support Obama's candidacy, leading to his Democratic primary victory and his election in November 2008.

## VOTER REGISTRATION

Minority groups have traditionally trailed behind whites when it comes to registering to vote and actually voting. In 1993 Congress enacted the National Voter Registration Act, which became popularly known as the Motor Voter Act, because it included provisions to enable driver's license applicants to simultaneously register to vote. In "Big Increase in New Voters" (October 15, 1997, http://www-cgi.cnn.com/ALLPOLITICS/1996/news/9610/15/motor.voter/), CNN reports that in the two years after the law went into effect (in January 1995) approximately 9 million people had registered to vote.

To be eligible to vote, a person must be a U.S. citizen and at least 18 years of age. The U.S. Election Assistance Commission states in *The Impact of the National Voter Registration Act of 1993 on the Administration of Elections for Federal Office, 2005–2006* (June 30, 2007, http://www.eac.gov/assets/1/Page/NVRA%20Reports%20and%20Data%20Sets%202006-2005.pdf) that in 2006 the voting-age population numbered 225.7 million. Of that number, 172.8 million (76.6%) were registered to vote, a 7.5% increase over the number of registrants in the 2002 midterm elections. However, following the presidential election in 2004 the number of registered voters had decreased from 176.2 million voters, reflecting a normal drop in registration after a presidential election, when states remove some nonvoters from the registration rolls. Each state determines for itself how long an individual may remain on the list of registered voters without voting.

In November 2008 (a presidential election year) there were 151.3 million non-Hispanic white U.S. citizens eligible to vote. (See Table 8.1.) Of this number, 111.2 million (73.5%) were registered to vote, which was a slight decrease from the presidential election in November 2004. Kelly

**TABLE 8.1**

**Reported rates of voting and registration among native and naturalized citizens, by race and Hispanic origin and region of birth, November 2008**

[In thousands]

| Nativity status, race and Hispanic origin, and region of birth | Total citizen population | US citizen | | | | | | | |
|---|---|---|---|---|---|---|---|---|---|
| | | Reported registered | | Not registered | | Reported voted | | Did not vote | |
| | | Number | Percent | Number | Percent | Number | Percent | Number | Percent |
| **United States** | | | | | | | | | |
| All races | 206,072 | 146,311 | 71.0 | 59,761 | 29.0 | 131,144 | 63.6 | 74,928 | 36.4 |
| White alone | 169,438 | 122,020 | 72.0 | 47,418 | 28.0 | 109,100 | 64.4 | 60,338 | 35.6 |
| White non-Hispanic alone | 151,321 | 111,215 | 73.5 | 40,106 | 26.5 | 100,042 | 66.1 | 51,279 | 33.9 |
| Black alone | 24,930 | 17,375 | 69.7 | 7,555 | 30.3 | 16,133 | 64.7 | 8,797 | 35.3 |
| Asian alone | 7,059 | 3,901 | 55.3 | 3,159 | 44.7 | 3,357 | 47.6 | 3,702 | 52.4 |
| Hispanic (of any race) | 19,537 | 11,608 | 59.4 | 7,930 | 40.6 | 9,745 | 49.9 | 9,792 | 50.1 |
| White alone or in combination | 171,798 | 123,628 | 72.0 | 48,170 | 28.0 | 110,500 | 64.3 | 61,298 | 35.7 |
| Black alone or in combination | 25,768 | 17,960 | 69.7 | 7,808 | 30.3 | 16,674 | 64.7 | 9,094 | 35.3 |
| Asian alone or in combination | 7,562 | 4,225 | 55.9 | 3,337 | 44.1 | 3,627 | 48.0 | 3,935 | 52.0 |
| **Native citizen** | | | | | | | | | |
| All races | 190,683 | 137,001 | 71.8 | 53,682 | 28.2 | 122,839 | 64.4 | 67,844 | 35.6 |
| White alone | 160,266 | 116,375 | 72.6 | 43,891 | 27.4 | 104,005 | 64.9 | 56,262 | 35.1 |
| White non-Hispanic alone | 146,906 | 108,438 | 73.8 | 38,467 | 26.2 | 97,538 | 66.4 | 49,367 | 33.6 |
| Black alone | 23,442 | 16,431 | 70.1 | 7,011 | 29.9 | 15,249 | 65.0 | 8,193 | 35.0 |
| Asian alone | 2,654 | 1,353 | 51.0 | 1,301 | 49.0 | 1,194 | 45.0 | 1,460 | 55.0 |
| Hispanic (of any race) | 14,461 | 8,574 | 59.3 | 5,886 | 40.7 | 6,995 | 48.4 | 7,466 | 51.6 |
| White alone or in combination | 162,511 | 117,910 | 72.6 | 44,601 | 27.4 | 105,341 | 64.8 | 57,170 | 35.2 |
| Black alone or in combination | 24,211 | 16,965 | 70.1 | 7,246 | 29.9 | 15,738 | 65.0 | 8,472 | 35.0 |
| Asian alone or in combination | 3,114 | 1,641 | 52.7 | 1,473 | 47.3 | 1,433 | 46.0 | 1,681 | 54.0 |
| **Naturalized citizen** | | | | | | | | | |
| All races | 15,390 | 9,310 | 60.5 | 6,080 | 39.5 | 8,305 | 54.0 | 7,085 | 46.0 |
| White alone | 9,171 | 5,645 | 61.6 | 3,526 | 38.4 | 5,095 | 55.6 | 4,076 | 44.4 |
| White non-Hispanic alone | 4,415 | 2,776 | 62.9 | 1,639 | 37.1 | 2,504 | 56.7 | 1,912 | 43.3 |
| Black alone | 1,488 | 943 | 63.4 | 544 | 36.6 | 884 | 59.4 | 604 | 40.6 |
| Asian alone | 4,405 | 2,548 | 57.8 | 1,857 | 42.2 | 2,163 | 49.1 | 2,242 | 50.9 |
| Hispanic (of any race) | 5,077 | 3,033 | 59.8 | 2,043 | 40.2 | 2,751 | 54.2 | 2,326 | 45.8 |
| White alone or in combination | 9,287 | 5,718 | 61.6 | 3,569 | 38.4 | 5,159 | 55.6 | 4,128 | 44.4 |
| Black alone or in combination | 1,557 | 995 | 63.9 | 562 | 36.1 | 936 | 60.1 | 621 | 39.9 |
| Asian alone or in combination | 4,448 | 2,584 | 58.1 | 1,864 | 41.9 | 2,194 | 49.3 | 2,254 | 50.7 |
| **Region of birth** | | | | | | | | | |
| Total | 15,390 | 9,310 | 60.5 | 6,080 | 39.5 | 8,305 | 54.0 | 7,085 | 46.0 |
| Europe | 2,725 | 1,712 | 62.8 | 1,013 | 37.2 | 1,562 | 57.3 | 1,163 | 42.7 |
| Asia | 5,340 | 3,021 | 56.6 | 2,319 | 43.4 | 2,555 | 47.8 | 2,785 | 52.2 |
| Northern America | 255 | 207 | 81.2 | 48 | 18.8 | 194 | 76.2 | 61 | 23.9 |
| Latin America | 6,304 | 3,889 | 61.7 | 2,415 | 38.3 | 3,558 | 56.4 | 2,746 | 43.6 |
| Africa | 637 | 430 | 67.5 | 207 | 32.5 | 389 | 61.1 | 248 | 38.9 |
| Other | 129 | 50 | 38.8 | 79 | 61.2 | 47 | 36.3 | 82 | 63.6 |

Note: Federal surveys now give respondents the option of reporting more than one race. Therefore, two basic ways of defining a race group are possible. A group such as Asian may be defined as those who reported Asian and no other race (the race-alone or single-race concept) or as those who reported Asian regardless of whether they also reported another race (the race-alone-or-in-combination concept). This table shows data for people who reported they were the single race white and not Hispanic, people who reported the single race black, and people who reported the single race Asian. Use of the single-race populations does not imply that it is the preferred method of presenting or analyzing data.

SOURCE: "Table 13. Reported Voting and Registration among Native and Naturalized Citizens, by Race and Hispanic Origin, and Region of Birth: November 2008," in *Voting and Registration in the Election of November 2008—Detailed Tables*, U.S. Census Bureau, July 2009, http://www.census.gov/hhes/www/socdemo/voting/publications/p20/2008/tables.html (accessed December 29, 2011)

Holder of the U.S. Census Bureau notes in *Voting and Registration in the Election of November 2004* (March 2006, http://www.census.gov/prod/2006pubs/p20-556.pdf) that in November 2004, 111.3 million (75.1%) non-Hispanic whites were registered to vote. Of the 24.9 million African-American citizens in November 2008, 17.4 million (69.7%) were registered to vote, up from the November 2004 figure of 16 million (68.7%). Of the nearly 7.1 million Asian-American citizens in November 2008, 3.9 million (55.3%) were registered to vote, up substantially from the 3.2 million (51.8%) who were registered to vote in November 2004. Of the 19.5 million Hispanic citizens in November 2008, 11.6

million (59.4%) were registered to vote, up from 9.3 million (57.9%) in November 2004. In other words, registration among non-Hispanic white citizens was down slightly as the election of Barack Obama approached, whereas registration among minority citizens was up.

Voter registration tends to decline during nonpresidential election years. In November 2010, 210.8 million citizens were eligible to vote in the congressional election; only 137.3 million (65.1%) reported that they were registered to vote. (See Table 8.2.) However, this proportion of registered voters varied by race and ethnicity. In

## TABLE 8.2

### Reported rates of voting and registration among native and naturalized citizens, by race and Hispanic origin and region of birth, November 2010

[Population 18 years and older, in thousands]

| Nativity status, race, and Hispanic origin | Total citizen population | Reported registered | | Reported not registered | | No response to registration[a] | | Reported voted | | Reported did not vote | | No response to voting[b] | |
|---|---|---|---|---|---|---|---|---|---|---|---|---|---|
| | | Number | Percent | Number | Percent | Number | Percent | Number | Percent | Number | Percent | Number | Percent |
| **All citizens** | | | | | | | | | | | | | |
| All races | 210,800 | 137,263 | 65.1 | 38,516 | 18.3 | 35,021 | 16.6 | 95,987 | 45.5 | 81,105 | 38.5 | 33,707 | 16.0 |
| White alone | 172,447 | 114,482 | 66.4 | 30,788 | 17.9 | 27,176 | 15.8 | 80,554 | 46.7 | 65,838 | 38.2 | 26,054 | 15.1 |
| White non-Hispanic alone | 152,929 | 104,316 | 68.2 | 25,064 | 16.4 | 23,549 | 15.4 | 74,372 | 48.6 | 55,939 | 36.6 | 22,618 | 14.8 |
| Black alone | 25,632 | 16,101 | 62.8 | 4,288 | 16.7 | 5,243 | 20.5 | 11,149 | 43.5 | 9,352 | 36.5 | 5,131 | 20.0 |
| Asian alone | 7,639 | 3,765 | 49.3 | 2,152 | 28.2 | 1,721 | 22.5 | 2,354 | 30.8 | 3,613 | 47.3 | 1,672 | 21.9 |
| Hispanic (of any race) | 21,285 | 10,982 | 51.6 | 6,266 | 29.4 | 4,037 | 19.0 | 6,646 | 31.2 | 10,808 | 50.8 | 3,831 | 18.0 |
| White alone or in combination | 175,090 | 116,115 | 66.3 | 31,398 | 17.9 | 27,577 | 15.8 | 81,614 | 46.6 | 67,045 | 38.3 | 26,432 | 15.1 |
| Black alone or in combination | 26,602 | 16,684 | 62.7 | 4,498 | 16.9 | 5,421 | 20.4 | 11,498 | 43.2 | 9,795 | 36.8 | 5,309 | 20.0 |
| Asian alone or in combination | 8,246 | 4,136 | 50.2 | 2,287 | 27.7 | 1,822 | 22.1 | 2,615 | 31.7 | 3,863 | 46.8 | 1,768 | 21.4 |
| **Native citizen** | | | | | | | | | | | | | |
| All races | 193,897 | 128,098 | 66.1 | 33,829 | 17.4 | 31,970 | 16.5 | 89,740 | 46.3 | 73,413 | 37.9 | 30,744 | 15.9 |
| White alone | 162,609 | 109,074 | 67.1 | 28,079 | 17.3 | 25,456 | 15.7 | 76,696 | 47.2 | 61,534 | 37.8 | 24,378 | 15.0 |
| White non-Hispanic alone | 148,465 | 101,758 | 68.5 | 24,001 | 16.2 | 22,706 | 15.3 | 72,495 | 48.8 | 54,183 | 36.5 | 21,787 | 14.7 |
| Black alone | 23,780 | 15,003 | 63.1 | 3,887 | 16.3 | 4,890 | 20.6 | 10,385 | 43.7 | 8,616 | 36.2 | 4,778 | 20.1 |
| Asian alone | 2,748 | 1,273 | 46.3 | 682 | 24.8 | 793 | 28.9 | 842 | 30.6 | 1,119 | 40.7 | 787 | 28.7 |
| Hispanic (of any race) | 15,535 | 7,938 | 51.1 | 4,509 | 29.0 | 3,087 | 19.9 | 4,541 | 29.2 | 8,081 | 52.0 | 2,914 | 18.8 |
| White alone or in combination | 165,166 | 110,661 | 67.0 | 28,655 | 17.3 | 25,851 | 15.7 | 77,715 | 47.1 | 62,707 | 38.0 | 24,745 | 15.0 |
| Black alone or in combination | 24,713 | 15,562 | 63.0 | 4,090 | 16.5 | 5,061 | 20.5 | 10,717 | 43.4 | 9,046 | 36.6 | 4,949 | 20.0 |
| Asian alone or in combination | 3,333 | 1,628 | 48.9 | 812 | 24.4 | 893 | 26.8 | 1,089 | 32.7 | 1,360 | 40.8 | 883 | 26.5 |
| **Naturalized citizen** | | | | | | | | | | | | | |
| All races | 16,903 | 9,165 | 54.2 | 4,686 | 27.7 | 3,051 | 18.1 | 6,247 | 37.0 | 7,692 | 45.5 | 2,963 | 17.5 |
| White alone | 9,838 | 5,408 | 55.0 | 2,710 | 27.5 | 1,720 | 17.5 | 3,858 | 39.2 | 4,304 | 43.7 | 1,676 | 17.0 |
| White non-Hispanic alone | 4,464 | 2,558 | 57.3 | 1,064 | 23.8 | 843 | 18.9 | 1,877 | 42.0 | 1,756 | 39.3 | 832 | 18.6 |
| Black alone | 1,852 | 1,098 | 59.3 | 401 | 21.6 | 353 | 19.1 | 763 | 41.2 | 735 | 39.7 | 353 | 19.1 |
| Asian alone | 4,890 | 2,492 | 51.0 | 1,470 | 30.1 | 929 | 19.0 | 1,512 | 30.9 | 2,494 | 51.0 | 884 | 18.1 |
| Hispanic (of any race) | 5,750 | 3,044 | 52.9 | 1,756 | 30.5 | 950 | 16.5 | 2,106 | 36.6 | 2,727 | 47.4 | 917 | 15.9 |
| White alone or in combination | 9,924 | 5,454 | 55.0 | 2,743 | 27.6 | 1,726 | 17.4 | 3,899 | 39.3 | 4,338 | 43.7 | 1,687 | 17.0 |
| Black alone or in combination | 1,889 | 1,122 | 59.4 | 408 | 21.6 | 360 | 19.0 | 781 | 41.3 | 749 | 39.6 | 360 | 19.0 |
| Asian alone or in combination | 4,913 | 2,508 | 51.1 | 1,475 | 30.0 | 929 | 18.9 | 1,525 | 31.0 | 2,502 | 50.9 | 885 | 18.0 |
| **Region of birth** | | | | | | | | | | | | | |
| All naturalized citizens | 16,903 | 9,165 | 54.2 | 4,686 | 27.7 | 3,051 | 18.1 | 6,247 | 37.0 | 7,692 | 45.5 | 2,963 | 17.5 |
| Europe | 2,522 | 1,536 | 60.9 | 591 | 23.4 | 395 | 15.7 | 1,169 | 46.3 | 965 | 38.2 | 389 | 15.4 |
| Asia | 6,067 | 3,055 | 50.4 | 1,817 | 30.0 | 1,195 | 19.7 | 1,869 | 30.8 | 3,038 | 50.1 | 1,160 | 19.1 |
| North America | 289 | 208 | 71.9 | 36 | 12.5 | 45 | 15.6 | 185 | 64.1 | 56 | 19.5 | 47 | 16.4 |
| Latin America and Mexico | 7,043 | 3,850 | 54.7 | 1,985 | 28.2 | 1,208 | 17.2 | 2,656 | 37.7 | 3,219 | 45.7 | 1,169 | 16.6 |
| Africa | 800 | 436 | 54.5 | 215 | 26.9 | 149 | 18.7 | 309 | 38.6 | 349 | 43.6 | 142 | 17.8 |
| Other | 181 | 80 | 44.4 | 42 | 23.1 | 59 | 32.5 | 60 | 33.0 | 65 | 36.1 | 56 | 30.9 |

Notes: Federal surveys now give respondents the option of reporting more than one race. Therefore, two basic ways of defining a race group are possible. A group such as Asian may be defined as those who reported Asian and no other race (the race-alone or single-race concept) or as those who reported Asian regardless of whether they also reported another race (the race-alone-or-in-combination concept).

[a] "No response to registration" includes those who were not asked if they were registered as well as those who responded "don't know," and "refused."

[b] "No response to voting" includes those who were not asked if they voted as well as those who responded "don't know," and "refused."

SOURCE: "Table 11. Reported Voting and Registration among Native and Naturalized Citizens, by Race, Hispanic Origin and Region of Birth: November 2010," in *Voting and Registration in the Election of November 2010—Detailed Tables*, U.S. Census Bureau, October 2011, http://www.census.gov/hhes/www/socdemo/voting/publications/p20/2010/tables.html (accessed December 29, 2011)

November 2010, 68.2% of non-Hispanic whites were registered to vote, compared with 62.8% of African-Americans, 51.6% of Hispanics, and just 49.3% of Asian-Americans. These figures had declined substantially from November 2008 among all groups.

Minority voter registration habits tend to vary by region. For example, Obama's candidacy increased African-American voter registration in some regions of the country more than in others. African-American voter registration was particularly increased in the Northeast, where 62.1% of African-American citizens were registered to vote in November 2008, compared with 54.9% in November 2004; and in the South, where 71.9% of the African-American population was registered to vote in November 2008, up from 65.3% in November 2004. (See Table 8.3.) Rates of voter registration among African-Americans increased only slightly in the West (66.2% in November 2008 compared with 64.3% in November 2004) and stayed the same in the Midwest (71.5% in November 2008 compared with 71.6% in November 2004).

Since the 1960s the number of minority registered voters in the South has increased. This increase is due in large part to the passage of the Civil Rights Act of 1964 and the Voting Rights Act of 1965. These laws removed voting restrictions and led to often volatile and dangerous voter registration campaigns that were conducted during the 1960s and 1970s. Before these changes many southern states enforced poll taxes, charging citizens for the right to vote and knowing that many poor African-Americans could not afford to pay. Some southern states had so-called grandfather clauses that permitted voting rights only to those whose grandfathers had been able to vote. Many elderly African-Americans were the grandchildren of slaves who had not been able to vote, so these clauses restricted their rights. Furthermore, because they did not have the right to vote, their own children and grandchildren were also prevented from voting under the grandfather clauses. It took more than laws to open voting booths to southern African-Americans—it took marches, demonstrations, and the loss of a number of lives.

The Census Bureau notes that Asian-American citizens living in the West were the most likely to be registered to vote in November 2008—59.8% of them were registered to vote. (See Table 8.3.) In the Midwest 57.9% of Asian-American citizens were registered to vote, in the South 52.4% were registered to vote, and in the Northeast 45.7% were registered to vote. Hispanic citizens were also the most likely to be registered to vote if they lived in the West, where 60.2% were registered to vote in November 2008, followed closely by the Northeast, where 59.7% were registered to vote, and the South, where 59.2% were registered to vote. Hispanic citizens living in the Midwest had the lowest rate of voter registration, at 56.2%.

## VOTER TURNOUT

Registering to vote is one thing, but actually going out to the polls on election day is another. Often, people will register to vote but fail to exercise their right to vote when the time comes. However, Sam Roberts reports in "No Racial Gap Seen in '08 Vote Turnout" (*New York Times*, April 30, 2009) that according to a Pew Research Center analysis the rates of minority turnout on election day in November 2008 were historically high. Turnout among non-Hispanic whites declined 1.1%, but turnout among minorities rose. Among African-Americans, the turnout rose by 4.9%, making it the most diverse voter turnout in U.S. history.

Even though African-Americans are somewhat less likely to vote than whites, both groups are much more likely to vote than Hispanics and Asian-Americans. In November 2008, 66.1% of non-Hispanic white citizens voted, down from 67.2% in the previous presidential election. (See Table 8.1.) Among African-Americans, 64.7% of eligible citizens voted, compared with 60% in November 2004. Among Hispanic citizens, 49.9% voted, up from 47.2% in November 2004. Results were similar among Asian-American citizens: in November 2008, 47.6% voted, up from 44.1% in November 2004.

African-Americans living in the Midwest were more likely to vote in November 2008 than were African-Americans living in other parts of the country. Two-thirds (67.3%) of African-American citizens in the Midwest voted that year, and nearly the same proportion (66%) voted in the South. (See Table 8.3.) The lowest turnout of African-American citizens was in the Northeast, where only 58.6% voted. Hispanic turnout was best in the West, where 53.1% of Hispanic citizens voted in November 2008, whereas the lowest turnout of Hispanics was in the South, where only 46.4% voted. Asian-Americans living in the West were also the most likely to vote—52.5% of them did so—whereas the lowest turnout of Asian-Americans was in the Northeast, at 39.9%.

Unsurprisingly, voter turnout was lower among all groups during the November 2010 congressional election. Whereas 66.1% of non-Hispanic white citizens voted in November 2008, only 48.6% reported that they voted in November 2010. (See Table 8.1 and Table 8.2) Voting dropped among minority groups as well. Only 43.5% of African-Americans voted in November 2010, compared with 64.7% in November 2008; 31.2% of Hispanics voted in November 2010, down from 49.9% in November 2008; and 30.8% of Asian-Americans voted, down from 47.6% in November 2008.

### A General Decline in Voting Participation

Since 1964 there has been a decline in the percentage of Americans who vote in presidential elections. The Census Bureau (November 1964, http://www.census.gov/population/

**TABLE 8.3**

## Voting and registration rates by race and Hispanic origin by region, November 2008

[In thousands]

| Race, Hispanic origin, age, and geography | Total population | Total citizen population | US citizen | | | | | | | | Total population | |
|---|---|---|---|---|---|---|---|---|---|---|---|---|
| | | | Reported registered | | Not registered | | Reported voted | | Did not vote | | Reported registered | Reported voted |
| | | | Number | Percent | Number | Percent | Number | Percent | Number | Percent | Percent | Percent |
| **All races** | 225,499 | 206,072 | 146,311 | 71.0 | 59,761 | 29.0 | 131,144 | 63.6 | 74,928 | 36.4 | 64.9 | 58.2 |
| Northeast | 41,543 | 37,886 | 26,455 | 69.8 | 11,431 | 30.2 | 23,837 | 62.9 | 14,049 | 37.1 | 63.7 | 57.4 |
| Midwest | 49,396 | 47,209 | 34,897 | 73.9 | 12,311 | 26.1 | 31,306 | 66.3 | 15,903 | 33.7 | 70.6 | 63.4 |
| South | 82,402 | 75,984 | 53,988 | 71.1 | 21,996 | 28.9 | 47,536 | 62.6 | 28,448 | 37.4 | 65.5 | 57.7 |
| West | 52,158 | 44,994 | 30,971 | 68.8 | 14,023 | 31.2 | 28,465 | 63.3 | 16,529 | 36.7 | 59.4 | 54.6 |
| **White non-Hispanic alone** | 154,472 | 151,321 | 111,215 | 73.5 | 40,106 | 26.5 | 100,042 | 66.1 | 51,279 | 33.9 | 72.0 | 64.8 |
| Northeast | 30,403 | 29,436 | 21,449 | 72.9 | 7,987 | 27.1 | 19,310 | 65.6 | 10,126 | 34.4 | 70.5 | 63.5 |
| Midwest | 40,418 | 39,891 | 29,995 | 75.2 | 9,896 | 24.8 | 26,864 | 67.3 | 13,027 | 32.7 | 74.2 | 66.5 |
| South | 53,122 | 52,284 | 38,117 | 72.9 | 14,168 | 27.1 | 33,690 | 64.4 | 18,594 | 35.6 | 71.8 | 63.4 |
| West | 30,529 | 29,710 | 21,654 | 72.9 | 8,056 | 27.1 | 20,177 | 67.9 | 9,532 | 32.1 | 70.9 | 66.1 |
| **Black alone** | 26,528 | 24,930 | 17,375 | 69.7 | 7,555 | 30.3 | 16,133 | 64.7 | 8,797 | 35.3 | 65.5 | 60.8 |
| Northeast | 4,710 | 4,081 | 2,533 | 62.1 | 1,548 | 37.9 | 2,389 | 58.6 | 1,691 | 41.4 | 53.8 | 50.7 |
| Midwest | 4,630 | 4,467 | 3,194 | 71.5 | 1,273 | 28.5 | 3,006 | 67.3 | 1,462 | 32.7 | 69.0 | 64.9 |
| South | 14,698 | 14,001 | 10,071 | 71.9 | 3,930 | 28.1 | 9,238 | 66.0 | 4,762 | 34.0 | 68.5 | 62.9 |
| West | 2,490 | 2,381 | 1,577 | 66.2 | 805 | 33.8 | 1,500 | 63.0 | 882 | 37.0 | 63.3 | 60.2 |
| **Asian** | 10,455 | 7,059 | 3,901 | 55.3 | 3,159 | 44.7 | 3,357 | 47.6 | 3,702 | 52.4 | 37.3 | 32.1 |
| Northeast | 2,346 | 524 | 697 | 45.7 | 827 | 54.3 | 608 | 39.9 | 916 | 60.1 | 29.7 | 25.9 |
| Midwest | 1,175 | 676 | 392 | 57.9 | 284 | 42.1 | 326 | 48.2 | 351 | 51.8 | 33.4 | 27.7 |
| South | 2,146 | 276 | 669 | 52.4 | 607 | 47.6 | 545 | 42.7 | 731 | 57.3 | 31.2 | 25.4 |
| West | 4,788 | 3,583 | 2,143 | 59.8 | 1,440 | 40.2 | 1,879 | 52.5 | 1,704 | 47.5 | 44.8 | 39.3 |
| **Hispanic (of any race)** | 30,852 | 19,537 | 11,608 | 59.4 | 7,930 | 40.6 | 9,745 | 49.9 | 9,792 | 50.1 | 37.6 | 31.6 |
| Northeast | 4,059 | 2,786 | 1,663 | 59.7 | 1,123 | 40.3 | 1,445 | 51.9 | 1,341 | 48.1 | 41.0 | 35.6 |
| Midwest | 2,490 | 1,496 | 840 | 56.2 | 656 | 43.8 | 703 | 47.0 | 792 | 53.0 | 33.7 | 28.2 |
| South | 11,571 | 7,475 | 4,424 | 59.2 | 3,051 | 40.8 | 3,466 | 46.4 | 4,010 | 53.6 | 38.2 | 30.0 |
| West | 12,731 | 7,780 | 4,680 | 60.2 | 3,100 | 39.8 | 4,131 | 53.1 | 3,649 | 46.9 | 36.8 | 32.4 |

SOURCE: Adapted from "Table 3. Reported Voting and Registration, by Race, Hispanic Origin, and Age, for the United States, Regions, and Divisions, November 2008," in *Voting and Registration in the Election of November 2008—Detailed Tables*, U.S. Census Bureau, July 2009, http://www.census.gov/hhes/www/socdemo/voting/publications/p20/2008/tables.html (accessed December 29, 2011)

socdemo/voting/p20-143/tab01.pdf; February 27, 2002, http://www.census.gov/population/socdemo/voting/p20-542/tab01.pdf) reports that in 1964, 69.3% of the voting-age population voted, compared with 54.7% in 2000. In 2004 this rate increased to 58.3%, and in 2008 the rate stayed about the same, at 58.2%. (See Table 8.3.) These figures include the resident voting-age population that is not eligible to vote, such as noncitizens.

A general decline in the proportion of Americans who vote was also seen across racial and ethnic groups, although voting was sharply up in 2008 among these populations. In *Historical Voting and Registration Reports* (August 26, 2008, http://www.census.gov/hhes/www/socdemo/voting/publications/historical/index.html), the Census Bureau reports that only among non-Hispanic whites (who were counted separately from Hispanic whites starting in 1980) did the percentage of the voting-age population that votes rise; after dropping from 62.8% in 1980 to 60.4% in 2000, it rose to 65.8% in 2004. However, voting among this group dropped in 2008 to 64.8%. (See Table 8.3.) In 1968, the first year African-Americans were counted separately from other races, 57.6% of the African-American voting-age population voted. This percentage dropped to 53.5% in 2000, but rose again to 56.3% in 2004 and then skyrocketed to 60.8% in 2008, the highest rate since recording began. Among Hispanics, 37.5% of the voting-age population voted in 1972, whereas in 2000 only 27.5% voted—and this percentage rose only slightly, to 28%, in 2004. However, voting among this population was up sharply in 2008 as well, to 31.6%. The number of Asian-Americans who vote has been tracked only since the 1992 presidential election. In 1992, 27.3% of the Asian-American voting-age population voted, down to 25.4% in 2000 but up to 29.8% in 2004 and to 32.1% in 2008.

### Reasons for Not Voting

Age seems to affect one's likelihood to vote. Traditionally, the demographic group between the ages of 18 and 24 has the lowest percentage of voters. This may partially explain the low voter turnout of Hispanics, because they are on average younger than other segments of the U.S. population. According to the Census Bureau, in *Voting and Registration in the Election of November 2008* (July 2009, http://www.census.gov/hhes/www/socdemo/voting/publications/p20/2008/tables.html), only 44.3% of young adults between the ages of 18 and 24 voted in November 2008. Obama had mobilized young voters in ways that previous candidates had been unable to accomplish; 41.9% of this population had voted in November 2004, and only 32.3% had voted in November 2000. Scott Keeter, Juliana Horowitz, and Alec Tyson of the Pew Research Center for the People and the Press report in "Young Voters in the 2008 Election" (November 12, 2008, http://pewresearch.org/pubs/1031/young-voters-in-the-2008-election) that the young vote during the November 2008 election made a

significant difference: 66% of voters under the age of 30 years voted for Obama. As citizens age, however, they are more likely to vote. The Census Bureau indicates that in November 2008, 51.9% of the voting-age population between the ages of 25 and 44 years voted, 65% of those between the ages of 45 and 64 years voted, and 70.1% of those between the ages of 65 and 74 years voted.

According to the Census Bureau, in *Voting and Registration in the Election of November 2008* (July 2009, http://www.census.gov/hhes/www/socdemo/voting/publications/p20/2008/tables.html), the number-one reason people gave for not voting in the 2008 presidential election was that they were too busy, an excuse that was given by 17.5% of registered nonvoters. Other leading reasons were illness or disability (14.9%), no interest (13.4%), dislike of candidates or campaign issues (12.9%), and out of town (8.8%). Asian-Americans and Hispanics were especially likely to state that they were too busy to vote (26.9% and 24.8%, respectively), and African-Americans were especially likely to say that they were ill or out of town (20.3% each).

The Census Bureau indicates that the reasons for not voting were similar in the congressional election of November 2010, except that two reasons—disinterest and simply forgetting—were much higher in the nonpresidential year. A large proportion (16.4%) of people said they did not vote because they were not interested and 8% said they forgot to vote. (See Table 8.4.) About 26.6% of registered voters said they were too busy, 11.3% did not vote because of illness or disability, and 9.2% said they were out of town. Nearly one out of 10 (8.6%) stated they did not vote because they did not like the candidates or the campaign issues.

## AFRICAN-AMERICAN POLITICAL PARTICIPATION

### Elected Officials

The number of African-Americans elected to public offices at all levels of the U.S. government has increased significantly since the 1980s. The largest gain has been in city and county offices, which include county commissioners, city council members, mayors, vice mayors, and aldermen/alderwomen. Obama became only the fifth African-American to serve in the U.S. Senate and only the third since the period of Reconstruction (1865–1877), when he was sworn in as a senator from Illinois on January 4, 2005. He had received international media coverage after delivering a stirring keynote address at the 2004 Democratic National Convention. In November 2008 he won the presidency and became the first African-American president in U.S. history.

Despite Obama's landslide victory in November 2008, he faced a tough reelection challenge in November 2012. Jeffrey M. Jones of the Gallup Organization reports in *Obama 49%, Romney 45% among Registered Voters Nationwide* (April 2,

## TABLE 8.4

**Reasons for not voting, by selected characteristics, November 2010**

[Population 18 years and older, in thousands]

| Characteristic | Total | Illness or disability | Out of town | Forgot to vote | Not interested | Too busy, conflicting schedule | Transportation problems | Did not like candidates or campaign issues | Registration problems | Bad weather conditions | Inconvenient polling place | Other reason | Don't know or refused |
|---|---|---|---|---|---|---|---|---|---|---|---|---|---|
| | | | | | | Percent distribution of reasons for not voting | | | | | | | |
| **Total** | **39,453** | **11.3** | **9.2** | **8.0** | **16.4** | **26.6** | **2.4** | **8.6** | **3.3** | **0.1** | **2.1** | **9.0** | **3.1** |
| **Age** | | | | | | | | | | | | | |
| 18 to 24 years | 5,863 | 3.4 | 12.4 | 10.1 | 15.4 | 30.4 | 2.1 | 4.7 | 5.6 | 0.0 | 2.3 | 8.4 | 5.1 |
| 25 to 44 years | 16,633 | 5.7 | 7.6 | 8.7 | 16.9 | 33.7 | 1.9 | 7.6 | 3.6 | 0.1 | 2.6 | 8.9 | 2.6 |
| 45 to 64 years | 11,782 | 12.2 | 10.6 | 7.4 | 16.4 | 24.1 | 2.3 | 10.6 | 2.2 | 0.1 | 1.8 | 9.2 | 3.1 |
| 65 years and over | 5,176 | 36.4 | 7.1 | 4.6 | 15.5 | 5.1 | 5.0 | 11.5 | 2.1 | 0.5 | 0.7 | 9.5 | 2.2 |
| **Sex** | | | | | | | | | | | | | |
| Male | 17,974 | 8.3 | 11.7 | 7.9 | 17.6 | 27.1 | 1.9 | 8.9 | 2.8 | 0.1 | 2.3 | 8.1 | 3.3 |
| Female | 21,480 | 13.8 | 7.1 | 8.0 | 15.3 | 26.1 | 2.9 | 8.3 | 3.7 | 0.2 | 1.9 | 9.7 | 2.9 |
| **Race and Hispanic origin** | | | | | | | | | | | | | |
| White alone | 32,526 | 11.1 | 9.4 | 7.8 | 16.6 | 26.4 | 2.1 | 9.2 | 3.2 | 0.1 | 1.9 | 9.1 | 3.1 |
| White non-Hispanic alone | 28,727 | 11.3 | 9.7 | 7.0 | 16.7 | 26.3 | 2.0 | 9.4 | 3.3 | 0.1 | 1.9 | 9.2 | 3.1 |
| Black alone | 4,658 | 13.9 | 7.5 | 8.5 | 16.4 | 24.9 | 5.1 | 4.9 | 3.3 | 0.5 | 3.5 | 8.7 | 2.8 |
| Asian alone | 1,326 | 8.0 | 10.2 | 6.0 | 12.5 | 39.7 | 2.0 | 5.6 | 3.6 | — | 1.4 | 6.8 | 4.3 |
| Hispanic (of any race) | 4,137 | 9.1 | 7.3 | 14.0 | 15.6 | 27.0 | 2.7 | 7.6 | 2.8 | 0.2 | 2.3 | 8.5 | 2.9 |
| White alone or in combination | 33,073 | 11.1 | 9.4 | 7.9 | 16.5 | 26.3 | 2.1 | 9.3 | 3.3 | 0.1 | 1.9 | 9.1 | 3.1 |
| Black alone or in combination | 4,869 | 13.5 | 7.3 | 8.8 | 16.3 | 25.2 | 5.0 | 5.0 | 3.3 | 0.5 | 3.3 | 8.9 | 3.0 |
| Asian alone or in combination | 1,430 | 7.6 | 10.1 | 8.1 | 12.7 | 37.9 | 1.9 | 6.0 | 3.5 | — | 1.4 | 6.7 | 4.0 |
| **Educational attainment** | | | | | | | | | | | | | |
| Less than high school graduate | 4,300 | 22.4 | 5.8 | 8.2 | 17.8 | 15.0 | 5.6 | 8.1 | 2.5 | 0.3 | 1.6 | 9.4 | 3.4 |
| High school graduate | 12,798 | 12.4 | 6.9 | 9.3 | 19.4 | 22.8 | 3.1 | 9.6 | 2.6 | 0.2 | 1.9 | 8.3 | 3.6 |
| Some college | 13,067 | 9.1 | 9.6 | 8.2 | 14.5 | 29.4 | 1.7 | 8.6 | 3.5 | 0.1 | 2.3 | 9.6 | 3.3 |
| Bachelors degree or more | 9,289 | 7.8 | 13.1 | 5.8 | 14.2 | 33.2 | 1.2 | 7.4 | 4.3 | 0.1 | 2.2 | 8.9 | 1.9 |
| **Nativity** | | | | | | | | | | | | | |
| Native-born citizen | 36,705 | 11.3 | 9.0 | 8.0 | 16.5 | 26.4 | 2.5 | 8.7 | 3.3 | 0.2 | 2.1 | 9.1 | 3.1 |
| Naturalized citizen | 2,748 | 11.4 | 11.2 | 8.2 | 14.6 | 29.2 | 1.9 | 7.7 | 3.2 | — | 1.7 | 7.5 | 3.4 |
| **Duration of residence** | | | | | | | | | | | | | |
| Less than 1 year | 6,655 | 6.5 | 8.8 | 9.7 | 13.9 | 26.8 | 3.4 | 5.2 | 9.8 | 0.1 | 2.2 | 10.9 | 2.8 |
| 1 to 2 years | 6,288 | 6.9 | 7.0 | 8.4 | 16.7 | 30.5 | 2.3 | 7.4 | 5.0 | 0.2 | 2.7 | 10.6 | 2.3 |
| 3 years or longer | 26,005 | 13.7 | 9.8 | 7.5 | 17.0 | 25.5 | 2.2 | 9.8 | 1.2 | 0.1 | 1.9 | 8.1 | 3.0 |
| Don't know or refused | 505 | 8.0 | 7.3 | 4.8 | 10.8 | 28.3 | 3.7 | 5.8 | 3.0 | 0.5 | — | 7.8 | 20.0 |
| **Region** | | | | | | | | | | | | | |
| Northeast | 7,335 | 11.8 | 10.3 | 5.1 | 17.7 | 27.8 | 1.6 | 9.9 | 2.4 | — | 1.4 | 8.5 | 3.5 |
| Midwest | 9,534 | 10.8 | 8.9 | 6.6 | 16.4 | 27.2 | 2.6 | 9.4 | 3.4 | 0.0 | 2.3 | 9.8 | 2.6 |
| South | 16,182 | 12.5 | 8.7 | 8.9 | 16.9 | 26.2 | 3.1 | 7.4 | 2.8 | 0.3 | 2.2 | 7.8 | 3.2 |
| West | 6,403 | 8.4 | 9.5 | 11.1 | 13.3 | 25.3 | 1.6 | 8.9 | 5.4 | 0.1 | 2.3 | 11.3 | 3.0 |

**TABLE 8.4**

**Reasons for not voting, by selected characteristics, November 2010** [CONTINUED]

[Population 18 years and older, in thousands]

| Characteristic | Total | Illness or disability | Out of town | Forgot to vote | Not interested | Too busy, conflicting schedule | Transportation problems | Did not like candidates or campaign issues | Registration problems | Bad weather conditions | Inconvenient polling place | Other reason | Don't know or refused |
|---|---|---|---|---|---|---|---|---|---|---|---|---|---|
| | | | | | | | | Percent distribution of reasons for not voting | | | | | |
| **Income** | | | | | | | | | | | | | |
| Total family members | 27,909 | 10.2 | 9.2 | 8.2 | 16.5 | 27.9 | 2.2 | 8.9 | 2.9 | 0.1 | 2.1 | 8.6 | 3.2 |
| Less than $10,000 | 1,349 | 15.0 | 5.7 | 11.4 | 12.9 | 21.5 | 7.5 | 7.0 | 4.8 | — | 1.1 | 10.7 | 2.4 |
| $10,000 to $14,999 | 1,225 | 16.2 | 5.8 | 11.4 | 20.4 | 19.3 | 5.5 | 7.4 | 2.8 | 0.6 | 1.1 | 6.2 | 3.3 |
| $15,000 to $19,999 | 1,101 | 19.2 | 3.1 | 11.2 | 16.1 | 19.4 | 4.4 | 6.3 | 1.9 | 0.2 | 2.0 | 14.2 | 2.0 |
| $20,000 to $29,999 | 2,660 | 15.9 | 5.2 | 9.7 | 16.0 | 23.8 | 3.0 | 9.0 | 3.3 | 0.2 | 1.8 | 8.8 | 3.3 |
| $30,000 to $39,999 | 2,716 | 11.3 | 5.4 | 10.1 | 17.3 | 24.3 | 2.8 | 10.4 | 4.3 | 0.3 | 2.4 | 8.8 | 2.7 |
| $40,000 to $49,999 | 2,030 | 8.5 | 7.3 | 8.9 | 19.9 | 27.0 | 1.1 | 9.2 | 3.8 | — | 1.7 | 8.0 | 4.5 |
| $50,000 to $74,999 | 5,109 | 8.1 | 7.9 | 8.2 | 16.1 | 30.0 | 1.4 | 9.7 | 2.6 | 0.1 | 2.8 | 9.8 | 3.3 |
| $75,000 to $99,999 | 3,233 | 5.7 | 10.4 | 8.3 | 16.3 | 33.8 | 0.8 | 10.4 | 1.6 | — | 2.5 | 8.2 | 2.0 |
| $100,000 to $149,999 | 2,927 | 5.1 | 15.1 | 6.3 | 16.7 | 32.1 | 0.1 | 7.4 | 3.5 | — | 2.0 | 8.0 | 3.8 |
| $150,000 and over | 2,155 | 7.6 | 20.8 | 3.6 | 13.9 | 33.9 | 0.8 | 5.5 | 2.6 | — | 1.8 | 7.0 | 2.4 |
| Income not reported | 3,403 | 12.7 | 9.6 | 5.9 | 16.2 | 27.1 | 2.7 | 10.1 | 2.0 | 0.1 | 1.8 | 7.2 | 4.6 |

Notes: Federal surveys now give respondents the option of reporting more than one race. Therefore, two basic ways of defining a race group are possible. A group such as Asian may be defined as those who reported Asian and no other race (the race-alone or single-race concept) or as those who reported Asian regardless of whether they also reported another race (the race-alone-or-in-combination concept).

Family income is limited to persons who report income or refuse to answer the income question. Respondents who report not knowing their income are not included in this table, which includes only the reference person with relatives in the household or people with the following relationship to the householder: spouse, child, grandchild, parent, sibling, or other relative. This table excludes foster children, unmarried partners, non-relatives, and roommates.

Total figure is the number of registered citizens who reported not voting. If a respondent answered "don't know" or "refused" to either the voting or registration question they were not included in this table.

SOURCE: Table 10. Reasons for Not Voting, by Selected Characteristics: November 2010, in *Voting and Registration in the Election of November 2010—Detailed Tables*, U.S. Census Bureau, October 2011, http://www.census.gov/hhes/www/socdemo/voting/publications/p20/2010/tables.html (accessed December 29, 2011)

2012, http://www.gallup.com/poll/153668/Obama-Romney-Among-Registered-Voters-Nationwide .aspx) that if the 2012 presidential election was held in April, Obama would receive 49% of the vote, while Mitt Romney (1947–), the presumptive Republican nominee, would receive 45% of the vote. In "With Voters Focused on Economy, Obama Lead Narrows" (April 17, 2012, http://www.people-press.org/2012/04/17/with-voters-focused-on-economy-obama-lead-narrows/), the Pew Research Center for the People and the Press reports similar results, identifying the continued troubled economy as a weakness for the Obama campaign.

### African-Americans and Political Parties

According to the Pew Research Center for the People and the Press, in *Evenly Divided and Increasingly Polarized: The 2004 Political Landscape* (November 5, 2003, http://people-press.org/reports/pdf/196.pdf), African-Americans are the strongest supporters of the Democratic Party. In 2003, 64% of African-Americans described themselves as Democrats, another 21% said they leaned toward the Democratic Party, and only 7% identified themselves as Republicans. Even though many Americans shifted toward the Republican Party after the terrorist attacks against the United States on September 11, 2001 (9/11), African-Americans did not. The Pew Research Center for the People and the Press notes that across regions, socioeconomic groups, and ages, the preference for the Democratic Party among African-Americans is uniform; the most affluent African-Americans' party affiliation is almost identical to the least affluent, and the Democratic advantage is only slightly smaller among younger people.

By November 2008 disillusionment with the administration of George W. Bush (1946–) and excitement over the candidates in the Democratic primary had drawn more Democratic voters to the polls. The Pew Research Center for the People and the Press notes in "Inside Obama's Sweeping Victory" (November 5, 2008, http://pewresearch.org/pubs/1023/exit-poll-analysis-2008) that even though equal numbers of Democrats and Republicans had voted in November 2004, in November 2008 Democrats had the advantage, 39% to 32%. Obama won 60% of those with low or moderate incomes of less than $50,000 per year. He also won 66% of the Hispanic vote, which was 13 percentage points higher than the Democratic candidate had won in November 2004, and 95% of the African-American vote, which was seven percentage points higher than the Democratic candidate won in November 2004.

The traditional African-American political goals, as presented by the 13 original members of the Congressional Black Caucus (CBC; April 2012, http://www.cbcfinc.org/cbc.html), are to "promote the public welfare through legislation designed to meet the needs of millions of neglected citizens." In April 2012 there were 42 members of the CBC. The CBC encourages and seeks out African-American participation in government, especially as elected officials, to correct the ills of the disadvantaged, many of whom are minorities.

As the African-American middle class continues to grow, party loyalties may change. Some younger professional African-Americans who may not have experienced poverty or the deprivation of the inner cities may be attracted to the Republican Party platform of less government and lower taxes. A vast majority of African-Americans embraced the programs of President Lyndon B. Johnson's (1908–1973) Great Society and his War on Poverty during the 1960s. In the 21st century a small minority believe that reliance on government has actually disempowered many African-Americans and other underprivileged people.

However, any movement toward the Republican Party before the 2008 election was slowed by Obama's election in November 2008. In "Strong Confidence in Obama—Country Seen as Less Politically Divided" (January 15, 2009, http://www.people-press.org/2009/01/15/strong-confidence-in-obama-country-seen-as-less-politically-divided/), the Pew Research Center for the People and the Press finds that in 2009 nearly four out of five (79%) African-Americans believed that "people like themselves" would gain influence under the Obama administration. This was more than the African-Americans who believed they would gain influence under the Bush administration, which took office in January 2001, or even under the Democratic Clinton administration, which took office in January 1993. Only 30% of African-Americans believed they would gain influence under Bush, and only 67% believed they would gain influence under Bill Clinton (1946–). The Pew Research Center for the People and the Press finds in "Obama: Weak Job Ratings, but Positive Personal Image" (January 19, 2012, http://www.people-press.org/files/legacy-pdf/1-19-12%20Obama%20Release.pdf) that in 2012, 92% of African-Americans maintained their favorable view of Obama.

## HISPANIC POLITICAL PARTICIPATION

### Factors Contributing to Low Political Participation

There was a tremendous increase in the Hispanic population in the United States during the late 20th century. According to the Census Bureau, by 2010, 50.5 million Hispanics lived in the United States. (See Table 1.3 in Chapter 1.) However, the Hispanic community has not attained political power equal to its proportion of the population. Two characteristics of Hispanic demography help account for this. First, even though the Hispanic voting-age population grew during the 1970s and 1980s, Hispanics have a young population, with many in the 18- to 24-year-old category—the age group that is the least likely to vote. In addition, a smaller proportion of Hispanics than of society as a whole are in the 55-years-and-older category—the age group that is the most likely to vote. The second and perhaps more important characteristic is the issue of U.S. citizenship. The 2010 census counted 50.5 million Hispanics living in the United States; however, just 21.3 million Hispanics were citizens. (See Table 8.2.) Therefore, 29.2 million (57.8%) Hispanics were not U.S. citizens and could not vote.

## Political Participation

Civil rights gains of the 1960s, such as the 24th Amendment eliminating the poll tax, the extension of the Voting Rights Act of 1965 to the Southwest, and the elimination of the English literacy requirement, helped a number of Hispanics attain political office. During the 1970s both major political parties started wooing Hispanic voters and drafting Hispanic candidates. Advocacy groups, such as the Mexican American Legal Defense and Education Fund, the Southwest Voter Registration Education Project, and the Puerto Rican Legal Defense and Education Fund, were formed. All these groups helped develop the political influence of the Hispanic community.

The National Association of Latino Elected and Appointed Officials (NALEO; 2012, http://www.naleo .org/aboutnaleo.html) is a research, policy, and education organization that is made up by over 6,000 Latino elected and appointed officials. The organization's mission is to facilitate the integration of Latino immigrants into U.S. society, to develop leadership abilities among Latino youth, and to support the nation's Latino elected and appointed officials. In 2004 the NALEO Educational Fund announced that it was collaborating with Univision Communications Inc. in a campaign aimed at mobilizing Hispanic voters throughout the United States. The "Voces del Pueblo" campaign included nonpartisan public service announcements on radio and television as well as voter education forums, phone contact, and targeted mailings. The campaign was an attempt to develop the political influence of the Hispanic community in part by encouraging Hispanics to become citizens. NALEO notes in *2008 Latino Election Handbook* (2008, http://www.naleo.org/downloads/NALEO _LEH_2008_final.pdf) that the significant rise in naturalized Latinos in 2006 and 2007 translated into an increased political influence at the polls. It argues that Latinos played a crucial role in Senator John McCain's (1936–) Republican primary victory in Florida and in keeping the primary campaign of Democrat Hillary Rodham Clinton alive in California, Texas, and Puerto Rico.

## Hispanics and Political Parties

As a group, Hispanics have been important supporters of the Democratic Party. Like many other Americans in the aftermath of 9/11, many Hispanics shifted their party affiliation to the Republican Party, although by 2007 that trend had reversed itself. Paul Taylor and Richard Fry of the Pew Research Center report in *Hispanics and the 2008 Election: A Swing Vote?* (December 6, 2007, http://pewhispanic.org/

files/reports/83.pdf) that even though Democrats outnumbered Republicans among Hispanics by more than two to one during the 1990s, after 9/11 Democrats led by a smaller margin. In fact, Bush received an estimated 40% of the Hispanic vote in 2004, a record for a Republican presidential candidate.

However, between 2006 and 2007 the shift of Hispanic voters to the Republican Party reversed course. Taylor and Fry find that in 2006, 28% of Hispanics said they supported Republicans and 49% said they supported Democrats. Within a year, only 23% of Hispanics identified as Republicans and 57% identified as Democrats. According to Taylor and Fry, more Hispanics believed the Democratic Party showed greater concern for Latinos and thought the Democrats were doing a better job on the issue of illegal immigration. In addition, 41% of Hispanics surveyed believed the Bush administration's policies had been harmful to Latinos, whereas only 16% believed these policies had been helpful.

Taylor and Fry suggest that Hispanics had the potential to be a swing vote in helping decide the 2008 presidential election. Latino voters represented a sizable share of the electorate in four of the six states that Bush carried by margins of five percentage points or fewer in the 2004 election: New Mexico, Florida, Nevada, and Colorado. The Pew Research Center predicted that the Hispanic vote in Florida, in particular, would play a strong part in the 2008 presidential election. Even though Cuban-Americans in southern Florida had been traditionally Republican, the Latino vote in central Florida had grown. Much of this population was from Puerto Rico. In addition, the state had a growing population of Latinos from South America, Central America, and Mexico. The Pew Hispanic Center notes in the fact sheet "Among Hispanics in Florida, 2008 Voter Registration Rolls Swing Democratic" (October 29, 2008, http://pewhispanic.org/files/factsheets/44.pdf) that by mid-2008 more Hispanics in the state were Democrat (35.3%) than Republican (33.5%), and that a third had chosen to remain Independent. In "How Hispanics Voted in the 2008 Election" (November 5, 2008, http://pewre search.org/pubs/1024/exit-poll-analysis-hispanics), Mark Hugo Lopez of the Pew Research Center reports that Obama won 57% of the Hispanic vote in Florida, a significant shift from 2004, when Bush carried 56% of the Hispanic vote in that state.

The case of Florida highlights the difficulties that the Republican Party faces during the 2012 presidential election. Florida has the third-largest Hispanic population in the nation. The Pew Hispanic Center notes in the fact sheet "Latinos in the 2012 Election: Florida" (January 23, 2012, http://www.pewhispanic.org/2012/01/23/latinos-in-the-2012-election-florida/) that as recently as 2006 more Hispanics in Florida were registered as Republican than were registered as Democrat. By 2008 Hispanics favored the Democratic Party, and as the 2012 presidential election approached, that gap was widening. Some political observers argue that Romney will not win the presidential election unless he broadens his appeal among Hispanic voters. Furthermore, Romney's promise to veto the Development, Relief, and Education for Alien Minors Act was believed to have hurt his chances among that demographic. According to a Univision News/ABC poll (http://faculty.washington.edu/mbarreto/ld/jan_national.html), in January 2012 Hispanic registered voters overwhelmingly favored Obama over Romney for president (67% and 25%, respectively).

## RACE, ETHNICITY, AND ELECTORAL DISTRICTS

The design of electoral districts can have a tremendous impact on the political power of minorities. Depending on how the lines are drawn, an electoral district might have a large concentration of minorities, enhancing their political power, or minority populations may be split up between many electoral districts, weakening their political influence.

Designing electoral districts to favor one group over another is known as gerrymandering, named after the Massachusetts governor Elbridge Gerry (1744–1814), who became notorious for the salamander-shaped district he approved in 1812. During the first half of the 20th century gerrymandering was widely used as an attempt to prevent African-Americans and other minorities from gaining true political representation. Another practice was creating at-large districts, in which the entire population of a large area elected several representatives. The alternative, having several smaller districts each elect only one representative, allowed concentrated populations of minorities to elect their own representatives.

Under the requirements of the Voting Rights Act of 1965, jurisdictions with a history of systematic discrimination (such as a poll tax or literacy test) must create districts with majorities of African-Americans or Hispanics, wherever the demographics warrant it. At the same time, they must avoid weakening existing "minority-majority" districts (i.e., districts "in which a majority of the population is a member of a specific minority group"). This law helped eliminate some districts that had been designed to favor whites. At the same time, however, it superseded the traditional criterion of compact districts and made for some oddly defined districts in the name of creating Hispanic- or African-American–majority districts.

### Computerized Redistricting

Douglas J. Amy notes in *Real Choices/New Voices: How Proportional Representation Elections Could Revitalize American Democracy* (2002) that with computer software, gerrymandering in the 21st century has become highly sophisticated. Redistricters can now incorporate a variety of information—party registration, voting patterns, and ethnic makeup—from a variety of sources, including census data, property tax records, and old district lines. This information allows them to produce a number of potential scenarios in an instant. Contemporary gerrymandering techniques are called "packing" (concentrating a group of voters in the fewest number of districts), "cracking" (spreading a group of voters across districts), and "kidnapping" (remapping so that two incumbents from the same party are now located in the same district and vying for the same seat). Gerrymandering in the past was essentially self-correcting; by attempting to control as many districts as possible, parties risked losing, should a small percentage of voters shift allegiances. However, contemporary software has become so sophisticated, and politics have become so partisan, that the concept of self-correction is no longer applicable. As a result, few seats in the U.S. House of Representatives are now competitive, with incumbents enjoying a locked-in advantage that is almost impossible to overcome.

The article "Political Gerrymandering 2000–2008: 'A Self-Limiting Enterprise'?" (*Harvard Law Review*, vol. 122, March 2009) also argues against the idea that gerrymandering will always be "self-limited." By looking at seven cases of redistricting schemes after the 2000 census, the article finds that the most damaging gerrymandering occurs in areas where a very strong party is in control and attempts to push its advantage to the limit, and in places where the two political parties collude in gerrymandering in an attempt to keep their own incumbents in office. In particular, "big party gerrymanders at least leave open the possibility of self-correction, but bipartisan gerrymanders make the idea fanciful." Whether voters want a change or not, the bipartisan gerrymanders fix incumbent parties in place for 10 years.

### Challenges to Electoral Districting

Redistricting has become a major source of contention between Republicans and Democrats since the 2000 census. One notorious case took place in Texas. The state's lawmakers were unable to agree on new congressional districts because Republicans controlled the state senate and Democrats controlled the state house of representatives. A compromise plan was forced on the parties by a panel of federal judges, essentially leaving the current partisan balance in place. However, after Republicans took control of the state house in 2002, they sought to reopen the redistricting question, breaking an unwritten rule that remapping was to be a matter dealt with once every 10 years to avoid incessant wrangling on the subject. To resist, Democrats in both the state house and senate fled to Oklahoma and New Mexico to prevent the creation of a quorum (the minimum number of representatives present to conduct business) and thwart the ability of the Republicans to push through their redistricting plan.

Eventually, the Democrats gave in and the congressional districts were redrawn, with the potential that the Republicans would pick up seven seats in the 2004 elections. Staff lawyers in the U.S. Department of Justice approved the plan, even though lawyers for the department had concluded that the redistricting plan undercut minority voting rights. In fact, Republicans won 21 of Texas's 32 seats in the U.S. House of Representatives in 2004, up from 15. The U.S. Supreme Court announced in December 2005 that it would consider the constitutionality of the redistricted congressional map. In June 2006 the court ruled that the redistricting violated the rights of some Hispanics, but did not violate the rights of African-American voters in the state. Furthermore, it ruled that nothing in the U.S. Constitution barred states from redrawing political lines at any time, and it established no timetable for reviewing the redistricting that had violated the rights of Hispanics.

A redistricting effort in Pennsylvania also drew a great deal of attention. After losing two seats in Congress due to a drop in population, Pennsylvania redrew its districts, a process that the Republican majority in the General Assembly openly sought to benefit the party through the latest techniques in gerrymandering. Some of the unusually shaped districts that resulted were called the "supine seahorse" and the "upside-down Chinese dragon." Even though a Democrat won the governor's race in Pennsylvania in 2002, Republicans took 12 of the 19 U.S. House of Representatives seats.

In *Vieth v. Jubelirer* (541 U.S. 267 [2004]), it was argued that the Republicans went too far in their efforts to favor their own party in redrawing congressional lines. However, the Supreme Court upheld the Pennsylvania map in a 5–4 decision. Justice Antonin Scalia (1936–) and others of the majority opinion maintained that it was the responsibility of Congress and not the court to define fair districting practices. Justice John Paul Stevens (1920–), a minority opinion holder, characterized the decision as "a failure of judicial will to condemn even the most blatant violations of a state legislature's fundamental duty to govern impartially."

# IMPORTANT NAMES
# AND ADDRESSES

**Alzheimer's Association**
225 N. Michigan Ave., 17th Floor
Chicago, IL 60601-7633
(312) 335-8700
FAX: 1-866-699-1246
E-mail: info@alz.org
URL: http://www.alz.org/

**American Heart Association**
7272 Greenville Ave.
Dallas, TX 75231
1-800-AHA-USA-1
URL: http://www.heart.org/HEARTORG/

**Bureau of Justice Statistics**
**U.S. Department of Justice**
810 Seventh St. NW
Washington, DC 20531
(202) 307-0765
E-mail: askbjs@usdoj.gov
URL: http://bjs.ojp.usdoj.gov/

**Center for Women's Business Research**
1760 Old Meadow Rd., Ste. 500
McLean, VA 22102
(703) 556-7162
FAX: (703) 506-3266
URL: http://www.cfwbr.org/

**Centers for Disease Control and Prevention**
1600 Clifton Rd.
Atlanta, GA 30333
1-800-232-4636
E-mail: cdcinfo@cdc.gov
URL: http://www.cdc.gov/

**Children's Defense Fund**
25 E St. NW
Washington, DC 20001
1-800-233-1200
E-mail: cdfinfo@childrensdefense.org
URL: http://www.childrensdefense.org/

**Civil Rights Project**
8370 Math Sciences, Box 951521
Los Angeles, CA 90095-1521

(310) 267-5562
E-mail: crp@ucla.edu
URL: http://
www.civilrightsproject.ucla.edu/

**College Board Educational Testing Service**
Rosedale Rd.
Princeton, NJ 08541
(609) 921-9000
E-mail: etsinfo@ets.org
URL: http://www.collegeboard.org/

**Congressional Black Caucus Foundation**
1720 Massachusetts Ave. NW
Washington, DC 20036
(202) 263-2800
FAX: (202) 775-0773
URL: http://www.cbcfinc.org/

**Congressional Hispanic Caucus Institute**
911 Second St. NE
Washington, DC 20002
(202) 543-1771
1-800-EXCEL-DC
FAX: (202) 546-2143
URL: http://www.chci.org/

**Lawyers' Committee for Civil Rights under Law**
1401 New York Ave. NW, Ste. 400
Washington, DC 20005
(202) 662-8600
1-888-299-5227
FAX: (202) 783-0857
URL: http://www.lawyerscommittee.org/

**League of United Latin American Citizens**
1133 19th St. NW, Ste. 1000
Washington, DC 20036
(202) 833-6130
FAX: (202) 833-6135
URL: http://www.lulac.org/

**National Association for the Advancement of Colored People**
4805 Mt. Hope Dr.
Baltimore, MD 21215
(410) 580-5777
1-877-NAACP-98
URL: http://www.naacp.org/

**National Association of Latino Elected and Appointed Officials Educational Fund**
1122 W. Washington Blvd., Third Floor
Los Angeles, CA 90015
(213) 747-7606
FAX: (213) 747-7664
URL: http://www.naleo.org/

**National Black Child Development Institute**
1313 L St. NW, Ste. 110
Washington, DC 20005-4110
(202) 883-2220
1-800-556-2234
FAX: (202) 833-8222
E-mail: moreinfo@nbcdi.org
URL: http://www.nbcdi.org/

**National Caucus and Center on Black Aged**
1220 L St. NW, Ste. 800
Washington, DC 20005
(202) 637-8400
FAX: (202) 347-0895
E-mail: support@ncba-aged.org
URL: http://www.ncba-aged.org/

**National Hispanic Council on Aging**
734 15th St. NW, Ste. 1050
Washington, DC 20005
(202) 347-9733
FAX: (202) 347-9735
E-mail: nhcoa@nhcoa.org
URL: http://www.nhcoa.org/

**National Indian Gaming Association**
224 Second St. SE
Washington, DC 20003

(202) 546-7711
FAX: (202) 546-1755
URL: http://www.indiangaming.org/

**National Urban League**
120 Wall St.
New York, NY 10005
(212) 558-5300
FAX: (212) 344-5332
URL: http://www.nul.org/

**Organization of Chinese Americans**
1322 18th St. NW
Washington, DC 20036-1803
(202) 223-5500
FAX: (202) 296-0540
E-mail: oca@ocanational.org
URL: http://www.ocanational.org/

**Pew Hispanic Center**
1615 L St. NW, Ste. 700
Washington, DC 20036
(202) 419-4300
URL: http://pewhispanic.org/

**Poverty and Race Research Action Council**
1200 18th St. NW, Ste. 200
Washington, DC 20036

(202) 906-8023
FAX: (202) 842-2885
E-mail: info@prrac.org
URL: http://www.prrac.org/

**Sentencing Project**
1705 DeSales St. NW, Eighth Floor
Washington, DC 20036
(202) 628-0871
FAX: (202) 628-1091
E-mail: staff@sentencingproject.org
URL: http://www.sentencingproject.org/

**Southern Poverty Law Center**
400 Washington Ave.
Montgomery, AL 36104
(334) 956-8200
URL: http://www.splcenter.org/

**U.S. Bureau of Labor Statistics**
**U.S. Department of Labor**
Postal Square Bldg.
2 Massachusetts Ave. NE
Washington, DC 20212-0001
(202) 691-5200
URL: http://www.bls.gov/

**U.S. Census Bureau**
4600 Silver Hill Rd.
Washington, DC 20233

(301) 763-4636
1-800-923-8282
URL: http://www.census.gov/

**U.S. Department of Education**
400 Maryland Ave. SW
Washington, DC 20202
1-800-872-5327
URL: http://www.ed.gov/

**U.S. Department of Health and Human Services**
200 Independence Ave. SW
Washington, DC 20201
1-877-696-6775
URL: http://www.hhs.gov/

**U.S. Department of Labor**
Frances Perkins Bldg.
200 Constitution Ave. NW
Washington, DC 20210
1-866-4-USA-DOL
URL: http://www.dol.gov/

**U.S. Equal Employment Opportunity Commission**
131 M St. NE, Fourth Floor, Ste. 4NWO2F
Washington, DC 20507-0100
1-800-669-4000
URL: http://www.eeoc.gov/

# RESOURCES

The U.S. Census Bureau collects and distributes the nation's statistics. Demographic data from the bureau include *Profiles of General Demographic Characteristics, Population Projections Program* (projections released periodically), and *American Community Survey* (released annually). Among the 2010 census publications that were used in this book were *The Black Population: 2010* (Sonya Rastogi et al., September 2011), *The Hispanic Population in the United States: 2010* (Sharon R. Ennis, Merarys Rios-Vargas, and Nora G. Albert, May 2011), and *Overview of Race and Hispanic Origin: 2010* (Karen R. Humes, Nicholas A. Jones, and Robert R. Ramirez, March 2011).

The Census Bureau releases the *Statistical Abstract* each year; the most recent edition is *The 2012 Statistical Abstract: The National Data Book* (September 2011). The bureau releases financial and family statistics in *America's Families and Living Arrangements: 2011* (November 2011) and *Income, Poverty, and Health Insurance Coverage in the United States: 2010* (Carmen DeNavas-Walt, Bernadette D. Proctor, and Jessica C. Smith, September 2011). The Census Bureau also compiles statistics on homeownership rates, business data, state and metropolitan population data, and voting data. Publications include *Voting and Registration in the Election of November 2008* (July 2009), *Voting and Registration in the Election of November 2010* (October 2011), and *Housing Vacancies and Homeownership Annual Statistics: 2010* (2011). The bureau periodically publishes the *Survey of Minority-Owned Business Enterprises*.

The U.S. Bureau of Labor Statistics (BLS) provides labor force data. The BLS publishes *Employment and Earnings, Household Data Annual Averages*, and the monthly *Employment Situation Summary*. The *Monthly Labor Review* provides detailed analysis of labor force statistics on a periodic basis. Other job-related sources are published by the U.S. Equal Employment Opportunity Commission, including *Enforcement and Litigation Statistics* (2011) and *2010 Job Patterns for Minorities and Women in Private Industry* (2011).

A variety of government resources on minority health proved invaluable. The National Center for Health Statistics produces *Health, United States, 2010* (2011) and the monthly *National Vital Statistics Reports*, which provide birth and mortality statistics. The Centers for Disease Control and Prevention publishes the annual *HIV Surveillance Report*. Another helpful source, *America's Children: Key National Indicators of Well-Being, 2011* (July 2011), is published by the Federal Interagency Forum on Child and Family Statistics. The *SEER Cancer Statistics Review, 1975–2008* (Nadia Howlader et al., 2011), published by the National Cancer Institute, provides invaluable data on cancer.

A number of U.S. Department of Health and Human Services publications were used in this book. The *National Healthcare Disparities Report, 2010* (March 2011) is helpful in examining differences in health care access and utilization among minority populations. *Indicators of Welfare Dependence, Annual Report to Congress, 2008* (Gil Crouse, Susan Hauan, and Annette Waters Rogers, 2008) examines the rates of utilization of a variety of social programs. *Results from the 2010 National Survey on Drug Use and Health: Detailed Tables* (September 2011) provides information on tobacco, alcohol, and illicit drug use.

The U.S. Department of Education's National Center for Education Statistics (NCES) publishes *The Condition of Education 2011* (Susan Aud et al., May 2011). Other NCES reports that proved helpful were *Digest of Education Statistics, 2010* (Thomas D. Snyder and Sally A. Dillow, April 2011), *Indicators of School Crime and Safety: 2010* (Simone Robers et al., November 2010), *Status and Trends in the Education of Racial and Ethnic Groups* (Susan Aud, Mary Ann Fox, and Angelina KewalRamani, July 2010), *The Children Born in 2001 at Kindergarten Entry: First Findings from the Kindergarten Data Collections of the Early Childhood Longitudinal Study, Birth Cohort* (Kristin Denton Flanagan and Cameron McPhee, October 2009), *Status and Trends in the Education of American Indians and Alaska Natives: 2008* (Jill Fleury DeVoe and Kristen E.

Darling-Churchill, September 2008), *Preschool: First Findings from the Preschool Follow-up of the Early Childhood Longitudinal Study, Birth Cohort* (Jodi Jacobson Chernoff et al., October 2007), and *American Indian and Alaska Native Children: Findings from the Base Year of the Early Childhood Longitudinal Study, Birth Cohort* (Kristin Denton Flanagan and Jen Park, August 2005). The College Board provides useful data in *2011 College-Bound Seniors: Total Group Profile Report* (August 2011).

The BJS produces *Homicide Trends in the United States* (James Alan Fox and Marianne W. Zawitz, January 2010) as well as numerous other reports. Other BJS reports used in this publication include *Capital Punishment, 2010* (Tracy L. Snell, December 2011), *Prisoners in 2010* (Paul Guerino, Paige M. Harrison, and William J. Sabol, December 2011), *Probation and Parole in the United States, 2010* (Lauren E. Glaze and Thomas P. Bonczar, November 2011), and *Criminal Victimization, 2010* (Jennifer L. Truman, September 2011). *Hate Crime Statistics, 2010* (November 2011) and *Crime in the United States, 2010* (September 2011) were published by the Federal Bureau of Investigation.

Finally, the Gallup Organization provides valuable polling information. Gallup publications used in this book include *Americans Divided on Whether King's Dream Has Been Realized* (Jeffrey M. Jones, August 2011), *One-Third in U.S. See Improved Race Relations under Obama* (Lydia Saad, August 2011), *Obama 49%, Romney 45% among Registered Voters Nationwide* (Jeffrey M. Jones, April 2012), *Little "Obama Effect" on Views about Race Relations* (Frank Newport, October 2009), *More Americans Say U.S. a Nation of Haves and Have-Nots* (Lydia Saad, July 2008), *Whites May Exaggerate Black-Hispanic Tensions* (Lydia Saad, July 2008), *Blacks Convinced Discrimination Still Exists in College Admission Process* (Frank Newport, August 2007), *Most Americans Approve of Interracial Marriages* (Joseph Carroll, August 2007), and *Whites, Minorities Differ in Views of Economic Opportunities in U.S.* (Joseph Carroll, July 2006).

# INDEX

Chinese Immigration,1800s, 10, 12–13
diet of, 121–122
geographic distribution, 13–14
history of immigration to/employment in
  U.S., 57–58
immigration of, 13
income of, 79
in labor force, 57–58, 64–65
occupations of, 71–73
overview of, 10
students, performance of, 38, 41–42
voter registration of, 148
in workforce, growth of, 68
Asian-Indians, 13
*Associated General Contractors of Ohio v.
  Sandra A. Drabik*, 75
Associated Press (AP)
  "Broad Opposition to Guest Worker
    Program," 59
  "Tribal Casinos No Longer Sure Bet in
    Washington," 76
Aud, Susan
  on Asian/Pacific Islander college
    enrollment, 52, 53
  on charter schools, 50
  on college drop-out rates, 52
  *The Condition of Education 2011*, 31
  on high school advanced placement
    courses, 51
  *Status and Trends in the Education of
    Racial and Ethnic Groups*, 43, 82–83

## B

Bachelor's degree, 52–53
Bacon, Perry, Jr., 145
Baker, Bryan, 4–5
*Bakke, Regents of the University of
  California v.*, 53
Balz, Dan, 145
Barnes, Patricia M., 122
Barnes, Robert, 43
Bartlett, Donald L., 75
Becker, Natalie Crow, 50
"Below the Bubble: 'Educational Triage'
  and the Texas Accountability System"
  (Booher-Jennings), 47–48
Beratan, Gregg, 44
Berger, Joseph, 7
Betts, Julian R., 50
Bickford, Eric, 10
"Big Increase in New Voters" (CNN), 145
Birthrates
  births for women 10–19 years, by age/
    race/Hispanic origin, 24*t*
  births to unmarried women, 21*t*
  among Hispanics, 4
  teen, 20–22
  for teenagers, 22*f*
  for teenagers, by race/Hispanic origin,
    23*f*

Births
  infant/neonatal/postneonatal mortality
    rates, by race/Hispanic origin of
    mother, 102*t*
  low birth weight/infant mortality,
    100–103
  low-birthweight live births, by race/
    Hispanic origin/smoking status of
    mother, 101*t*
  overview of, 99–100
  by race/Hispanic origin of mother, 100*t*
  *See also* Pregnancy
"Births: Final Data for 2009" (Martin
  et al.), 21, 100
"Births: Preliminary Data for 2010"
  (Hamilton, Martin, & Ventura), 21–22
BJS (Bureau of Justice Statistics), 129
Black codes, 57
Black colleges, 55
*The Black Population: 2010* (Rastogi et al.), 9
*Blacks Convinced Discrimination Still
  Exists in College Admission Process*
  (Newport), 54
"Blacks Getting Equal Health Care Are Still
  More Likely to Die from Some Cancers"
  (Stein), 105
"Blacks Shift to Obama, Poll Finds" (Balz
  & Cohen), 145
BLS. *See* Bureau of Labor Statistics
*A Blueprint for Reform: The
  Reauthorization of the Elementary* (U.S.
  Department of Education), 48
*Board of Education of Topeka, Kansas,
  Brown v.*, 43
*Bollinger, Gratz v.*, 54
Booher-Jennings, Jennifer, 48–49
Border fence, 59
Bracero Program, 58
Braveman, Paula, 103
Breast cancer, 104–105
Brenchley, Cameron, 48–49
*Briefing on U.S. Customs and Border
  Protection's Border Security Fencing,
  Infrastructure, and Technology Fiscal
  Year 2011 Expenditure Plan* (GAO), 59
"Broad Opposition to Guest Worker
  Program" (AP), 59
Bronchus cancer, 105–107
*Brown v. Board of Education of Topeka,
  Kansas*, 43
"Burden of Acting Neither White nor
  Black: Asian American Identities and
  Achievement in Urban Schools"
  (Lew), 38
Bureau of Justice Statistics (BJS), 129
Bureau of Labor Statistics (BLS)
  *Employment and Earnings*, 68, 71–73
  *The Employment Situation—March
    2012*, 60
Bush, George W.
  American Dream Downpayment
    Assistance Act, 28

guest worker program and, 59
Hispanic vote and, 154
No Child Left Behind Act and, 46
response of Democratic voters to, 153
Business
  minorities in, 74
  minority women-owned businesses, 74
  set-aside programs, criticism of, 74–75

## C

California Civil Rights Initiative, 53
"Can Obama Count on the Black Vote?"
  (Bacon), 145
Cancer
  breast cancer, 104–105
  breast cancer incidence/death rates, by
    race/Hispanic origin, 108*f*
  colon/rectum cancer, 107
  colon/rectum cancer incidence/death
    rates, by race/Hispanic origin, 111*f*
  lung/bronchus cancer, 105–107
  lung/bronchus cancer incidence/death
    rates, by race/Hispanic origin, 110*f*
  among minorities, overview of, 103
  mortality rates/trends, by race/Hispanic
    origin, 106*t*–107*t*
  prostate cancer, 105
  prostate cancer incidence/death rates, by
    race/Hispanic origin, 109*f*
  rates/trends, by race/Hispanic origin,
    104*t*–105*t*
*Capital Punishment* (Snell), 142
Carroll, Joseph
  *Most Americans Approve of Interracial
    Marriages*, 19
  *Whites, Minorities Differ in Views of
    Economic Opportunities in U.S*, 68
Casares, Whitney N., 22
Casinos. *See* Tribal casinos
Castagno, Angelina E., 44
Castro, Fidel, 7–8
Castro, Ida L., 66
Catalano, Shannan M., 129
Cataldi, Emily Forrest, 132–133
CDC. *See* Centers for Disease Control and
  Prevention
Center for Nutrition Policy and Promotion
  (CNPP), 121
Centers for Disease Control and Prevention
  (CDC)
  on diabetes, 112
  on HIV/AIDS, 113
  on illicit drug use, 122–123
  on obesity, 121
  on sickle cell disease, 113, 117
Chang, Shih-Chen, 22
"Characteristics and Risk Factors for
  Adverse Birth Outcomes in Pregnant
  Black Adolescents" (Chang et al.), 22
Charter schools, 50

"The Optimistic Immigrant: Among Latinos, the Recently Arrived Have the Most Hope for the Future" (Escobar), 83–84

Orfield, Gary, 43–44

O'Rourke, Sheila, 53

Ostrov, Barbara Feder, 66

# P

Pacific Islanders, diet of, 121–122

"Parental Involvement in Predicting School Motivation: Similar and Differential Effects across Ethnic Groups" (Fan, Williams, & Wolters), 41–42

Parents
  children living with grandparents, 26, 28
  children living with one parent, by race/Hispanic origin, 28f
  children's, 25t
  marital status of parents, by age/race/Hispanic origin, 27t
  of single-parent households, 23–24
  *See also* Families

*Parents Involved in Community Schools v. Seattle School District*, 43

Park, Jen, 44–45

Parole, adults on, 141(t7.11)

Patriot groups, 132

"The 'Patriot' Movement Explodes" (Potok), 132

Pavetti, LaDonna, 89

*Peña, Adarand Constructors Inc. v.*, 74–75

Pennsylvania, redistricting in, 156

Pepsi Beverages, 66

"Pepsi to Pay $3.13 Million and Made Major Policy Changes to Resolve EEOC Finding of Nationwide Hiring Discrimination against African Americans" (EEOC), 66

*Percent Plans in College Admissions: A Comparative Analysis of Three States' Experiences* (Horn & Flores), 54

Perry, Marc, 58

"Persistent Peril: Why African American Babies Have the Highest Infant Mortality Rate in the Developed World" (Kashef), 103

Personal Responsibility and Work Opportunity Reconciliation Act, 84

Petit, Charles W., 14

Pew Hispanic Center
  "Among Hispanics in Florida, 2008 Voter Registration Rolls Swing Democratic," 154
  "Cubans in the United States," 7
  "Hispanic Health," 101–103
  "Latinos in the 2012 Election: Florida," 154–155
  *Statistical Portrait of Hispanics in the United States, 2010*, 91

Pew Research Center for the People and the Press
  *Evenly Divided and Increasingly Polarized: The 2004 Political Landscape*, 153
  Inside Obama's Sweeping Victory, 153
  Obama: Weak Job Ratings, but Positive Personal Image, 153
  Strong Confidence in Obama—Country Seen as Less Politically Divided, 153
  "With Voters Focused on Economy, Obama Lead Narrows," 153

Physicians, visits to, 95

Picower, Bree, 44

Pike, John, 8

Planty, Michael
  *The Condition of Education 2009*, 43, 49
  *High School Coursetaking: Findings from the Condition of Education 2007*, 51

"The Political Economy of American Indian Gaming" (Cornell), 76

"Political Gerrymandering 2000–2008: 'A Self-Limiting Enterprise'?" (*Harvard Law Review*), 155

Political participation
  African-American, 150, 153
  Hispanic, 153–155
  overview of, 145
  race/ethnicity and electoral districts, 155–156
  rates of voting/registration among native/naturalized citizens, by race/Hispanic origin/region of birth, 2008, 146t
  rates of voting/registration among native/naturalized citizens, by race/Hispanic origin/region of birth, 2010, 147t
  reasons for not voting, 151t–152t
  voter registration, 145–146, 148
  voter turnout, 148, 150
  voting/registration rates by race/Hispanic origin by region, 149t

Political parties, African-Americans and, 153

Population
  African-American by region, 10f
  civilian noninstitutional, employment status of, 64t
  employment status of population by race/sex/age, 61t–62t
  by Hispanic origin, 6t
  Hispanic origin groups with population one million+, 7t
  of Hispanics by counties, 8f
  of Hispanics by state, 7f
  minority, by counties, 4f
  by race/Hispanic origin, 2t, 3t
  by/sex/age/Hispanic origin/race, 92t

Population Reference Bureau, 2

*Postethnic America: Beyond Multiculturalism* (Hollinger), 145

Potok, Mary, 132

Poverty
  children living below selected poverty levels, by age/family structure/race/Hispanic origin, 85t
  children living in, 81–83
  depth of, 80–81
  4th-graders eligible for lunch programs, by school location/race/Hispanic origin, 86f
  government programs, 84–85, 87–89
  haves/have-nots, 83–84
  number in poverty/poverty rate, 81f
  people/families in poverty, 82t–83t
  poverty guidelines, 2011, 80t
  status of minorities, 80
  TANF/Food Stamps/SSI, percentage receiving assistance from by race, Hispanic origin, and age, 87t

Powell-Griner, Eve, 122

Pregnancy
  births/fertility, 99–100
  prenatal care, 96–98
  prenatal care, by race/Hispanic origin of mother, 99t
  *See also* Births

"Pregnancy and Childbirth" (CDC), 113

Prenatal care, 96–98

Preprimary education, 33–34

*Preschool: First Findings from the Preschool Follow-up of the Early Childhood Longitudinal Study, Birth Cohort* (Chernoff et al.), 33

"Pressure Grows on Fannie and Freddie to Cut Principal on Loans" (Dewan), 30

Preston, Julia, 59

Prisoners under sentence of death, by region/jurisdiction/race, 143t

Prisons
  adults on parole, 141(t7.11)
  adults on probation, 141(t7.12)
  death row, minorities on, 142
  minorities in, 136–140
  Native Americans in, 140
  number of prisoners under state and federal jurisdiction, 138(t7.9)
  parole/probation, 140–142
  rate of prisoners under state and federal jurisdiction, 139t
  sentencing, racial disparities in, 140

Probation, adults on, 141(t7.12)

Proctor, Bernadette D.
  *Income, Poverty, and Health Insurance Coverage in the United States: 2010*, 80
  on numbers of uninsured, 93

Property crimes, 132

Prostate cancer, 105

Provasnik, Stephen, 51

"A Puerto Rican Rebirth in El Barrio; After Exodus, Gentrification Changes Face of East Harlem" (Berger), 7

# T

Taggart, William A., 75, 76

Tan, Joyce Beiyu, 41

TANF. *See* Temporary Assistance for Needy Families

Tang, Y. Emily, 50

Taylor, Paul, 154

"Teenage Pregnancy and Adverse Birth Outcomes: A Large Population Based Retrospective Cohort Study" (Chen et al.), 22

Teenagers
 birthrates for, 22*f*
 birthrates for, by race/Hispanic origin, 23*f*
 dropout rates of 16- through 24-year-olds, by race/Hispanic origin, 41*f*
 high school dropouts, 16- to 24-year-olds, by nativity/race/Hispanic origin, 42*t*
 high school dropouts, 16- to 24-year-olds who were, by sex/race/Hispanic origin, 41*t*
 pregnancy among, 20–22
 *See also* Children; Education

Temporary Assistance for Needy Families (TANF)
 criticism of, 87–88
 establishment of, 84
 numbers receiving, 87, 87*t*

"Temporary Worker Program Is Explained" (Fears & Fletcher), 59

Texas
 affirmative action in, 53
 redistricting in, 155–156

*Texas, Hopwood v.*, 53

"Texas Vote Curbs a College Admission Guarantee Meant to Bolster Diversity" (McKinley), 53

13th Amendment, 57

Tobacco
 health threat of, 117, 121
 tobacco product use by age/gender/race/Hispanic origin, 121*t*
 use by age/gender/race/Hispanic origin, 121*t*

"Tobacco Valley: Puerto Rican Farm Workers in Connecticut" (Glasser), 6

"Topic A: Obama's Compromise on D.C.'s School Vouchers Program" (*Washington Post*), 49

Treaty of Guadalupe Hidalgo, 5

Treaty of Paris, 6

"Trends in the Prevalence of Tobacco Use" (CDC), 117

Trends in the United States (Fox & Zawitz), 129–131

Tribal casinos
 economic recession and, 76
 monies earned from, 65
 overview of, 75–76

"Tribal Casinos No Longer Sure Bet in Washington" (AP), 76

"Tribes Hit the Jackpot" (Robinson-Avila), 96

Trounson, Rebecca, 54

Truman, Jennifer L.
 *Criminal Victimization, 2010*, 129
 on property crimes among lower income people, 132

Trump, Donald, 75

Tulalip Tribes, 95

"26 More States and D.C. Seek Flexibility from NCLB to Drive Education Reforms in Second Round of Requests" (Department of Education), 49

*2007 Survey of Business Owners* (U.S. Census Bureau), 74

*2010 Alzheimer's Disease Facts and Figures* (Alzheimer's Association), 112

"2010 Census Offends Some Americans with Handling of Race" (Sy), 2–3

"The 2010 Census Questionnaire: Seven Questions for Everyone" (Population Reference Bureau), 2

*2010 Yearbook of Immigration Statistics* (DHS), 5, 9, 13

"2011 SAT Trends" (College Board), 51–52

Tyson, Alec, 150

# U

UC (University of California), 53–54

Undocumented immigrants, dropout rates of, 38

Unemployment
 among African-Americans, 60
 among Asian-Americans, 65
 among Hispanics, 63
 among Native Americans, 65
 overview of, 60

*Uneven Justice: State Rates of Incarceration by Race and Ethnicity* (Mauer & King), 142

"The Unexamined Whiteness of Teaching: How White Teachers Maintain and Enact Dominant Racial Ideologies" (Picower), 44

University. *See* Higher education

University of California (UC), 53–54

University of Michigan, 54

University of Texas, 53

"Unpredicted Trajectories: The Relationship between Race/Ethnicity, Pregnancy during Adolescence, and Young Women's Outcomes" (Casares et al.), 22

U.S. Census Bureau
 on African-American income, 78–79
 *America's Families and Living Arrangements: 2011*, 17, 19, 25–26
 on Asian-American income, 79

 on decline in voting, 150
 on health of Hispanic population, 91
 on Hispanic income, 77–78
 *The Hispanic Population in the United States: 2010*, 5
 on homeownership, 28
 on number of minorities, 1
 on numbers of African-Americans in U.S., 9
 survey of business owners, 74

U.S. Department of Education, 48, 49, 55

U.S. Department of Health and Human Services (HHS)
 *AFCARS Report*, 25
 on assistance programs, 84–85, 87
 on diabetic services, use of, 112
 on health of uninsured people, 93
 on heart disease, numbers suffering, 107
 on HIV, 113
 on minorities access to health care, 92–93
 on quality of minorities health care, 91
 "Questions and Answers on the American Recovery and Reinvestment Act of 2009 (Recovery Act)," 89

U.S. Department of Homeland Security (DHS)
 on Asian immigrants, numbers of, 13
 on immigration statistics, 5–6
 on numbers of Cuban immigrants, 9

U.S. Department of Transportation, 74–75

U.S. Election Assistance Commission, 145

U.S. Equal Employment Opportunity Commission (EEOC), 66

U.S. government
 minorities in, 73–74
 programs for impoverished Americans, 84–85, 87–89

U.S. Government Accountability Office (GAO), 59

U.S. Office of Personnel Management, 73–74

U.S. Sentencing Commission (USSC), 140

USSC (U.S. Sentencing Commission), 140

"Utah Voters Resoundingly Defeat School Voucher Ballot Issue" (National School Boards Association), 49–50

# V

Vaught, Sabina E., 44

Vekshin, Alison, 30

Ventura, Stephanie J., 21–22

Very low birth weight, 100

Victims, of crime, 129

*Vieth v. Jubelirer*, 156

Vietnam, postwar immigration from, 58

Vines, Paula L., 14, 65

"Violence by Gang Members, 1993–2003" (Harrell), 142

Violent Crime and Law Enforcement Act, 132